Seeing Young Children:

A GUIDE
TO OBSERVING
AND RECORDING
BEHAVIOR

Third Edition

Warren R. Bentzen
State University of New York at Plattsburgh

Delmar Publishers

I(T)P® International Thomson Publishing

Albany • Bonn • Boston • Cincinnati • Detroit • London • Madrid
Melbourne • Mexico City • New York • Pacific Grove • Paris • San Francisco
Singapore • Tokyo • Toronto • Washington

NOTICE TO THE READER

Cover Design: The Drawing Board

Delmar Staff
Publisher: William Brottmiller
Senior Editor: Jay Whitney
Associate Editor: Erin J. O'Connor Traylor
Production Editor: Marah Bellegarde
Production Coordinator: Sandra Woods
Editorial Assistant: Glenna Stanfield

COPYRIGHT © 1997
By Delmar Publishers
an International Thomson Publishing Company

The ITP logo is a trademark under license.

Printed in the United States of America

For more information, contact:

Delmar Publishers
3 Columbia Circle, Box 15015
Albany, New York 12212-5015

International Thomson Publishing GmbH
Konigswinterer Strasse 418
53227 Bonn
Germany

Nelson Canada
1120 Birchmont Road
Scarborough, Ontario
Canada, M1K 5G4

International Thomson Editores
Campos Eliseos 385, Piso 7
Col Polanco
11560 Mexico DF Mexico

Thomas Nelson Australia
102 Dodds Street
South Melbourne, 3205
Victoria, Australia

International Thomson Publishing–Japan
Hirakawacho Kyowa Building, 3F
2-2-1 Hirakawacho
Chiyoda-ku, Tokyo 102
Japan

International Thomson Publishing Europe
Berkshire House 168-173
High Holborn
London, WC1V 7AA
England

International Thomson Publishing Asia
221 Henderson Road
#05-10 Henderson Building
Singapore 0315

1 2 3 4 5 6 7 8 9 10 XXX 02 01 00 99 98 97 96

Library of Congress Cataloging-in-Publication Data

Bentzen, Warren R.
    Seeing Young Children: a guide to observing and recording
behavior / Warren R. Bentzen. — 3rd ed.
        p.   cm.
    Include bibliographical references and index.
    ISBN 0-8273-7665-0
    1. Behavioral assessment of children. 2. Observation (Psychology)
3. Observation (Educational method)   I. Title.
BF722.B46 1996   96-11006
144.4'0723—dc20   CIP

Contents

Part 3 Observation Exercises

Part 4 Middle Childhood—The School-Age Years

Preface

In the preface to the second edition of *Seeing Young Children*, I commented about the tremendous satisfaction and sense of accomplishment I felt at having this work go into a second edition. The fact that it is now in yet a third edition could incite me to flowery hyperbole. But I will resist that temptation and simply express my heartfelt thanks and appreciation to Delmar Publishers, to Delmar's extremely competent and patient editorial staff, and to you, the reader, for making this book a continuing success.

Unlike the second edition, bringing the third into being was a difficult and time-consuming task. I believe this was partly so because this time around the reviewers' recommendations were more exacting than in the past. This is not a disparagement of the previous reviewers: The time and the book were different then and called for different assessments and different corrective measures.

Much of the revision process was taken up with adding a bit here and deleting a bit there. In no small number of instances I had to expand on a point or an issue. I must confess that thanks to the reviewers' astuteness and dedication to their task, *Seeing Young Children* is now a much better book than it would otherwise have been.

Let me deal first with what some might consider relatively minor changes. Some features of the format of the observation exercises have been modified. The earlier editions called for a columnar layout for the observation report, where the objective behavioral descriptions were in the left-hand column and the interpretations were in the right-hand column. This seems a trivial change, indeed, but for those who followed my instructions to the letter in the previous editions, managing to construct side-by-side columns must in some instances have been a challenging task.

Other small changes add to the effectiveness of the observation exercises. For example, each objective behavioral description (OBD) subheading is followed by a place to indicate when the behavioral episode began and when it ended. This should help not only to prevent errors of transmission, but should provide the observer with useful information regarding the duration of behavioral episodes. I saw the deficiency of the earlier editions when I was instructing my own students to indicate the beginning and ending of each OBD, even though there was no official place to mark the times.

Some of the exercises in the last edition were rather difficult to complete adequately. I am especially referring to all of the exercises that involve the Greenspans' emotional milestones. Again, my own students' relative difficulty in understanding this part of the assignment made me realize that something needed to be changed. I have provided some alternative exercises on emotional development that are more straightforward and "traditional." Discussions of groups based on the work of Martin and O'Connor were difficult for many readers to comprehend. Although I did not eliminate that material for the sake of those who would welcome and use it, I do provide the opportunity to observe groups that does not require such specialized information.

Sample exercises have been included in this edition, and I hope the reader finds them useful and informative. Corrections were also made in the sample recordings of behavior used to illustrate several of the recording techniques. Better ways of describing and interpreting the behavior of hypothetical children are used in the illustrations than what was provided in the last edition.

I am vitally concerned with the ethical issues associated with observing and working with young children, and there is a discussion of such issues in Chapter 3. I also recommend that readers consult the National Association for the Education of Young Children's (NAEYC) official protocol and guidelines regarding the ethical treatment and study of children. For the purposes of this text I simply assume that most observations will take place within some formal setting or other, and, consequently, that the student/observer will receive sufficient instruction on the issue and practice of ethical conduct. My assumption notwithstanding, a complete version of the Code of Ethical Conduct & Status of Commitment can be obtained by contacting the NAEYC. In a similar vein, there is the issue of developmentally appropriate practice in relation to young children, which is another deep concern of the NAEYC.

Two basic premises have governed the conception and writing of *Seeing Young Children*: First, I was not writing a set of guidelines by which to operate a child care center, nor an instruction manual on how to teach young children, or on appropriate classroom practice. Second, there is the premise that observation *qua* observation, as well as its requisite skills, is *fundamentally* independent of specific subject matter. This latter proposition, however, must be taken in the proper light. Obviously, one must observe something, and to observe effectively, one must have some knowledge of what is being observed. Without knowing what dependency behavior is, for instance, it would be hard to *meaningfully and comprehensively* observe and record examples of such behavior. One wouldn't know what it was in the first place, nor could one accurately interpret the behavior as being dependent behavior. But the central aim of this text is to help the reader and potential or prospective observer to learn and apply the skills and techniques upon which good observation depends. The content of the observations, as well as their specific locations or settings, are not the focus of this edition, even though I have provided some content and a set of observation sites. Such provision, of course, is a function of the text's intended audience, namely, early childhood educators, child care professionals, and others in whatever capacity who work with or care for young children ages 0–8.

The focus of this text is on the whole child, not on the facility or setting in which the child is observed. Therefore, one can learn (1) how to observe and record such things as the effects that developmentally appropriate (or inappropriate) practice has on children, or (2) how to observe and record actions and decisions and other dynamics that reflect developmentally appropriate practices, or (3) how to observe for both of these things. I have chosen the first of these objectives as the text's primary focus.

There are other changes that I will mention. Some are stylistic changes, but the two really major changes in this edition consist of the addition of two new chapters. Chapter 18 deals with the six-year-old, and Chapter 19 deals with the seven- and eight-year-old. This is in keeping with the National Association for the Education of Young Children's (NAEYC) designation of early childhood as comprising the period from birth through eight years. This extended coverage thereby conforms more closely to the connotations and denotations of the words "young children" in the book's title. I also think the reader will find this new material advantageous in many respects. It increases the number of potential observation sites, together with the increased variety that such new locations can provide—formal school settings, formal and informal peer groups, groups organized around specific activities, and so on, all of which are appropriate to the child in the beginning phases of middle childhood or the school-age years. In keeping with the reality that one must observe something, from a practical standpoint that "something" has been increased to include older children in more sophisticated settings than obtain with infants, toddlers, and preschoolers. Also increased, therefore, are the observer's opportunities to extend and hone his or her skills as well as to add to the knowledge that fosters skillful observation and recording of young children's behavior.

Since the first edition of *Seeing Young Children,* I have been concerned with keeping a proper balance between producing an observation text and producing a work that closely resembles a developmental textbook. It falls considerably short of a developmental text, and yet it seems to me that I sometimes approach the domain of the developmental psychologist. It's conceivable that an observation text could be written that includes hardly anything specifically developmental and that depends on the reader to find the appropriate information on which to base his or her observations. This would be a sort of "Learn-all-you-can-about-the-motor-skills-of-the-infant-and-then-observe-one-for-examples-of-the-same" kind of approach. This would be eminently undesirable in my view. There undoubtedly are those who will disagree with me on what I should or should not have included in the background information that accompanies the observation exercises. I wish I could please or accommodate everyone. But since that is an impossible task, I have had to select what I believe is at least reasonably suitable information on the various domains and aspects of young children's development and behavior. Let me emphasize that you are free to base your observations on information of your own choosing. The exercises and their background information are guidelines or suggestions only! My primary goal in writing *Seeing Young Children* is to provide information about observation as a process and about the recording techniques or formats that are available to you. Beyond that, you have the latitude to observe and record whatever behavior you want in whatever context you want. A "high tech" suggestion is to use a video. The only limitations are those that dictate proper, ethical conduct, and the resources that you have at your disposal.

A final comment concerns the bibliographic references and the issue of primary versus secondary sources. A large part of the bibliography has been updated to include material that has been published recently. Aside from what is presumably the greater accuracy and relevancy of recent compared to older information and research, there is a cosmetic appeal to dates that are only a few years old. However, "dated" material is not necessarily "outdated" material. There are classics in the field that probably will be cited in textbooks for years to come. I have not attempted, therefore, to eradicate all references prior to 1990 simply for the sake of enhancing the book's visual attractiveness. The older citations still have validity and relevance; moreover, I also take my lead from other writers whose scholarly ability and writing skills I concede are greater than my own and who dip generously into the "well of knowledge" that has been dug by members of an earlier generation.

Finally, I must acknowledge the writings of such people as Piaget and Vygotsky and others who have written about these great thinkers. If I were writing a scholarly thesis on Piaget's or Vygotsky's theories, their original writings would be mandated. I find that stating their ideas is sufficient for students and serves the essential purpose of *Seeing Young Children,* which is to instruct the reader on how to engage the observation and recording processes in a meaningful, effective way. I thank the following reviewers of my manuscript for more than they realize.

Anne O'Neill
College of New Rochelle
Rye, New York

Charlotte Madison
University of Connecticut
Storrs, Connecticut

Jeanne Roller
Mount St. Clare College
Clinton, Iowa

Nancy Maldonado
Lehman College
New York, New York

Patricia Schindler
Newcomb College Nursery School
New Orleans, Louisiana

Dedication

There are six beautiful, wonderful children to whom I want to dedicate this third edition. It makes eminent sense to dedicate to children a book that is about children. Five of the six children are my grand nephews and nieces; the sixth is the son of a very good friend. And so to you, Lauren Christie Riemersma, age eight; Joel David Riemersma, age five years and five months; Corey Benjamin Riemersma, age one year and seven months; Christian Andrés Ginez, age seven years and ten months; Sophia Michelle Ginez, age three years and seven months; and William Christopher Irving, age four years and nine months, to all of you, I dedicate this third edition of *Seeing Young Children.* I am grateful to your parents and grandparents that you are here on this earth, and I look forward to watching you grow into adults who are as loving and caring as they are.

Overview

PART 1

HAPTER ONE
Introduction

Objectives

After studying Chapter One, you will be able to

- describe the differences between seeing in a physiological way and seeing in an observational way
- analyze the importance of observation to early education
- analyze the importance of observation to science and to an individual
- examine the relationship between observation and the observer's personal and theoretical perspectives
- discuss in general terms what observation is and what it involves

Observation: Some Preliminary Thoughts

The scene is a preschool classroom, and you have come simply to visit, and to watch. You notice a small boy sitting at a table playing with a piece of clay. He is alone, and you want to get closer to see what he is doing. The boy (we will call him Robby) smiles as you approach, and asks you if you want to play with him. You say "yes," and he gives you his clay. As Robby watches very closely, you roll the clay into one large ball and then break it into two, roughly equal parts. You hand him his portion of the clay and tell him, "Now, we both have just as much to play with." Robby nods and smiles again, takes his ball of clay and rolls it around on the surface of the table. You take your part of the clay and proceed to flatten it out like a pancake. Robby is now very interested; he looks intently at your flattened piece and then shouts, "Hey, *your* piece is bigger! I want *that* one!" You are, after all, a guest, and you certainly do not want to quarrel with a three-year-old over a piece of clay, so you trade your piece for his. He smiles once more and goes back to his playing.

You have just observed a child's behavior in a particular situation. You have received information through your eyes and your ears. But what happened? What have you seen? What could you say about the observation process you have just gone through? What could you say about Robby?

Had you seen Robby through the eyes of an early education teacher, you could have seen a child in Piaget's preoperational stage of cognitive development. You could have seen a little boy who was unable to *conserve substance*. From that you would have seen Robby's inability to understand that if no clay was added and none was taken away, then the amount of clay must remain unchanged. You could have seen Robby being fooled by the outward appearances of the pieces of clay. Moreover, you could have predicted all of these things just by knowing that Robby was three years old. Questions and possible answers such as these are central to this manual. Think about observation and what it will mean when, in doing your observation exercises, you say, "I'm going to observe young children."

One might think that observing something is a fairly simple task. This belief is given support by the vital role our ears and eyes play in getting information about our environment. Observation appears to involve seeing or hearing some stimulus or set of stimuli coming from the external environment.

There is a difficulty, however, when we think of observing just as seeing or hearing. A problem arises because humans are not cameras or tape recorders; we do not merely take in sensory information through the eyes and ears. If we did, we would be as unable as the camera and recorder to use that information. It is precisely because we can do something more with sensory information after we obtain it that observation becomes complicated. Furthermore, what and how much information we perceive varies from person to person, and even within the same person, from one time to another. And so it is that two individuals can be visually aware of the same object or event, but visually aware in quite different ways (Hansen 1958). Here is an example.

Mrs. Delgado has enrolled her four-year-old son Phillipe in a community child-care center. It is the center's policy and practice to involve parents in some of the curricular activities that take place there. This is done partly in the hope that parents can carry on in the home what the center is trying to accomplish in just a few hours each day. One might say that the center takes a broad "systems" view of childcare, believing that home and school are interrelated, and that what happens in one of those places affects what happens in the other.

Phillipe is relatively new at the center, having been there about a week. Mrs. Delgado is at the center on a particular Monday morning to help the staff but especially to observe her son's "progress" in the program. Phillipe is in the big block area with two other boys, and they appear to be building a "house" together. Mrs. Delgado watches closely, being especially alert to Phillipe's interactions with the other two boys. Phillipe, you see, is, by his mother's perceptions, shy and seemingly tentative about initiating and maintaining social contacts. As she observes her son's behaviors, she wonders what value there is in playing with big wooden blocks. Because she is very interested in his social behavior, she concludes that his present activity is more appropriate to building muscle strength and coordination than it is to fostering interpersonal skills. Furthermore, she doesn't want the center to ignore or underemphasize skills and abilities that require thinking and planning and talking—"cognitive" and language skills.

Mrs. Hafner, the center director and head teacher, is also observing Phillipe in the big block area. As she looks at him, she doesn't "see" everything that

Mrs. Delgado sees, simply because, as his mother, Mrs. Delgado has had four years to get to know her son very intimately. Mrs. Hafner, on the other hand, has had only about three hours a day for merely a week to learn anything at all about the boy. But, Mrs. Hafner has at least one advantage over Mrs. Delgado: she can see and interpret events and behaviors that are relevant to Phillipe *in the context of the childcare center* that would go unnoticed and unappreciated by Mrs. Delgado. She can do this because she is professionally trained in early childhood education and in child development. Consequently, she "sees" all the boys in the block area acquiring and sharpening their spatial relations skills—learning how, for example, blocks of different sizes and shapes can fit together to form the particular structure they are trying to build. They are also acquiring a sense of weight and some understanding that size alone does not necessarily predict an object's heaviness or lightness. Big things can weigh less and be easier to lift than small ones—a somewhat large but light pine wood block as compared with a small but heavy cube of lead. Mrs. Hafner also will see the language and arithmetic skills that are being used—"Hey," says Phillipe, "give me *two* more blocks so that I can finish this bridge."

What Mrs. Hafner may not see, at least not at first, is the shyness and unwillingness on the part of Phillipe to enter into social situations. This may not be an immediate *interpretation* that Mrs. Hafner is likely to make, because she has not observed Phillipe in many other situations where he could exhibit his shyness. His mother, of course, might be inclined to "see" shyness in much of what Phillipe does in association with others.

The point of this hypothetical example is that Phillipe's mother and his teacher saw essentially the same *overt* behaviors as they watched him playing in the big block area. What we've depicted, however, is Mrs. Delgado seeing *only play* going on. *She does not fully understand the value of play and the many kinds of learning that are taking place.* Mrs. Hafner, on the other hand, does see *learning* taking place *in the context of a play situation.* Mrs. Delgado doesn't see spatial relationship or arithmetic skills being acquired and practiced, nor does she see Phillipe learning what she most wants him to learn—social interaction skills.

This use of the word "seeing" is a way of dealing with the observation process. It must be kept separate in some important ways from seeing in a physiological sense. When we look at an object, its image is projected on that part of the eye called the retina. For example, look at Figure 1-1. The image that figure forms on your retina will be identical with the image on someone else's retina. Physiologically, most individuals will see the same thing.

What distinguishes "seeing" in the observational way from seeing in the physiological way, also distinguishes what a physician and his patient see when each of them looks at an X-ray. Both the patient and the physician receive the same visual information; the X-ray picture is projected on each of their retinas. Because of the differences in their backgrounds and training, however, each perceives something different; each draws different meanings from the visual

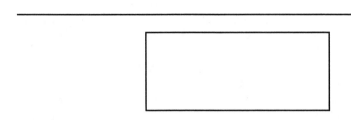

Figure 1-1   In a physiological sense, all persons with normal vision see the same thing when they look at this figure.

information taken in. The patient may see only shadows or vague outlines; the physician will see a tumor or a clogged artery.

The essential point here is that all of us look at and organize the objects and events in our world according to our past experiences, what we know, and what we believe.

Why Observation is Important

Goodwin and Driscoll (1980) give three reasons why observation is important in early childhood education. First, it allows measuring many behaviors of children that may otherwise be unmeasurable. Young children's verbal abilities are limited, which rules out the use of traditional information-gathering techniques such as interviews and paper-and-pencil tests. The area of emotions is especially suitable to observational methods; the observer can see the child as he actually behaves, without the shortcomings of limited test-taking ability, unreliable understanding of test instructions, and eagerness to please adults by responding in the way they think the adults want them to respond. In more recent scholarship, Morrison (1995) speaks to this characteristic by also referring to the ability of observation to "gather data that cannot be gleaned by conducting paper-and-pencil tests or questioning a young child" (p. 45). Morrison comments on the overall importance of observation, noting that

> Professionals recognize that children are more than just what is measured by a particular test. Utilizing more "authentic" means for assessing children, professionals realize that observation is one of the most authentic means of learning about children and what they know and are able to do, especially when it occurs in *naturalistic settings* such as classrooms, child care centers, playgrounds, and homes. (p. 45, italics original)

He states further that "Observation enables professionals to gain information directly that could otherwise be gathered only indirectly" (p. 45). We would note that, generally speaking, if you observe a child yourself, the information you get is likely to be more accurate and reliable for your purposes than if you use someone else's observation data.

Critical to all of this, however, is Morrison's view that when looking at children, professionals and parents sometimes "do not really see what they [the children] are doing or understand why they are engaging in a particular behavior or activity.... This is why it is important for early childhood professionals to understand the importance of and how to use observation to gather data about young children" (p. 45).

Second, formal testing procedures are not typically viewed as seriously by children as by adults. Goodwin and Driscoll (1980) believe that young children do not take to heart adults' advice that the test is serious business and that they should try as hard as they can, an attitude formal testing relies on for its success. There are other criticisms leveled against the formal testing of young children. It's argued, for example, that formal testing is developmentally inappropriate for young children. Some also contend that rather than *not* taking testing seriously, as Goodwin and Driscoll claim, children in fact become severely stressed under formal testing conditions. The National Association for the Education of Young Children (NAEYC), for example, cites as a developmentally *inappropriate* practice the evaluation of children ".... only against a predetermined measure, such as a standardized group norm or adult standard of behavior. All are expected to perform the same tasks and achieve the same narrowly defined, easily measured skills" (cited in *Early Childhood Education 88/89*, Annual Editions. Guilford, Connecticut: Dushkin Publishing Group, Inc., p. 111).

Spodeck and Saracho (1994) also discuss the issue of the standardized testing of young children as well as from the perspective of the NAEYC. They write that "While some form of assessment is important as an indicator of the effectiveness of programs, standardized tests may be the wrong instrument for this purpose" (p. 240). It is not our purpose to become embroiled in the controversy regarding such tests. Nonetheless, the fact that standardized testing is coming under serious scrutiny, together with the resulting stress on the importance and appropriateness of naturalistic observation, makes refining one's skills in observing young children's behavior all the more critical.

Fortunately, naturalistic observation shares none of these disadvantages with formal testing. The observer wants to see children's behavior as it occurs without adult interference. Nor does the observer want to generate anxiety or other emotions that might affect inappropriately the children's behavior.

Third, Goodwin and Driscoll believe that even when they know they are being observed, young children feel less threatened or anxious than do older children and adults. Young children presumably are also less likely than older children or adults to change their behavior in response to being observed. The assumption here is that, in the case of older children and adults, if someone knows he is being watched, it is harder for him to behave normally than if he thinks he is alone. It has been said that if we were observed behaving in what we thought were private moments, most of us would be judged insane. Observation of young children, then, supposedly yields behavior that is relatively unaffected by the process of observing it.

We need to add, however, that this assumption is subject to empirical verification or refutation in any given situation and with any given child or group of children. Perhaps the wisest course of action is *not to take it for granted that young children do not react adversely to being observed.* This admonition really is related to the general principle to remain as inconspicuous as possible when in the observation setting (see Chapter 3). It's an incontrovertible fact, however, that it is impossible to remain invisible to the children or to keep them ignorant of your presence under all circumstances. Consequently, you will be seen by the children, and they either may come to know what you are doing on their "turf," or they will develop a perception or belief as to what you are doing. This must be handled carefully, most importantly for the sake of the child's well-being, and secondarily for the sake of the successful and "honest" completion of your observation.

Aside from these reasons, there are others that give importance to the observation process. You may find yourself observing children who are in a variety of settings (e.g., in preschool classrooms, playgrounds, the home, or public school classrooms). Our knowledge of children and how they change over time ultimately depends on someone (actually, many people) studying children, observing them doing various things in various situations at various ages. There are two aspects to the relationship between theory and observation. First, theories, which attempt to explain development, have to be *tested* and shown to be useful or not useful in understanding the developmental process. In this case, such testing must ultimately involve observation. Although it is unlikely that you will have to test a theory in any formal or "official" manner, we think it is safe to say that observing and interpreting children's behavior *does* result in theory testing of a sort. Let's look at an example.

Piaget's theory of cognitive development has given rise to a huge amount of research, both for its own sake and for the sake of developing, for instance, preschool curricula and programs. Piaget argued that egocentrism, which essentially is defined as the inability to take another person's point of view or perspective, is a basic characteristic of the young child. His "mountain view" task is a classic in the field of egocentrism research, and it's from children's performances on tasks such as the mountain view that Piaget derived his essential conclusions about the extent of children's egocentrism. Nonetheless, for some time now researchers have been finding evidence that young children are *not* as egocentric as Piaget thought. Murray Krantz (1994), a writer and researcher, reports that when materials and situations that are familiar to the children are substituted for Piaget's essentially unfamiliar mountain task, their responses are consistently *non*egocentric (p. 295). Laura Berk (1993) offers a general statement regarding Piaget's conclusions. She writes that "New evidence indicates that Piaget underestimated the competencies of infants and preschoolers" (p. 21). She further states that "This discovery has led many investigators to conclude that the maturity of children's thinking may depend on their familiarity with the investigator's task and the kind of knowledge sampled" (pp. 21–22). The point here is that if you are looking for examples of egocentrism in preschoolers' typical behavior, you may instead observe instances of nonegocentric behavior, an event that would in effect put Piaget's conclusions and theory to the test.

The second aspect of the relationship between theory and observation has to do with the fact that your observations can help you better understand the theories that you may be studying. Put another way, there is a relationship between what you might learn from books, for example, and your observation experiences. On the one hand, involvement with real children can help you understand what you read and hear about them; on the other hand, what you are learning about children and their development will influence what you see as you complete the observation exercises. For example, what you know in general about language development will affect what you learn and understand about a particular child's language development. The nature of your understanding, and how you explain what you see, will depend on your knowledge, your observation skills, and the theoretical and personal perspective(s) from which you view growth, development, and even people in general. This is true in areas other than early childhood education. A Freudian therapist is very likely to see a client's problem as involving psychic conflict, whereas a behavioral therapist is more likely to see the same problem in terms of the client's reinforcement history. Each therapist, because of his professional training, sees that behavior from a different point of view and is sensitive to different aspects of the individual's behavior. If you work with children in a professional capacity, your particular training will incline *you* to see children in certain ways and to interpret their behavior in a way that agrees with your point of view or theory. This manual is designed to help you sharpen your observation skills. It also emphasizes the need for a conceptual framework from which to observe and make sense out of what is seen.

To finish our earlier reference to Morrison's discussion of the importance of observation, he cites the value of observation for assessing children's abilities, which in turn "determines areas in which they need additional support and help" (p. 45). He mentions observation being used to assess children's "performance over time," and finally, observation enables professionals to gather information that can be used in parent conferences and in reports to parents about their children. (p. 45).

We want to emphasize, however, that this manual is *not* a source book for learning in great detail about such things as child development, early childhood education curricula and classroom practices, or procedures for intervening in the lives of children who present particular problems. Rather, this text focuses on the processes of observing and recording behavior, processes or techniques that can be applied to virtually any situation or set of circumstances in which observation and recording skills are needed. Except for the practice exercises provided in this manual, we leave it to you to find the occasions for such application and thereby also to find the specific content of your observation and recording activities.

The preceding discussion has much to do with the importance of observation. There is, however, a broader aspect to the importance of observation. Observation is crucial, because so many of the sciences—social and physical—must gather data that can be seen, heard, smelled, touched, or tasted. Such data are called *empirical* data, which are data that depend on experience or observation rather than abstract theory. A psychologist must eventually leave abstract theories of human behavior and explore and measure the "real" behavior of "real" people. This exploring and measuring require observation. A psychologist interested in studying children's aggressive behavior, must at some point stop thinking about aggression in just theoretical terms, and identify what she means by aggression in empirical terms. In this example, the psychologist must observe and record visible behaviors exhibited by children—behaviors she believes indicate aggression. It is likely she will accept as aggression behaviors such as hitting, pushing, calling names, or taking a toy away from another child. But regardless of its definition, the idea of aggression must ultimately be linked to something directly observable. Based on that observable behavior, the psychologist assumes the presence or existence of aggression.

What is Observation?

In a very real sense, you will be acting as a scientist when you observe children. You will be doing what every scientist or researcher must do if she is to learn about the real world. Because of the purposes that are part of their occupations, scientists and researchers have to work with ideas that are abstract or removed from everyday life. But all of us deal with abstract ideas at some time. Examples can be found in our everyday language. We use words as symbols that stand for something else. For instance, the word 'chair' stands for a piece of furniture that one sits on (usually). In ordinary conversation, most of us can agree on what is meant by 'chair.' A problem arises, however, when we move away from casual conversation and toward descriptions of abstract ideas such as truth or beauty.

The generally acknowledged goals of science are description, explanation, prediction, and control. Being able to explain something indicates that one understands it, knows how it operates, and why it operates in that manner. Explanation first requires description. The explainer must know what he is looking at; he must be able to show the phenomenon to others, if only through a verbal description or "picture." In some instances, the explainer may have to make it clear as to why he thinks he will see what he is looking for in the specific phenomenon chosen for observation. In your case, you will be looking at children, some of whom will be a phenomenon for you to describe, explain, maybe predict and, consequently, understand.

You may decide to observe a three-year-old child for evidence of egocentrism. It probably will seem reasonable to do this, because according to Piaget, a child of this age is typically egocentric in some behavior and thinking. You might recall, however, our earlier discussion regarding recent findings that children are not as egocentric as Piaget thought. This new evidence might change your views of egocentrism and how and where to look for it. Nevertheless, if you were to pursue egocentrism among three-year-olds, you will first have to define it so that you will recognize it when it occurs. You will describe those behaviors that fit your definition of egocentrism, or from which you infer its presence.

Participation as an observer is not just a matter of watching children play, for example, and then writing down what you have seen. What you have observed must make sense and must be given meaning. *There is no guarantee, however, that your meaning will be the only valid one or that you will even take notice of everything of significance in the situation.* Validity (accuracy) and completeness depend on the perspective from which you observe and on your skill as an observer. Observation, most simply put, refers to the noting and recording of "facts." We refine this meaning to include the idea of looking for something in a *controlled, structured* way. The importance of the words "controlled" and "structured" will become apparent as you read further and when you perform some observations in an actual setting. For now, "controlled" most simply means that your observations are not random or haphazard. You know beforehand *what* you want to observe, *where* you want to observe, and essentially *how* you want to observe. These factors all contribute to the "structured" character of your observations. You will, at least some of the time, use predetermined observation forms, whether those provided in this manual or others constructed by yourself or someone else.

Thus, it is what you do in the observation setting that will be distinctively different from what the average person will do when casually watching children play, or show emotion, and so on. Facts, however, are seldom if ever pure or self-evident. We must process them in some way. *Process* means to think about, to give a verbal label to, or to put the fact into some meaningful relationship with other facts. We seldom deal directly with the objects, events, and people in our world; rather, we deal with what is said about them. Saying something about an object, however, already involves interpretation and a perspective. Finding the appropriate words indicates knowledge of language, of the object, and the ability to place the object in a relationship with other objects or with other relevant information. Here is an illustration.

Think for a moment of what is involved in "watching children play." At the very least, you must have some idea of what play is. How do you know it is play you are observing rather than another kind of activity? If you believe that everything young children do is play, you will make no distinctions among the behaviors they exhibit. However, if your perspectives (ideas, views) on play are more sophisticated, you are likely to classify play and non-play activities according to criteria based, perhaps, on a theory. Or you may identify different types or characteristics of play, possibly using Craig's (1989) six categories or forms of play (see Chapter 17). Can you see how it is possible to view play (or anything else) in either a simple or a complex way? Let us look at one more illustration of this essential point.

Although the 1977 writings of early childhood educators Constance Kamii and Rheta DeVries may seem a bit outdated in the mid-1990s, what they have to say is still current and relevant. In their discussion of Piaget's ideas about the development of intelligence, they also deal with this necessary component of all observation, namely, the processing of facts. They use the example of a child understanding the concept of "capital" (specifically, as represented in the statement, "Washington, D.C. is the capital of the United States.") A sixth grader has some understanding of such a statement, but as Kamii and DeVries point out, with six more years of living, studying, and other maturing experiences, the statement will take on richer and more elaborate meanings. As a result, say the authors, free association to the word "Washington" might raise from the child such responses as "The White House, the Capitol, the Lincoln Memorial . . ." (1977). The adult's range of responses to Washington would be even broader than the child's (perhaps including "taxes," "an area of land 10 miles square," or the election in 1994 of predominantly Republican candidates to Congress.) Like the child's, the adult's response would be relevant to the particular word and its accepted set of meanings. They would not include a response such as "The price of eggs in China" or "Napoleon" (Kamii and DeVries 1977). The idea of putting one fact into a relationship with other facts (processing) is conveyed in the following passage

> These free associations illustrate Piaget's view that since knowledge is or-
> ganized in a coherent, whole structure, no concept can exist in isolation.
> Each concept is supported and colored by an entire network of other con-
> cepts (Kamii and DeVries 1977).

Please be aware that this example from Kamii and DeVries has to do with *you*, the observer, and your obligation to process what you perceive as facts. The authors' thesis simply is that no one can make sense of, say, Fact #1 without being able to put it into some kind of relationship with Fact #2, or Fact #3, and so on. It is this organizing of concepts that makes up the processing of facts and, again, it is guided by developmental or behavioral theories and personal perspectives.

You realize by now that observing is not simply looking *at* something. Disciplined, scientific observation is looking *for* something in a particular way (or ways). These particular ways of observing children are discussed in Chapters Four–Twelve.

There is a final aspect of observation you should be familiar with. The phrase "observation process" has been used several times. That phrase has two meanings of interest to us. First, process refers to a series of related activities that require time to accomplish. Thus, to observe a child involves a number of activities and behaviors on the part of both the child and the observer. The child has to exhibit the behaviors of interest to the observer, and the observer has to do something with those behaviors. He must see them, then record and interpret them. Process also involves structure of some sort. Structure may be inherent in the situation itself, to the extent that certain activities have to follow a particular sequence or time order. For example, you have to observe a behavior *before* you can record and interpret it. Other kinds of structure can be imposed on the situation by an observer, as when she chooses a particular method of recording behaviors or a particular theoretical perspective from which to interpret and explain the behaviors.

In its second meaning, process can be used as a noun, where it refers to a sequence or series of actions or changes that bring about some kind of result or consequence. *The American Heritage Talking Dictionary* (1995) also includes in its definition of process "a series of operations performed in the making [or treatment] of a *product*" (italics added). We may not usually think of others or ourselves as "products," but we are indeed that. And, of course, change is always involved in the making of any product, including the product that is you—your skills, values, attitudes, and personality. Change is part of observation (and vice versa), since the child will not remain the same even in the short period of time required to do an observation exercise, let alone over a period of weeks and months. You too will change. You will learn about developmental theories, norms, and research studies. You will acquire knowledge of observation techniques and skill in performing them. Your knowledge of theory and your observation experiences will interact with each other and be enhanced or improved. Your attitudes concerning children—how they grow and develop, who they are, where they "fit" in the life cycle—may also change.

I wish you success on your journey.

Summary

Observation is something we do continually, whether we are aware of it or not. We observe largely through our eyes and ears, taking in various kinds of sensory information. All observation, however, whether casual or scientifically rigorous, consists of more than the physical reception of stimuli. We truly observe or "see" when what we have received through our senses has meaning for us. We see when we can put our observations into a mental framework that has personal relevance. All of us have personal frameworks within which we describe and interpret what happens in our world. These frameworks can be called our personalities. It is also possible to have more formal frameworks to describe and interpret observed phenomena. These formal frameworks can be called theories.

Observation is critical for a number of reasons. The most basic reason is that ultimately we learn about reality by observing it, by having contact with it through one or more of our five physical senses. It logically follows, then, that if we are to understand children, we must watch them, listen to them, and touch them. Moreover, we must think about the information we have gotten in these ways and make some sense of it in order to act with and toward children in appropriate and meaningful ways.

Study Questions

1. What is the importance of seeing in a physical sense and seeing in an observational sense? How are these two kinds of seeing related?
2. Do you think observational skills are important or unimportant to being a good teacher or child care worker? Defend your position with specific reasons. Do the same regarding the importance or unimportance of observation to science

and the individual. Are your three sets of reasons like or unlike each other? That is, is observation for the teacher, scientist, and the ordinary person actually three different activities, or do they share some commonalities?

3. With respect to the last part of question two above, how might observation done by a scientist in an *experimental setting* differ from observation done, say, by a preschool teacher in a *natural setting* or context? If there are any differences, what form would they likely take?

4. This chapter argues that observation is affected or determined by our personalities (i.e., our knowledge, values, attitudes, and experience). How could you show this argument to be true or false?

5. It's been said that it is *impossible not to communicate*. Is it also impossible not to observe? Take the broadest possible view of observation to answer this question.

Practical Exercise: Chapter One

What we would like you to get out of this first chapter is some sense of how much our personalities or our experiences influence the observation process when we engage in it, which is most of the time. Although to complete this exercise will require you to do some work, we believe it will be well worth your time and effort.

The essential theme or purpose of this exercise is to ask several individuals to describe or explain some object, sound, or event and compare their responses in the context of their professions or occupations. Select two or three individuals whose professions or occupations are very different from one another's and to whom you could have access for discussion or interviewing. For instance, you could play a taped recording of a piece of music (classical, jazz, rock), or you could show each person a photograph of a building or some other object. The key to successfully performing this exercise is to match the task with the individuals' respective professions in such a way as to emphasize the differences in their responses.

For example, playing the opening bars of Beethoven's Fifth Symphony to a professional musician, an attorney, and an automobile mechanic would likely result in very different comments, explanations, or understandings. One would predict that the musician's responses would be quite detailed, informed, and sophisticated, whereas the responses of the other two individuals would be more general and less knowledgeable regarding the finer points of Beethoven's music. This would precisely point up how who we are determines how we see (hear) things and interpret their meaning or significance.

This same general procedure could be done using, say, a picture of a building. Again, one would expect an architect's responses to be very different from those of a land developer or an historian.

CHAPTER TWO
Overview of Developmental Theories

Objectives

After studying this chapter, you will be able to

- define the concepts of growth and development
- discuss levels of explanation
- discuss the meaning of interpretation and its role in the observation of children
- describe various characteristics and principles of development
- discuss the different views that are held regarding certain characteristics of development
- discuss the relationship between one's views on development and what one sees when observing children

Development and Explanation: Some Preliminary Thoughts

The purpose of this chapter is to introduce you to the concepts of child growth and development, as well as to the idea of explaining or interpreting behavior within the context of growth and developmental change. The nature of your involvement requires us to present more than one point of view. The important characteristics that define developmental change and the different perspectives and interpretations that are associated with various theoretical positions will be included. Be prepared for the possibility of explaining or interpreting your observational data in several ways, depending on what theoretical "filter" you are using.

Explanation, which is heavily influenced or determined by one's perspectives on development (and on people in general), is also included in this chapter.

Development and Growth

The term *development* refers to change over time—change in the structure, thought, or behavior of an individual that comes about from biological and environmental influences. This is probably the simplest sense we can get of the concept of development. Kathleen Berger (1991) offers the same uncomplicated idea when she writes that " . . . *the study of human development is the study of how people change over time, as well as how and why they remain the same*" (p. 2; italics original).

Sroufe and Cooper (1988) offer a slightly more sophisticated conceptualization of development. They write that "Development during childhood and adolescence refers to certain age-related changes that are orderly, cumulative, and directional" (p. 7). *Orderly* change is change that follows a predictable (Sroufe and Cooper use the term "logical") sequence, where each change paves the way for future changes and makes sense with respect to what has previously taken place. These authors define *cumulative* as meaning that any given phase of development encompasses everything that has already occurred, but the "new" or emerging phase includes something additional that was not present in the earlier phases or stages. By *directional* Sroufe and Cooper mean that "development always moves toward greater complexity" (p. 7).

These same authors identify several other aspects to development that deserve mention at this time. They call development "dramatic and predictable" (p. 9). But, they ask, how does this dramatic, predictable process occur in the first place? Three factors provide an answer to their question. First, there is a genetic/maturational factor, "a preexisting developmental plan built into the organism" (p. 9). Second, the development that has already occurred provides an ongoing and necessary foundation for all subsequent development. And third, development needs a supportive environment, what Sroufe and Cooper identify as "all of the nutrients, inputs, circumstances, and challenges the developing organism encounters" (p. 9).

The team of Mussen, Conger, Kagan, and Huston (1984) identify three basic goals of developmental psychology. These goals are related to Sroufe and Cooper's three factors discussed immediately above. They also provide a rationale by which to assess the observed behavior of children. (See Table 2-1) Mussen *et al.* cite as one goal the understanding of changes that "appear to be *universal* —changes that occur in all children regardless of the culture in which they grow up or the experiences they have" (p. 7; italics original). A second goal is to explain *individual differences* in behavior. Why are some children more skillful than others in social relationships, for example, or why do children react differently to stress or changes in routine? The third goal of developmental psychology identified by Mussen and his colleagues is that of determining the influence of *context* or *situation* on a person's behavior. One child's imitation of another child's aggressive behavior might be a result of some specific contextual or situational influence, for example. Mussen *et al.* give us a useful summary of the significance of development and its various emphases or perspectives. For further reference, see NAEYC's Developmentally Appropriate Practice.

These three ways of examining children's behavior—searching for universal patterns, individual differences, and situational or contextual influences—are all necessary for a full understanding of development. The emphasis placed on any one of the three depends on the theoretical orientation of the investigator and on the type of question being studied. (Mussen *et al.*, 1984, p. 8)

The last sentence in the above quotation will be particularly important later on because, among other reasons, your observations will be put into a particular the-

Table 2-1 Goals of Developmental Psychology: A Comparison

Sroufe and Cooper's Three Factors Explaining Development	Mussen et al.'s Goals of Developmental Psychology
Genetic-Maturational Factor: "A preexisting developmental plan built into the organism"	To Understand *universal* developmental changes ithat occur in spite of individual experiences
Current level of development provides basis for future development: *Development is cumulative*	To explain *individual differences*
Development needs a *supportive environment*	To understand the effects of context or situation on a person's behavior

oretical perspective, which will consequently put a particular emphasis on your observational data.

Development is of two general kinds: normative and individual (Sroufe and Cooper, 1988). *Normative development* consists of general behavioral changes that are shared by all children across various ages. One might consider normative development as changes that occur simply because we belong to the human species. This is comparable to the idea of universal changes touched on above. *Individual development* has two meanings. On the one hand, it consists of "variations around the average, or normative, course of development of a certain ability" (Sroufe and Cooper, 1988, p. 8). Individual development therefore occurs within a range of possible variations. On the other hand, individual development involves the element of uniqueness, the distinctiveness that every person possesses that separates him or her from every other person with respect to such things as temperament, behavioral capacities, or put most broadly, personality. Such uniqueness concerns the issue of individual differences.

Development also involves age, which most appropriately viewed, is the amount of time one has been alive (see again Sroufe and Cooper's definition of development as involving "age-related changes"). Although time and developmental change are related, the relationship is not perfect. We cannot precisely predict any person's developmental level knowing only her age. Furthermore, the importance and relationship of age to development depends on one's point of view. For example, it's likely that a physician (pediatrician) will be quite interested in a child's age, primarily because doctors tend to rely on age as a general marker of where a child should be developmentally. Therefore, a two-year-old child would be compared with other two-year-old children through the use of norms, which, as will be discussed, are a sort of average, general trend, or pattern that is exhibited by, in this case, most two-year-olds. Therefore, if Marsha is significantly "behind" her age-peers in some area of functioning, the physician will look for possible causes of her slower development, which may be biologically, physically, or medically based.

On the other hand, an early childhood teacher, although concerned that Marsha is developing more slowly than her age-mates, will not likely emphasize her age as such, but will focus on Marsha's *developmental level*. The teacher will want to provide Marsha with experiences, challenges, and opportunities that are appropriate to what Marsha is actually able to do rather than what she should be able to do according to the developmental norms. When put into practice, this is what developmentally appropriate education is all about.

Stage theories (such as Piaget's) see development as heavily based on maturational processes, which are processes that are primarily controlled biologically or genetically. Dworetzky (1987) defines maturation as "a genetically determined biological plan of development, one relatively independent of experience" (p. 101). Maturation, in turn, is age-related because, like age, it occurs over time. In contrast to the stage viewpoint, the environmentalist perspective does not believe age is especially relevant to development. For the environmentalist, age serves mostly as a convenient way of marking points in the life span where change has occurred.

The role of age in understanding development is like the role of a stopwatch in timing a sprinter. As the runner moves along the track, the watch can indicate how long he took to run a certain distance. There is a relationship between the speed at which he runs and how much distance he covers in a specific amount of time. This is like the relationship between a child's developmental level (where he is on the "track") and how long he has been alive ("running"). The watch cannot explain why the runner is as fast as he is; it can only mark how long it took him to get to a certain point. This is worth keeping in mind as you observe children of various ages, lest you be tempted to think that Susan behaves as she does *because* she is three. Bear in mind, however, that there are behaviors, characteristics, and developmental patterns that children of particular ages tend to share with one another. If this were not so, norms would not be possible. The point here is that age, in and of itself, does not explain development or behavior.

In spite of its limitations, age can be a useful estimator of where any given individual is likely to be with respect to various areas of development (intellectual, social, emotional, physical). This notion of average gives us what psychologists call *norms*, an important but sometimes misused concept and body of information about the growth and developmental patterns of humans. Richard Lerner (1976) captures the essentially invariant meaning of the concept of norms when he describes them as "statements about when in people's lives a particular behavior is typically seen . . . ." Other writers use words such as "average" to express the meaning of norms. Berns (1994), for instance, refers to norms as "scientifically established averages . . . at which most children reach specific developmental milestones" (p. 22). This use of "average" best allows us to think in terms of a large number of individuals, in which case age is most meaningfully viewed as an estimate of the developmental characteristics likely to be possessed by most of the persons in any given group.

Growth is easier to understand than development. This manual uses the term growth to mean changes in size or number, which are *quantitative* changes. Physical growth is the simplest kind of quantitative change to recognize and measure. A child becomes taller, heavier, and larger in circumference. These changes represent increases in the amount of bone and muscle tissue. Guy R. Lefrançois (1992) offers a good definition of growth, which, he says, "ordinarily refers to physical changes, which are primarily quantitative because they involve addition rather than *transformation*" (p. 8; italics added). The term "transformation" will be discussed in more detail later in this chapter.

Explanation *or* Interpretation

The concept and study of development can be quite complex. This is especially true when one tries to explain (or interpret) development and answer questions such as, "How does development occur?" Even though explanation is not always easy, it is an essential activity and one of the major goals of the empirical sciences. Explanation is part of observation. Even the simplest descriptions involve putting information into some kind of conceptual framework. Consequently, description, pure and simple, is virtually impossible. By merely describing a behavior, one has already begun the process of interpretation, of putting new facts into a relationship with other facts already known or understood. Because of its importance, time and space will be devoted to some perspectives on interpretation and its relation to observing and understanding children.

Some Definitions and Conceptions of Explanation: To explain behavior, for instance, is to make it clear or understandable. Making behavior clear or understandable can, in turn, involve interpreting that behavior so as to go beyond the actions performed or the words spoken and give those actions or words meaning or significance for some purpose and within some context. In this case, to explain means "to offer reasons for or a cause of " [something] (*The American Heritage Talking Dictionary*, 1995).

In addition to the dictionary definition just offered, there is a conception of explanation that is especially relevant to the basic theme of this manual. It is a conception proposed by Don Ihde (1977) who says that "explanation is any sort of theory, idea, concept . . . that attempts to go *behind* phenomena, to give the reasons for it in terms other than what appears" (italics in original).

Although it may be a bit confusing at this point, Ihde's conception of explanation gets at the heart of what is involved in observing and explaining behavior and developmental change. How is this so, and what bearing does it have on your observations?

Observation is the cornerstone of the empirical sciences, which are those that rely on the physical senses to take in relevant data and measure that data in some way. Science also goes one step further. It tries to find a relationship among the data it acquires. It is not enough simply to gather information; one must try to see how the facts science acquires fit into a broader theoretical framework. Indeed, as Brandt (1972) puts it, "Observational data possess little meaning by themselves. They allow only inferences to be made about people on the basis of their behavior." More recently, Neuman (1994) confirms Brandt's point when he writes that "Displays of behavior do not give meaning; rather, meaning is inferred, or someone figures out meaning" (p. 334). Theories provide scientists with the means to make such inferences. What a scientist (or parent or teacher) first requires are data; and data frequently are in the form of descriptions. Descriptions are a central part of your observation exercises. In addition to simply describing, you will try to interpret or explain, i.e., give a meaning to what you have seen and described. How will you do that? One way is by looking at your descriptive data through a particular theoretical perspective, which will, in a sense, "tell you" what meaning could be put on what you have observed. But, (and this is an important "but") that meaning, that explanation suggested by the theory, goes behind the phenomenon and is not itself experienced. You have supplied the meaning, but you have not experienced the meaning in the same way you have experienced the observed behavior, event or object. In fact, your observed and objectively described data are connected to your explanation by an abstract conceptual framework, possibly a theory or your own personal beliefs.

Let us look at a simple example of how Idhe's notion of explanation might work. The example is given only to illustrate Idhe's concept of explanation; in a real situation, you would want a much larger and more representative sample of behavior before drawing any final conclusions. You are observing a group of four-year-olds playing outside on a playground, and the following is an example of your objective behavioral description.

Samuel walks over to Tommy, who is driving a truck around the sandbox on a road he's made by putting blocks of wood in the sand. "Can I play with you?" "OK," says Tommy, "but *I'm* the boss. This is *my* construction company, and you work for me!" Samuel nods affirmatively and asks, "Wha d'ye want me to do, boss?"

You have *seen* Samuel approach Tommy at the sandbox; you have *seen* Tommy playing with a truck in the sand; you have *heard* their brief verbal exchanges. You could have described more than what is given in the example; but even this extremely small amount of information raises questions: What might this behavior signify? What meaning does it have beyond its mere occurrence? Now you are faced with that "something that is not itself experienced." You might offer one of several explanations or interpretations of the two boys' behavior and interaction. Suppose you knew that Tommy's father owns a construction company. You could tentatively interpret Tommy's actions toward his play materials and toward Samuel as an indication of *imitation* or *identification* with his father. Tommy pretends to have some of his father's characteristics and behavior—he is the boss; he tells people what to do; and he behaves in an authoritative manner. In such an explanation, you would rely on a historical perspective—Tommy's family background—and would apply to it the psychological concepts of imitation and identification. You could also argue that Tommy is engaging in *anticipatory socialization*, which involves practicing some of the behaviors, values, and attitudes that are part of the adult role Tommy imagines himself filling when he grows up. You could see Samuel as a follower or as emotionally dependent on Tommy in this particular interaction. There are other ways you could explain or interpret Tommy's and Samuel's behavior. Whatever they might be, however, they would not be visible, hearable, touchable, tasteable, or smellable.

That is what is meant by an explanation giving reasons for something in terms of other than what appears. What appears are the things you saw and heard take place between Tommy and Samuel. The "other than what appears" are the abstract ideas you used to explain what occurred—the ideas of identification, imitation, anticipatory socialization, and emotional dependency. You have not, however, experienced identification. You have experienced some small portion of Tommy's behavior that, to you, indicated a particular psychological process. This general idea cannot be stressed too much. The sense we make of our world—at whatever level of sophistication—is formed through inferences that are founded on any number of factors or variables.

Each of us brings to any situation our own personalities, experiences, and even personal theories about how the world operates. What we observe is filtered or processed through our theories and beliefs, and we draw conclusions based on what gets through the filter. Each of us notices different information (stimuli, events) because each of us is sensitive to different aspects of our environment. As one writer states it, "Observation is based on attention and attention is *ipso facto* (by the fact itself) selective" (Brandt 1972, italics in original). Or, to put it into another context, teachers (child care workers) are more likely to see those aspects of children's behavior that fit into, let's say, their professional interests or training, than those that do not. For instance, if a teacher is particularly interested in children's social development, she might tend to overlook, "not to see," or at least to de-emphasize, motor behavior. Or, perhaps more likely, she will see motor behaviors as a means to promote social skills; she will see these behaviors in light of their relevance to social behavior. In contrast, a teacher whose special interests or concerns lie with children's physical/motor development is more apt to "overlook" social behaviors in favor of observing how they walk, run, jump, tumble, use their hands, and so on.

On a more general level, a teacher trained in the Montessori method will likely see many opportunities for children to experience self-discovery learning. Another teacher whose approach to early childhood education (or beyond) is based on behavioral analysis will see occasions where structure and teacher-directed activities are required. And yet, if in the same classroom with the same children, both teachers will have access to what is objectively the same situations and information, each will simply attend to different aspects of the situation.

The very real possibility that observers will hold different perspectives justifies, if not demands, the gathering of different viewpoints before making judgments or decisions about a child. This will help to reduce the undesirable effects of bias, although bias itself cannot be eliminated.

Some biases and perspectives are personal, and none of us can completely escape or avoid them; for that reason, they are important. If you place a high value on neatness, for example, you should be alert to the presence and potential influence of this value when you observe children who do not fit your idea of how children should look when they come to school. There are other biases or perspectives that are directly related to the observation situation or are formalized as theories or philosophies.

The theory type of bias or perspective is of some concern in this manual. Our intention ultimately is to have you bring together your knowledge of developmental theories and your observation skills, so that you can look at, describe, and interpret various aspects of children's behavior in ways that suit your particular purposes. To accomplish this goal, you must be familiar with the concept of development, some of its general characteristics, and the differing ways psychologists and theories view these characteristics.

Levels of Explanation: Mussen, Conger, and Kagan (1979) identify several levels of explanation. You can explain or interpret a child's behavior in terms of immediate circumstances. For example, Johnny leaves the big block area after his playmate Billy pushes him and says, "Go 'way, I don't wanna play with you anymore!" Johnny's leaving is a response to a present stimulus that immediately preceded his leaving the block area. This level of explanation is common, because, we all react to the demands the environment makes on us at any given moment.

The second level of explanation goes behind the present situation to deal with historical reasons. Another child might have responded differently to Billy's command to "go 'way," perhaps telling Billy he should go away or even striking out at him. Johnny's reaction has an explanation that lies somewhere in his past experiences. His parents may have taught him that he should respond to aggression by walking away; or maybe in his past encounters with aggressive children, Johnny lost fights or arguments, and so he avoids those situations. This level of explanation perhaps is relevant to Sroufe and Cooper's second factor required to explain developmental change, namely that present development is dependent on the development that has already occurred. In turn, future development is dependent on present development, and so on.

Mussen and his colleagues point out, however, that neither of these reasons explains the "purpose of the child's behavior." For purpose, we must look at the adaptive reason for the behavior: How does the behavior help the child to function within his physical-social setting or within the limits of his own personality and temperament? In the case of Johnny and Billy, there could be a number of adaptive reasons for Johnny's walking away. He might want to avoid the guilt he would feel if he violated his parents' or teacher's admonitions not to fight; he might want to avoid being punished by his parents or his teacher for fighting; or he might be afraid to fight, because in the past, he had been hurt by other children and wants to avoid being hurt again.

The last level of explanation offers reasons on an *evolutionary* basis. Evolutionary reasons are concerned with how we have come to be what we are, as a species, and why we exhibit some of the behaviors that we do in particular circumstances. Mussen *et al.* (1979) give the informative, but perhaps somewhat distressing example, of a human baby crying when punished—distressing because, as some would argue, babies should not be punished—in contrast to young monkeys that tend to "cower and assume a submissive posture when punished by their parents." The critical point here, according to Mussen *et al.*, is that the two species, human and monkey, display different responses to punishment because of genetic forces that operated during our respective evolutionary histories. This is also significant in that each species is capable of certain kinds of behavior, abilities, and learning that are not necessarily possible for other species. A classic example is that of learning a "true" language, an ability that is possible only for human beings, even though other animals can communicate with one another through signs and signals.

Characteristics of Development

To say that development is change over time is not to say that just any kind of change counts. As Vimala Pillari (1988), a social worker, points out, "An accident in a house can bring about changes in people's lives, but these are nondevelopmental changes: random, unorganized, and unsystematic" (p. 3). Pillari also calls nondevelopmental changes *nonnormative life events* (p. 3), by which she apparently means those events that are not expected or for which one is not prepared. She includes such things as the death of a young child or even a "sudden financial inheritance" (p. 3) among these nonnormative life events. Psychologists believe that developmental change has certain special characteristics. The picture is made more complicated by the fact that psychologists themselves differ as to how to define or describe development or as to what characteristics or features it must possess. These disagreements result in a variety of theories and perspectives on development and behavior, as well as in a variety of opinions regarding how best to explain them. Because this manual tries to present varying points of view of the developmental process, some of the basic issues associated with the concept of development are presented now.

Development as a Continuous Phenomenon: Let us begin with the belief that developmental change takes place throughout the life cycle. Physical growth seems to stop, of course, and further change in size is more the case of putting on or taking off weight than it is the continuation of physical growth as a process. As Craig (1989) puts it, "Any single structure or capability usually has its point of optimal maturity. *Growth* usually refers to the increase in size, function, or complexity to that point of maturity" (p. 8; italics in original). Many psychologists agree, however, that we do continue to develop socially, emotionally, intellectually, and so on, until we die. This view was expressed earlier in this chapter when we cited Sroufe and Cooper's (1988) assertion that developmental theories essentially agree that there is a continuity to development, although such continuity operates against a background of ongoing developmental change. This agreement regarding the continuous aspect of development occurs despite the fact that various theories take different perspectives or approaches. Some focus on innate or inherited characteristics, whereas others focus on environmental experiences. Still others argue for the interaction between heredity and environment.

Whatever view you take, continuity explains why it is that certain characteristics possessed at one stage in life are likely to be present at later stages, even though developmental changes have occurred that in other respects make the individual different from what she was before. Shyness, for instance, is a characteristic that tends to show continuity from one developmental period to another, perhaps even persisting through adulthood.

Qualitative vs. Quantitative Change: "Qualitative" and "quantitative change" are important concepts. As Lawrence Schiamberg claims (1985) "the study of human development emphasizes two types of change in human beings over time: *quantitative* change and *qualitative* change" (p. 5; italics original). The term "quantitative" is often used when talking about physical growth, where it is the quantity or amount of something measurable—such as height or weight—that changes with maturation. Growth changes can also include such other things as "number of years of education and size of family" (Schiamberg, 1985, p. 5). Qualitative change, on the other hand, often refers to changes in psychological functions, such as speech, emotions, and intelligence. Here, there is not the adding-on process that characterizes quantitative change. In qualitative change, the basic nature or organization of the child's behaviors and behavior patterns changes. For instance, speaking in three- to four-word sentences is not just more of the child's earlier cooing or babbling; nor is solving relatively complex arithmetic problems simply more of the earlier ability to match up one set of objects with another set to get the same number. In attaining these higher-level skills or capacities, it is believed that some kind of reorganization or basic modification has occurred in the way the child thinks, the way she perceives and reasons about the world. Piaget called such a reorganization a change in the child's cognitive structure. Lefrançois (1992), you will recall, defined growth as a process of addition rather than a process of transformation. Transformation is here equivalent to the idea of reorganization. Addition and transformation, therefore, address respectively the difference between quantitative and qualitative change. Jerome Kagan (1971) described quantitative and qualitative change like this: "The phenomena of growth fall into two patterns: enlargement and change. The leaf expands as it grows, but it does not alter its essential form. The butterfly, on the other hand, passes through dramatically different stages en route to adulthood." The leaf exemplifies quantitative change; the butterfly, qualitative change.

The Cumulative and Directional Aspects of Developmental Change: Although some psychologists believe that development leads to behaviors that are qualitatively different from earlier behaviors, they do not say that later behavior patterns have no connection with earlier ones. Some believe quite the opposite: Every stage or behavior within a stage builds on what has gone before, and it forms the foundation for what is yet to come. In more technical language, development is said to be cumulative. This characteristic is one of the three factors that Sroufe and

Figure 2-1   The change from this fetal hand to a fully-formed hand is an example of differentiation.

Cooper (1988) say are needed to explain how development takes place. In this view, all developmental change contributes to the essentially forward direction of the developmental process. The idea of a "forward direction" to development apparently can involve at least two ideas or approaches: One can ask whether development leads to some "ideal goal" or "most mature level of functioning" (Mussen, Conger, and Kagan, 1979, p. 34). Or one can more simply define "directional" as meaning that "development can always move toward greater complexity" (Sroufe and Cooper, 1988, p. 7), a concept we shall discuss below.

Not all psychologists believe that development moves toward some ideal goal. As Mussen *et al.* (1979) point out, "Learning theorists do not assume that the child is necessarily traveling in any special direction, even though his behavior is changing every day." In this context, behavior and development lead to the ability to survive in an environment—to adapt to the demands of a particular physical and psychological environment. Piaget, on the other hand, thought of the individual as progressing toward a state of developmental maturity characterized by certain mental abilities such as the ability to reason and deduce logical conclusions. What is relevant to your observations is the question of how you will interpret differences among children of various ages, as well as differences that a given child will exhibit in his behavior. Will differences and changes be most meaningfully explained as quantitative or as qualitative ones? Will you see the child as progressing toward some optimum goal or end state of development in which all behaviors build onto one another and ultimately contribute to the child's reaching that optimum goal? Or will you see the child as changing because of the continual learning of responses, but which do not necessarily lead to any particular goal or developmental objective?

Complexity, Differentiation, and Hierarchical Integration: There is another characteristic of development that most psychologists would agree on regardless of their theoretical orientations: Development, as a reflection or manifestation of its "directional" aspect, results in increasing complexity in organization and functioning. As a child gets older and more mature, his behavior, emotions, motives, abilities, and language become more sophisticated and refined, not less so. This increase in complexity is partly the result of the child's learning how to do more things, but there is something else. The child's knowledge and abilities increasingly form a unified, integrated whole. Psychologists speak of differentiation and hierarchic integration when referring to this movement toward complexity. *Differentiation* means that behaviors that initially are expressed in a diffuse way, eventually separate out and become more skilled, more specific, and more independent of one another. "More specific" means that previously unspecialized body parts and responses become specialized; they take on particular functions or play particular roles. For example, the very young infant exhibits seemingly random muscle movements; she moves almost her entire body when responding to even a specific, focused stimulus such as a pin prick to the foot. Later on, however, she is able to move just her foot, thus indicating that body movements and muscle groups have become differentiated and capable of responding more precisely to specific stimuli.

Hierarchic integration takes place when the child can combine various skills, behaviors or movements and have them work together as a harmonious unit. Thus, finger movements become differentiated from larger arm movements, and although each type of movement can serve a different purpose and be brought into play independently of the other, the arms and fingers can also work together as an integrated unit. This coordination permits the child to reach for and grasp an object. Reaching and grasping generally also involve visual functioning, which illustrates even greater integration. As another example, the child initially differentiates single words as she acquires a speaking and listening vocabulary; eventually, she combines those words into complex, grammatically correct sentences. With this integration, he can express increasingly more complex thoughts and ideas.

One can think of developmental change as occurring in an orderly and lawful fashion; it can also be viewed as occurring in a sequential manner. There most likely is a general consensus that development is not haphazard or random, but not everyone agrees that it unfolds sequentially. The environmentalists—learning theorists—for example, are not likely to adopt this conception of development. Stage theory best depicts development as a sequential, orderly movement. Development is seen as occurring in a stair-like manner; the general timing, rate, and order of the stages are determined by genetic or maturational factors. Piaget's theory, for example, maintains that there are four such steps: (1) the sensorimotor, (2) the preoperational, (3) the concrete operational, and (4) the formal operational stages, in that order. Freud and Erikson also proposed stage theories, but with different content. The sequential nature of development also imposes several restrictions on how change can occur:

a. The various stages or steps cannot be skipped—the child cannot go from the sensorimotor stage to the concrete operational stage, for instance.
b. Their essential order cannot be disturbed—the child cannot go from the sensorimotor stage to the concrete operational stage, and then go back to "pick up" the preoperational stage.

Figure 2-2 Physical-motor development occurs along cephalocaudal (head to tail) and proximodistal (center-to-edge) principles.

c. The order of the stages as well as their content are universal—they are found in children everywhere regardless of their social or cultural backgrounds.

These restrictions, by the way, appropriately fall under the universal aspect of development as proposed by Sroufe and Cooper (1988) and Mussen *et al.* (1984).

The limitation on the order that stages must follow does not account for the fact that not all children progress equally far through all the stages. Not everyone reaches Piaget's final stage of formal operations, for example, which could be the result of individual differences, a particular genetic inheritance, or we suppose, situational factors.

One important feature of stage theories is that they allow us to recognize certain principles or laws by which change can be described, explained, and predicted. It is the orderliness and predictability of change—within certain limits—that help make possible the scientific study of children.

Perhaps the most evident sequences that take place in a child over time are those that describe physical-motor development. The sequences in which motor abilities emerge have been designated as *principles*, which means that they operate predictably in all children in all cultures. The *cephalocaudal principle* (head-to-tail) of motor development says that the child first gains control over the movements of his head and neck (lifting the head up off the mattress, for example), whereas control over foot movements comes last. A second principle, the *proximodistal principle*, says that the child first gains control over those body parts closest to the body's midline—the shoulders, upper arms, and chest; then he gains control over the more distant parts such as the fingers. These sequences also describe a pattern that progresses from gross (large) muscle control to fine (small) muscle control. This genetically preprogrammed sequence of motor skills can be observed as the child accomplishes the milestones in motor development depicted in Table 2-2.

Table 2-2 Selected Developmental Milestones

Age	Postural Control	Locomotion	Manual Control
2–3 Months	Holds head steady when in upright position. While in prone position, lifts head up far enough to see what is in front of her.		Starts to reach for objects, but efforts are poorly coordinated. Holds on to objects for short time.
4 Months	Holds chest up while in prone position. Head control more stable than before.	Rolls over from back to stomach and from stomach to back.	Shows better-coordinated visually directed reaching, but attention alternately shifts from hand to object (Faw & Belkin, 1989).
5–8 Months	Gets into a sitting position by himself; sits by himself unsupported. Most can stand while holding on to something.	Some can move in a *side-stepping* fashion while holding on to furniture. From 5–8 months, most learn to crawl with the body on the ground, or creep on hands and knees; some scoot in a sitting position.	Craig and Kermis (1995) put-visually directed reaching at 5 months. Up until that time, infant has the individual component skills but cannot put them together in a coordinated fashion. Eight-month-olds like to pass things from one hand to the other.
9–12 Months	By 12 months, about half of all infants can stand by themselves (Craig & Kermis, 1995).	By 9 months most can pull themselves to a standing position; some can "cruise" while holding on to to furniture. Most babies walk alone between 11 and 13 months (Craig & Kermis, 1995).	Most 12-month-olds can oppose the thumb and forefinger in a *pincer grasp*. They can open drawers, turn handles and knobs, insert things into small openings (Craig & Kermis, 1995).
18 Months	Almost all children of this age have enough postural control to walk alone; however, cannot kick a ball because of unsteadiness.	Nearly all children of this age walk alone. Some still have trouble climbing stairs; kicking a ball is hard for most, and pedaling a tricycle or jumping virtually impossible (Craig & Kermis, 1995).	Most can stack blocks to build a small tower. Can scribble with a crayon or pencil. They are better at feeding themselves and some may be able to partly undress themselves.
24 Months	Can balance briefly on one foot. Balance during locomotion is good.	Can walk and run, pedal a tricycle, jump with both feet, climb up steps.	Can throw a ball overhand; will put things into and take things out of containers; they manipulate objects of all kinds.

Compiled largely from Craig and Kermis (1995). Table format original by this author.

Three Controversies or Recurring Themes

Discussion of the remaining characteristics of development will take a slightly different track from that taken with the preceding material. Following such writers as Berger (1991) and among others, we shall identify the developmental characteristics to be presented as basic issues or themes in developmental psychology. Berger (1986) deals with two traditional issues and adds a third that perhaps is not as well known as the other two. She phrases these issues as questions: Nature or Nurture?, Continuity or Discontinuity?, and Deficit or Difference? Lefrançois (1992) refers to "recurring questions", which he identifies as the "nature-nurture controversy"; the question " . . . is development a continuous, relatively uninterrupted process or does it consist of separate stages"; and "is it best to view children as an active, exploring organism . . . [or as] a more passive recipient."

Some of the following discussion should be familiar to you. We have already touched on such topics as stage theory, the environmentalist perspective, and maturation. Now, we present some of these issues again within the broader context of "controversy" or "recurring questions."

Hereditary-Environment Controversy (Nature vs. Nurture Issue): The nature-nurture debate centers around the question of what is the primary source or cause of developmental change. There are typically three answers or perspectives to this question:

1. Developmental change comes from genetically determined processes of *maturation*, which are those changes that are "built into" the individual and unfold naturally and sequentially with the passage of time. This view, representing the *nature* side, is Arnold Gesell's maturationist theory of development;
2. Developmental change is caused by experiences (stimuli) that come from the external environment; the child responds to these stimuli, and he learns according to the principles of reinforcement. This view is represented by learning theory, or what is also referred to as the environmentalist or behaviorist view. This is the *nurture* side of the issue.
3. That the source of developmental change comes from the *interaction* between the environment and the forces of maturation. This view is represented by Piaget's, Freud's and Erikson's theories.

As Berger (1991) so aptly points out, "whether it is nature or nurture that yields the greater impact, the implications [of the answer] are significant" (p. 11). She goes on to describe some of the potential consequences of taking one or the other side of this issue. For instance, math aptitude appears to be roughly equal in boys and girls in elementary school, but at about eighth grade, boys on average, begin to perform at higher levels than girls. Berger asks whether this discrepancy is the result of maturation or of differences in experience. She argues that if the seeming difference in math performance is the result of genetically related differences in fundamental ability, then it would be foolish and frustrating to push young women to do as well in math as men. On the other hand, if such differences are the result of learning or socialization, then "precious mathematical talent" would be wasted "by not encouraging girls to develop their full math potential" (Berger, 1991, p. 11).

Development as Sequential in Nature—The Continuity vs. Discontinuity Issue: We have already discussed the term "continuity" as one of the characteristics of development. In that discussion, however, continuity meant *stability over time*; the persistence of certain traits from one stage or period of developmental change to another; or the fact that development is considered to occur throughout the entire life span, with any given level of development being dependent on, or partly a function of, whatever development has occurred up to the present moment.

In the continuity vs. discontinuity issue, a different meaning is needed. Here, continuity refers to a more or less gradual growth or developmental progression, where what seems to be an abrupt change—a baby's first step—is actually not abrupt at all, but is, as Berger (1991) puts it, "the final event in weeks of growth and practice" (p. 12). Incidentally, continuity is frequently associated with the concept of quantitative change, which again, is change characterized by gradual increments or additions to some trait, ability, or physical structure.

Discontinuity, in contrast, proposes the emergence of identifiable stages, with each stage showing qualitative differences from all previous stages. Thus, discontinuity is linked with qualitative change in a manner parallel with the link between continuity and quantitative change mentioned above. "Milestone" events, such as taking a first step or learning to talk, are considered the beginning of a new stage. It's critical to understand that in the discontinuity view of development, walking and talking are *not* just more of the earlier crawling or creeping and cooing and babbling stages. Instead, these new capacities are the result of the transformation, reorganization, or restructuring brought about by the interaction of maturation and experience. Furthermore, new potentials for behavior are opened up as a consequence of such reorganization. The discontinuity view of development, which is a stage-oriented view, is often represented by a drawing of a set of stairs.

In an earlier publication, Stone and Church (1979) also dealt with this issue, but within the context of the question "How does one describe behavioral changes—what terms does one use—and how detailed are those descriptions?" Although the term "development" seems to imply that all individuals undergo the same changes, there are individual differences in the way change occurs and expresses itself. Everyone changes, and some aspects of change are shared by all human beings. Stone and Church (1979) refer to development as "changes in the structure and properties of behavior which take place in the course of a lifetime." Changes in the "structure and properties of behavior" involve some common and basic occurrences. For example, all "normal" children eventually walk, talk, control their bodily functions, learn to solve problems and make decisions, acquire a self-concept, and so on. As Stone and Church (1979) point out, however, ". . . no two people's lives follow the same course, even though there are some common features to be found in the life histories of almost everybody."

Development is the result of such factors as each person's unique personal characteristics (intelligence, attitudes, personality traits, health, temperament), family characteristics (size, parental discipline and rearing techniques, socioeconomic status), and the events that take place in her life. As Stone and Church indicate, each individual reaches maturity partly in his own way; what we all have in common is our humanity, and it is our humanity that provides developmental change with the common characteristics it possesses.

There are some variations in the viewpoints regarding description and individual differences. For the behaviorist (mechanistic or environmentalist model), change is described as the acquisition of a new association, a new connection between a stimulus, a response, and the consequences of that response. For example, if six-month-old Roberta smiles at her mother during meal time, and if that smile brings a pleasant reaction from her mother, Roberta is more likely to smile again during meal time. Roberta will have acquired what is called a *stimulus-response bond*. At some point, Roberta may smile at other persons and in other situations; if smiling again leads to positive reinforcement, another link will have been added to the learning chain. Those who believe the learning theory point of view believe that learning, and therefore development, is a matter of accumulating more and more of these new connections or stimulus-response bonds. According to the learning theory perspective, individual differences are quite easy to account for: different children have different experiences, different sets of associations, and different learning histories.

Those who support the interactionist (Piagetian, cognitive) perspective claim that one must describe development and its accompanying behavior "in great detail," and must "demonstrate how it (the behavior) differs from what was present before, and try to infer the change in mental mechanisms leading to the change in behavior" (Mussen *et al.*, 1979). "Change in mental mechanisms" involves qualitative change. From the stage theory or interactionist perspective, differences between individuals are accounted for in several ways. "The Piagetian view, insofar as it addresses the issue, can only explain individual differences in terms of exposure or nonexposure to the conditions that will permit maturational possibilities to fulfill themselves" (Mussen *et al.*). According to Piaget, cognitive development depends on the biological process of maturation together with the amount and kinds of stimulation and experiences needed to grow intellectually and cognitively. A deprived environment may stifle cognitive development; but inadequate genetic potential can have the same effect. A somewhat different position is reported by Richard Lerner (1976), who states that according to stage theory, people may differ from one another in only two ways: (1) in the *rate* or speed at which they progress through the various developmental stages, or (2) in the final level of development attained. Thus, individuals can differ in how fast they develop or in how far they develop. Not all children take two years to get through Piaget's sensorimotor stage, for example; nor does everyone reach the period of formal operations, Piaget's final stage of cognitive development.

The above discussion can put individual differences and universal patterns of development into something of an adversarial relationship, although it is not

Figure 2-3   Children need stimulation to grow intellectually and cognitively.

one that will unduly concern us. We bring it to your attention so that you can at least observe children and possibly draw conclusions based on the assumptions of individual differences within the broader framework of universal patterns.

Activity vs. Passivity in Development—Which Role Does the Child Play?:   Are children active or passive during their development? Is the child an active participant in her own development, or does she, sponge-like, simply "soak up" stimulation and experiences from the external environment? The distinction is crucial, especially when one is considering the education and socialization of children. The environmentalist point of view sees the child as essentially passive. According to this theory, it is the environment, and how it is arranged with regard to reinforcements, that produces learning and, therefore, development. Put another way, the child (and adult) is a reactor to environmental stimuli and depends a great deal on the consequences of those reactions.

In contrast, for stage theorists such as Piaget, " . . . humans spontaneously initiate their actions; they play a constructive role in their own psychological experience and development" (Langer, 1969). Humans are therefore actors who seek stimulation. Again, it is the contributions of both heredity and environment that result in developmental change. One of the contributions of heredity is to pre-program humans to initiate interactions with their surroundings.

Deficit or Difference?:   Berger's (1991) "deficit or difference" issue is an interesting one. She asks "Is there one pattern of human development that is the usual or normal one? Or are there as many paths of development as there are individuals" (p. 13). She notes that the idea of "one universal pattern [of development] was held by many of the first scientists interested in development" (p. 13). The concept of norms came out of the early studies that were based on this belief in universal development.

But Berger (1991) points out that the idea of universality is being questioned by another perspective. She writes that

> differences have increasingly come to be seen as alternative paths of development rather than inferior ones ... Contemporary developmentalists are much more likely to recognize the unique characteristics of each child, each family, each culture, than they are to stress the universal generalities that apply to all of them. (p. 13)

Stone and Church (1984) said much the same thing as Berger in this regard. Following a discussion of continuity and regularity in development, they state that

> What we are saying is that our account of development must acknowledge the common path of human development, yet still recognize that there are many different ways of becoming human. (p. 6)

This is evidenced by the different beliefs psychologists hold about development. Even the developmental changes we observe in real children are not always readily understood or unambiguous, particularly when we compare children with one another and find sometimes marked, and sometimes subtle, differences among them.

This is not to say that there are no predictable aspects to developmental change. Psychology has discovered principles and regularities that govern and define growth and development in particular areas of functioning. Recall, for example, the **cephalocaudal** and **proximodistal** priciples of motor development. Other regularities include, among others, the emergence of first teeth at about six months of age on average; the rapid growth of the brain during the first several years, with especially rapid myelinization and the laying down of neural connections between parts of the brain; or the best time to begin toilet training, which for most children is "the end of the second or beginning of the third year" (Berk, 1996, p. 189). But such regularities notwithstanding, what you observe, and the sense you make out of your observations, are influenced by the various issues that have been discussed. For example, do you believe children are active participants in their own development, or passive reactors to environmental stimuli? Do you conceive of change as the adding on of more and more stimulus-response associations, or as the progressive acquisition of qualitatively different abilities? You can supp¹⁄ _____ ₐal questions.

An important point here is that these differences in beliefs have a strong influence on what you "see." But perhaps even more important, they have an influence on what you do to, with, or for children.

Egocentrism and Autonomy: Salkind (1981) notes that development and maturation result in a lessening of *egocentrism*. This is an important concept in

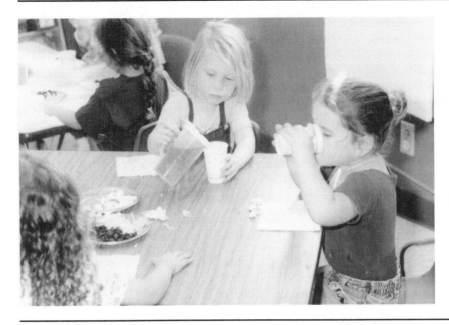

Figure 2-4   Self-help behavior.

Piaget's theory. Egocentrism is the young child's inability to view the world from perspectives other than her own. As Papalia and Olds (1993) put it, egocentrism *"is a form of centration: these children are so centered on their own points of view that they cannot take another's view at the same time"* (p. 303). Egocentrism is a "limitation of thought, something preventing children from imaginatively stepping outside themselves and seeing from a different viewpoint" (Papalia and Olds, 1987, p. 281). Egocentrism can be demonstrated in many ways. A three-year-old, for example, begins to tell you about what happened to her before she came to school that morning. In her story, she mentions names of people you do not know and have never heard of. The child does not realize that "Billy" has no meaning for you; she does not bother to explain who Billy is so you can follow her tale of adventure. As the child matures, she becomes less egocentric and more *sociocentric* or capable of seeing the world from different points of view. You should note here that childhood egocentrism, as proposed by Piaget, is not the same as egotism, which is often applied to adults who are unwilling (rather than unable) to take another person's point of view.

The second trend noted by Salkind is the *development of social autonomy*. This refers to the child's increasing independence and ability to rely on himself for the satisfaction of various needs and desires. In short, the child becomes more self-sufficient. This aspect of change and of children's behavior will certainly be

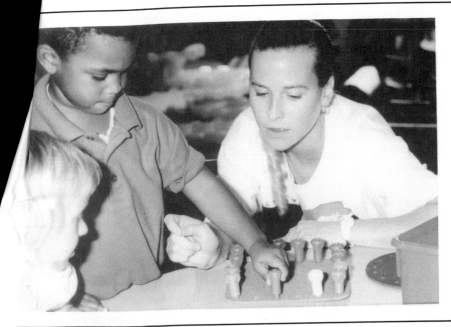

Figure 3-1 Teachers observe for various reasons. What might this teacher's observational goals be?

Observational objectives are numerous. An objective might be to gain experience in observing children of various ages. Gaining experience in observing children, on the other hand, ultimately can serve further purposes that are more specific and sharply defined. Learning how children behave in particular situations, and why they behave as they do, is such a purpose. Such information could be used to change the equipment and materials in a classroom, or to change the arrangement of the equipment and materials. Modification of seating patterns during story time might be made because of a teacher's observation that certain children, when together, seem to foster arguments or inattentiveness to the teacher. Or, a teacher and her staff may want to assess the effectiveness of their efforts to bring a shy four-year-old out of his "shell" and to encourage him to interact more with the other children. Some observational objectives are not specifically identified beforehand. Nonetheless, as in the above example of children's disruptive behavior during story time, certain behaviors and events are noticed, because a teacher and staff are alert to the general objective of using observation to promote the well-being of the children in their care.

In relation to the exercises in this manual, you have to know why you are in a particular observational setting. What are you supposed to see there? The success of your efforts to see what you are looking for depends only partly on your knowledge, values, experiences, and skill. Objectives have to be matched with resources, settings, and recording methods. For example, if an exercise calls for observing an infant's reflexes, it would be inappropriate to ob-

a noticeable one, especially as you observe children through various periods in the life span. Erikson's theory also addresses the notion of autonomy. His second stage of *psychosocial development*—which lasts roughly from one to three years of age—is called the stage of "autonomy versus shame and doubt." During this stage, children want to use their newly acquired mental and physical skills by choosing and deciding things for themselves. The ability to walk, to reach for and grasp objects with well-coordinated movements, the desire to make decisions for himself, all contribute to the child's solution to the psychosocial crisis as theorized by Erikson. If the child is granted reasonable independence and is permitted to use his new-found motor abilities, he will resolve this second psychosocial crisis by acquiring a basic sense of autonomy. If the child is prevented from exercising his skills, he will develop a basic sense of shame—shame for not being able to do what he perceives he should be able to do. A sense of doubt will result if the child comes to believe that he is *unable* to perform adequately his various motor skills.

Whatever conceptualization of autonomy you care to use, this aspect of change and of children's behavior will certainly be a noticeable one, especially as you observe children through various periods of the lifespan. Ordinarily with age and developmental maturity come increasing independence and the ability to take care of oneself. Again, however, keep in mind that autonomy is always relative to any individual's level of competence, which means that children's efforts to be independent must be weighted against their respective abilities and level of developmental maturity.

Summary

In this chapter, we have discussed some of the conceptual and theoretical characteristics of development; characteristics that vary, depending on which theory or viewpoint one is using. Development is not a simple, straightforward concept with consistent, uniform properties. This is evidenced by the different beliefs psychologists hold about development. Even the developmental changes we observe in real children are not always readily understood or unambiguous, particularly when we compare children with one another and find sometimes marked, and sometimes subtle, differences among them.

This is not to say that there are no predictable aspects to developmental change. Psychology has discovered principles and regularities that govern and define growth and development in particular areas of functioning (recall the discussion of the principles of motor development, for example). Such regularities notwithstanding, what you observe, and the sense you make out of your observations, are influenced by the various issues that have been discussed. For example, do you believe children are active participants in their own development, or passive reactors to environmental stimuli? Do you conceive of change as the adding on of more and more stimulus-response associations, or as the progressive acquisition of qualitatively different abilities? You can supply additional questions.

An important point here is that these differences in beliefs have a strong influence on what you "see." Perhaps even more important, they have an influence on what you do to, with, or for children.

Study Questions

1. What is a major difference between growth and development? Do you think the difference is an important one with regard to observing and understanding children? Why or why not?
2. Mussen and his colleagues identified four levels of explanation: immediate, historical, adaptive, and evolutionary. Describe three imaginary observation situations where the first three levels of explanation might be used to understand or explain a child's behavior.
3. Describe in your own words what is meant by the statement that explanation attempts to go *behind* a phenomenon. What does this statement have to do with observing and interpreting children's behavior?
4. A teacher believes that children are passive with respect to their development; another teacher believes they are active. What differences might you observe in the respective classrooms of these two teachers? What kinds of interactions might take place in the two contexts?
5. Of the two concepts, individual differences and universal patterns of development, which one do you think would be easier to base conclusions on after observing some children's behavior?

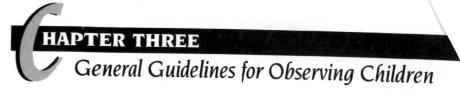

CHAPTER THREE
General Guidelines for Observing Children

Objectives

After studying this chapter, you will be able to

- discuss the steps that must be taken to prepare to observe
- discuss the role of inconspicuousness in observing children
- analyze the role of professional ethics in observation
- identify factors that affect observation
- discuss the three categories of errors in observation
- discuss the three aspects that affect the accuracy and reliability of observation
- analyze the potential dangers of evaluating the worth of children's behavior
- distinguish several kinds of groups
- discuss several approaches to group observation

The following guidelines provide a framework within which you can formulate your own thinking and behavior for various observation situations.

Preparation for Observing

Preparation involves several organizational steps that must be taken before you enter the observation setting.

What Are Your Purposes?:   There are many reasons to observe young children You should have yours clearly in mind as you approach your exercise Identifying your objectives is a central task, because everything else depends on it. Objectives must be defined precisely enough to bring the observation activity down to a manageable size. Brandt (1972) confirms the importance this issue when he points out that the sheer complexity of behavior in naturalistic settings "makes it virtually impossible to study all significant factors time." He goes on to note that the task of the observer ("investigator") is not of studying the total "complex of activity" in a given setting, but rather "isolating and then studying the most important components of that complex Brandt's advice relates to the statement made in Chapter One—scientific servation is not merely looking *at* something; it is looking *for* something.

serve preschoolers. If you are to observe behaviors that occur infrequently, time sampling should not be the method you choose, because time sampling is best used with behaviors that occur often (see Chapter Seven).

Other questions must also be answered before you begin to observe. What developmental area or behaviors are the focus of the observation (social, physical/motor, language)? How much time are you to spend observing those behaviors (an hour, several minutes, for as long as they occur)? Whom are you to observe (individual children, a group, a particular child, several particular children)? How are you to record your observations (check list, duration record, narrative description, time sampling)? What kind of interpretations are you to make (based on a given theory, on what has taken place in the setting)?

Some of these questions are directly related to the specific recording technique you use. Let us look at the question of how long to observe. On the one hand, a time sampling procedure requires observing and recording for intermittent but uniform and relatively short time periods of several seconds or minutes. On the other hand, event sampling and the narrative description call for observation over longer periods of time. In event sampling, the length of the time you observe and record depends on how long the child exhibits the desired behavior, or what is called the **event**. In the narrative description, the length of time you observe depends mostly on such things as how much information you want or need and how long you are physically and mentally able to observe and record behavior. As you shall learn later on, the narrative description tries to capture as much information as possible, and the observer makes no prior judgments or decisions as to what is or what is not proper "grist for the mill," so to speak.

Where Are You Going to Observe?:   The site of your observations is related to your objectives, and as they change, the site may have to change. If a limited number of facilities is available, the observations, or certain aspects of the observations, will also be limited. Under those conditions, your observations will have to fit the possibilities afforded by the setting. For example, if the only structured environment in which to observe children is one local child-care center that provides care to children from three through five years of age, then you will not be able to observe two-year-olds. Your observation exercises are limited to the children accessible to you and to the characteristics and abilities typical of those age groups. In other cases, you might have access to a number of facilities and opportunities, such as child-care centers, nursery schools, kindergartens, elementary schools, and public playgrounds, which offer a wide range of ages and environments. Under those conditions, you will have more flexibility. You will need to carefully match observation exercises and purposes with specific settings.

What May You Do in the Setting?:   Knowing why you are in the observation setting includes knowing what you may or may not do there. Some settings may give you considerable leeway to do what is necessary to accomplish your objectives. Others may be more formal and not allow certain behaviors. For example, some center directors or teachers may not allow you to sit out of the way

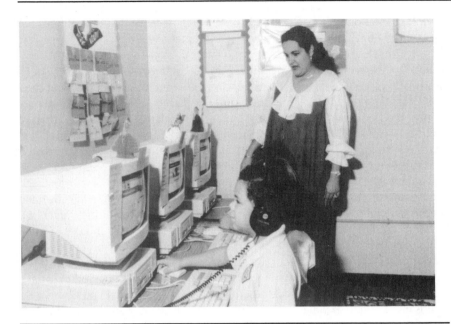

Figure 3-2   Observation can take place inside the classroom.

just observing and recording; instead, you may be asked to help the children during toilet time, snack time, or when they dress to go out. You may be required to step outside the classroom to take notes. In those cases, you will have to rely on your memory until you can get to your notebook and record your data. What you may do can be affected by the recording technique you choose. A checklist, for example, would not prevent some participation on your part. A teacher might have fewer objections to in-classroom recording with a brief checklist than with a more elaborate narrative description. You need to learn what is allowed and expected of you as an observer *before* you take on that role. This is made doubly important by the fact that child care center directors, school directors and classroom teachers differ widely in their expectations regarding acceptable behavior.

It is possible that you may experience difficulties in completing some observations because of limitations imposed by the setting. Therefore, if there are other options open to you, you may want to select a more compatible observation setting.

There is another important aspect to the issue of what you may do in the setting. In many child care centers and schools, anyone not officially associated with the facility has to have a signed permission slip before being allowed to enter the faculty to observe or conduct any kind of business. This is a matter that you will have to determine ahead of time and plan accordingly.

Figure 3-3   Some schools have observation rooms with one-way windows and counter top desks.

Inconspicuous Observation

Why Be Inconspicuous?:   There is a principle that says that observing a phenomenon changes it. Observing people *can* change their behavior, although we may not know how much their behavior changes. Their awareness of the observer's presence can distract them or motivate them to behave in ways they believe will please the observer. Behavioral changes brought about by the act of observing are of deep concern to researchers who want to study groups such as gangs, families, or nonindustrialized societies. Such researchers—anthropologists and sociologists, for example—sometimes attempt to minimize these unwanted effects by engaging in what is called *participant observation*. This means that the observer becomes part of the group and participates in as many of its activities as is appropriate for the circumstances. Teachers are participant observers as a matter of course, and there is little doubt that they are accepted by the children and can observe them without unduly influencing their behavior in ways that fall outside the planned goals and general intentions of the child care center. We recognize that, as one person communicated to us, education precisely involves changing behavior. But the term "unduly," as used above, refers to what is akin to the unintended effects of socialization. The unfamiliar person in the center or classroom can affect children's behavior, feelings, performance, etc., in ways that are not in the children's or the facility's best interests or within their stated objectives. It can be quite different in the case of an observer who is not perceived as part of the group or setting, particularly someone who comes and goes. Some believe that eventually, the observer will blend into the group and be accepted, which reduces the impact of being watched by an outsider. One can argue that it is virtually impossible for an observer to mask her reasons for being in the group well enough for the group to forget those reasons. In short, the argument goes, those being watched will always "perform" for the person doing the watching.

There may be some exceptions to this influence. Thorndike and Hagan (1977) write that "the young child has not developed the covers and camouflages to conceal himself from public view as completely as has his older brother and sister, so there is more to be found out by watching him." Inconspicuous observation tries to prevent or minimize unwanted influence on behavior. It remains a debatable point whether being observed continues to have an influence on behavior after the observer has become an accepted member of the group. Anecdotal reports on the issue do indicate that young children adapt well to the presence of unfamiliar persons. It might be prudent to advise the observer to determine empirically whether or not the children in a particular setting and under particular circumstances do in fact adjust to the presence of unfamiliar persons. This determination should guide or at least contribute to any further decisions regarding your observations.

The Difficulty of Remaining Inconspicuous: Being inconspicuous is not always easy. Any unfamiliar person in the classroom is likely to capture the attention of the children until the novelty has worn off. Sometimes observation booths are available, which allow you to observe without being seen (through the use of two-way mirrors). Their use is based on the assumption that the children do not know there is anyone behind those mirrors, or that if they do know, an unseen observer interferes less with normal behavior than one who is visible. The author's experience has been that children learn all too quickly about the existence of observation booths, as well as whether anyone is inside watching them. It is also likely, however, that if engrossed in play, children will rather quickly forget that there is anyone in the observation booth watching them, or maybe even that there is an observation booth at all, although we don't want to put too fine a point on the issue.

It is also true that children can become very curious about someone writing in a notebook, perhaps especially so if they are not used to seeing other, familiar adults who also write in notebooks. The best advice we can give you if a child asks what you are doing is simply to reply "I am working," or some other such brief but true explanation. Do not tell the child, however, that you are watching him and writing down everything he does. This serves no legitimate purpose, but it might make the child nervous, self-conscious, or otherwise cause him or her unnecessary discomfort.

There are additional problems when observation objectives call for recording behaviors that cannot be observed from a distance. Language behavior, for instance, requires you to be close enough to a speaker to hear him.

Naturally, getting that close, as well as having to be there with notebook (or if permissible, tape recorder) in hand, brings with it the possibility of calling attention to yourself. Problems can also arise when there is uncertainty concerning whether you should intrude into a situation. The role of the participant observer comes into play here. Teachers, center directors and staff members, and other similar individuals are necessarily participant observers at some time or other, and being a participant brings with it a potential problem that the "detached" observer may not have to face—namely, how to carry out one's responsibilities with the children and, if it is necessary or desired, at the same time observe and record behavior. Krogh (1994), for example, stresses the importance of teachers observing children in the classroom, but she also points up one of the difficulties. She writes:

> Take advantage of every opportunity to observe each individual child. Observation can be formal: make notes on what you see and keep a record for future reference. *Much of the time, however, formal observation isn't possible because interaction with the class is necessary and desirable.* (p. 89, emphasis added)

How and When to be Inconspicuous: In spite of the difficulties mentioned above, reliable and inconspicuous observation is possible within the requirements and limitations of the given situation. In this writer's view, an extremely important part of being inconspicuous is remaining as detached as possible or necessary from the children and their activities. This does not mean you should be cold and aloof, but only that you not try to influence behavior beyond what is required by the observation objectives or beyond what you are permitted to do in the setting. This advice should be followed according to its intent and within its appropriate context. For example, naturalistic (or informal) observation depends on the subjects of study exhibiting behavior spontaneously, and not at the prompting of the observer. There are occasions, however, when children are asked to behave in particular ways, such as in testing situations or formal research studies. In those contexts, the observer has to intrude into the children's environment in a way dictated by the purposes of the study or test. More generally, however, nearly every environment demands some particular behaviors from the individuals in it. Most environments, for example, require individuals to behave in a socially conforming manner. Even young children must learn to conform to the demands imposed by various environments or settings. Naturally, they are just learning about such things as what behavior is appropriate under what circumstances—when it is permissible to run and shout, where and when one may go to the bathroom, and so on. This writer would contend, however, that at the earliest ages, children begin to acquire some understanding of what is and what is not acceptable behavior. The key, of course, is to match one's demands to the child's ability to meet them; adults' expectations should be developmentally appropriate.

Morrison (1995) speaks to this issue in the context of adults modeling appropriate behavior for children to imitate. He cites four specific techniques the

Figure 3-4   This observer is engaging in "participant observation". By becoming part of the group she has become inconspicuous as an observer.

early childhood professional can use " ... to help children learn through the modeling," and two of these techniques are of immediate interest here: modeling and supervision. Briefly, "modeling occurs when the professional practices the behavior expected of the children." "Supervision," in turn, "is a process of reviewing, insisting, maintaining standards, and following up" (p. 480). In any child care setting, therefore, adults hold certain expectations regarding children's behavior. It's important to keep in mind that those same adults will hold expectations regarding *your* behavior while you are in the setting doing your observations.

Other kinds of demands are made, too, depending on the purpose and characteristics of the setting. In other words, our actions are almost always structured in some way; they occur within some set of acceptable boundaries. Inconspicuousness can be achieved by not further structuring or affecting children's behavior beyond what is already part of the setting and situation. Consider a brief example.

Suppose you want to observe a child's language behavior. This could require writing down word for word what the child says, to whom she speaks, and any other important circumstances surrounding her use of language. Language is a complex phenomenon, however. One can study just the language itself, that is, such things as vocabulary, sentence structure, and sentence length. One can also examine the conditions under which the child uses language and for what purposes—to ask for help, to give commands, to ask questions, to self-regulate behavior, or to persuade others. All of these are part of language development and usage.

If you are interested, for example, in seeing how Jenine uses speech under naturalistic or non-test conditions, you would have to allow her language to occur on its own. Thus, Jenine might speak very infrequently and not say very much when she does speak. If so, you may be unable to tell much about her language proficiency, but a great deal more about the social and psychological aspects of her speech—the circumstances under which she tends to talk, to whom, to what ends, and so on. What do you do in such a case?

You could remain inconspicuous by accepting Jenine's speech behavior as it naturally occurred. But, if the circumstances warrant it, you could also "test" Jenine by engaging her in a conversation and trying to draw out of her more speech than she had demonstrated up to that point. In such an instance, you would be trying to determine her level of language ability, the level at which she is able to communicate with speech. Here a distinction is made between learning (ability, skill, proficiency) and performance. The distinction is important and useful, for it points out that a child may know how to do something, but may not necessarily exhibit his ability. Most of us know how to hit, for example, but we do not go around hitting; we do not ordinarily demonstrate this skill.

If you test the child in any way, but your objectives do not justify testing, then you have unnecessarily sacrificed inconspicuousness. You have entered into the setting and changed what occurred there. Again, however, merely being present in an observation setting sacrifices some inconspicuousness. Of equal concern is how much freedom you will have to test or interfere in any way with what is going on. In a preschool, for instance, the teacher may not allow you to interact with the children; you may have to be a nonparticipant observer. The freedom issue is directly related to the process of prior preparation. Consequently, how much you are allowed to participate, or how much influence you are allowed to exert, should not take you by surprise. Participation is an aspect of observation that you should always discuss with the person in charge of the setting before you begin to observe.

In summary, think of inconspicuous observation as observation that imposes or introduces nothing into the observation setting, or on the persons and objects in the setting, beyond what is necessary to achieve legitimate objectives. Your objectives must never conflict with the objectives, philosophy or procedures of the preschool, school, or any other location in which you are doing the observing. Nor must your objectives and procedures violate the rights or privileges of any individual or group. There will be some contexts where the restrictions are fewer than those in private facilities. Public places, such as government buildings, playgrounds, and parks, are governed by laws, regulations, and even a philosophy. But these are different from the regulations and philosophies governing child-care facilities, if only because the latter have the specific goals of caring for and fostering the growth, development, physical safety, and psychological security of young children.

Some of the above concerns and issues also apply to professional ethics and confidentiality.

Professional Ethics and Confidentiality

Professional ethics and confidentiality are concerns that are inseparable from all observation activities. When you go into a particular place, you are, in some cases, a guest, (such as in a private preschool or a public elementary school). In all cases, you are a representative of your school or institution. Your behavior therefore reflects not only on yourself, but on your school and your department. If you are not a student, you still have obligations to those whom you are observing. You also have obligations to others who might have come before you and laid the groundwork and good will so necessary for observation and research activity. You also have an obligation to anyone who might come after you. One person's improper behavior can spoil it for everyone else.

The full scope of the ethical conduct issue, although an extremely important issue, cannot be covered in its entirety in this text. A copy can be obtained from NAEYC. It is a document to which you should refer whenever you are uncertain of how you may behave in any child care setting or, for that matter, *in any situation that involves children.*

What we present below is an abbreviated treatment of professional ethics and confidentiality—enough information, we trust, to get you started on your observations. Bear in mind, however, that every child care facility will have its own set of principles by which you must conduct yourself, principles that are relevant to the unique circumstances that exist in that particular setting. It is hoped, of course, that if you are in a "formal" child care setting, the staff there will be familiar enough with the broader aspects of ethical conduct to direct you toward all the proper behavior.

The Need for Professional Ethics: Research using human subjects is open to intensive scrutiny today. Gone are the times when a researcher is at liberty to do almost anything he wants in the name of science. The rights, safety (physical and psychological), and privacy of the individual are now of extreme importance when conducting research. These restrictions sometimes make the study of human behavior difficult; nonetheless, protection of rights and safety justifies that difficulty and must be preserved. Your observations are, strictly speaking, a form of research; they provide the methods and data for answering research questions. You are trying to learn about children, to understand their behaviors and how they change over time. In doing this, you will ask yourself questions; you will construct a written record of what certain children do in various situations; you will make interpretations, and might even evaluate their behaviors. In short, you are getting information about people, which must always be done with care and sensitivity. Care and sensitivity are often best served and achieved by being objective rather than subjective. An accurate description of behavior—i.e., simply conveying what happened, what was said, and what actions were performed—

is usually preferred over making judgments about the desirability or "value" of the behavior. It's imperative that you keep in mind that even so-called "objective descriptions" can sometimes reveal information that is potentially embarrassing or could be misused to characterize unfavorably an individual or group, which is a situation that is unacceptable under any circumstances. Even positive or seemingly harmless information, however, places the child and her behavior at the focus of attention, and that can cause some parents and teachers discomfort or even alarm. This concern can be partly alleviated by not using the children's real names, thus assuring parents and teachers that your observation reports will not reveal the real identity of any child. This is an assurance that is required by the ethical concern for privacy and confidentiality.

There are other concerns that involve ethics. Parents may feel distressed at the possibility of an outside observer discovering any deficiencies in their child. Parents often compare their child with other children: Does Aletha talk as well as her age mates, her family might ask? Carl's father may ask if he is as coordinated physically as the other children in the preschool—especially the other boys. Renee's mother may express concern about whether Renee is socially popular, a leader, bright, and so forth. Parents might be touchy about anyone other than the school staff observing and recording their child's behavior and developmental progress. This is especially true if the child has any characteristics that set him apart from others in a way the parents view as unfavorable. Such sensitivity on the parents' part must be matched by your own equal, if not greater, sensitivity. You must protect the child's and the parents' privacy, and you must give careful consideration to their feelings.

There is one guiding principle that is worth mentioning, perhaps because it is so easily and so frequently violated, and because it seems to cover so many situations in which ethics play a part. The principle is this: Do not communicate (talk, write, use nonverbal gestures) about any child to anyone other than the person who gave you permission to observe. ("Anyone" here includes your roommate, your best friend, your parents . . .). Furthermore, if you do discuss a young child with some appropriate individual, be certain that the child in question, any of the other children, or any other adult, do not overhear what you say. Remember, when it comes to young children, "Little pitchers have big ears."

This principle does not rule out discussing a child privately with an instructor or in a formal classroom setting, when the purpose is to aid your understanding of the child or the observation process, or to solve problems you may be encountering in doing the observations. Such discussions can still be carried on without violating the child's and the parents' rights to privacy and confidentiality.

Privacy, confidentiality, and rights also include the right of parents not to have their child be a subject of observation. Therefore, if any parents do not want their child observed and information about him recorded, you are obligated not to do so. It may be less obvious, but if a child does not want to be observed, the same ethical constraints apply as when parents refuse their child's participation. This leads to the issue of permission.

Permission extends beyond just the specific target of observation and study. You should not—indeed may not—walk unannounced and uninvited into a classroom to do your exercises. Prior permission is always necessary; at the very least, it is a sign of courtesy and respect for the teachers, staff, and children. In some instances, it can also be a matter of trespassing on private property. Gander and Gardiner (1981) suggest that written permission be obtained when observing in schools. The district supervisor or principal and the teacher can grant such permission. Gander and Gardiner also point out that school officials act in what is called *in loco parentis* ("in place of the parents"), and additional permission from the parents is therefore not necessary.

In situations where adult roles are less clearly defined than they are in the schools (e.g., in clubs, Sunday schools, and similar organizations), Gander and Gardiner recommend that permission (written and signed) be obtained from those in charge and from the parents. If you observe in a public place, such as a park, swimming pool, or playground, permission is not necessary. Nonetheless, even public settings require that you be unobtrusive; you are not permitted to disturb others, to try to get children to perform for you, or in any way to violate the rights of others in the setting. It is further suggested that, in a public place, if you are going to record the behaviors of children whose parents are present, you explain what you are doing and ask their permission (Gander and Gardiner, 1981). Asking is a gesture of courtesy, and it may help avoid suspicion.

Professional Behavior: Professional ethics demand that you behave at all times in a professional manner. This is a significant and weighty obligation, for it requires that, when necessary, you set aside your own personal preferences and wishes. Always act in accordance with the legitimate requirements and expectations (1) of the observation setting, (2) of those individuals in that setting and, in the case of minors, of those persons responsible for them, (3) of the faculty and institution whom you represent, and (4) of the observation exercises themselves. This last item refers to being intellectually honest in the performance of your exercises. In other words, be faithful to the discipline and subject matter of which your observations are a part.

Factors That Affect Observation

Observation consists of seeing certain things and recording what you have seen in a way that can be used for a particular purpose. Making meaningful, useful observations is not an easy task. There are a number of factors that can affect your observations.

Sensitivity and Awareness: Earlier, we discussed how sensitivity to children changes with experience and training, which are long-term influences. There are, however, more immediate influences that can limit your sensitivity and awareness and possibly bias your observational data and interpretations. At this very moment, you possess a particular understanding or, as Lay and Dopyera

(1977) put it, a "set of understandings or discriminations that you are capable of making about any child you encounter" (p. 70). Whatever your level of skill or understanding, there will be times and conditions when you will not observe at the level of which you are capable. Certain things will interfere with how you see the subject of your observations.

Fatigue, Illness, and Discomfort: Fatigue is an obviously limiting condition, as are illness, physical discomfort, and psychological disturbances. These conditions can distract you and take your attention away from the task at hand. You can also be distracted by psychological disturbances such as personal problems, anxieties and fears, or trying to do too much at once. Sometimes disturbances will come from the external environment and can limit your perception—noise, temperature extremes, poor lighting, or crowded conditions. Many of these variables will be beyond your personal control, but your ability to recognize the effects they have on you can be invaluable. At the very least, you will be able to identify potential sources of distraction and other types of error and, if possible, offset them in some way.

One way to offset the effects of these conditions is to try to avoid them altogether. For instance, fatigue, illness, or discomfort might justify postponing your observation until those conditions are remedied. If that is not possible or feasible, you might try doing several observations at different times. In either case, the chances are that your observations and written reports will be more objective and accurate than they would otherwise be. Keep in mind that children also suffer from fatigue, illness, and discomfort. Although these conditions are part of being human, and they certainly are of concern to all early childhood educators and other professional child care workers, sometimes the bias they impose on children's behavior and general functioning will work against you meeting your observation purposes or goals. Again, taking the above steps might alleviate the situation.

The Influence of Self or Personality: Perhaps one of the most difficult factors influencing observations is your own self or personality, a problem Lay and Dopyera (1977) refer to as "sorting out 'you' from what you view" (p. 72). Our individual experience, attitudes, needs, desires, and fears tend to act as "filters" through which we not only process what we observe, but which also affect what we notice in the first place. An observer may, for example, have a tendency to project his own feelings onto a child; he may believe that the child feels what he thinks he felt as a child or would feel in the present situation. Or, a teacher may tend to dislike or like someone who has certain characteristics or exhibits certain kinds of behaviors. These biases can influence the teacher or observer to pay either too little or too much attention to certain aspects of the child's behavior or personality, and obstruct perception of other equally important features. This seems to be especially true when the behaviors or characteristics are disliked or considered taboo by the observer. In such a case, there is an inclination to be turned off by a child who displays these traits. Such a negative reaction can be a powerful determinant of how you see and interpret that child's behavior. This becomes important again during the evaluation process.

Controlling our Biases: We all have biases, and although they cannot be completely eliminated, we can be conscious of them and take steps to control them. It is very important that the traits or characteristics that we like or dislike, easily accept or do not easily accept, do not cause us to lose our objectivity. It is particularly important not to pass judgment on children or make evaluative statements that reflect poorly on their character or worth.

To say, as an example, that a child is aggressive or dependent, meaning that he is to be thought of forever thereafter as having an aggressive or dependent personality, is not part of your observation exercises. You may, however, describe aggressive or dependent *behavior* when a child displays it. The focus on behavior can be illustrated by the now well-known advice to parents on how to respond to a child's misbehavior: Do not tell the child that she is a bad girl. Tell her that what she did is wrong. The behavior is the focus of criticism, not the basic worth and character of the individual. Positive self-esteem should always be reinforced in the child's mind, despite lapses into behavior that adults find undesirable.

Although it was stated previously that "we can be conscious of [our biases] and take steps to control them," we must also say that one of the problems with biases is that they don't necessarily jump up and bite us on the nose. They often operate outside of our conscious awareness, similar to the way we can be critical or sarcastic and express sincere surprise and disbelief when a friend (or enemy) tells us that we *are*, in fact, critical or sarcastic. It's not always possible (and certainly not easy) to identify our biases or the reasons we have them. But maybe there are occasions when it's more important to recognize *other behaviors* that might be founded on an unconscious bias and deal with those rather than with the bias itself.

For example, suppose that for whatever reason, you particularly dislike aggressive children, or aggressive behavior of any kind, no matter who displays it. (Or it might be dependent behavior that especially irks you. Or perhaps you dislike children who do not come to school looking as neat and clean as you think they should; select your own bias.) You might, therefore, have a tendency to overgeneralize from your observations a child's aggressive *behavior* and *label* the child *as aggressive* (or dependent or dirty). In other words, you have gone from seeing an aggressive episode to judging a child's personality or character. Although you may not understand why you dislike aggressiveness, you can always search for and root out language that reflects an overgeneralization or hasty conclusion based on very limited evidence.

Influence of the Setting or Situation: Other factors that could influence your observations are those imposed on you by the setting and the individuals in it. These include such things as the size and arrangement of the physical space; the equipment and materials available to the children and, in some cases, to you; and the characteristics, skills, and personalities of the children. The size and arrangement of the space can limit your observations by making it difficult to stay close to a given child or to be inconspicuous. Equipment and materials have an influence by providing children the means of exercising their skills and pursuing their interests. Characteristics of the children affect what you can do in the setting, because they help determine the kinds of behaviors that will be exhibited. Some children may be active physically, others passive and inactive; some may talk a lot, others little; some may interact a great deal with their peers, others hardly at all. The presence of various behaviors can provide you with examples of what you want to observe. Whether the absence of certain behaviors is to your disadvantage depends on your objectives. For example, if Tasha typically avoids her classmates, that avoidance might give you valuable information about her self-concept, her social skills, or her status among her peers. If, however, your aim is to observe "normal" or more extensive social behaviors and interactions, you may have to select another child.

Categories of Errors in Recording Observations

There are three categories of errors you can make in recording your observational data: (1) errors of omission; (2) errors of commission; and (3) errors of transmission (Richarz, 1980).

Errors of Omission: Errors of omission occur when you leave out information that is helpful or necessary to understanding a child's behavior. If your objectives call for it, you should include enough information to provide a complete picture of what happens during a behavioral episode. Such a picture helps you form broader and more generalized conceptions of a particular child than would otherwise be possible. Consider the following example.

Millard, a four-year-old preschooler, is playing by himself in the sandbox with a small dumptruck. While he is playing, Kent comes over and without saying a word, grabs the truck out of Millard's hand. You happen to look over toward the sandbox just as Millard hits Kent and grabs the truck. How might you describe and interpret this episode? You could decide that Millard had behaved aggressively toward Kent, and you might continue to observe the behaviors of the two children. The point here is that something important would be missing if you had accepted the incident as it appeared. Your interpretation of Millard's behavior as aggressive would be premature and not quite correct. You would have left out the critical incident of Kent initiating the aggressive action. Some would call Millard's response assertiveness. Missing part of a behavioral sequence or interaction may not make your objective description invalid; you could record very accurately the behaviors and events you did happen to observe. But remember it is not just the descriptions that are important; they must acquire a meaning that will help you understand the child and his behavior. In the above case of Millard, the meaning of his actions toward Kent would have been significantly altered, if not distorted, by leaving out the critical segment of behavior. You will describe for a purpose, and part of that purpose will be to understand the broader context of the behavior.

There are many reasons why errors of omission are made: various distractions, simply missing behaviors that have already occurred (as in the above example), or poor note-taking. Note-taking is heavily influenced by the passing of time. You may not be able to take a lot of (or any) notes during the observation session and may therefore have to rely on memory. The longer you wait to record your observations, the more you are likely to forget. Naturally, this argues for writing up your notes as quickly as possible. A very important factor is the particular way you see what you are observing: what and how much you perceive; whether what you notice is meaningful to you and, in your opinion, worth writing down; and the relationship between what you see and the purpose of your observations at the time.

Errors of Commission: In contrast, errors of commission occur when you include more information than is actually present in the situation. This involves such things as reporting that behaviors, speech, or interactions took place when in fact they did not; or reporting that certain persons were in the sitting/situation when again, in fact, they were not present at all. These errors are also made for a number of reasons, including inattention, relying on a faulty memory, and those factors that contribute to errors of omission. It is not always easy to catch these errors, particularly when they stem from your individual way of seeing. We all have gaps in our perception and understanding; at least they may be thought of as gaps by someone who sees things differently from the way we do.

Errors of Transmission: The third category is called errors of transmission. In this case, the fault lies in recording the behaviors you observe in improper sequence. This can be a serious mistake, for it is frequently the order of events that gives them meaning: What happens at 9:20 A.M. can influence what happens at 9:35 A.M., and so on. The chances of making this type of error can be reduced if you record the time at which you observe a particular behavior. Under some circumstances, you can record the times at which a given behavior begins and ends, or the time at which you start and stop observing and recording a behavior. This can be done for each behavior, event, and interaction that you observe throughout the entire period. Besides reducing errors of transmission, timing behaviors gives you information about such aspects as the length of the child's attention span and the proportion of time the child spends on particular activities.

Three Aspects of the Observation Process

If you are careful to avoid these errors, accurate and reliable observation is possible. There are three aspects to the observation process, which, if you keep them clearly in mind, will increase your accuracy and reliability. These aspects are (1) objective description, (2) interpretation (inference or explanation), and (3) evaluation.

Objective Description: This is the foundation of observation, since so much else depends on it. Objective description, sometimes referred to as reporting, consists of recording what you see as precisely and completely as possible. The term 'completely' must, however, be considered in relation to your specific purposes. There are occasions when you will want a great deal of information, which will therefore require a great deal of recording. On other occasions, your purpose may be satisfied by just recording whether a specific response has occurred, as in the case of recording how often children act "aggressively." The key word here is objective, which the *American Heritage Talking Dictionary* (1995) defines as "... Having actual existence or reality....Uninfluenced by emotions or personal prejudices: *an objective critic.*" Objective reporting leaves out your interpretations, evaluations, impressions, and speculations, and the descriptions of what you see and hear would be agreed to by anyone observing the same scene. For instance, the statement "Carlita climbed on a tricycle and rode across the room for about ten feet. The trike tipped over, Carlita fell off and began to cry" is an objective description. Another observer would describe the events much the same way. It is important to remember that absolute objectivity is not possible. Each of us views the world from a bias or perspective that differs from someone else's. In the case of the above example, just being able to describe Carlita as "riding a trike across the room" requires knowledge of tricycles and of what is meant by "riding." An acceptable level of objectivity is possible, however, in part because we in this culture share common language, values, norms, and experiences; therefore, most of us understand riding trikes.

Interpretation/Explanation: Interpretation means going beyond your objective descriptions and trying to explain or give them some meaning. If, in the above example, you were to add "because she was hurt," that would be an interpretation, especially if Carlita herself had not indicated that she was hurt. The "because she was hurt" is an interpretation (possibly an accurate one) because it goes further than simple description. You and your roommate, for example, might disagree about whether Carlita was hurt; your roommate could interpret her crying as resulting from fear or frustration rather than pain or injury.

Interpretation or explanation, then, involves attempts to identify the cause of some behavior or event; to assign motives to an individual; to determine the objectives of a behavior; in short, to provide any additional information that might make your objective descriptions more meaningful than they would otherwise be. Such additional information also includes or comes from one's knowledge of child development and developmental theory. The role of theory becomes rather obvious, for example, when, in the context of interpretation, one tries to offer some possible reasons or explanations for a child's behavior. The main point is that wherever the information comes from, it moves the observer from *what* has been observed to—it is hoped—some *deeper understanding* of the behavior's *meaning or significance.*

Evaluation: This third aspect of observation is possibly the most dangerous part of the observation process, for it is at this point that you apply your values and

Figure 3-5   A peer group.

attitudes to the child's behavior, characteristics, and personality. Evaluation refers to placing a value on, or judging the worth of, something. Unfortunately, it is all too easy to make hasty judgments or to form stereotypes about someone. Once we have the stereotype, there seems to be no need to learn more about the individual and possibly to modify our opinion of him based on further contacts and interactions.

The groundwork for evaluation is already laid during the observation and recording process, for it is there that terms such as "dependent," "aggressive," and "anxious" are used to describe and explain behavior. What is critical here is that terms such as these are often used in careless ways. They can be legitimate concepts, but they should always be strongly linked with observable behavior. Moreover, labeling a child as "lazy," for example, does not explain the child or his behavior. "Lazy" is a convenient way of summarizing one's views or attitudes about a child. What has to be described are the behaviors that led to the decision to call him lazy. What has to be explained are the reasons for those behaviors.

Derogatory labels such as lazy, dull, and unattractive should not be in the observer's written vocabulary. Any conclusions concerning a child's general characteristics or traits should be based on frequent, representative, and objectively described samples of behavior. This advice applies to both positive and negative attributes.

Group or Individual Observation

The distinction between individual and group observation is an important one. It represents a distinction between data that are useful for one purpose and data that are useful for quite a different purpose.

Limitations of Group Observation

First it is virtually impossible to observe a group and gain significant information about specific individuals. Meaningful observation of specific individuals is similar to having a meaningful conversation. You can listen only to one person at a time, and only one person can speak at a time, otherwise the conversation becomes incomprehensible. If you wish to observe even as few as two children simultaneously, you must watch first one child, then the other, shifting your attention back and forth between them.

Observing more than one individual at a time makes sense when there is an interaction going on. When two individuals are influencing or responding to each other, the interaction and its context also become important. There is an inseparable relationship between behavior and the setting in which it occurs. Behavior is influenced and governed by the characteristics of the setting, which include the nature, purpose, and location of the interaction, and the specific persons involved. Your comments in a conversation are governed in part by the other person's comments, by where you are, and by the topic of conversation.

Keep in mind that if you observe a group, you will be unable to obtain much information about individuals. You can study the behavior of groups as well as the behavior of individuals in groups, but it is necessary to consider the differences. Some of what we have just said can be qualified by considering the use of today's available technology. Videotaping, for instance, provides nearly unlimited repeated observation of a group's (or a child's) behavior and activities. The "rewind" mode of the VCR means that you can concentrate on the behaviors of every child in a given group, and you can do so at your leisure. The potential loss of information that results from having to shift your attention back and forth between children has been remedied by the videotape. Nonetheless, we would still point out that even with videotape viewing, each rewind and replay represents an actual shift in your attention from one child to another. The tape has simply greatly expanded the time you have to make the shift, thereby allowing observation for as long as is necessary to obtain the information you desire or need. Schickedanz *et al.* (1993), for example, corroborate this advantage of videotaping when, in discussing the specimen record [narrative description] technique of recording observations, they write that "This technique was extremely difficult before audio and video technology gave the researcher the tools with which to observe a moment in a child's life over and over again" (p. 26).

A word of caution, however; it is easy to become enthralled by technology, especially if it appears to make our jobs easier to perform, or if it appears to give us data of a depth and scope that are not otherwise possible. It is our contention that a videotape can never take the place of a skilled observer, no matter how sophisticated the technology might eventually become. For one thing the tape that has recorded young children's behavior in a child care setting is no better than the individual viewing that tape. It is not the video camera that does the "seeing" or the "hearing." It is human eyes, ears, and brains that ultimately have to make sense out of what the camera has captured. Videotaping is extremely limited when compared to the freedom and flexibility an observer has to have when applying his or her skills "while on the move," so to speak. It is difficult, and in some cases impossible, to take a camera into all observation environments, nor would it always be desirable to do so. With a videotape, you have frozen in time a relatively small segment of the behavioral stream, but you can't "freeze" the entire stream, any more than you can with more mundane observational techniques. However, this is not the purpose of observation. The best we can hope for is to find representative samples of children's behavior from which we can draw reasonable, meaningful conclusions that help us better understand the children in our care.

In the final analysis, *you* have to do the observing, not the camera. Whatever use videotaping has in the observation of young children, its use, in this writer's view, is at best secondary with respect to acquiring and refining personal observational skills.

What is a Group? Perspective One: A group is sometimes defined as a collection of individuals who are assembled in a particular place. This simplest of groups has no purpose around which it is formally structured; it merely consists of a number of persons who happen to be in the same place at the same time. You will recognize, however, that they could gather together for common reasons, such as to shop or watch a sporting event. Of much greater interest is the true group, which is a collection of individuals who are organized around a common purpose and who have an identifiable social structure.

Some groups are formed by an outside authority or agency. A school system establishes kindergartens, elementary and high schools; a community agency, church, or parents' group sets up a nursery school, and so on. Such groups can be referred to as *institutional groups* (Brandt 1972). This kind of formal group can contain subgroups that are spontaneously formed by the members themselves. Membership is often determined by mutual interests and common characteristics. "Mutual interests and common characteristics" can include age and developmental level, two factors specified by Bukatko and Daehler (1995), when they define a peer as "a companion who is approximately the same age and developmental level" (p. 564). Their further comments on peers and peer groups are instructive:

> Peers, however, usually function as equals, and it is primarily among equals that children can forge such social skills as compromising, competing, and cooperation. Thus, experiences with peers afford the child unique opportunities to construct social understanding and to develop social skills. (p. 564)

The above description suits those settings where the children tend to be homogeneous with respect to age and developmental level. But such homogeneity does not always prevail, thus limiting the usefulness and applicability of the concept of the peer group.

A preschool class, for example, could be an institutional group; a public kindergarten and elementary school class are clearly institutional groups because of their connection to the larger educational system. The third grade classes of two city schools could comprise peer groups. But, three children who play together in Mrs. Martin's preschool are also a peer group. This kind of group can be the focus of your observations.

The following discussion of the question "What is a group? Perspective Two" might require a background or an interest that some readers may not have. Therefore, Martin and O'Connor's (1989) systems approach to the study of groups can be omitted without doing harm to the reader's overall understanding of groups or to his or her ability to observe them. We offer the lengthier treatment of a group's characteristics for those who want to delve more deeply into the dynamics of group functioning.

What is a Group? Perspective Two: There is another way of defining or looking at the concept of group that is worth a little bit of discussion. Patricia Yancey Martin and Gerald G. O'Connor (1989), who take a systems perspective on social phenomena, identify the characteristics of small groups based on what they define as a group's four *components*. These are of interest because they can provide a framework within which to put your observations of children's group behavior. We shall adapt these authors' broad and somewhat theoretical views on groups to fit the case of children.

Component One: Member Characteristics

"*Member characteristics* are the properties, or qualities, of individuals who belong to groups" (Martin and O'Connor 1989, p. 165; italics original). The authors cite a number of individual characteristics that are of significance to observers of young children.

There are the demographic characteristics of age, gender, race, ethnic and cultural heritage, and religious commitment. They also cite the extremely important factors of "unique family and developmental biography and a distinctive psychological makeup and style" (p. 165). Also included in member characteristics are "feelings of self-concept or self-esteem . . . " (p. 165). These feelings translate into differences in assertiveness, in how loudly or persistently a child will talk, and so on. The length of time a child has belonged to a specific group is also important and can have a bearing on how that child behaves in the group.

The premise here is that these member characteristics affect how a group will engage in various activities, as well as the outcomes of those processes. Think of this "premise" as essentially meaning that all stimuli to which the group responds; all behaviors displayed by the group, as a group, fundamentally depend upon the characteristics, abilities, personalities, and so on, of its individual members. They are the filters through which all inputs come into the group and outputs leave the group. Think of it this way: there can be no track team if the persons who are to make up that team cannot run. A group of preschoolers cannot be a goal-striving group if the individual members don't have the wherewithal to accomplish the necessary tasks leading to the final goal.

Consider the following illustration: A group of four four-year-olds wants to engage in some imaginary play in which one of the children is a doctor, another is a nurse, and the other two are patients. It may matter very little whether or not these children have accurate knowledge about what physicians and nurses actually do; it is, after all, *their* fantasy, and they have no obligation to conform precisely to reality. The "doctor" can do doctor things as he or she sees fit. But, it may make a difference to the success of their play if they can agree on who will assume each of the required roles. If each child wants to be the doctor, or the nurse, or the patient, and if each is unyielding in his or her insistence on playing that specific role, the imaginary play will never happen. It is then that "all behaviors displayed by the group, as a group, fundamentally depend upon the characteristics, abilities, personalities, and so on, of its individual members."

Component Two: Member Behaviors

Member behaviors are defined very simply by Martin and O'Connor (1989) as "the actions of individuals in a group," although they add "during group meetings" (p. 165). We can replace this last phrase by "during group activities" or "during group interactions." Martin and O'Connor emphasize that member behaviors will differ according to the basic purpose of the group—a task group, for instance, as opposed to a play group. It's essential to note that, according to the authors, "member behavior is necessary for group development" and that "without member behaviors, individuals remain isolated and a group never forms" (p. 165).

Member behaviors appear so basic a requirement that you might wonder why Martin and O'Connor even mention it. For our purposes, we would only ask you to keep in mind that it's not just any collection of individuals that constitutes a group. There must be some consistent behaviors that "connect" members in some meaningful way. Furthermore, as we shall discuss below, an essential characteristic of a group is the relationships, or relationship patterns, that eventually form and distinguish not only one group from another, but also distinguish a group from a "non-group."

Component Three: Group Contextual Characteristics

"*Group contextual characteristics* are the properties of a group as a system that are relatively constant or enduring" (p. 167, italics original). These characteristics "include the social, relationship, and procedural phenomena that *emerge* through members' individual and interpersonal behaviors" (p. 167, italics original).

Group contextual characteristics depend upon the interactions among group members, which lead to the development of such things as "group goals, rules, procedures, a common identity, shared standards for assessing both each other's and the group's actions and progress, and so on" (p. 167). Martin and O'Connor (1989) identify three contextual characteristics of small groups: group norms, group climate, and "a group's normal round of procedures" (p. 167). These deserve some discussion.

Group norms are shared standards for appropriate behavior. As Martin and O'Connor put it, "norms have a *should* quality to them" (p. 167, italics original). It's important to point out that norms are often associated with *roles*, which are recurring patterns of behavior that are in turn associated with a position in a social group. (For example, the social position of *teacher* requires such role behaviors as giving instructions, handing out assignments, and giving grades.) Of potential interest to the observer of young children is Martin and O'Connor's claim that "certain aspects of the *role of group member* are normative, that is, they are required because of shared expectations for members' behavior, whereas others are not" (p. 167; italics original). For example, a preschool group may have the (adult-generated) expectation that there be no behaviors such as pushing or other forms of aggression, but there may be no particular expectation regarding the kinds of games or activities the group should engage in.

Group climate is very close if not identical in meaning to our concepts of setting, situation, and context. Martin and O'Connor (1989) define group climate as "the shared socioemotional atmosphere or mood of a group" (p. 168). You should recognize that a group's climate can remain relatively stable or it can change. Changes can be the result of things that happen within the group as such, or that affect the group in relation to its environment (Martin and O'Connor, 1989, p. 168). For example, an especially dominant child might leave a group, which could leave the group without an effective leader. The effects of that situation depend, of course, on a number of factors; but the broad effects could be a dramatic change in how the group behaves, the goals or tasks it undertakes, and even whether the group stays together at all.

Moving the group to another environment (climate) can also change the dynamics and relationship patterns for the better or for the worse. Different equipment and materials in the new setting, for instance, might change the group's behavior and possibly even its leadership. In a former setting, one child may have been the leader because of his or her skill with a particular piece of equipment. In a new setting, a different child may be especially competent with yet a different piece of equipment, thus gaining the group's deference with respect to its use and role in the group's functioning. The possibilities are great indeed.

A *group's normal round of procedures* is, according to Martin and O'Connor, "the agenda of typical or routine activities that a group follows to accomplish its goals" (p. 168). Preschool groups may establish such rounds of activities if they exist long enough for the members to reach this kind of agreement and settled routine. Of course, it's also possible that the simple addition of a new but dominant member might change the "round" for as long as that individual is present in the group. That is to say, a group's normal round of procedures depends on the group's purposes as well as on all of the components being discussed.

Component Four: Group Episodes

Group episodes, say Martin and O'Connor (1989), are "shared, system-level events, incidents, or happenings that occur in groups that are characterized by continuous activity" (p. 168). The authors present an informative analogy for thinking about group episodes. They write that "Episodes are like scenes in a play; each has distinctive content and meaning but can be understood fully only in relation to the total 'drama' or group context" (p. 168). The concept of episode reflects the extreme importance of context in understanding behavior. Indeed, it can be said that an individual's behavior ultimately has meaning *only* in some social context or other. This is so because human beings can seldom, if ever, totally remove themselves from the social environment or from the already existing influences of such an environment.

It's assumed here that as "a series of shared events," episodes "are more than the discrete acts and behaviors of individual members" (Martin and O'Connor, p. 168). Essentially, this means that episodes depend for their meaning or significance on the *relationships among the group members*, rather than on the actions of any particular person or persons in the group. Martin and O'Connor (1989) give episodes the very important role of giving "meaning to members' behavior and help(ing) them interpret and make sense of what is said and done" (p. 168).

Use will be made of the episode concept in your observation exercises. According to the concept, children's behavior, *as individuals,* can make sense only when viewed from the perspective of the larger group and its influence on each individual member. Each member's behavior "connects" with someone else's behavior, which is how relationships are established. Ultimately, a network is constructed, in which the behavior of a number of individuals combines or interacts to produce what we call a group. Sarah's behavior while in the group is affected by, say, Mark's behavior. Staying with Martin and O'Connor's analogy, Sarah and Mark are actors in a play. One does or says something as a result of what the other has done or said. It's like following the directions of a script. Most importantly, Sarah's behavior, as an individual, makes the most sense when it is considered *in relation to Mark's behavior.* This relationship is the group episode, or it forms part of a larger group episode. Relationships also make behavior social; their absence effectively leaves behavior *asocial* (or nonsocial).

Some Approaches to Group Observation: Almy and Genishi (1979) point out that "Teachers have always known that every group of children has its own distinctive qualities. Like individuals, each group or class is unique." Each group also has distinctive influences on its members; therefore, the group is part of the setting. Here is an example.

> Julie, Erica, and Floyd often form a small play group. Their activities are varied, ranging from dramatic play, where Floyd nearly always plays the "daddy" and Julie and Erica take turns being the "mommy," to building with

big blocks, where there is no set or consistent pattern of interaction among the three children. They seldom quarrel, and any disagreements tend to be short-lived. None of the three children seems to emerge as a leader.

From time to time, Erica also participates as a member of another group, this one consisting of herself, Roger, and Tanya. These three children, however, seem more restricted in their activities. They seldom play house because arguments usually break out between Erica and Tanya over who will play the mother. Roger does not like to build with blocks, and the girls do not press for that activity. Tanya seems more of a leader than a follower, although Erica will occasionally challenge her attempts to lead. This second group does not play together for the relatively long periods of time that characterize the play of the first group.

How could you approach these two different situations?

One way would be to concentrate on the behaviors of each child as an individual. You would notice the different responses, play patterns, and peer relationships, but they would be put solely in the context of the individual. Thus, you could describe Erica's behavior in each of the two groups: what she said and how she said it, her gross and fine muscle activities, her social and emotional responses, and so on.

A second approach would be to observe individual behaviors, as before, but place them within the larger framework of the three-person groups in which they occurred. Now Erica's behavior is seen in light of its group context. You might notice, for instance, that her language usage differs, depending on which group she is in at the time. You might try to describe the relationship between her language and the characteristics of the group and its members. It would also be of interest to examine other interaction patterns and attempt to explain them, perhaps on the basis of the children's differing personalities or the different way the teacher treats the two groups.

A third approach would be to look primarily at the group itself, taking less account of the behaviors of each single member and more account of how the three children are acting as a single unit. You could describe the group as though it were an individual, even attributing to it characteristics or traits—a friendly group, a hostile group, or a hard-working group.

Behavior can be significantly influenced by the larger group, although such influence is not always dramatic. Some children take very little part in the group life of their peers, seemingly preferring to focus their attention and energy on trying to please adults (e.g., see Almy and Genishi 1979). Groups, in turn, react differently to different individuals. Some children are not readily accepted into a group, while others are not only accepted but quickly become the leader. As illustrated in the previous example, children behave differently in different groups and situations. We have all known someone who acted so differently from what we are accustomed to, that we tried to explain the unusual behavior by saying it was her companions that caused the change in her personality.

Your Goals in Observing Groups: The above discussion emphasizes the need to observe children in context and to determine how their actions might change in various settings. All of us belong to a number of groups—a family, school, work organization, and social organizations—and our positions and behaviors vary from one group to another.

Your goals in observing groups will vary, depending on what you want to learn. A goal could be to determine how a child's behavior differs in various groups. In our opinion, leadership and follower patterns in various groups are especially worthy topics for observation. We believe this because in human groups a leader usually either naturally emerges or an individual is selected to lead the group. This being so, it stands to reason that leaders must have characteristics that set them apart from followers. A child may have "charisma," which the *American Heritage Talking Dictionary* (1995) defines as "a rare personal quality attributed to leaders who arouse fervent popular devotion and enthusiasm." In the case of children, such a definition may be an overstatement, but the basic meaning applies. A child might assume the role of leader because of his greater physical size and strength, because he has special expertise or skill, or because he has personality characteristics (friendliness, generosity, an outgoing nature) that make him popular with the other children. Strictly speaking, we suppose, it may be somewhat inaccurate to say that young children really possess the kinds of qualities that are possessed by adults who are considered leaders. On the other hand, leadership must be viewed in the context in which it occurs. It would be equally inaccurate, therefore, to assess children's leadership behaviors from the perspective of situations and characteristics that tend to define or characterize adult leadership. The same argument is valid for assessing patterns of "follower" behavior and the characteristics of children who are followers in specific situations.

All of this notwithstanding, you may want to look for answers to such questions as: How do leaders emerge in different situations and groups? How does leadership change in a given group? How does a particular child express his or her leadership (e.g., through size and strength, skillfulness in social manipulation, and so on.) Is a particular child a leader in all situations or only in some? How do the other children respond to a child's attempts to be a leader? Can you identify specific behaviors or approaches taken by children who try to lead but fail? What seems to turn off the other children to the efforts of these would-be leaders? What behaviors or approaches appear to be successful when used by a particular child?

Sometimes group patterns of behavior might be of interest. These can be discerned through a frequency checklist that records how many children use a particular space or engage in a particular activity (e.g., see Table A in the Appendix). A checklist will not tell you about the dynamics of group interaction, but it will tell you which classroom areas or activities are the most popular and draw the heaviest traffic. This information is important in planning future activities or arranging the physical environment. Very useful information can also be obtained by keeping a record of the particular areas and activities that are used by specific children. A teacher may notice, for instance, that Jonathan usually spends his free play time in the big block area. Repeated observations reveal that Jonathan's fine motor coordination is poor. He therefore feels uncomfortable in activities that require skilled hand-eye coordination. As a result, he plays with equipment and materials that involve large muscle groups. Here you have an example of a child matching his abilities with the opportunities provided by a given environment. This data would be relevant to a group observation if the teacher concluded prematurely that Jonathan plays in the big block area because of the other children who play there. In other words, Jonathan's play and social behavior might erroneously be interpreted in terms of group membership, rather than in terms of his difficulty in performing fine motor tasks.

Groups and individual behaviors within groups are important aspects of understanding children. Your overall objectives for observing will determine where and how groups fit into your specific observation activity.

Summary

There are a number of steps that must be taken before entering the observation setting. The most important step is determining the purpose of your observation; this will affect everything else you do. Selecting the site of the observation and knowing what you may do in the observation setting are also steps in the preparation process.

A series of questions was presented that you are to ask and answer before you even enter the observation setting.

1. Which developmental area or behaviors are the focus of your observation (physical/motor, social, language, etc.)?
2. How much time are you to spend observing the selected behaviors (several minutes, an hour, for as long as they occur)?
3. Whom are you to observe (individual children, a group, a particular child, several particular children)?
4. How are you to record your observations (checklist, duration record, narrative description, time sampling, event sampling)?
5. What kind of interpretations are you to make (based on a given theory, on what has taken place in the setting)?

Being inconspicuous when observing is very important. Naturalistic observation requires as little interference with children's behavior as possible. There are times, however, when children are asked to behave in particular ways, such as in testing or formal research studies. Your overall observation objectives will determine whether you remain completely separated from the children's ongoing behavior or intervene in some way.

The need for professional ethics cannot be too heavily stressed. Ethics and confidentiality protect the rights and well-being of everyone associated with your observations. Professional ethics was discussed under the general notion of professional behavior.

Making meaningful, useful observations is not easy, and several factors that affect observation were discussed. Your sensitivity to children, fatigue, illness, and discomfort all contribute to what you see when you look at children. The most difficult factor influencing observations, however, is your personality—your values, attitudes, experiences, knowledge, and so on. These attributes act as filters through which you process what you see and that affect what you notice in the first place.

The influence of the setting and situation was also discussed. Space size, equipment, materials, and people in the space, and how they are arranged will affect your observations.

Three categories of errors were covered in the chapter. There are errors of omission, commission, and transmission. These errors affect the accuracy and reliability of your observational data. In spite of the possibility of error, however, accuracy and reliability can be achieved, and three aspects of observation were discussed in this regard: objective description, interpretation, and evaluation. Evaluation was characterized as possibly the most "dangerous" part of the observation process. It is in evaluating a child that you attach a value to her behavior, character, and even her worth as an individual. Extreme caution was advised, and even positive evaluations must be supported by frequent, representative, and objectively described samples of behavior. In any case, derogatory labels and descriptions must never be part of a child's observation record.

Distinctions were made between individual and group observations. The limitations of observing groups of children were presented, with a significant limitation being the loss of information about specific individuals. It was pointed out that one can study the behavior of groups and the behavior of individuals in groups, but the differences should be borne in mind. Several kinds of groups were defined, but peer groups are the most likely focus of your observations. Several approaches to observing groups were discussed. Some goals of group observation include issues such as documenting changes in children's behavior as they functioned in different groups, leadership and follower behavior patterns in various groups, and assessing the effect of a group on a particular child's behavior.

The concept of group was also discussed by way of viewing a group as characterized by four components: (1) member characteristics, (2) member behaviors, (3) group contextual characteristics, and (4) group episodes. Three specific contextual characteristics of small groups were also discussed, namely (1) group norms, (2) group climate, and (3) a group's normal round of procedures.

Study Questions

1. Your overall purpose for observing is a key element to success. Identify and discuss some of the problems an observer might encounter if she did not

have her objective clearly in mind before entering the observation setting.

2. List some questions concerning professional behavior that *you* think should be answered before starting to observe in a preschool. How would you answer them?

3. How are interpretation and evaluation related? Which one has to be done first, and why?

4. Why is objective description important to the accuracy and reliability of observation?

5. Give some examples of when group observation is more valuable than individual observation. How would you actually do the observing?

Practical Exercise: Chapter Three

Chapter Three contains a great deal of important information, but most of it is fairly easy to grasp. There is one topic, however, that might cause some problems, and that is the topic of groups and how to observe the behavior that occurs in groups. Therefore, it may be useful for you to try out a practical assignment before you get to the more formal observation exercises later on in the text.

On pages 60 and 61, we describe two groups of three children each. One group consists of Julie, Erica, and Floyd; the other consists of Erica, Roger, and Tanya. A key element here is the fact that Erica belongs to both groups, but the other children are members of only one of the groups. We discuss three approaches one could take to study these two groups and the different situations they present: (1) observe the behavior of each child as an individual, (2) observe individual behaviors but put them within the larger framework of the three-person groups, and (3) look primarily at the groups themselves and de-emphasize the behaviors of the individual members.

For your practice exercise, try the following. Go into a setting where groups are likely to occur and identify two groups of three to four children each. Be careful not to select too large a group or else the observation and recording tasks may become too difficult. It's critical that one of the children be a member of both groups, so that in some manner he or she will move back and forth between them as the occasion requires or allows.

Having completed the groundwork, try each of the three approaches mentioned above. Reread the more detailed description of these approaches found on pages 52 and 53 of the text so that you have a complete idea of what each approach entails and how each is accomplished. It may also be useful to have a discussion with others who are doing the same exercise and to compare your findings, the problems you may have encountered, and so on.

The Elements of Observation

PART 2

Introduction and Preparation

As a real, practical activity, observation is "all of a piece": it possesses its own integrity or unity, especially when it's done with skill. But like any process, observation consists of parts or elements, each of which must fit well with all of the other parts if it is to be successful.

The eleven chapters in Part 2 discuss what we have chosen to call the elements of observation. The distinction between Parts 1 and 2 is somewhat arbitrary, for, in fact, developmental theories and the general guidelines for observing children (Chapters 2 and 3) are every bit as much the elements of observation as are the various methods of recording behavior. The term 'elements,' however, is particularly appropriate in this case, because it describes those special components of observation that make possible the *objective* recording of behavior and the keeping of more or less permanent records. Without such "elements," observation remains merely casual watching similar to what one does while sitting on a park bench or in a restaurant. Unfortunately, this kind of "observation" is subject to all of the adverse effects of no predetermined observation plan and a fallible memory.

The intent of Part 2 is to provide you with at least seven ways of recording behavior in virtually any setting or situation. We must stress, however, that none of the methods is of much use without careful prior preparation—preparation that ranges from knowing where you are going to observe, to having some understanding of how children develop, to familiarity with your method of choice and how to use it properly and effectively.

Given all of the above, we believe that these elements of observation, judiciously studied and reasonably mastered, will, with persistent application, help to make you a skilled and astute observer of the behavior of young children.

CHAPTER FOUR
Methods, Behavior, Plans, and Contexts

Objectives

After studying this chapter, you will be able to

- relate the concept of method to observation
- identify the role of behavior in observation
- interpret the relationship of a plan to observation
- analyze the relationship between observation and the context in which it occurs

How To Do It:
Some Preliminary Thoughts and Cautions

This chapter discusses the concept of methods of observing and recording children's behavior. Methods are the "how-to-do-it" aspects of the observation process.

We go through our lives using methods of one kind or another to accomplish tasks. Any method is in some ways similar to observation—it depends for its success on an individual's skills, knowledge, experience, and other factors that go into making that person who he is. Just as there is more to observation than what meets the eye, there is more to a method than what one reads in a book or hears from a teacher.

A method is a way of doing something. The *American Heritage Talking Dictionary's* (1995) definition gets at some important features of method, to wit: "A means or manner of procedure, *especially a regular and systematic way of accomplishing something*" (italics added). The words "regular" and "systematic" exemplify the essential character of the methods of observation discussed in this text. The term "methodology" is also useful in understanding the concept of method. The *American Heritage Talking Dictionary* (1995) defines methodology as "... [the] orderly arrangement of parts or steps to accomplish an end. ... The procedures and techniques characteristic of a particular discipline or field of knowledge."

As defined, methodology actually can refer to the total observation process, which includes all of the preparatory steps necessary to successfully observing and recording behavior. Method addresses the specific recording technique to be used. Given all of this, then, a method specifies a procedure by which one can accomplish a goal. In this text, a *method* is considered a set of instructions with two major characteristics: (1) it must specify what one has to do to achieve some objective, and (2) it may also describe how to do what one needs to do to achieve the objective. "What" provides the objective of the instruction, and "how" describes the actions or steps that lead to the accomplishment of the objective. In short, methods are designed to give one the skill, understanding, and knowledge necessary to achieve some end.

Methods can be applied in almost any context and for any reason, as long as some goal or task has to be accomplished. Methods can range from the simple to the relatively complex. Spodek and Saracho (1994) make the following claim: "Other ways to characterize a good teacher of young children include identifying what such teachers know *as well as what they should be able to do*" (p. 3, emphasis added). "Able to do," for this writer, specifies the need for some kind of method, or for what Spodek and Saracho call "techniques." They identify four areas of knowledge that are critical to being a good teacher: "Knowledge of basic health and safety measures; techniques to present activities to children; classroom management techniques; and knowledge of the content of early childhood curriculum" (pp. 3 and 5).

The methods associated with keeping children safe and healthy might be considered relatively simple to implement, even though the knowledge on which the method is based may be relatively complex or sophisticated. As Spodek and Saracho state, "[Teachers] must understand the nature of disease and infection, proper handling of food and materials, and proper sanitary procedures, especially in relation to toileting" (p. 3). Being able to *do* what is necessary, for example, to keep food preparation areas antiseptic, involves a method, but a rather simple one.

As a more complicated, contrasting example, suppose that you were asked to intervene in a child care center situation. It's your first day on the job in a local center, and some of four-year-old Margaret's behavior is disruptive and possibly harmful to the other children. Suppose further that this particular center uses behavior modification principles and techniques to change undesirable behavior as well as to establish desirable behavior in the children in its care. The head teacher tells you first to determine a frequency baseline for Margaret's target behavior. Then she instructs you to weaken or eliminate the target behavior through the use of non-reinforcement. Finally she tells you to establish a new behavior, initially on the basis of a continuous reinforcement schedule and gradually going to a variable ratio schedule of reinforcement. Could you do this? Again, it would depend on your understanding such concepts as *baseline frequency, nonreinforcement,* and *continuous* and *variable ratio schedules of reinforcement*. It would depend further on your ability to implement or apply these principles, to translate them into actual practice.

Consequently, the directions on how to observe and record behavior will be useful only if, first, you understand what the directions mean and how to use them, and second, you know something about the subject to which the method is being applied. You must already have knowledge to acquire more knowledge, skill to acquire more skill. Descriptions of methods will not provide an unerring path to successful observation; none of the techniques is self-evident or self-explanatory, not even to observation experts. Instructions are potentially a means of developing the skill and knowledge needed to use a particular observation and recording method. If that use becomes a "natural" part of you, your reading about observation methods will have been successful.

Again, critical relationships exist between you and what you see, and between you and any "how-to-do-it" approach to an activity.

Behavior: A Central Element of Observation and Recording

Behavior is the major object or focus of everything you will do in observing and recording. What is absolutely crucial to your understanding the meaning of behavior, however, is that with respect to *observing* it, you will be focusing on the *actions* of children as they respond to various stimuli, stimuli that come either from outside themselves or that originate from within their own bodies or minds. Pillari (1988), a social worker, captures the essence of behavior—for our purposes—when she defines it as "everything that is potentially *observable* about a person or event" (p. 2, italics added). To put it most simply, therefore, behavior will be considered anything an individual does that can be directly seen, heard, smelled, tasted, or touched. The word directly means that the behavior you are observing is right there or immediate. Walking, running, eating, and speaking are examples of directly observable behaviors. They involve visible or hearable muscular actions or responses. It is behavior then, that one observes: a child walking around the room, talking to a friend, or painting at an easel.

Behavior Sampling and Observation Plans: Behavior has an important characteristic: It occurs continuously, without ceasing, for as long as one is alive. Even sleeping is a behavior, although it is not as exciting as a hockey game. If one is alive, one is behaving. Herbert F. Wright (1960) captured the continuous quality of behavior when he referred to it as a "stream." He wrote: "The behavior of a person is a lifelong continuum. It is in the nature of a stream that it can never be seen in its entirety."

Wright's behavior-as-a-stream metaphor is a useful one. Observation can be thought of as entering that stream at some point and taking a sample of the behaviors that are flowing by. However, entering the stream and taking a sample is somewhat like going shopping. You need a plan to do it successfully. Deciding what to buy and where to buy it is analogous to deciding what behaviors to observe in children (aggression, dependency, language), and where you might find those kinds of behaviors—in a preschool classroom or a public playground. Deciding how much you are going to buy is like deciding how much of the behavior stream you are going to try to observe on a given occasion. Finally, you must decide how to get to the store and bring home your purchased goods. This is comparable to choosing an observation method, a way to enter the child's stream and take a sample of the behavior you want.

Figure 4-1   The observation setting—a preschool in action.

A question may arise as to what should drive or motivate one's observation objectives. Some might argue that children's needs determine what one observes or why one observes in any child care or early education setting. This is far too restrictive a criterion; it does not account for legitimate purposes for observing young children's behavior other than meeting their immediate needs. To be sure, child care staff are obligated to hold needs as their primary concern, and much of what they observe will be directed toward that end. However, there are students who must observe young children's behavior simply to learn how to do it and do it well. And on occasion, even professional early childhood educators and child care workers conceivably may want and need to observe and record young children's behavior only to refine and hone their observational skills and techniques. To expand on the shopping example above, parents may shop for food and clothing specifically for their children, and those needs "drive" the shopping list. But it's equally true that these parents at some time must shop to meet their own needs as well.

The method you choose will determine some of the other details required by your plan, such as how much of the behavior stream is to be observed, and the form the observational data will take. A narrative description, for example, covers a large portion of the child's behavior stream, and the data are in narrative, or raw form. Time sampling deals with smaller portions of the behavior stream, and the final data can be just a checkmark indicating whether a given behavior or category of behaviors has occurred.

Your overall plan must always come first. All other decisions will follow from that plan.

Settings and Situations

Setting and situation can have different meanings. Setting, for some (Wright, 1960) covers tangible factors such as physical space, the objects in that space, and opportunities and resources that permit individuals to behave in certain ways. An early childhood classroom is a setting because it has observable and measurable physical dimensions located in a specific place. A classroom setting contains equipment and materials the children can use to behave in particular ways, such as blocks to build with, tricycles to ride, and books to read. For further reference, see NAEYC's Developmentally Appropriate Practice (Bredekamp).

In contrast to setting, situation is mainly concerned with the social and psychological conditions in the setting. What is the nature of the children's play—active and cooperative, or active and individualized? What kinds of activities are being encouraged by the teacher (or by the children themselves)? What unexpected event may temporarily capture the children's attention, and thereby change the ongoing stream of behaviors?

Settings and situations are related to one another in a special way—situations occur within settings. Settings have physical and social-psychological characteristics. Physical spaces generate feelings in us. We do not respond the same way to every environment. Different people also create different atmospheres.

Wright (1960) made three assumptions concerning the relationship of setting to situation. First, he assumed that some settings are more conducive to certain situations than to others. Some settings, for example, promote certain social interactions better than others. Something as simple as seating arrangements can work for or against children talking to one another.

Second, he assumed that the relationship is not fixed. He noted that although the same setting can support different situations, identical situations can occur in different settings. As an example, two groups of children could use the same setting at different times and both groups could be active, outgoing, and cooperative. Or, in contrast, one group could be subdued and withdrawn, showing little interaction with materials or among themselves.

The idea of identical situations occurring in different settings is illustrated by the following example. Think of two Head Start classrooms. Each is conducted in a different setting, and yet many of the same activities can take place, and much the same warm, supportive atmosphere may characterize both situations.

Finally, Wright assumed that "the behavior of the child at a particular time does indeed depend more directly upon the situation than upon the setting in which it takes place." Wright's third assumption has the most implications for us as observers.

Context: The word context is more suitable than setting or situation, because context includes setting and situation. Context involves place, time, circumstances, other people, and even psychological and physical conditions. Places, times, and people determine or influence how we behave and feel. Places allow some behaviors, but not others. Compare what you may do on the beach with what you may do in an office. Physical space permits some activities, while excluding others. (Can you swim in a bowling alley, for example?) Personal interactions are also affected by context. Individuals occupy *statuses* within social groups, and those statuses require certain behaviors or *roles*. These statuses and roles regulate individuals' behavior toward one another. Think of the relationship between a teacher and a student. The status of teacher requires certain kinds of role behaviors, such as teaching, grading, and counseling students. Student is a different status, with different role behaviors, such as attending class and doing homework. The nature of the student-teacher interaction is largely determined by these statuses and roles.

If you observe children in a preschool classroom, the classroom is the broad context for the children's behavior. But there are smaller settings and situations within the overall classroom context, and these smaller settings may occupy some of your attention during observations. Snack time, story time, free play time, nap time, and the block, art, and sandbox areas are examples of these smaller physical and social environments. These smaller contexts can determine what the children are allowed to do and the behaviors they exhibit.

Summary

This chapter discussed the idea of method, which was defined as a set of instructions that tell us what to do to accomplish some task or objective. It was pointed out, however, that methods do not guarantee success. The effectiveness of any method depends on the skills and knowledge of the individual using it. Thus, to acquire knowledge and skill, one must already have knowledge and skill.

Behavior is the central element in all observation of children. Behavior is anything a person does that can be directly seen, heard, smelled, tasted, or touched. Behavior was also discussed in metaphorical terms as a stream that never stops as long as one is alive. Sampling involves entering the child's behavior stream and catching a portion of the behavior flowing by. Plans are the prearranged steps one takes to enter the stream and sample the desired behavior.

Setting and situation were also covered in the chapter. Setting is the physical aspects of the child's environment; situation is the social and psychological characteristics of the environment. Both of these terms were combined into the general term context, which includes all the factors that pertain to setting and situation.

Study Questions

1. Describe a method you use in a common daily activity. What skills and knowledge are required to use this method? How is the method you have described similar to an observation method. Do they share any characteristics?

2. Why is visible behavior a central part of observation, rather than such things as thoughts or feelings?
3. What is the relationship between plans and methods? Are they similar or dissimilar? How?
4. Describe an imaginary context. How might the characteristics of that context affect the observation of behavior?
5. If you wanted to observe and record such things as thoughts or feelings, how would you have to go about it? What would you have to do to make such observation and recording possible?

CHAPTER FIVE
An Introduction to Observation and Recording Methods

Objectives

After studying this chapter, you will be able to

- discuss the differences between formal and informal methods of observation
- compare open versus closed methods of recording behavior
- describe the relationship between the degree of selectivity and the type of method used for recording behavior
- identify the role of inference of interpretation in the observation process

Methods of Observing and Recording Behavior: Some General Characteristics

Seven methods for observing and recording behavior are covered in this manual: (1) narrative description, (2) time sampling, (3) event sampling, (4) anecdotal records, (5) diary records, (6) frequency counts, and (7) checklists. Each of these procedures has its own characteristics, uses, advantages and disadvantages; each is best used under certain conditions for certain objectives. Before learning about each method, it is useful to consider several general characteristics of observation methods.

Goodwin and Driscoll (1980), among others, distinguish between the broad categories of formal and informal observation methods. These authors also describe several distinctions among formal methods, which they label (1) open versus closed, (2) degree of selectivity, and (3) degree of observer inference required.

Because of their importance in understanding the different methods, the general features of formal and informal methods and of the distinctions among formal methods will be discussed.

Formal and Informal Observation

Formal and informal methods of observation differ mainly in how strict the conditions are for using them. Formal methods are conducted in a highly structured manner, which is why they are usually chosen for research studies. Goodwin and Driscoll (1980) outline some of the factors involved in using formal observation methods within a research context.

It typically involves defining categories carefully, constructing elaborate data forms, training observers and establishing their interreliability, and recording, analyzing, and interpreting data using relatively sophisticated procedures.

This statement emphasizes the careful way in which formal observation is carried out and data are analyzed and used.

The relationship between formal observation and research studies is conveyed by the term controlled, which is an alternative to the term formal. Research is a highly controlled activity, and when observation is used in research studies, it is also controlled.

Informal methods, in contrast, involve a "less structured and less elaborate" approach to observation (Goodwin and Driscoll 1982). The strict research format is missing in informal observation; informal methods are therefore more suited to "instructional planning and day-to-day program operation . . . ." They are also more suited to an immediate, intuitive use than formal methods. This does not mean that attributes such as accuracy and dependability may be sacrificed when using informal methods. But, compared to formal methods, informal ones may be easier and more appropriate to use under some circumstances. Informal observation is also called "naturalistic observation," a name that captures the ideas of ease of use and lack of tight control.

Open vs. Closed

Recording techniques can be classified according to whether they are open or closed (see Wright 1960, Goodwin and Driscoll 1980). Open and closed methods differ in whether they preserve the *raw data* for later analysis. A distinction is appropriate here. Raw data are descriptions of behavior and events as they originally occurred. Pillari (1988), citing Coombs (1964), describes raw data as "the bits of information that are selected and constructed by the investigator as empirical facts for further analysis" (p. 2). *Data*, on the other hand, are described as "a body of facts that have already undergone interpretation according to the investigator's chosen method" (Pillari 1988, p. 2). So, for example, a narrative description of two children playing together in the big block area is raw data. But, if that description is reduced to a checkmark on an observation sheet, the raw data are lost even though, by Pillari's definition, you have preserved data. In short, then, open methods preserve raw data, closed ones do not.

Please note the important connection between *data, method,* and *interpretation*. It should be clear that preservation of *raw data* can be significant, inasmuch as different interpretations can be made of the raw data, thereby yielding different sets of data. Loss of raw data, however, results in the loss of any data other than that provided by the investigator or observer through interpretation according to some method.

The contrast between open and closed methods can be illustrated by an analogy to two books. Imagine a book containing information about children. Imagine further that, although you are permitted to look in this book to learn its contents, you have been given a limited time to do so. The best you can do, therefore, is summarize some of the information using a coding scheme. Furthermore, once you leave the book, it is closed and locked up; there is no going back to read more. Later, you look at your notes and you see that the book talked about aggressive behavior thirteen times, dependency behavior eight times, and not at all about language behavior. Your summary record might mention children's names, but there is no description of how the aggressions were expressed. You cannot go back to the book and figure out how you came to the decision to note Melinda's hitting Johnny as an aggressive event. Indeed, you have no record of Melinda hitting Johnny at all; you have only a checkmark to indicate that aggression occurred. There is no information on the circumstances surrounding behavior. This is a description of a closed method. The raw data are still in the book, out of your reach.

Imagine a second book that, like the first, contains information about children. You are again permitted to use the book, but this time you are given longer to read. Rather than summarize, you record what you read in as much detail as you can. Now, instead of noting how many times one child behaved aggressively toward another, you describe those aggressive behaviors—who aggressed against whom, in what specific setting and situation, the consequences of the behavior, and so on.

When you leave this second book, it remains open to you. You brought with you so much of the second book that you can examine and reexamine your records and notes. You may come to conclusions about the children and their behaviors that would not have been possible from your summary of the first book. The second book is like an open method—the raw data are in your hands, to use as you wish.

Degree of Selectivity

Degree of selectivity, which is closely related to openness and closedness, determines how many behaviors are targeted for observation and recording. Some methods are very unselective; no specific behaviors are chosen ahead of time, and almost everything that occurs is acceptable for observing and recording. Other methods are the opposite; the observer records only specific behaviors that she has chosen before entering the observation setting. For example, only instances of dependency behavior or of interpersonal exchanges between a child and an adult might be recorded in a closed method. Instances of motor behavior would be disregarded.

Degree of selectivity is comparable to the size of the holes in a fishing net. If the holes are small, you can catch fish of all sizes and kinds. If the holes are large, only the bigger fish will be caught, and the smaller ones will escape through any hole larger than they are. Similarly, if an observation method's degree of selectivity is low, it is like fishing with a small-holed net. You will catch the small details of behavior, context, and sequence. If the degree of selectivity is high, of course, the holes in the observation net are large and will capture only certain behaviors.

This analogy also points up the close relationship between selectivity and the characteristics of openness and closedness. The number of details that can be recorded with a particular method is comparable to the number of fish that can be caught with a particular net. The bigger the holes in the net, the fewer the number of fish; the smaller the holes, the larger the number of fish since the net is capable of catching big fish as well as small ones.

Degree of Observer Inference Required

Inference means drawing a conclusion based on data, premises or evidence. For our purposes, inference means the same thing as interpretation or setting out the meaning of something. Inferences or interpretations are essentially conclusions based on directly observable data, but are not themselves directly observable. The conclusion is reached through a mental process; a connection is made between information we can perceive directly through our physical senses, and some other condition that we cannot learn of in that way.

You say "hello" to a friend, and she makes no response. You might infer—interpret her behavior to mean—that she is (1) angry with you, (2) angry with someone else, (3) preoccupied, (4) ill, or (5) teasing you, among a number of other possibilities. Whatever the case, your friend's anger, preoccupation, illness, or teasing is not what you observe. You can only observe the fact that she walked by without speaking to you. The rest is inference.

To put it into the context of children, think of all the times in the past when a child on some given day behaved in ways that were not typical of him or her. The child may have been sluggish or apathetic, or perhaps appeared to have been overstimulated and demonstrated an activity level that was much higher than usual. What did you do? What did you think? It's almost certain that at the very least, you attempted to make some sense out of the child's unusual behavior. You wanted to know the reasons for the behavior. Suppose that the child's seeming listlessness was caused by the fact that her parents had argued before she left for the child care center. What you will have seen, however, is not the parents' quarrel, but the child's response to the quarrel. Learning about the incident may give you a basis for understanding the child's behavior, but it nonetheless may still remain an inference on your part until you learn firsthand from the child (or from someone else) why she is listless or overstimulated (or whatever mood the child may display).

Various methods require different degrees of inference. Methods also differ as to when in the observation process inferences must be made. Some methods require no initial inference, since they involve no preselection of the behaviors to be recorded. Considerable inference may be involved if one wants to give meaning to the behaviors after they are recorded. In a case like this, inference takes place after the fact. It is not involved in decisions regarding behaviors to record, or categories a behavior should be in, at the time of the observation. Some methods do require inferences at the time of initial observing and recording. Making inferences during the recording phase of observation does not rule out making inferences later on. The inferences made during and after observing and recording serve different purposes.

If you do not care what kinds of fish you catch, you will use a net that will get you all kinds of fish, and there is no need to be choosy while you are fishing. Once you have hauled in your net, however, you might be interested in examining your catch. What kinds of fish are they? What does it mean to have caught them in these particular waters, under these particular conditions? Of what significance is it to have found this species of fish in the same area as this other species?

Suppose, though, that you do care what kind of fish you catch; you want a fish of one particular species. In this case, you have to know something about that fish; you have to be able to recognize it when you see it. Consequently, you throw out your net when that particular fish swims by, and not at any other time. Can you see the similarity to observation methods, and degree of inference required? With an open, unselective method, you do not worry over what behaviors are being caught in your net; indeed, you trap or record as many of them as you can. If you wish, you can examine your data and make inferences after the fishing is done. But, with a closed and selective method, you make an on-the-spot decision or inference as to whether Betsy's taking a toy away from Susan is an example of aggressive behavior. Is it the kind of "fish" you are looking for? If it is, then you record it; furthermore, once you have it and many others like it in your net, you can analyze and use the data. For example, the number of times various children exhibit aggression can form the basis for a behavior modification program in the classroom. Frequent aggression by a child, as documented by observation records (frequency counts, for example), can give the teacher a measurable basis for judging whether her efforts to eliminate the behavior have been successful.

The issue of when during the observation process inferences are made, is covered in the discussion of the methods themselves.

Summary

This chapter covered some important characteristics of methods of observing and recording behavior. Two types of methods were discussed: formal and informal. These types differ primarily in the strictness of the conditions that govern their use. Formal methods are characterized by careful prior preparation and strict control of all aspects and phases of the observation and recording process. Informal methods involve a less structured and less elaborate approach to observation, and for this reason, they are often used by teachers in the classroom.

Formal methods can be described along the dimensions of openness versus closedness, degree of selectivity, and degree of inference required. Openness versus closedness refers to whether or not the method preserves the original (raw) observational data. An open method was compared to a book that one is allowed to read and take extensive notes on, which can then be used at a later time. The notes preserve much of the original book (the raw data). A closed method was compared to a book that one is given only limited time to read, thus requiring brief note-taking in the form of a code. These notes omit the details of the book's content, thus failing to preserve the raw data. Degree of selectivity refers to whether the observer may record anything that occurs during the observation session or is restricted to certain predesignated behaviors and events. Selectivity was presented as analogous to a fish net with holes of varying sizes: the larger the holes, the greater the degree of selectivity; the smaller the holes, the less selective a method is. Degree of inference required was discussed in terms of whether inferences are made at the time of initial observing and recording or at a later time. Some methods require immediate inference at the time of recording; others use inference when the observing and recording are completed.

Study Questions

1. What do the terms "formal" and "informal" mean with regard to observation? What do they mean with regard to a social gathering, for example? Are the meanings similar or different in the two situations?
2. To what, other than observation and recording methods, might the characteristics of openness and closedness be applied? Do the essential meanings of openness and closedness change or remain the same in the different applications?
3. How are openness and closedness related to degree of selectivity? Could they be independent of each other; that is, could a method be closed without also being selective, or open without also being unselective?
4. What is the difference between observation and interpretation?
5. Why is the distinction between "raw data" and "data" an important one? What is the significance for you, an observer, of the difference between these two kinds of information? What role do the two kinds of data play in your own observation activities?

CHAPTER SIX
Narrative Descriptions

Objectives

After studying this chapter, you will be able to

- define the role of narrative descriptions in the observation process
- identify the relationship between the recording technique and the selectivity of the narrative description
- determine the limitations of narrative descriptions
- explain the role of inference in narrative descriptions
- identify the advantages and disadvantages of narrative descriptions

General Description

The first formal method of observation to be discussed has a rather confusing history with respect to its name. We shall call it the *narrative description*, although it is also labeled "specimen record" and sometimes, if a distinction is not made, "running record." These other names are not particularly relevant to our purposes, and so we shall not dwell on them. But we do need to point out that our term "narrative description" is a modification of Lay-Dopyera and Dopyera's (1982) term "descriptive narrative," which apparently is their version of the specimen record. Our decision to make this change is based on our desire to emphasize as clearly as possible the essential characteristics of this method: it is first of all a *narrative* in its basic form, and it *describes* behavior.

The narrative description is a formal method of recording behavior because it requires what Irwin and Bushnell (1980) describe as "more rigorous detail and predetermined criteria" (p. 103). It is the rigorous detail and predetermined criteria that impose *structure* and *control* on the narrative description; these are among the characteristics of formality. The informal counterpart of the narrative description, which can be referred to as the "running record," is described by Cohen and Stern (1958, 1978) as a "classroom observational technique for teachers and it involves taking on-the-spot records of behavior as it is occurring" (1958, p. 7; cited in Irwin and Bushnell, 1980, p. 100). The narrative description also records behavior as it is occurring, and usually on the spot. Consequently, the difference between the narrative description and the running record may be difficult to preserve in actual practice. Schickedanz *et al.* (1993) write that "The specimen record [narrative description] is used mainly to get a detailed picture of some aspect of a child's everyday behavior" (p. 26). This text's use of the narrative description will include getting a detailed picture of *children's* behavior and will permit one to go beyond "everyday behavior" to include atypical or unusual behavior, if the circumstances warrant it and call for detailed descriptions. For practical purposes, however, we shall recommend the format and intent of the narrative description technique, especially to stay in keeping with Irwin and Bushnell's assertion that narrative descriptions are usually based on predetermined criteria such as the time of day, the person, and the setting. We believe that the observation exercises impose criteria such as these, and, therefore, it is technically more correct to speak of the narrative description than of the running record.

The predetermined criteria mentioned just above refer to such things as *when, where, who, how,* and *why* you are going to observe. (All of these issues are to be resolved, of course, during the planning process as discussed in Chapter 3.) As you can see, an informal approach to, or application of, the narrative description would *not* rely on knowing *all* of these things ahead of time. Obviously, a child care center worker or an early childhood educator directly participating in the facility's ongoing activities, and responsible for the children's welfare, may only "discover" who she wants to observe as she notes a particular child's—or group of children's—behavior that she decides merits further attention.

In any case, in the narrative description technique, you continuously record in as much detail as possible what the child does and says, by herself and in interaction with other persons or objects. The chief goal of narrative recording is to obtain a detailed, objective account of behavior without inferences, interpretations, or evaluations. It is an important feature of the narrative description in that it details not only behaviors, but also the context (setting and situation) of the behaviors and the sequence in which they occur. It is also essential that the behaviors be *described* and not simply referred to in broad terms. A good description should enable the reader to close his eyes and get a mental picture of the scene. To say, "John played with the big blocks for 20 minutes" tells very little about John, the big blocks, played, or where all of these events took place. The potential completeness and inclusiveness of the narrative description is seen in Goodwin and Driscoll's note that "the permanent record itself might consist of just movies, videotapes, or audiotapes, if mechanical observation means have been used, or some combination of mechanical recording and observer's notes." Although the written narrative description is not as capable as movies and videotapes of "mirroring" the original raw data of the observation, it is capable of yielding rich, detailed information. Narrative descriptions "provide a comprehensive, descriptive, objective, and permanent records of behavior as it occurs" (Goodwin and Driscoll, 1980). (See Table 6-1.)

The narrative description in theory has no time limits. But practical considerations such as fatigue do impose limits on any single observer. In practice, therefore, the narrative description uses limited observation periods of approximately an hour. The observing and recording are continuous during that period. Longer records can be obtained by several observers recording on a rotating basis.

Open vs. Closed

The narrative description is the most open of all the observation methods. Its openness is a result of its unselectiveness and the amount of information it enables you to gather. The record preserves the description of behaviors, chronological sequences, and contexts. Consequently, those data are available in their original, unprocessed form for further examination and analysis.

Degree of Selectivity

The narrative description is not selective at all. Everything that occurs within an observation period is fair game for the recorder's pen. One observes and records with a small-holed net, being perfectly willing to haul in any kind of behavior that happens by.

We should emphasize, however, that strictly speaking, *selectivity is inherent in all recording methods.* This is because an observer can't see everything and must decide from among any number of persons and events exactly who and what to watch. Degree of selectivity, therefore, is relative and depends upon the specific recording method you are using. When we say that the narrative description "is not selective at all," we mean only that selectivity operates minimally compared with other methods.

Degree of Inference Required

At the time you are observing and recording, little inference is required, because everything that takes place is targeted for recording. When observing with the narrative description, therefore, you do not have to consider whether the behavior or the context is the "right one," just as when fishing with a small-holed net, there is no concern about whether you have trapped a carp or a minnow. One is as good as the other. Again, however, interpretations may be attempted after the fact. If you want to give to the original data any meaning that goes beyond that provided solely by objective description, inferences become necessary. In other words, you may want to examine your fish once you have brought them into the boat. You may wonder why carp and minnows got trapped in the net at the same time. Or you may want to examine your descriptions and try to determine why Beth Ann is friendly toward Jane, while in the same context she is hostile toward Mark. In this case, your "recording net" has "trapped" two different kinds of behavior on the part of Beth Ann: friendliness and hostility. Seeking a possible reason for these two different behaviors ("fish") might lend insight into some or all of the children involved.

Advantages

Some of the advantages of the narrative description stem precisely from its openness and lack of selectivity. Because of these characteristics, the method can provide a complete account of what has occurred during the time you were in a child's behavior stream. Furthermore, the narrative description has the important advantage of capturing context (setting and situation) along with behavior. Wright (1960) placed considerable importance on this combination. "Everyone knows, at least intuitively, that the meaning and significance of an action and even its occurrence depend directly ... upon the coexisting situation." Information concerning what and where can be especially useful when trying to understand individual children and how they behave in various contexts. As is well known, every child has his own unique style, attitudes, fears, and abilities. The narrative description, like a fishing net with small holes, catches these differences, these nuances in children's behavior, and permanently preserves them. Furthermore, it catches all of these behaviors, contexts, and styles under naturalistic conditions, without the artificial influences of experiments in a laboratory.

The permanence of the narrative description is also an advantage. Such records get more valuable as they get older. It is useful to compare narrative descriptions obtained at an earlier time with more recent records. This comparison helps us learn about changes in children's behavior and development across time and place (see Wright 1960; Gaver and Richards 1979).

Narrative descriptions are usable under many circumstances. They require no prepared observation sheets or coding schemes, nor any special language or jargon. The richness and subtlety of plain language is a major strength of the narrative description, although it is a strength that depends on the observer's language skills.

The narrative description allows considerable variations in the amount of time spent in the behavior stream. Narratives may describe behaviors ranging from several seconds to twelve hours or more (see, e.g., Barker and Wright 1951). The extended record usually involves several observers taking turns recording.

Disadvantages

The narrative description can cost a great deal in staff energy and time. The method can be inefficient for obtaining representative samples of behavior quickly. Part of the inefficiency comes from the failure to quantify behavioral data ahead of time through a predetermined coding scheme. For example, you cannot record the frequency of a behavior at the time you observe it. Narrative descriptions can be analyzed for such things as frequency counts, but these analyses would have to be done after the observation session. They would also be time consuming.

Skill and effort are needed to notice and get down on paper the numerous details that are the goal of narrative description. Lay-Dopyera and Dopyera (1982) comment that because "the writing load is intense, many observers restrict themselves to a brief episode," which suggests the method of time sampling.

Table 6-1 Narrative Description

Observer's Name   <u>Alice Thompson (Teacher)</u>

Child/Children Observed   <u>Melissa L.</u>

Child's/Children's Age(s)   <u>4 years, 3 months</u>   Child's/Children's Sex   <u>Female</u>

Observation Context (home, child care center, preschool, school)   <u>Children's Delight Preschool</u>

Date of Observation <u>January 10, 1996</u>   Time Begun <u>9:20 A.M.</u>   Time Ended <u>9:30 A.M.</u>

Brief Description of Physical and Social Characteristics of Observation Setting

Children are busily engaged in various free play activities. The overall mood seems upbeat. Of the usual 15 children who are enrolled, only 12 are here today—three are ill, according to the parents' telephone communications with the director this morning. Although the children's moods seem good, they are more quiet than usual—not as much loud talking as sometimes takes place.

Objective Behavioral Descriptions (OBD) and Interpretations: *Narrative Description*

OBD 1: [Time Begun 9:20 A.M.   Time Ended 9:22 A.M.]
Melissa (M) arrives about 35 minutes after the other children have arrived and started their activities. She puts her coat in her cubby and then stands in the doorway of the main classroom and looks around; she remains motionless for about 1/2 minute, moving only her eyes as she glances at other children and their activities.

Interpretation 1:
Melissa seems shy, almost withdrawn. From moment of arrival, she seemed reluctant to enter into things. May be because she didn't want to come in first place; her reluctance was mentioned by her mother several days ago. No specific reason was offered.

OBD 2: [Time Begun 9:22 A.M.   Time Ended 9:24 A.M.]
M. now walks toward reading area on far side of the room from the cubbies. As she walks, she scrapes the toe of her right foot at each step, doing this for about 5 feet. She passes by the puzzle table where 2 children are seated; no communication is exchanged. She now walks to a table with some books lying on it. Tina, José, and Miguel are seated at the table; José and Miguel are sharing a book, Tina (T) is watching them "read." Melissa says nothing to the three children as she sits down.

Interpretation 2:
Melissa still seems uncertain; even her motor behaviors seem restricted; she walks slowly, shuffling, as though unsure of herself and of her relationship with the other children or her environment. Seems to have trouble deciding what to do. Not at all communicative; makes no overtures to any of the children who were "available" for such.

OBD 3: [Time Begun 9:24 A.M.   Time Ended 9:29 A.M.]
José and Miguel don't look up or acknowledge Melissa in any way. Tina says "Hi, Melissa, wanna read a book with me?" M. cocks her head to one side and says, "I don't know how to read." T. replies "We can look at the pictures" M. looks over toward the big block area and without looking at T., says "OK." Tina smiles and goes to a shelf containing a number of books. M. picks up one of the books already on the table and flips through the pages. T. returns with a book and says "I like this one, let's look at this one" M. merely nods; T. sits down close to M., but M. moves slightly, keeping a distance of about 6–8 inches between her and Tina.

Interpretation 3:
Tina seems outgoing and friendly as Melissa approaches; M. is still uncommunicative; still seems shy and uncertain; speaks softly as though afraid of being heard. Tina persists in spite of M.'s ap-

parent lack of enthusiasm. M. also seems distractable or inattentive. She shies away from T.'s efforts to get close physically. Tina moves at a quick pace—much more energetic than M.

OBD 4: [Time Begun 9:29A.M. Time Ended 9:30A.M.]

José looks up and says "Hey, you two, wha'cha doin'?" Tina tilts her head upward, thrusts out her chin slightly and says "Never mind, we're busy." Melissa says nothing, but gets up from the table and walks toward big block area. Miguel still reads.

Interpretation 4:

Tina is much more outgoing and sure of herself than M. T. didn't interact too much w/ José and Miguel; may have felt left out of their activity. T. definitely seemed pleased to see M.; displayed no unfavorable response to M.'s "unsocial" behavior. T.'s response to José was quite assertive, but in a friendly way; almost like she claimed Melissa as her playmate, maybe in retaliation for the two boys ignoring her earlier. M. still seems uninterested, even uncertain of what to do.

Summary

The narrative description is a formal method of observation. In this technique, you record in as much detail as you can everything that occurs in the way of behavior and its context. The record is objective, without any evaluations or interpretations in the narrative description itself. The narrative description is the most open of all the observation methods. It is not at all selective, and it involves no inferences at the time of initial recording.

There a number of advantages to the narrative description. It provides a rich, detailed account of a child's behavior and the circumstances in which it occurred. The record is permanent and can be used for a later comparison with more recent records. The method is costly in time and effort, however, and is not very efficient for quickly gathering representative samples of behavior. The technique also requires skill because of the many details that are the targets of narrative description.

Study Questions

1. What is a distinguishing characteristic of the narrative description? What are some advantages and disadvantages of this characteristic?
2. How does the narrative description's degree of selectivity affect the way one specifically records observational data?
3. Under what conditions would you probably not want to use the narrative description? Under what conditions would you probably want to use the method?
4. What is the role of interpretation in the narrative description? When is interpretation most likely to be used or needed?
5. When would what you intended to be a narrative description actually turn out to be a running record? Would the data differ significantly between the two reports?

CHAPTER SEVEN
Time Sampling

Objectives

After studying this chapter, you will be able to

- relate the importance of the representativeness of behavior to the time sampling method
- determine the most appropriate coding system to use in a particular time sampling observation
- identify the characteristics of time sampling in relation to the dimensions of open versus closed, degree of selectivity, and degree of inference required
- analyze the advantages and disadvantages of the time sampling method of observation

General Description

If you select one piece of candy from a box containing 50 pieces of candy, you have *sampled* that candy. One of the purposes of such sampling might be to help you decide whether or not you will like the candy that *you have not tasted* (sampled). Sampling spares you the necessity of eating the whole box while at the same time allowing you to judge the overall quality of the whole box based on the quality of the piece you have eaten. Consequently, sampling can be economical of time and effort.

These same principles apply to *time sampling*: out of the total amount of time a child is in the observation setting, the observer selects or samples a relatively small amount of that total time and observes the child during that time period. What is essential to understand, however, is that *you are also sampling behavior* and not just time, because you are observing to see whether a *particular behavior* occurs. What must happen, therefore, is that the two samples of time and behavior must coincide, that is to say, a particular behavior is recorded as having occurred only if it is observed during the preselected period of time. If the behavior takes place outside of the selected time frame or interval, it is ignored or disregarded. So, for example, you might decide to observe each of 15 children for one minute and record—by a checkmark—all instances of aggressive behavior. If, during "Sarah's minute," she displays aggressive actions, you would so indicate on your time sampling observation form. If while observing Karl, however, you happen to see Sarah display aggression, you would not record

it, since your focus is on Karl and not on Sarah, and since her aggressive behavior did not occur within the preselected time period that you had set aside
to observe her.

Although seemingly dated, Irwin and Bushnell's (1980) discussion of
time-sampling still offers some valuable insights into the time sampling technique. First of all, these authors make an interesting statement that adds to the
meaning of time sampling. They write that "Using observation to *sample, rather
than to describe behavior. . .*" (p. 148, emphasis added). This distinction is a vital one, since one must understand the difference between (1) merely recording a mark on a form every time a particular behavior occurs, and (2) actually
describing that behavior in considerable detail (as in the narrative description).
Irwin and Bushnell complete the partial sentence previously quoted with
". . . made it necessary to place some restrictions on what would be observed"
(p. 148). One of these restrictions is that ". . . the behavior occur frequently enough
that the observer could be reasonably sure of being able to see it" (p. 148). Citing another much earlier source, they write that ". . . if the behavior to be observed occurs less than once in fifteen minutes on the average, time sampling
should not be used" (pp. 148–149). This writer sees no reason to depart from
that prescription. All of this, by the way, has to do with the notion of *representativeness.*

Representativeness of the time sample is extremely important. "The
length, spacing, and number of intervals are intended to secure representative
time samples of the target phenomena" (Wright 1960, italics in original). Brandt
(1972) also notes that behavior samples are chosen . . . "in order to be representative of a population of behavioral units larger than that of those observed."
Brandt points out, however, that representativeness is only possible for those
behaviors that occur frequently.

The probable or likely frequency of various behaviors is not too difficult
to estimate or predict, and again, Irwin and Bushnell are very helpful. They identify as infrequent such behaviors as grief, hysteria, and tree climbing, which, on
reflection, make sense. More frequent behaviors include such actions as talking, eating, smiling, and playing (Irwin and Bushnell, p. 149). They also note
that if uncertain about the relative frequency of various behaviors, the observer
may have to do some preliminary observations in order to determine which ones
can reasonably be recorded with a time-sampling technique.

A time sampling session might be structured in the following manner.
The observer spends three minutes on each of 15 children in a preschool classroom. She observes the first child for three minutes. Using a previously coded
observation sheet, she records each instance of dependency or cooperative behavior exhibited during that period. The observer then moves on to the second
child and repeats the process, until she has observed and recorded the dependency and cooperative behaviors of all 15 children.

Variations on the time sampling procedure are numerous. Variations are
possible not only in the length and distribution of time intervals, but also in
recording techniques. For instance, an observer might decide to spend six

minutes on each child, but follow an on-off, observe-record procedure. This is especially appropriate when using a combination of coding scheme and narrative description. Here, he could observe the child for one minute, indicating only whether the target behavior(s) occurred. The second minute could be used to write a brief narrative description of the behavior and its context. The remaining one-minute intervals would be used in the same on-off fashion until the six minutes of observation were completed. The time periods could be divided in some other way—for example, observe for 10 seconds and record for 50 seconds. The variations possible are revealed by Goodwin and Driscoll's (1980) report of studies in which observation and recording took place as frequently as every three or six seconds.

Certain behaviors are always preselected as targets for observation—for example, the children's dependency, speech utterances, or attentiveness to assigned tasks might be chosen. Coding schemes are often used with the time sampling method. These schemes require making an appropriate mark on an observation sheet whenever the child displays the behavior of interest. There are two kinds of coding systems: category and sign systems (Irwin and Bushnell 1980; Goodwin and Driscoll 1982). A sign system, say Irwin and Bushnell, "requires that the categories of behavior be mutually exclusive...." This means that no given behavior can be placed in more than one category, for each category chosen excludes all others. The category system also requires "mutually exclusive categories of behavior but, in addition, the categories must be *exhaustive*. They must include the total range of behaviors so that anything the child does can be tallied" (Irwin and Bushnell 1980). Exclusiveness, for instance, would be *violated* if a respondent to a survey questionnaire were asked to indicate his or her religious preference using the following format:

Christian	☐	Muslim	☐
Baptist	☐	Jewish	☐
Catholic	☐	Other	☐

As you can see, Baptists and Catholics are also Christians, which leaves open the opportunity for the respondent to place a checkmark in at least two places (if he or she is also either a Baptist or a Catholic). The criterion of exhaustiveness would be violated if all of the possibilities were not accounted for in the behavior recording form. So, for instance, the form in the previous example would be both exclusive and exhaustive if it read:

Christian	☐
Jewish	☐
Muslim	☐
Other	☐

Here, provision is made for any respondent to indicate his or her religious preference—or no preference at all—because the category "Other" takes into account those individuals who are Christian, Jewish, Muslim, Hindu, Sufi, atheist, agnostic, or what have you. It is generally easier to construct an exclusive set of categories than an exhaustive one. Let us look quickly at a coding scheme that uses a sign system.

Examine Table 7-1. In this example, several facets of a child's behavior are defined for notice and recording. The categories are Task Orientation, Cognitive, Motility, and Interpersonal Behavior. These broad categories are further divided into specific behavioral characteristics. Thus, if you observe what you interpret as interpersonal behavior (broad category 4), you would then determine the direction or pattern of the behavior—Child to Teacher, Child to Other Child, or Other Child to Child. From there, you would have to make yet another decision as to the nature of the interpersonal behavior using the descriptions provided in the checksheet: Complies, Ignores, Resists, and so on. Table 7-1 gives you enough space to record the behaviors of eight children, or of one child over eight time intervals, whichever best suits your purpose. Space is provided at the end of the table for doing either one or both of the following: (1) briefly describing the context of the recorded behaviors, and/or (2) recording the names of the children observed and using the line numbers as codes to quickly identify the child being observed at any particular time. (If John's name is recorded on line 1, then the numeral "1" thereafter refers to John. This eliminates the need to repeatedly write "John.")

This format is easy to use. You must first specify the time intervals you will use. Your choices are almost unlimited, but they must be tempered by the purpose of your observation and the practicality of any given interval. For instance, it wouldn't make much sense to observe for a minute and then wait ten minutes before observing and recording again. This scheme would waste precious time. It would also be difficult to observe for one second and record for one second. The time intervals are far too short to be manageable and adhered to with any accuracy, and one second is not long enough to fully comprehend what a child is actually doing.

A reasonable format, for example, would be eight one-minute intervals. Or you could observe eight children for one-minute periods (or five-minute periods, or whatever makes sense with respect to your observation goals). The following procedure would work very well when doing the actual recording. Let's say that Aliya is the first child you will observe. Aliya's name is written on line 1 of the chart at the end of Table 7-2; Aliya is subsequently referred to by the numeral 1. You observe Aliya (# 1) for, say, five minutes. If she exhibits any of the behaviors specified in the four general categories, you indicate this by writing the numeral 1, followed by the numeral and letter that identifies the behavioral category and subcategory.

To illustrate how an actual time sample would be done, Table 7-2 provides you a hypothetical example of three equally hypothetical children. Notice that we have modified slightly the children's identification numbers by circling them; this avoids confusing the child's number with the numbers that identify the various behavioral categories (1 for Task Orientation, 2 for Cognitive, and so on).

Table 7-1 An Example of a Time Sampling Format: Sign System

BEHAVIORAL SIGNS	1	2	3	4	5	6	7	8
1. *Task Orientation: A.* Attentive to Teacher; *B.* Intent indiv. work; *C.* Disinterest; *D.* Attentive to other children; *E.* Social work; *F.* Intent non-teacher prescribed work; *G.* Aimless wandering; *H.* Verbal disruptive; *I.* Physical disruptive.								
2. *Cognitive: A.* Seeking information; *B.* Offering information; *C.* Curiosity and experimentation; *D.* None								
3. *Motility: A.* Expansive; *B.* Average; *C.* Constricted								
4. *Interpersonal Behavior:*								
4.1 *Child to Teacher: A.* Absent; *B.* Present								
Response to Teacher Initiation: A. Complies; *B.* Ignores; *C.* Resists; *D.* None								
Seeks Help, Support, Approval: A. Absent; *B.* Present								
Verbalization to Teacher: A. Confident; *B.* Hesitant; *C.* Whine; *D.* None								
4.2 *Child to Other Child: A.* Absent; *B.* Present								
Type: A. Active interchange; *B.* Approaches tentatively; *C.* Passive watching; *D.* Imitates; *E.* Avoids								
Tone: A. Friendly; *B.* Neutral; *C.* Hostile								
Control: A. Dominates; *B.* Neutral; *C.* Passive								
	1	2	3	4	5	6	7	8

Children Observed and/or Brief Description of Situation

1. _____   5. _____
2. _____   6. _____
3. _____   7. _____
4. _____   8. _____

Reprinted with permission from Dr. Donald S. Peters

For a practical exercise, look at Parten's six classifications of play or social interaction found in Table 7-3c. Parten's classification is an example of a category system, which, again, means that her scheme possesses both exhaustiveness and mutual exclusiveness. Construct a time sampling format that allows you to record the occurrence of Parten's play behaviors. This can be done

Table 7-2 Hypothetical Example of a Time Sampling Format: Sign System

BEHAVIORAL SIGNS	1	2	3	4	5	6	7	8
1. *Task Orientation:* A. Attentive to Teacher; B. Intent indiv. work; C. Disinterest; D. Attentive to other children; E. Social work; F. Intent non-teacher prescribed work; G. Aimless wandering; H. Verbal disruptive; I. Physical disruptive.	① 1D	② 1B	③ 1G					
2. *Cognitive:* A. Seeking information; B. Offering information; C. Curiosity and experimentation; D. None	① 2A,B	② 2C	③ 2D					
3. *Motility:* A. Expansive; B. Average; C. Constricted	① 3A	② 3B	③ 3B					
4. *Interpersonal Behavior:* 4.1 *Child to Teacher:* A. Absent; B. Present	① 4.1A	② 4.1A	③ 4.1A					
Response to Teacher Initiation: A. Complies; B. Ignores; C. Resists; D. None	① 4.1D	② 4.1D	③ 4.1D					
Seeks Help, Support, Approval: A. Absent; B. Present	① 4.1A	② 4.1A	③ 4.1A					
Verbalization to Teacher: A. Confident; B. Hesitant; C. Whine; D. None	① 4.1D	② 4.1D	③ 4.1D					
4.2 *Child to Other Child:* A. Absent; B. Present	① 4.2A	② 4.2A	③ 4.2A					
Type: A. Active interchange; B. Approaches tentatively; C. Passive watching; D. Imitates; E. Avoids	① 4.2A	—	—					
Tone: A. Friendly; B. Neutral; C. Hostile	① 4.2A	—	—	① 4.2A				
Control: A. Dominates; B. Neutral; C. Passive	① 4.2B	—	—					
	1	2	3	4	5	6	7	8

Children Observed and/or Brief Description of Situation

1. Aliya
2. Corinne
3. Carlita
4. _____
5. _____
6. _____
7. _____
8. _____

Reprinted with permission from Dr. Donald S. Peters

by building a table consisting of "cells" that accommodate each of the six play categories and each of the children that you will observe. When completed, the form might look something like Table 7-3a.

Choose a time sampling interval (such as 10 seconds for observing, 10 seconds for recording, and 40 seconds of waiting before moving on to the next

Table 7-3a Sample form for recording play

Parten's Play Categories	Eiswari	Michael	Sun Lee	Jethro	Beth	Ibraham	Miguel
Unoccupied Behavior							
Onlooker Behavior							
Solitary Play							
Parallel Play							
Associative Play							
Cooperative Play							

child). If you observe Eiswari engaging in any one of Parten's six play categories, put a checkmark in the cell (box) under Eiswari's name and to the right of the category that applies to it. Then move on to Michael and repeat the same process until you have observed all of the children listed on the form. Of course, you may enlarge the form to include more children, or reduce it to include fewer children than are allotted space in the example. You can also draw vertical lines down the columns to make spaces for repeated observations of the same children. Thus, if you divide each cell into, say, four equal parts, then you can observe each child four different times without having to construct more forms.

Yet another procedure can use the numbering technique to identify the children—as described above—and this modified form might look like Table 7-3b.

Table 7-3b Modified sample form for recording play

Parten's Play Categories																								
Unoccupied Behavior																								
Onlooker Behavior																								
Solitary Play																								
Parallel Play																								
Associative Play																								
Cooperative Play																								

Children Observed

1. Eiswari
2. Michael
3. Sun Lee
4. Jethro
5. Beth

6. Ibraham
7. Miguel
8. Ronald
9. Melissa
10. Juan

In this format, you follow the same time sampling procedure as described above (or one devised by you), but in this case, if Eiswari displays parallel play, for example, you simply write the numeral "1" in the box or cell to the right of the cell that contains the parallel play category. Again, you proceed in this fashion until you have observed all of the children listed below the time sampling form. Since there are twenty-two (22) columns in this example form, you could repeat this process 22 times for each of the 10 children, or you could observe and record the behavior of as many as 22 children. There are a number of possible combinations, although not all of them are equally desirable or practical.

Much simpler coding schemes are available. Gander and Gardiner (1982), for instance, note a procedure where each minute is divided into fifteen-second intervals that are represented in some kind of graphic form. During each fifteen seconds of observation, if the selected behavior occurs, an "X" is placed in the appropriate spot on the form; if the behavior does not occur, an "O" is recorded. Over a period of three minutes, the record could look something like the following, where each / marks off a fifteen-second interval and each I marks the end of one minute (adapted from Gander and Gardiner):

1 Min.	2 Min.	3 Min.
X / O / O / X	X / O / O / O	X / X / X / O

The form could be made more elaborate if prepared and printed ahead of time. It could look like the following:

1 Min.	2 Min.	3 Min.
X O O X	X O O O	X X X O

The shaded portions mark off or separate each fifteen-second interval—they replace the diagonal lines in the example just above. They are clearly discernible and make for easy recording, since the blank spaces in which the Xs and Os are to be put are also clearly delineated. The issue here is not how elaborate or fancy a form one can construct, but rather how clear and easy the form is to use. This could be repeated any number of times for any number of children.

It may be helpful if you can think of time sampling in relation to the concept of a behavior stream. A person's life consists of a continuous stream of behavior that flows through time. The time sampling method looks for samples of certain kinds of behavior in a child's behavior stream; but, it looks for those behaviors only in specific parts of the stream identified by intervals of time. So, an observer using the time sampling method might reason along the following lines:

> I am going to look for aggressive behavior in this group of children; but I want to observe all of the children, and I'm interested in how often aggression is displayed among the group. Therefore, between the hours of 9:00 and 10:30 A.M., a one and one-half hour segment of these children's behavior streams will flow by. I want to enter into that one and one-half hour

---

Table 7-3c Parten's Six Classifications of Play or Social Interaction

---

1. Unoccupied Behavior	Here the child is not engaging in any obvious play activity or social interaction. Rather, she watches anything that is of interest at the moment. When there is nothing of interest to watch, the child will play with her own body, move around from place to place, follow the teacher, or stay in one spot looking around the room.
2. Onlooker Behavior	Here the child spends most of her time watching other children play. The child may talk to the playing children, may ask questions, or give suggestions, but does not enter into play. The child remains within speaking distance so that what goes on can be seen and heard; this indicates a definite interest in a group(s) of children, unlike the unoccupied child, who shows no interest in any particular group of children but only a shifting interest in what happens to be exciting at the moment.
3. Solitary Play	This is play activity that is conducted independently of what anyone else is doing. The child plays with toys that differ from those used by other children in the immediate area—within speaking distance—and she makes no effort to get closer to them or to speak to them. The child is focused entirely on her own activity and is not influenced by what others are doing.
4. Parallel Play	Here the child is playing close to other children but is still independent of them. The child uses toys that are like the toys being used by the others, but he uses them as he sees fit and is neither influenced by or tries to influence the others. The child thus plays *beside* rather than with the other children.
5. Associative Play	Here the child plays with the other children. There is a sharing of material and equipment; the children may follow each other around; there may be attempts to control who may or who may not play in a group, although such control efforts are not strongly asserted. The children engage in similar but not necessarily identical activity, and there is no division of labor or organization of activity, or of individuals. Each child does what he or she essentially wants to do, without putting the interests of the group first.
6. Cooperative or Organized Supplementary Play	The key word in this category is "organized." The child plays in a group that is established for a particular purpose—making some material product, gaining some competitive goal, playing some formal games. There is a sense of "we-ness," whereby one definitely belongs or does not belong to the group. There is also some leadership present—one or two members who direct the activity of the others. This therefore requires some division of labor, a taking of different roles by the group members and the support of one child's efforts by those of the others.

part of their lives and see what is happening. To do this, I'm going to divide up the total 90 minutes among all 15 children, which gives me six minutes for each child. To get a reasonably representative sample of behavior, however, I'll probably repeat this entire process several times over the course of a week so that I'll end up with, say, three six-minute recorded samples of behavior for each child. I will also need to observe the children during different times of the day and during different activities, which will contribute further to the representativeness of my sample.

Open vs. Closed

Both Wright (1960) and Goodwin and Driscoll (1980) classify time sampling as a closed method. They consider it closed because of its use of coding schemes or "at the point of initial data collection" (Goodwin and Driscoll 1980). A coding scheme applied at the time of observation loses raw data; it is that loss that defines a closed method.

Time sampling methods are not always closed, nor need they be completely closed. We have considered the possibility of combining a closed coding scheme and an open narrative description or event sampling method. But even the use of only narrative descriptions is acceptable. Lay-Dopyera and Dopyera (1982), for example, describe the "on-off" sequence we discussed earlier as " . . . observation, note-taking, and note expansion." Although time sampling often uses a coding scheme to record behaviors, the terms "note-taking" and "note expansion" indicate that a form of narrative record can also be used. The principal feature of time sampling is the use of precisely and uniformly defined time intervals, and not the specific recording technique used. Consequently, we will consider time sampling an open method to the extent that it preserves the raw data.

Degree of Selectivity

The time sampling method is very selective; it "fishes" with a large-holed net, and the net is cast only when the preselected behavior appears in the child's behavior stream. It is not like the narrative description, which, you will recall, fishes with a small-holed net that stays in the stream throughout the observation period.

Degree of Inference Required

Time sampling does require initial inferences or interpretations. This is so because the method requires you to make an immediate decision concerning whether to record a behavior. That decision is based on whether you see the behavior as falling under a particular descriptive category, as an example of aggression, cooperative play, or what have you.

As with the narrative description or any of the other methods to be discussed, time sampling can require inferences at other points in the observation process. Once you have collected your data, you may want to use them to draw conclusions about such things as the relationship between the observed be-haviors and certain characteristics of their context. For example, you may dis-cover that Billy seems to behave aggressively when he is in the big block area during free play. Drawing conclusions about such relationships, however, re-quires information on context and behaviors that is not ordinarily obtained with coding schemes. Therefore, some narrative description may have to be a part of your recording technique. In any case, such inferences would be made after the observations were completed; so, they are not an inherent part of the method, but part of the use made of the recorded data.

Advantages

Time sampling has many advantages. There are no restrictions on the kinds of behaviors that can be studied with this method. Wright (1960) cites the range of behaviors that have been time sampled as early as the 1930s. He refers to behaviors ranging from "imaginative behavior" to "friendships and quarrels" to "tics or 'nervous habits'." The method has a long history, which attests to its reliability and usefulness.

The method is economical in terms of required time and energy. Time sampling is efficient because it regulates precisely the content of the observa-tion and the amount of time one observes (Wright 1960; Irwin and Bushnell 1980). Efficiency is also achieved by using preestablished coding schemes, which reduces variability in observer judgments and inferences. This potential elimination of differing judgments contributes to an agreement among several observers, thereby increasing *inter-observer reliability.*

Time sampling also provides representative and reliable data, if one gath-ers a large number of observations related to a particular research problem. Large numbers of recordings are possible because of the method's efficiency and the ease with which data can be recorded using coding schemes. Early childhood educators and other professional child care workers may never need to gather data for formal research projects, thus limiting, for some readers, the usefulness of learning about time sampling in a research context. Nonetheless, one can still be informed about the varied purposes for which this technique can be used, thereby conceivably resulting in other creative uses of the time sampling format.

Yet another advantage of the time sampling method is its ability to com-bine several different techniques for recording—coding and narrative descrip-tion, for example. This allows the observer to use two different nets; one net catches limited kinds of data (whether the behavior has occurred at all), the other net catches the details of context and behavior. One can also use event sam-pling or some other form of narrative description by itself.

Disadvantages

This last advantage is an important one, for it also points up a significant disadvantage of a time sampling format that uses only coding schemes. Coding schemes do not capture the details of context, what the behaviors look like, how the behavior sequence turns out, how the behaviors change over time, or how the behaviors are related to each other (Wright 1960; Irwin and Bushnell 1980). Brandt (1972) points out these same weaknesses when he writes that "Time samples lack the continuity, contextual completeness, and perhaps naturalness of event samples . . . ." From this perspective, then, time sampling is chiefly used to measure the frequency of behaviors.

Frequency of occurrence of a given behavior is a limiting factor, however. Behaviors are not displayed equally often, nor do all behaviors occur with great frequency. It makes no sense to record every 15 seconds whether a particular behavior took place, when that behavior occurs every 28 minutes on the average. Gander and Gardiner (1982) address this problem when they relate behavior frequency with decisions concerning the length of the observation periods and the length of the recording intervals. If a behavior can be expected to occur fairly often, it may make sense to set aside several segments of time for observing and recording and to specify recording intervals that are relatively frequent and short. Gander and Gardiner use the example of a child's social interaction and suggest that "you might decide to observe for three five-minute sessions at five-minute intervals, and note whether your target behavior is occurring every fifteen seconds." This procedure assumes that social interactions take place frequently enough to justify dividing your recording intervals into such small segments. It therefore follows that longer recording intervals should be adopted when the behavior of interest occurs less frequently. But as Gander and Gardiner point out, these decisions take "a little experience." These decisions may also depend on the observer doing some preliminary observations to determine the frequency of the behaviors. Again, Irwin and Bushnell (1980) indicate that for time sampling to be an effective method, a behavior should occur at least once every 15 minutes on the average.

Time sampling does not treat behavior as it naturally occurs. When using predefined and restricted units of time, it is inevitable that the natural length of the behaviors will not correspond exactly to the somewhat arbitrary length of the observing and recording intervals. It is as though you throw your net into an entire school of fish, but you haul in only a very small number of them. From that very small number you will be able to tell almost nothing about the ones that got away. This has been referred to as "the observation of action fragments" (Wright 1960). A problem arises if these fragments do not accurately represent what is going on in the larger behavior stream. Here is an illustration.

You are observing a classroom, and you watch each child for five-second intervals and record on a precoded sheet any occurrences of aggressive behavior. After each interval, you move on to another child, repeating this procedure until every child has been observed. The process is then repeated, until you have obtained some predetermined total number of observations. Suppose that while you are giving your five seconds of attention to Jean, she screams at Harold, "Get out of here, you bad boy!" You decide this is an example of verbal aggression, and you appropriately mark it as such on your recording sheet. You then shift your attention to the next child. What you may have missed from this sequence were the preceding dramatic play behaviors, in which Jean was the "mommy" and Harold was her "son." "Mommy" was simply scolding her "son" for misbehaving, symbolically speaking. You may also have missed Harold's response: "I'm sorry mommy, please don't spank me." In this illustration, Jean's remarks taken out of context, misrepresented the larger sequence of which they were a part. This example argues for gathering a number of time samples to ensure the representativeness and validity of your data. One could also argue that sampling for longer time periods would increase the accuracy and representativeness of your data. But if your intervals are too long, you might as well use event sampling, since you are sacrificing the economy and efficiency associated with time sampling. To observe for, say, five-minute periods to ensure the accuracy of your interpretation, but only to record the behavior with a checkmark, would indeed be rather wasteful of your time. Our goal here, however, is to inform you of the advantages and disadvantages of time sampling, not to prescribe precisely when you should or should not use the technique and for what precise time intervals. As with many human endeavors, some judgment is required—and sometimes some experimentation.

Irwin and Bushnell (1980) also report that the use of predetermined categories might bias what the observer sees. As they put it, "you look for things to fit the categories rather than describe what is occurring, and [use of predetermined categories] can cause you to overlook behaviors that might be important in helping understand the behavior or pattern under study." This weakness of time sampling is found in any method that is highly selective and closed.

A final comment on time sampling may have to do with either advantages or disadvantages, depending on your point of view. Coding schemes impose certain problems and obligations on the observer. Look again at Table 7-1. The categories (actually signs) in Table 7-1 may appear straightforward, but their simplicity is deceptive. Before you could use Table 7-1 as a time sampling technique, every one of those signs would have to be defined. How would you recognize "curiosity and experimentation" if you saw them? How would you know whether a child's verbalizations to her teacher were confident, hesitant, or whining? These decisions require inferences; moreover, they require consistent inferences. It is improper to accept a set of behaviors as verbally disruptive at one time, then a few minutes later put similar behaviors into a different category. Defining such descriptive categories as precisely as you can is a strength of the time sampling method; but at the same time, such definition requires a lot of prior preparation.

Summary

The time sampling method has two distinguishing features. It observes and records selected samples of a child's behavior, and it does so only during predetermined intervals of time. Time sampling aims at representative samples of behavior. To achieve this requires you to observe over a large enough number of intervals to capture the typical quality of the stream from which the sample is taken.

The variations on the time sampling method are numerous. Although coding schemes are usually used with time sampling, narrative description can be combined with such schemes. There are two general types of coding schemes: category and sign systems. A sign system of coding requires mutually exclusive categories of behavior. No given behavior can be included in more than one category. A category system requires mutually exclusive categories and exhaustive categories. The categories must include the total range of behaviors.

Time sampling varies on the dimension of open versus closedness. If only coding schemes are used, the method is closed; if combined with narrative description, it is open to that degree. The method is very selective and records only specific behaviors. Time sampling requires inferences at the time of initial recording; a decision must be made as to whether to record a particular behavior. Inferences may also be needed after the data are collected, depending on your purposes.

Time sampling is economical of time and effort. It regulates precisely the content of the observation and the amount of time you observe. An important disadvantage of time sampling is that it does not capture the details of behavior and context. It also is not a useful method for recording infrequent behaviors. The amount of preparation needed to define the behavioral categories used in the coding scheme can be an advantage or a disadvantage, depending on your point of view.

Using the narrative description data, Table 7-4 depicts what a time sample might look like. This format uses a sign system, and the data are restricted just to Melissa, Tina, José, and Miguel. Because this time sampling data are obtained from the previous narrative description (focusing primarily on Melissa), there will be no information recorded for Tina, José, and Miguel until the recording interval matches the time in the narrative description when their behaviors would actually have been observed. In a real time sampling session, of course, the observer would have recorded Melissa's behavior (if appropriate), then he would have observed Tina, then José, then Miguel, and so on, for the entire class. The present illustration merely simplifies the description.

Again, only data for Melissa are recorded in the example. Melissa is identified by the numeral "1" with a circle around it. This is obtained from the list of "children observed" that is located at the end of the sample recording form; we simply and arbitrarily put Melissa first on the list, thus assigning her the numeral "1." Under Recording Interval 1, and to the right of the category "General Response to Setting," we have put Melissa's identification number ("1") and circled it to distinguish it from the numbers that specify the various possible responses. We have enterd the numeral "2" in the same cell, because we interpreted Melissa's general response to the setting as "Enters setting reluctantly." The remainder of the recorded data should be reasonably clear.

Table 7-4 Example of a Time Sample Formation on One Child.

Observer's Name   Carmen Gonzalez

Child/Children Observed   Melissa (Tina, Miguel, and José are also involved, but only data on Melissa are included in this example)

Child's/Children's Age(s)   4 years, 3 months   Child's/Children's Sex   Female

Observation Context (home, child care center, preschool, school)   Mother's Love Child Care Center

Date of Observation   February 12, 1996   Time Begun   9:30 A.M.   Time Ended   9:45 A.M.

Brief Description of Characteristics of Physical and Social Environment:
Children seem in a good mood; some are physically active, others are engaging in sedentary activities. All 15 children are present today. Some children are playing with children with whom they do not ordinarily play.

Recording Intervals

Behavior Category	1	2	3	4	5	6	7	8	9	10
General Response to Setting										
1. Enters setting willingly (specify which areas are involved—big block area [BBA], reading area [RA], Snack Area [SA], Free Play [FP], Art Area [AA], Main Classroom [MC], etc.)		②	③	④						
2. Enters setting reluctantly	①2									
3. Refuses to enter setting										
General Response to Environment										
4. Uses equipment/materials freely										
5. Limited or sporadic use of equip-ment/materials					①5					
6. No use of equipment/materials										
General Response to Others										
7. Seeks or is in contact with peer(s)										
8. Seeks or is in contact with adult										
9. Avoids or breaks contact with peer(s)										
10. Avoids or breaks contact with adult										
11. Reluctant contact with peer(s); contact lacks motivation or concentration on part of child					①11					
12. Reluctant contact with adult; contact lacks motivation or concentration on part of child										
	1	2	3	4	5	6	7	8	9	10

Children Observed

1. Melissa   3. José
2. Tina   4. Miguel

The procedure for this example could have been the following: Procedure—Observe the child for 30 seconds, record during the next 10 seconds, and wait for 20 seconds, for a total of one minute. The 20-second waiting period might well be necessary to locate the child who is to be observed next—in the example, this would be Tina.

Study Questions

1. What does it mean to say that a sample of behavior is representative? Why is representativeness a potential problem in time sampling? How can this problem be solved or at least minimized?
2. What is a coding system? When is a coding system necessary in time sampling?
3. Describe an example of a coding system. What are its characteristics?
4. What makes time sampling a closed and highly selective method? When might time sampling not be closed?
5. Why is inference necessary in time sampling? When does it occur?

CHAPTER EIGHT
Event Sampling

Objectives

After studying this chapter, you will be able to

- examine the differences and similarities between time sampling and event sampling
- identify behaviors that could constitute an event
- identify procedures to record an event
- identify the characteristics of event sampling in relation to the dimensions of open versus closed, degree of selectivity, and degree of inference required
- analyze the advantages and disadvantages of event sampling

General Description

Event sampling is the last formal method of observation to be discussed. Just as the word "time" is central to time sampling, the word "event" is central to event sampling. Although both methods use the word "sampling," their procedures and results can be quite different.

The notion of an event is not difficult to understand, nor is the notion of event sampling. We would argue that life is a continuous stream of events; an event of some kind or other is taking place every second of every day. At least, that is how events may be conceptualized. Put differently, an event is essentially anything that occurs somewhere in the "real" world. Some events can be observed in a particular way, whereas other events either go unnoticed or cannot be noticed or observed in the normal course of things—for example, various kinds of electromagnetic radiations (X-rays, gamma rays), sound waves that are not within hearing, and so on.

As a formal recording technique, event sampling simply takes advantage of the pervasive occurrence of events by defining which specific events are of interest and waiting until they occur in the observation setting. In the context of observing children, therefore, events are behaviors that can be placed into particular categories. For instance, a quarrel is an event that is made up of specific observable behaviors such as loud speech, certain kinds of facial expressions, or arguing over such things as the possession of a toy. You observe two children exhibiting certain behaviors, and you must decide whether those behaviors belong to the category labeled quarrels. Put another way, do those behaviors represent the *event* called quarreling?

Recall that in time sampling, preselected behaviors are the targets of observation and recording. Whether you come away with any recorded instances of these behaviors, however, depends not only on whether they occur, but also on whether they occur within specified intervals of time. So, you can see that time sampling methods take two different samples out of the child's behavior stream: (1) specifically defined segments of time, and (2) specifically defined behaviors. The limiting condition here is that these two samples must occur at the same time. The designated behavior must be displayed sometime during the designated time interval, otherwise, the behavior either escapes notice or it is not recorded because it did not occur at the proper time.

Event sampling differs from time sampling in that it takes only one sample from the child's behavior stream, namely, specifically defined behaviors or events. Events are behaviors that can be placed into particular categories. For example, quarrels, as stated previously, can be an event. You observe two children exhibiting certain behaviors, and you must decide whether these behaviors belong in the category labeled quarrels. The event must have certain characteristics if it is to be labeled a quarrel.

Event sampling seems simple. You select an event for observing, whether it be quarrels, social interactions, or dependency behavior. Again, you define the event in terms of the behaviors you will accept as examples of that event. You position yourself in the observation setting where the children can be seen, and you wait for the event to occur. When it does, you can do one of three things. Goodwin and Driscoll (1982) summarize the recording technique used with event sampling as immediate coding of the occurrence of certain events. Lay-Dopyera and Dopyera (1982), and Gander and Gardiner (1981), however, write of describing the event in detail. Gander and Gardiner say "... you should record the entire sequence of behavior from beginning to end in as much detail as possible to provide a rich body of information to use in drawing inferences." Therefore, you can choose a (1) coding scheme, (2) narrative description, or (3) combination of these two. The previous discussion of coding schemes in time sampling also applies to event sampling. When using narrative description, you will observe and record for as long as the event lasts. (Note how this differs from time sampling, where observing and recording are limited to predetermined amounts of time.)

Just as a point of information, time sampling is in some respects similar to event sampling. Refer to Chapter 7 (Table 7-1), for example. Each of the behavioral categories represents an event. As an observer, you record whether the event has occurred. You already know the two characteristics or conditions that have to be present for time sampling to "work." It is also characteristic of time sampling, however, that very often no data describing the behavior are recorded, only whether the child has exhibited the behavior of interest. At the risk of confusing you, can you see how a time sample is in some instances very much like a checklist? Note, however, that checklists are usually concerned only with whether a behavior has occurred, not with when it occurred.

Event sampling, on the other hand, is very much like the narrative description, except that the event sample disregards any behavior that does not fit into the definition of the particular event. The narrative description records everything, without considering into which specific category the behavior can be put. Furthermore, unlike time sampling, event sampling cares nothing about when a behavior occurs; it's not boxed in by having to record only behaviors that take place during predetermined time intervals.

Open vs. Closed

Both Wright (1960) and Goodwin and Driscoll (1982) classify event sampling as a closed method. For our purposes, though, it can be open or closed. Detailed narrative description preserves the raw data, thus fulfilling the requirements of openness. If only coding schemes are used, the method is closed.

Degree of Selectivity

There is a high degree of selectivity, since only specific events chosen beforehand are observed and recorded.

Degree of Inference Required

The degree of initial inference is high, just as in the time sampling method. Remember that an inference is any decision as to whether a behavior or set of behaviors belongs to a particular category. Does Ralph's clinging to the teacher's hand belong in the category "emotional dependency?" Also remember that even the simplest of these inferences is not self-evident. One must recognize clinging behavior and must know or decide whether clinging is an accurate or appropriate element of emotional dependency.

Advantages

Event sampling shares some of the advantages of both the narrative description and time sampling. The potential for rich, detailed descriptions of behavior and its context is an advantage, just as it is in the narrative description. Event sampling can also be very practical; it is a very suitable method to use with behaviors that do not occur frequently. Of course, the infrequent observer may not find this an advantage; the odds are against infrequent behaviors occurring at the same time as infrequent periods of observation. Thus, teachers or others who are in the observation setting often and for relatively long periods of time may find event sampling a useful method.

Wright (1960) points out that event sampling "structures the field of observation into natural units of behavior and situation." These "natural units" allow you to study the relationships between behavior and its context. The narrative description does the same thing, but it captures "everything" in the behavior stream. Therefore, specific behavior episodes—the natural units of behavior—have to be gotten from the larger body of information. Even though event sampling deals with natural behavior units, it is limited because it still breaks up the continuity of behavior. As a result, the inability of event sampling to preserve large segments of the behavior stream may be regarded as a disadvantage.

A final advantage of event sampling is that it can combine narrative description and coding schemes, thus gaining the efficiency of immediate coding and the completeness of the narrative description. Because events are predefined patterns of behaviors, you can use a coding scheme such as a checklist to record features of the context that are predictably related to the event. For example, in a preschool setting, various locations within the room (e.g., big block area, dramatic play area), kinds of equipment and materials (paints, crayons, puzzles, trikes, and so on), official activity at the time the event occurs, and the children and adults present at the time, can be listed for easy checking and coding. The narrative description can be structured around questions that relate directly to the particular event. Positive social interchanges, for instance, have certain behaviors associated with them. Therefore, you can be prepared to record information concerning what the children said during the social episode; what physical actions the child performed (hugging, smiling, giving a toy); what immediately preceded the social behavior; or the outcome of the event (adapted from Wright 1960).

Disadvantages

Some of the disadvantages of event sampling have already been mentioned. The most notable disadvantage is its unsuitability for studying infrequently occurring behaviors. This limitation, however, also applies to time sampling. Also, if full details of behavior and context are desirable or necessary, event sampling may not be the appropriate method.

Summary

Event sampling differs from time sampling in that it takes specifically defined behaviors or events from the child's behavior stream, but is not concerned with when the behaviors occur or with the length of the recording period. Events were defined as behaviors that can be placed into certain categories; for example, loud speech and certain facial expressions could be put into the category of quarrels, which constitutes an event. The event must be carefully defined before beginning the observation (see Table 8-1).

Event sampling was discussed as being either open or closed, depending on whether you use narrative description or coding schemes. A combination of both is also possible. This method is highly selective, and the degree of initial inference is high.

Event sampling shares some of the advantages of both the narrative description and time sampling. There is the potential for detailed behavioral descriptions and the use of efficient coding schemes. Infrequently occurring behaviors can be suitable targets for event sampling, if you are in the setting often or for relatively long periods of time. There is the disadvantage that although

Table 8-1 Event Sampling—Social Behavior

Observer's Name   Ursula Ostertag

Child/Children Observed   Melissa

Child's/Children's Age(s)   4 years   Child's/Children's Sex   Female

Observation Context (home, child care center, preschool, school) Preschool (FunTime Care Center)

Date of Observation October 13, 1996   Time Begun 9:20A.M.   Time Ended 9:35A.M.

Brief Description of Characteristics of Physical and Social Environment

The children are fairly active today—seem to be in a good mood. The teachers and aides also share the children's mood. The activity areas are in a bit of disorder—equipment and materials are strewn about, which might reflect the general emotional mood of the class. The general demeanor is in somewhat sharp contrast with yesterday's emotional climate.

Objective Behavioral Descriptions (OBD) and Interpretations:
Event Sampling

OBD 1: [Time Begun 9:24A.M.   Time Ended 9:29A.M.]
Melissa slowly approaches the reading table where Tina, José, and Miguel are seated. M. sits down, but says nothing to the others. Tina responds immediately to M.'s presence; greets her with "Hi, wanna read a book with me?" M. replies that she (M.) can't read. T. replies that they can look at the pictures. M. agrees with a soft spoken "OK." Tina smiles and goes for a book. M. does not look at or speak to José and Miguel, nor they to her. T. comes back and tries to sit close to M., who responds by moving away slightly, keeping about 6–8 inches between them. José speaks to the two girls, asking them what they're doing. T. responds, "Never mind, we're busy." M. says nothing but gets up from the table and moves slowly toward the cubby area.

Interpretation 1:
Melissa seems shy, withdrawn, apathetic. She doesn't respond to Tina's greeting, barely even looks at her; seems not even to notice José and Miguel, who also ignore her. M. avoids close contact with Tina; seems to reject physical or psychological proximity. M. is easily distracted, does not focus well socially, as evidenced by her lack of eye contact with Tina and by her looking around the room as T. tries to engage her in a social exchange. M.'s actions don't appear to stem from any dislike of Tina; no evidence of hostility—indeed, M. is emotionally bland. Appears to have no interest in the company of others.

OBD 2: [Time Begun 9:29A.M.   Time Ended 9:30A.M.]
M. breaks contact with Tina and José and walks toward the big block area.

Interpretation 2:
Melissa still seems withdrawn and uninterested; she makes no response to José's friendly overture.

event sampling records details of behavior and context, it still breaks up the overall continuity that characterizes all behavior.

Study Questions

1. How are time sampling and event sampling similar? What are some important differences?

2. What is an event? Give two examples of events and identify some of the behaviors that make up each event.
3. Describe how you might prepare for and carry out an observation session using the event sampling method.
4. Compare the narrative description and the event sampling methods. How are they alike and how do they differ?
5. Under what circumstances would you want to use event sampling rather than another method?

CHAPTER NINE
Diary Description

Objectives

After studying this chapter, you will be able to

- describe the characteristics of the diary description method of observation
- discuss the characteristics of the diary description in relation to the dimensions of open versus closed, degree of selectivity, and degree of inference required
- describe the advantages and disadvantages of the diary description

General Description

Diary description is an informal method of observation, and it is considered the oldest method in child development (Wright 1960). Traditionally, it is used over extended periods of a child's life (*longitudinally*). In this technique, daily records are made of selected aspects of the child's growth and development. It is not as inclusive as the narrative description, because continuous contacts with the child over a period of weeks, months, or years, prohibit the intense writing load required by the narrative description.

The diary record has the objective of "recording in sequence *new* behavioral events in the behavior continuum of one subject, usually an infant or a child of preschool age" (Wright 1960; italics in original). Goodwin and Driscoll (1982) confirm this use of the diary, indicating that "Emphasis is on recording new behaviors demonstrated by one child." These new behaviors are often part of a particular developmental area such as intellectual functioning, language behavior, and social-emotional behavior. This type of diary description has been referred to as a *topical diary*. (Wright 1960). Piaget's records of his own children's cognitive development are a classic example of a topical diary. A broader focus is maintained by what Wright called a *comprehensive diary*, which "records in order as much of everything new as it can. . . ." The general intent of the diary description is to chart a child's step by step progress over a period of time.

The diary description demands a close and almost continuous contact between the child and the observer. Such closeness is rarely achieved except by a parent or guardian.

Open vs. Closed

Diary description is classified as an open method, because it captures the details of the child's behaviors, behavioral changes, and their context. It preserves those details as raw data that can be examined, analyzed, or compared later with other records.

Degree of Selectivity

Although the comprehensive diary as described by Wright appears to be unselective, it does limit itself to new behaviors that add to the recorder's understanding of the developing child. It is therefore not as undiscriminating as the narrative description. The topical diary is even more selective than the comprehensive diary; it limits itself to new behaviors that occur only within specific areas of growth and development.

Degree of Inference Required

The inference required in the diary record is much like that required in the time sampling and event sampling methods. At the least, the observer must make judgments as to whether a particular behavior is indeed new and whether it legitimately belongs in the topical area that is the focus of study. For example, is the smile displayed by two-month-old Rebecca a true indication of social behavior or is it merely gas pains? Any later use of the completed record can require further inference.

Advantages

The diary description shares with the narrative description a richness of detail, breadth of coverage, and the permanency of the written record (Wright 1960). The breadth of its coverage includes the context of the behaviors as they occur at a given time, and their sequence. Thus, rather than isolated incidents, behaviors become connected to one another within an unfolding developmental framework. This connectedness is part of the longitudinal character of the diary description. It should also be noted that longitudinal techniques, i.e., the observation and recording of behavior over relatively long periods of time, yield more reliable data than do observations over relatively short periods of time. This is partly because the observations become more representative of the individual's "true" or typical behaviors and behavior patterns.

Permanency of the record allows future comparisons with other forms of observational data, including developmental norms.

Disadvantages

The obvious disadvantage of the diary description is its limited usefulness to most observers. The need for continuous and close contact with the child rules out almost everyone but parents or other members of the child's family.

Even teachers seldom have such an extensive relationship with a particular child (Goodwin and Driscoll 1982).

Summary

The diary description is an informal method of observing and recording. It is considered the oldest method in child development. Historically, the diary description has been used over relatively long periods of a child's life to record selected aspects of her growth and development. Two types of diary descriptions were discussed: the topical diary, and the comprehensive diary. The first type emphasizes new behaviors demonstrated by the child; these new behaviors are often part of a developmental area such as intellectual functioning or language behavior. The comprehensive diary is broader in scope than the topical diary, and it records "as much of everything new as it can" (Wright 1960).

The diary description is considered an open method; it preserves the details of the child's behaviors and their context. The diary is limited to new behaviors that add to the observer's understanding of some aspects of the developing child, and so it is somewhat selective. The diary description requires inferences regarding whether a given behavior is new and belongs in the topical area being studied.

The diary shares with the narrative description the advantage of providing rich, detailed descriptions of behavior, breadth of coverage, and the permanency of the written record. Its major disadvantage is that not everyone can use it because it requires close, continuous contact with the child.

Sample Diary Description: Case Study Use

January 12, 1997. Jon L., male, age 3 years, 4 months.
Area of Observation: Social Development

Today, Imran initiated play in the big block area with Isela, a three-year-old girl. This is very unusual for Imran; in the three months (since September 1996) he's been attending the preschool, he has typically been shy and rather aloof. He is smaller than most of the other boys in the class, and the staff suspects that he is intimidated by their greater physical size. We have not, however, witnessed any bullying by the other boys.

Imran has an older, bigger brother, who may be contributing at home to Imran's apparent fearfulness or shyness in the company of the larger, stronger children. This is a possibility we should check out in our next parent conference.

Mrs. Owens (teacher) also witnessed Imran's behavior with Isela. She showed her pleasure with his actions by commenting on how nicely the two of them played together. Imran reacted positively to her remarks; he smiled and appeared to increase his efforts to interact with both Isela and the blocks. They played together for about 7 minutes, when Adrian, one of the bigger boys in the class, tried to join them. Imran almost immediately left the big block area and sat down with a book at one of the reading tables. No further interactions between Imran and any of the other children occurred for the remainder of the morning.

January 18, 1997

A real breakthrough seems to be taking place in Imran's social behavior. Since the observation of Jan. 12, the staff and I have been seeing what we think are glimmerings of a desire on Imran's part to be with at least a few of the other children. Today, about 10:00 A.M., Imran "timidly" asked Michael K., who is not much bigger than Imran, if he would play in the sandbox with him. Michael agreed. The two boys played amicably with two trucks, driving them on "roads" they constructed with wooden blocks. Play lasted for about 9 minutes; it ended when time came for snacks.

It must be noted that during their play, Imran was not assertive. Michael pretty much dictated or directed what was to happen, who was to "drive" which truck, and where the "roads" were to be placed in the sand. Nonetheless, Imran didn't appear to be especially anxious or intimidated by Michael's leadership role. He must be observed again to see whether he attempts to be more forceful in expressing his own desires or goals.

Study Questions

1. When are diary descriptions typically used?
2. How does the selectivity of the diary description compare with that of the narrative description and event sampling methods? To which of the latter two methods is the diary description most similar? Why?
3. How is inference involved in the diary description? In which other method or methods is inference involved in the same way as in the diary description?
4. Why is the diary description not a likely method for most observers?
5. The above example of a diary description most appropriately illustrates the diary's use as a *case study* (see Irwin and Bushnell, 1980, p. 85). First, find out about some of the purposes for which a case study is used. How do the purposes of the case study conform to the characteristics of the diary description? What specific criterion of the diary description method is met in the above example?

CHAPTER TEN
Anecdotal Records

Objectives

After studying this chapter, you will be able to

- discuss the characteristics of the anecdotal record method of observation
- discuss the characteristics of the anecdotal record in relation to the dimensions of open versus closed, degree of selectivity, and degree of inference required
- describe the advantages and disadvantages of the anecdotal record

General Description

The anecdotal record is another method of informal observation. It is a method often used by teachers, and the record may follow a child from grade to grade and teacher to teacher. It is a record that teachers make for future reference and as an aid to understanding some aspect of the child's personality or behavior.

Goodwin and Driscoll (1982) list five characteristics of the anecdotal record. First, the record is the result of direct observation of a child. This is important, for it legitimately rules out records based on rumors. Second, the record is a prompt, accurate, and specific descriptive account of a particular event. This confirms the necessity of direct observation. Third, the anecdotal record supplies the context of the child's behavior; it identifies setting and situation so that the behavior is not separated from the events that influenced or caused it. This context includes accurate accounts of what is said by the child or other appropriate participants. Fourth, if any inferences or interpretations are made by the observer, they are kept separate from the objective description and are clearly identified as inferences or interpretations. Finally, the anecdotal record concerns itself with behavior that is either typical or unusual for the child being observed. If the behavior is unusual, it should be so indicated. Irwin and Bushnell (1980), however, note that anecdotal records "are not limited to highlighting new behaviors" and that such records "report whatever seems noteworthy to the observer, whenever that behavior occurs."

Arguments have been made for recording only "events highlighting personality characteristics or adjustment rather than those bearing on achievement, creativity, intelligence, or problem solving" (Goodwin and Driscoll 1982). The reason for this selectivity is that there are other more effective ways of documenting behaviors such as achievement. These authors, however, go on to recommend that even cognitive areas should be documented in the case of very young children.

Open vs. Closed

The anecdotal record is an open method, assuming it preserves the raw data provided by detailed description.

Degree of Selectivity

The anecdotal record can be highly selective, especially if the observer records only, as Goodwin and Driscoll phrase it, "strikingly unusual behavior." If one follows other criteria for the anecdotal record, however, selectivity decreases, and whatever is of interest can be the target for observation and recording.

Degree of Inference Required

Inferences or interpretations can be made in an effort to explain an event or behavior, especially if the behavior is not typical for the child. Again, determining whether a behavior is ordinary or unusual requires a decision that goes beyond immediate sensory information.

Advantages

An important advantage of the anecdotal record is that it gives the teacher a running account that helps him understand a child's behavior in particular situations and settings. It also allows continuing comparisons of a child's behavior, which then provides a way of documenting changes—for example, changes in the way a child handles stressful conditions or in his social interaction patterns with children or adults. Irwin and Bushnell (1980) say that the anecdotal record is the easiest to do of the recording methods, since it needs no special setting, codes or categories, or time frame. This claim has also been made for the narrative description.

Disadvantages

Despite their common use, anecdotal records are not necessarily easy to write. They have been criticized because of the relative ease with which bias can affect the selection of events to be recorded (bias that could creep in because the observer likes or does not like certain characteristics); the vulnerability of the record to improper wording, thereby leading to misinterpretation or negative value judgments about the child by the reader; and the obligation to use the record productively, which is not always easy.

One final comment regarding this method's disadvantages has to do with the uses to which it is sometimes put. The anecdotal record is a controversial technique in some quarters, partly because it is so easy to record negative biases or judgments about a child, a disadvantage discussed immediately above. The consequences of such biases, however, do not stop with the record per se. A child's anecdotal record sometimes follows her from grade to grade and from teacher to teacher, as part of her permanent, cumulative records. As each subsequent teacher inherits the child's records, the opportunity is created for the self-fulfilling prophecy (or for the Pygmalian effect) to operate. That is to say, there is sometimes a tendency on the part of teachers—and anyone else, for that matter—to perceive and treat a child in accordance with what has been said (written) about him. Sadly, if these perceptions and treatments are negative or derogatory, the child can also behave in ways that confirm others' expectations regarding his behavior, ability, self-worth, and so on. It should go without saying that this is a totally unacceptable use and consequence of the anecdotal record, and this note of caution must not be taken lightly.

Summary

The anecdotal record (Table 10-1) is often used by teachers to help them understand some aspect of a child's personality or behavior. Five characteristics of the anecdotal record are: (1) it is the result of direct observation; (2) it is a prompt, accurate, and specific description of a particular event; (3) it gives the context of the child's behavior; (4) inferences and interpretations are kept separate from the objective description; and (5) it records behavior that is either typical or unusual for the child being observed. Some writers maintain, however, that anecdotal records may report anything of interest to the observer.

The anecdotal record is an open method. Its selectivity varies somewhat, depending on whether you record everything of interest or only unusual behaviors. Inferences are required if you try to explain the meaning of a particular behavior or event. The method's important advantage is that it gives the teacher a running record to help him understand a child's behavior in particular situations and settings. It also allows ongoing comparisons of behaviors, which provide a way of documenting changes in the child's behavior. An important disadvantage is that they are not easy to write, and some critics argue it is easy for bias to enter into the selection of events and behaviors to be recorded.

Table 10-1 A Hypothetical Anecdotal Record

Child Observed   *Melissa*
Observation Setting   *Preschool Classroom, during free play*
Observer   *Mrs. Thompson*
Date   *1/23/93*

Melissa came to school late today. She stood in the doorway to the main classroom and just looked around for about half a minute at the other children involved in various activities. She finally walked across the room toward the reading table, scraping the toe of her right foot for about 6 steps or so. She then picked up her pace a bit and, on reaching the table, sat down. Tina, José, and Miguel were already seated at the table. Tina had been watching the two boys "read" a book together; she greeted Melissa with a bright "Hi, Melissa, wanna read a book with me?" The boys neither looked up nor said anything. Melissa told Tina that she (Melissa) couldn't read, but Tina replied that they could look at the pictures. Melissa agreed with a softly spoken "ok"; she made no eye contact with Tina—in fact, she looked over toward the block area as she spoke her consent. As Tina went to get a book from the shelf, Melissa began idly flipping through some pages of a book that was lying on the table. Tina returned with a book, saying "I like this one; let's look at this one." She tries to sit close to Melissa, but she moves away slightly, putting 6–8 inches distance between them. José asks, "Hey, you two, wha'cha doin'?" Tina responds with "never mind, we're busy." As she says this, she tilts her head upward and sticks out her chin slightly. Melissa makes no response; she gets up from the table and walks slowly toward the big block area. Mrs. Johnson announces clean-up time, but Melissa again does not make any relevant response; she doesn't participate in clean-up.

Comments

This is the second time in three days Melissa has been late for school. As I recall, on the other occasion, she also seemed different from her "usual self."

Melissa stood in the doorway as though reluctant to leave her position there. I sensed that, momentarily at least, she would have rather been somewhere else.

M's response to Tina's suggestion to look at pictures uncharacteristically lacked enthusiasm. She usually likes to look at books.

I can't understand M's reaction to Tina's trying to sit close to her. It's almost as though M. is rejecting Tina. The contrast between Melissa's and Tina's behavior seems especially marked.

Note: I'll have to do some follow-up observations of Melissa. Her seemingly apathetic, unsocial behavior needs to be checked—it may just be a bad day for her. Must check with some of my staff; they may have noticed she's become somewhat withdrawn over the past several days. Bring this up at next staff meeting.

Study Questions

1. Why is the anecdotal record popular with teachers? How are such records used by teachers?
2. If the anecdotal record is used to record unusual behavior, how might records of such behavior be useful to a teacher? How might records of typical behavior be useful to a teacher?
3. On what does the degree of selectivity depend in the anecdotal record?
4. What makes the anecdotal record easy to use? Another method also claims to be easy to use for the same reasons? What method makes the same claim as the anecdotal record, and at the same time, how are these two methods different?

CHAPTER ELEVEN
Frequency Counts or Duration Records

Objectives

After studying this chapter, you will be able to

- determine the relationship between frequency records and duration records
- examine the uses of frequency counts and duration records
- identify the relationships between frequency counts or duration records and event or time sampling
- determine the method of observation, degree of selectivity, and degree of inference required in using frequency counts or duration records
- explore the advantages and disadvantages of frequency counts and duration records

General Description

The term frequency immediately identifies this method's primary characteristic. The observer simply makes a mark on an observation sheet every time a particular behavior occurs. A variation of the frequency count is the *duration record.* As Goodwin and Driscoll (1982) indicate, there are occasions when the length of a behavior is more useful to know than just its frequency.

One use of frequency counts is in the establishment of *baselines* in behavior modification. Baselines are simply frequency counts of a behavior that the teacher, experimenter, or therapist wants to modify. The effectiveness of the particular modification procedure is measured by whether the frequency of the behavior after the procedure is less than or greater than the baseline frequency. (Less than or greater than, depending on whether an undesirable behavior is to be reduced or eliminated, or a desirable behavior is to be increased.)

Both frequency counts and duration records require you to define, in advance, the behaviors you want to observe and record. The specific behaviors of interest are often dealt with as categories; for example, cooperative behavior, dependency behavior, aggression, or perhaps the various play classifications (parallel play, associative play, and so on). Frequency counts and duration records are similar to event sampling because the behavior or category must occur before it can be recorded. However, as verified by Goodwin and Driscoll's account, the frequency count can also follow a time sampling procedure, where one or more observers watch a child for designated periods and lengths of time. This affords the most economical use of time, as well as an opportunity to gather a representative sample of a given behavior. Of course, when you use a time or event sampling format, you also take on the advantages and disadvantages of those methods.

Open vs. Closed

Frequency counts and duration records are decidedly closed. Neither preserves any raw data.

Degree of Selectivity

Both methods are highly selective. If you are going to count something, you first have to specify what that something is. The same is true for measuring how long something lasts. Nevertheless, it is conceivable that frequency counts and duration records can be incorporated into some of the other methods already discussed. It can be very useful to time the duration of behaviors when using event sampling, for example. As discussed in Chapter 3, this can help prevent errors of transmission and give you relevant information about the child's attention span, level of interest in an activity, and so forth. Narrative descriptions can also make use of frequency counts, although it is likely that they would be made after the recording was completed.

Degree of Inference Required

Inferences and definitions are required in these methods since you must define ahead of time what specific behaviors are included in the category you want to observe and record. Such definitions are a form of inference; you are interpreting specific behaviors as indicating a category (cooperation, social interaction, and so on). Further inference is required as you observe a child doing various things. Do you see specific actions and responses as cooperation, dependency, aggression, or do you see something quite different? Furthermore, it happens that even with the most carefully defined categories, children will display behaviors that do not exactly fit a category, or the behavior happens too quickly to be seen in its entirety. These conditions will call for a judgment from the observer.

Advantages

The most obvious advantage of the frequency count or duration record is its simplicity. Nothing seems easier than making a tally mark every time a particular behavior or event occurs. The recording technique itself is simple to use and entails very little effort from the observer. The duration record is more complicated than the frequency count, since it involves using a watch to time the behavior. This is not in itself difficult, but it is an extra step that requires you to watch the behavior carefully to know when it begins and ends. This careful notice is also necessary in event sampling, but unlike event sampling, duration records do not involve the writing of narrative descriptions.

We want to emphasize here that "ease of use" refers primarily to the amount of effort one has to expend to record the observation data, as well as the amount of time and effort needed to construct a form on which to record the frequency or duration of various behaviors. If, however, one figures in the skill required to recognize the behaviors at issue and to make judgments concerning whether or not to mark a behavior as having occurred, the frequency count and duration record are no easier to use than any of the other recording techniques. It is not the techniques or the particular form on which you record your data that enable you to observe with skill and discernment. Rather, it is your skill, discernment, and *understanding* of the various techniques, that enable you to properly use those techniques. Moreover, in this writer's view at least, the neatness and formality of the forms on which you record observations mostly concern either personal preference, or what a particular recording format contributes to orderly record keeping.

Frequency counts have the advantage of giving almost immediate quantifiable data, which can in turn be used or represented in a number of ways. Goodwin and Driscoll (1982) mention representing the frequency of the behavior by bar graphs and using the data to calculate rates of behavior per some unit of time (such as the number of instances of aggression per minute), or to calculate the percentage of time a child spent in a particular behavior. For example, you could determine that of the total time observed, a child spent 30 percent of her time in cooperative play and 20 percent in solitary activity. Although a much more elaborate "picture" than most observers would construct, Figure 11-1 illustrates how these (hypothetical) percentages of time spent in co-

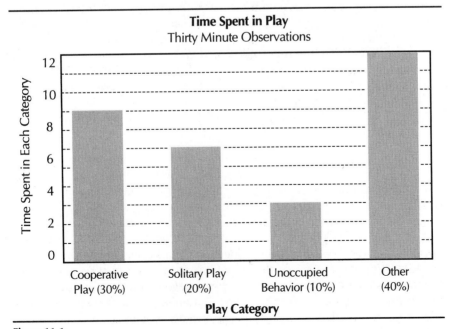

Time Spent in Play
Thirty Minute Observations

Figure 11-1

operative and solitary play derived from duration record data could be depicted by a bar graph. Of course, other types of graphic representation can be used.

Frequency counts and duration records are also useful in noting changes in behavior over time. Duration records are appropriately used when the extent of the child's involvement is most important. The fact that a child exhibits a behavior may be less significant than how long she exhibits it. Social participation, for example, might be better evaluated in terms of the length of the interactions a child has than in terms of how often she has them. Frequent but very short social contacts might indicate an inability to sustain social behaviors. In this case, a simple frequency count could mislead the observer to the conclusion that the child is highly social.

Disadvantages

The primary disadvantages of frequency counts and duration records lies in their closedness. They reveal nothing about the details of the behavior or its context. Again, one might be recording action fragments that are not descriptive or indicative of the larger behavior stream.

Summary

The frequency count tallies the occurrences of a particular behavior. The duration record, a variation of the frequency count, measures the length of a behavior. The duration record is used when the extent of a child's behavior is more important than just its frequency.

Frequency counts and duration records are closed and highly selective; if you are going to count something, you have to know what that something is. Inferences are required in these methods, because you must define beforehand what behaviors will fit the category you want to observe and record—for example, cooperation, social exchanges, and so on. Frequency counts have such advantages as simplicity of use, provision of immediate quantifiable data, and usefulness in noting changes in behavior over repeated observations. The chief disadvantage lies in their closedness; they reveal virtually nothing about the details of behavior and its context.

A Sample Frequency Count Format for Four Categories of Behavior

Name/Time	Aggression	Cooperation	Dependency	Autonomy
Barbara K.	| | | | | | /	| | | | | | | /	| | | | | | /	| | | | | |
Jason P.	| | | | | | /	| | | | | | | /	| | | | | | /	| | | | | |
Brian L.	| | | | | | /	| | | | | | | /	| | | | | | /	| | | | | |
Alice W.	| | | | | | /	| | | | | | | /	| | | | | | /	| | | | | |
Darius H.	| | | | | | /	| | | | | | | /	| | | | | | /	| | | | | |

This sample frequency count format is only one of many possible formats. You will see that you could record only five instances of each of the four behaviors designated for study. Five might be sufficient, however, if you were observing and recording for brief periods of time. It would probably be unlikely, for instance, that Brian would exhibit more than five aggressive behaviors within the span of one minute.

But, the form is merely a concept, and it is as flexible as you need it to be. Indeed, you can record frequencies on a blank sheet of paper. The spaces indicated above are simply to give you a visual reference as a guide to what is involved in recording how often a specific behavior occurs. A simple mark is recorded (IXI) whenever the child exhibits the behavior of interest. Perhaps the most difficult task is to keep accurate track of the time periods within which you want to record the behavior. For example, if you are watching Barbara K. for one minute between 9:00 and 9:01 A.M., and you want to move on to Jason P. for the minute between 9:02 and 9:03, you must make certain that you do observe for precisely that period of time. If, in fact, you devote a minute and a half to Barbara and only forty-five seconds to Jason, any differences in behavior frequency between the two children could be attributed to the differences in the amount of time you observed each child.

The above sample also limits you to five "slots" to record the occurrence of a behavior. But if you wanted to record behavior frequencies over a long period of time (an hour, or a morning, for instance) to establish a baseline on a particular child, an open-ended form would be appropriate. You would simply make a mark every time the behavior occurred. If the frequency of the behavior was greater or less than desired, steps could be undertaken to modify the behavior's frequency upward or downward.

A duration record is really quite simple. It has the qualities of a frequency count but also records the length of time the behavior lasts. The sample form given above can easily be modified into a duration record by providing spaces for recording time spans. In fact, you may eliminate the spaces for frequency checks, since every time record also indicates the occurrence of the target behavior.

Study Questions

1. When might a duration record give more important information than a frequency count? Will a duration record lose information about frequency?
2. For what purpose might a frequency count be the most useful method of recording? the least useful method?
3. What do time sampling and frequency counts have in common?
4. What advantages and disadvantages does the frequency count share with time sampling?

CHAPTER TWELVE
Checklists

Objectives

After studying this chapter, you will be able to

- determine appropriate uses of checklists
- examine the characteristics of checklists
- discuss the characteristics of checklists in relation to the dimensions of open versus closedness, degree of selectivity, and degree of inference required
- discuss the advantages and disadvantages of checklists

General Description

Checklists have many uses and are very simple to use. A checklist is any record that denotes the presence or absence of something. A shopping list and a class attendance sheet are simple checklists. When observing children, checklists are used to record the occurrence of specific behaviors in a given context. Key words here are "specific behaviors" and "given context." The first term simply indicates that the checklist has to be made up ahead of time before you begin observing. This being so, it stands to reason that you can't construct a checklist of any kind until you know what you want to include on that list. Think of it again in terms of a grocery shopping list, which, as we have pointed out, is really a type of checklist. As you put each item on the list into your cart, you check it off, thereby keeping track both of what items you have in your cart and what items you still have to find in the store. But you can't do that if you haven't prepared the list before you enter the store (or while in the store but before actually beginning to shop). "Given context" means that at least some of the behaviors on the list will likely occur in particular settings and situations. So, for instance, if your checklist concerns physical/motor behaviors, ideally you would want to observe for those behaviors in a setting where they are most likely to occur—the big block area, during outside play, and so on. This would increase the efficiency and productivity of your efforts. However, it must be emphasized that the checklist can be used almost anywhere—physical/motor actions at the snack table are just as legitimate as those displayed while climbing a jungle gym, even though they might differ in certain respects (e.g., fine versus gross motor activities).

Brandt (1972) notes two types of this recording method. One important class of items recordable by a checklist is what he calls *static descriptors*. Static descriptors are "a set of descriptive items pertaining to highly stable character- istics of research subjects or settings that are to be checked or filled out, thus ensuring systematic notation of the data." Age, sex, race, socioeconomic status, characteristics of the physical environment, and time of day are examples of common static descriptors.

A second class of items for checklist recording is *actions* (action check- lists, Brandt 1972). Actions are behaviors and are therefore of prime concern to observers of children. A typical action checklist records occurrences of specific behaviors during an observation period. A list of behaviors is made up for each child, and the observer marks the behaviors that the child exhibits anytime dur- ing the observation period. A checklist can also be used to record whether the child can demonstrate certain behaviors on request. In this case, the checklist becomes a form of assessment.

Examine Tables 12-1 and 12-2. These particular examples are checklists used in a local Head Start program known to the author (courtesy of Helen Chauvin, Director). As you can see from Table 12-1, behaviors can be checked off at any time; but the checker needs to observe that the child can perform the behaviors, or that the characteristics in question are true of the child. What is important and useful about this checklist is that the teacher or observer is not bound by time or context. He can record the information at any time. (This list, incidentally, is only partial; the original contains 166 items.) Table 12-2 com- bines a straightforward list of motor and self-help skills with normative data that indicate the age at which children typically acquire various skills. For example, the part of the Inventory called the "Blueprint" indicates that by three to four years of age on the average, children acquire the large motor skills described by items 24 through 32.

There are so many kinds of checklists that they may not be easily recog- nized as such. Consider the following example. The *Denver Developmental Screening Test*, although called a *test*, is also a checklist. The *Denver Test* pro- vides norms for various behaviors within four developmental areas. It also pro- vides the examiner with a series of questions, directions, and actions to elicit particular verbal, cognitive, or motor responses from the child. The examiner checks whether the child can answer the questions and demonstrate the desired behaviors. The child's performance is also matched against the norms for his age. Similarly, a preschool teacher might want to determine what specific skills the children in her class have: Who can hop on one foot, bounce a ball at least five times, count to ten? Such a checklist can be used to measure a child's skills when she first enters the preschool program, and again at a later time (see Table 12-3). Brandt (1972) says that checklists "are especially appropriate when the behavior alternatives with respect to a given problem are somewhat limited, mutually exclusive, and readily discernible to observers."

Checklists require a great deal of structuring; the items to be noticed in a behavioral situation are clearly established beforehand (Brandt 1972). This cri-

Table 12-1 Sample Checklist

Name _____ School or Agency _____

Age _____ Group _____ Sex _____ Time of Day _____

Birthdate _____ Observer _____

Directions: Check only those statements which you feel are really true of the child. Do not guess (if you are not certain) or make a premature judgment call.

1. ( ) Vigorous and energetic in his attack on a project
2. ( ) Overcautious, not venturesome, afraid to attempt the untried
3. ( ) Nearly always accomplishes tasks in spite of difficulties
4. ( ) Voice animated, alive
5. ( ) Does not become fatigued easily
6. ( ) Poor concentration (begins and ends activities quickly or abruptly)
7. ( ) Merely copies other children's reactions, not original
8. ( ) Concentrates well at his task
9. ( ) Original and inventive reactions
10. ( ) Curious and questioning
11. ( ) Expresses himself well for his age
12. ( ) Resourceful in dealing with difficult situations
13. ( ) Poor use of language for his age
14. ( ) Patient
15. ( ) Absorbed; self-sufficient in his activity
16. ( ) Restless; a certain dissatisfaction with his own activity
17. ( ) Retiring; wishes to be in the background
18. ( ) Even-tempered
19. ( ) Frequently disturbed; easily upset by the disagreeable or the exciting
20. ( ) Seldom disturbed; sudden changes in mood infrequent
21. ( ) Slow to adjust to a novel experience
22. ( ) Original in play
23. ( ) Is easily distracted from task at hand
24. ( ) Gives up easily; lacks persistence
25. ( ) Submits to any child who takes the initiative
26. ( ) Dominates children of his own age (either sex)
27. ( ) Will submit to a specific child only
28. ( ) Submits to a leader only after a struggle to dominate
29. ( ) Is a follower to one specific group only
30. ( ) Occasionally dominates a group
31. ( ) Usually leads a small group
32. ( ) Decides who shall participate in the group activities
33. ( ) Can organize the activities of a group to carry out a definite purpose
34. ( ) Leads or follows as the occasion demands
35. ( ) Neither leads nor follows; plays alone

Note: Checklists are from actual centers and are intended as examples; not necessarily ideals for all ages.

Table 12-2 Checklist with Some Developmental Norms

Child's Name _____ Date of Birth _____

Date _____ Teacher's Name _____

Directions: Check only those statements which you feel are really true of the child. Do not guess if you are not certain.

1. Puts together 3-piece puzzle	_____Yes	_____No
2. Snips with scissors	_____Yes	_____No
3. Picks up pins or buttons with each eye separately covered	_____Yes	_____No
4. Paints strokes, dots or circular shapes on easel	_____Yes	_____No
5. Can roll, pound, squeeze, and pull clay	_____Yes	_____No
6. Holds crayons with fingers, not with fist	_____Yes	_____No
7. Puts together 8-piece (or more) puzzle	_____Yes	_____No
8. Makes clay shapes with 2 or 3 parts	_____Yes	_____No
9. Using scissors, cuts on curve	_____Yes	_____No
10. Screws together a threaded object	_____Yes	_____No
11. Cuts out and pastes simple shapes	_____Yes	_____No
12. Draws a simple house	_____Yes	_____No
13. Imitates folding and creasing paper 3 times	_____Yes	_____No
14. Prints a few capital letters	_____Yes	_____No
15. Copies a square	_____Yes	_____No
16. Draws a simple recognizable picture (e.g., house, dog, tree)	_____Yes	_____No
17. Can lace shoes	_____Yes	_____No
18. Prints capital letters (large, single, anywhere on paper)	_____Yes	_____No
19. Can copy small letters	_____Yes	_____No
20. Cuts pictures from magazines without being more than 1/4 inch from edge of pictures	_____Yes	_____No
21. Uses a pencil sharpener	_____Yes	_____No
22. Folds paper square two times on diagonal, in imitation	_____Yes	_____No
23. Prints name on paper	_____Yes	_____No
24. Kicks large ball when rolled to him	_____Yes	_____No
25. Runs 10 steps with coordinated, alternating arm movement	_____Yes	_____No
26. Pedals tricycle five feet	_____Yes	_____No
27. Swings on swing when set in motion	_____Yes	_____No
28. Climbs up and slides down 4-6 foot slide	_____Yes	_____No
29. Somersaults forward	_____Yes	_____No
30. Walks upstairs, alternating feet	_____Yes	_____No
31. Catches ball with 2 hands when thrown from 5 feet	_____Yes	_____No
32. Jumps from bottom step	_____Yes	_____No
33. Climbs ladder	_____Yes	_____No
34. Skips on alternate feet	_____Yes	_____No
35. Walks balance beam forward without falling	_____Yes	_____No
36. Runs, changing direction	_____Yes	_____No
37. Jumps forward 10 times without falling	_____Yes	_____No
38. Jumps backward 6 times without falling	_____Yes	_____No
39. Bounces and catches large ball	_____Yes	_____No

Blueprint for Motor and Self-Help Skill Inventory

Developmental Levels	Large Motor			Fine Motor			Self-Help
3–4 Years	24	25	26	1	2	3	
	27	28	29	4	5	6	
	30	31	32				
4–5 Years	33	34	35	7	8	9	
	36	37	38	10	11	12	
	39			13	14	15	
5–6 Years							

terion should be familiar to you, because the idea of structuring and defining "items to be noticed" applies to many of the methods already discussed. Structuring and defining are also part of the characteristics of openness/closedness and degree of selectivity. It is important to recognize that any recording scheme that marks a category, item, or answer on an observation sheet, is a form of checklist; therefore, its categories must be carefully defined.

If validity and reliability are of concern when using a checklist, carefully defined categories will potentially enhance both of these characteristics. There are two kinds of reliability that are relevant here: *intraobserver* and *interobserver* reliability. If a checklist has *intra*observer reliability, repeated use of the checklist by the same individual will yield the same results. So, for example, if the checklist categories have been carefully defined and prove to be reliable, every time an observer sees aggression, for example, she will indicate on the checklist form that aggression has occurred. Of course, the observer has to know how aggression has been defined for the purposes of the observation, and she must be able to recognize aggression when she sees it. But the checklist also has to contain the proper descriptions of aggressive behavior so that its occurrence can be noted. If there are no items on the checklist that pertain to aggression, or if the items are not sufficiently descriptive, then reliability (and perhaps validity as well) will be reduced or sacrificed altogether.

*Inter*observer reliability deals with the stability or consistency of recordings made by more than one observer using the same checklist and observing the same child. That is, two or more observers have to make the same decisions regarding whether or not a particular behavior has occurred, and they must mark the same item on the checklist that indicates the occurrence of the behavior.

Validity is a bit more difficult to achieve. *Validity* means that the checklist is indeed measuring or capturing the behaviors, skills, or characteristics that you say it is. In other words, if a checklist claims to allow an observer to record instances of children's motor functioning, it is valid if it does just that. But if the

Table 12-3 Possible Checklist to Chart Developmental Progress

Child Observed _____

Child's Age _____

Observation Setting _____

Date _____

Time _____

1.	Imitates a 3-cube bridge	_____Yes	_____ No
2.	Uses both hands to steady a cube tower	_____Yes	_____ No
3.	Uses scissors to snip inaccurately	_____Yes	_____ No
4.	Copies a circle	_____Yes	_____ No
5.	Imitates a horizontal line and a cross	_____Yes	_____ No
6.	Feeds self independently with a spoon	_____Yes	_____ No
7.	Dresses/undresses with assistance for front, back, snaps, laces	_____Yes	_____ No
8.	Jumps in place	_____Yes	_____ No
9.	Pedals tricycle	_____Yes	_____ No
10.	Washes/dries hands	_____Yes	_____ No
11.	Bounces ball at least three times	_____Yes	_____ No
12.	Holds crayon between thumb and first two to three fingers	_____Yes	_____ No

items on the checklist really have nothing meaningful to do with motor functioning, then it is invalid and is of no use for its stated or intended purpose. It is perhaps easier to achieve validity in some behavioral areas than in others. It would appear to be easier to make valid recordings of motor functioning, for instance, than it would be for cases of certain areas or aspects of intellectual functioning. It is beyond the scope of this text to get into the technical aspects of validity and reliability. It is this writer's belief, however, that for most normal uses of the checklist in child care situations and settings, the issues of validity and reliability will resolve themselves, especially if repeated observations and recordings are made over some period of time by several individuals. And, of course, such repetition is itself part of the process of improving validity and reliability.

Open vs. Closed

Checklists are closed, because they reduce a raw data to a tally that indicates the presence or absence of a specific behavior.

Degree of Selectivity

The degree of selectivity is high, because the behavioral items to be recorded are identified and defined before beginning the observation.

Degree of Inference Required

The inferences required in using checklists by themselves are similar to those required when checklists are incorporated into other methods (for example, time sampling, event sampling, and frequency counts). You must define in advance the behaviors or events that properly belong in your observational categories. However, there will be times when you will see a behavior that is ambiguous and does not clearly fit the categories. In that case, you will have to decide then and there whether the behavior fits your definition.

Table 12-4 is an example of a checklist that would be appropriate for an infant one to four months of age. To construct the checklist, we first had to identify a range of behaviors and abilities that normally apply to a child this age. In a real observation situation, we would also have to decide what abilities, behaviors, and characteristics are important or relevant to our purposes. Obviously, it would make no sense to include in our list an item such as "Can walk five steps or more." The actual appearance of the checklist is less important than its overall clarity and ease of use. Finally, of course, anyone using the list has to understand what he or she is looking for and has to recognize it when it occurs. In this example, we do not use the format typically used throughout this manual. We are emphasizing only the kinds of checklist items that would be appropriate for an infant one to four months of age; furthermore, the list is very short and for purposes of illustration only. Naturally, you may add to it and use it as an observation exercise or for other legitimate reasons.

Advantages

Checklists have the advantage of being usable in many different situations and methods. They are efficient and easy to use. The checklist is efficient, because it reduces complex descriptive information to a single tally or notation, thus providing easily quantifiable data. The notation often signifies a category such as social exchanges, quarrels, or task-oriented activity. These categories are defined by a group of behaviors that share certain characteristics. The checklist eliminates the need to record all the details of behavior. It can also be an advantage that a checklist used in any format or method requires careful prior preparation. The checklist also has the advantage of providing what is called baseline information, which can then be compared with similar checklist records made during subsequent observations. The data can reveal the developmental gains or behavioral changes that have occurred from one time to the next. One final advantage we shall mention is that the checklist can also serve to identify behaviors, skills, and so forth, that one might want to observe and record in greater detail later on. This use of the checklist can save you a lot of time otherwise spent in waiting for a behavior to occur in order to record it using, say, a narrative description or event sampling technique. The checklist will tell you that the child can and does perform a particular behavior and that the behavior has become available for further, more intense observation.

Table 12-4 Sample Checklist for Infant One to Four Months of Age

Behavior, Characteristic, Ability	YES	NO	COMMENTS
Legs are slightly bowed in appearance			
Tears flow when crying			
Shows start of binocular vision (eyes move together)			
Displays well-developed rooting and sucking reflexes			
Grasps objects with whole hand in a palmar grasp			
Supports head and upper body on arms when in a prone (face down) position			
Can follow a moving object held 12 inches away			
Imitates gestures that are displayed by another			
Can locate the source of a sound			
Smiling at or speaking to infant evokes babbling and cooing			
Friendly face or voice evokes smile from infant			

Information adapted from Allen and Marotz, 1994

Disadvantages

As with any method that does not preserve raw data, the checklist loses the details of the observed behavior and its context. This means that the observation record will consist mainly of action fragments or isolated impressions of the children observed. This makes it important to match carefully any recording method with your observation objectives.

Summary

The checklist is a method with many uses and is very simple to use. A checklist is any record that denotes the presence or absence of something. Two types of this method were discussed. One type of checklist records static descriptors, which were defined as "a set of descriptive items" that pertain to "highly stable characteristics of research subjects or settings." Age, sex, race, and socioeconomic status are examples of static descriptors. The second type of checklist records actions, which are simply behaviors. An action checklist records the occurrence of a behavior during the period of observation. Several examples of checklists were discussed.

The number of checklists is so great that it might be difficult to recognize some of them as checklists. The *Denver Developmental Screening Test* was offered as an example of a test that is also a form of checklist but may not be easily recognized as such.

Checklists are closed and highly selective: they do not preserve raw data, and behaviors to be recorded are identified and defined before the observation begins. Inferences are required with this method, because prior decisions must be made concerning what behaviors or events fit the categories chosen for observation and recording. Further, as with other methods that involve inferences, behaviors will at times be ambiguous and not clearly fit the predetermined categories. An interpretation will therefore be necessary before recording or not recording the behavior.

Checklists have the advantage of being usable in many different situations and methods. They are efficient and require little effort. A chief disadvantage is their closedness; the checklist will provide a record that will be composed of action fragments and isolated impressions of behavior and context.

Study Questions

1. What characteristics do checklists share with frequency counts and time sampling? How are they different?
2. Describe or list five examples of checklists (different from any discussed in this manual). What does your list suggest about the possible uses and kinds of checklists?
3. Construct a brief checklist and then describe how you went about making it up, what use you had in mind, what factors you had to consider, and so on.
4. How might a multiple choice examination be considered a form of checklist? Could an essay examination also have any features of a checklist?

Practical Exercise: Chapter Twelve

As a practical exercise, design and construct a checklist based on some key developmental aspects of the one-year-old. Use it in a real observation. Have several individuals use it at the same time while observing the same child. You may want to repeat this process with several children. Compare your results. Did you achieve interobserver reliability? How could your checklist be improved?

CHAPTER THIRTEEN
Application: Recording Methods in Action

This chapter applies several recording methods to an imaginary child, Melissa. The intent is to illustrate how observational data might look in each method, and how the appearance of these data might change from one method to another. A narrative description (Table 13-1) will begin this illustration. Imagine that in each example, the observer sees the behavior and context described in the sample narrative description.

Bear in mind that this is one example chosen from among many possibilities. Depending on your objectives, these recording methods could follow different formats, and the final product could look quite different from what follows.

Table 13-1 Narrative Description—Social Behavior

Observer's Name   Carmen Gonzalez (Center Staff)

Child/Children Observed   Melissa

Child's/Children's Age(s)   4 years, 3 months   Child's/Children's Sex   Female

Observation Context (home, child care center, preschool, school) Mother's Love Child Care Center

Date of Observation February 12, 1996   Time Begun 9:20 A.M.   Time Ended 9:30 A.M.

Brief Description of Characteristics of Physical and Social Environment

The children are fairly active today—seem to be in a good mood. The teachers and aides also share the children's mood. The activity areas are in a bit of disorder—equipment and materials are strewn about, which might reflect the general emotional mood of the class. The general demeanor is in somewhat sharp contrast with yesterday's emotional climate.

Objective Behavioral Descriptions (OBD) and Interpretations:
Narrative Description

OBD 1: [Time Begun 9:20 A.M.   Time Ended 9:22 A.M.]
Melissa arrives about 35 minutes after the other children have arrived and started their activities; puts her coat in her cubby. She stands in the doorway of the main classroom and looks around; remains motionless for 1/2 minute, moving only her eyes as she glances at other children and their activities.

Interpretation 1:
Melissa seems shy, almost withdrawn. From moment of arrival, she seemed reluctant to enter into things. May be because she didn't want to come in first place.

OBD 2: [Time Begun 9:22 A.M.   Time Ended 9:24 A.M.]
M. walks toward reading area on far side of the room from cubbies. She walks scraping the toe of her right foot at each step, for about 5 feet. She passes by the puzzle table where 2 children are seated;

no communication exchanged. She now walks more briskly to a table with some books lying on it. Tina, José, and Miguel are seated at the table; José and Miguel are sharing a book, Tina is watching them "read." Melissa says nothing to the three children as she sits down.

Interpretation 2:

Melissa still seems uncertain; even her motor behaviors seem restricted; she walks slowly, shuffling, as though unsure of herself and of her relationship with the other children or her environment. Seems to have trouble deciding what to do. Not at all communicative; makes no overtures to any of the children who were "available" for such.

OBD 3: [Time Begun 9:24A.M. Time Ended 9:29A.M.]

José and Miguel don't look up or acknowledge Melissa in any way. Tina says, "Hi, Melissa, wanna read a book with me?" M. cocks her head to one side and says, "I don't know how to read." T. replies "We can look at the pictures." M. looks over toward the big block area and without looking at T., says "OK." Tina smiles and goes to a shelf containing a number of books. M. picks up one of the books and flips through the pages. T. returns with a book and says "I like this one, let's look at this one." M. only nods; T. sits down close to M., but M. moves slightly, keeping a distance of about 6–8 inches between her and T.

Interpretation 3:

Tina is outgoing and friendly as Melissa approaches; M. is still uncommunicative; still seems shy and uncertain; speaks softly as though afraid of being heard. Tina persists in spite of M.'s lack of enthusiasm. M. also seems distractible or inattentive. She shies away from T.'s efforts to get close physically, Tina moves at a quick pace, much more energetic than M.

OBD 4: [Time Begun 9:29A.M. Time Ended 9:30A.M.]

José looks up and says "Hey, you two, wha'cha doin'?" Tina tilts her head upward, thrusts out her chin slightly and says "Never mind, we're busy." M. says nothing, but gets up from the table and walks toward big block area. Miguel still reads.

Interpretation 4:

Tina is much more outgoing and sure of herself than M. T. didn't interact too much w/José and Miguel; may have felt left out of their activity. T. definitely seemed pleased to see M.; displayed no unfavorable response to M.'s "unsocial" behavior. T.'s response to José was quite assertive, but in a friendly way; almost like she claimed Melissa as her playmate, maybe in retaliation for the two boys ignoring her earlier. M. still seems uninterested, even uncertain of what to do.

Using the same narrative description data, let us see what a time sample might look like (Table 13-2). This format uses a sign system, and the data are restricted just to Melissa, Tina, José, and Miguel. Because these time sampling data are obtained from the previous narrative description (focusing primarily on Melissa), there will be no information recorded for Tina, José, and Miguel until the recording interval matches the time in the narrative description when their behaviors would actually have been observed. In a real time sampling session, of course, the observer would have recorded Melissa's behavior (if appropriate), then he would have observed Tina, then José, then Miguel, and so on, for the entire class. The present illustration merely simplifies the description.

The numbers in the cells (boxes) refer to the behaviors that define the major categories. The procedure for this example would have been the following: Procedure—Observe a child for 5 seconds, record for 5 seconds; wait 50 seconds, then repeat the process with the next child until all children have been observed.

Table 13-2 Time Sampling—Interactions with Others and with Environment

Observer's Name   Carmen Gonzalez (Center Staff)

Child/Children Observed   Melissa, Tina, José, Miguel

Child's/Children's Age(s)   4 yrs, 3 mos; 4 yrs, 5 mos; 4 yrs, 7 mos; 4 yrs, 4 mos
Child's/Children's Sex   F, F, M, M

Observation Context (home, child care center, preschool, school) Mother's Love Child Care Center

Date of Observation February 12, 1996   Time Begun 9:20 A.M.   Time Ended 9:30 A.M.

Brief Description of Physical and Social Characteristics of Observation Setting

The children are fairly active today—seem to be in a good mood. The teachers and aides also share the children's mood. The activity areas are in a bit of disorder—equipment and materials are strewn about, which might reflect the general emotional mood of the class. The general demeanor is in somewhat sharp contrast with yesterday's emotional climate.

Behavior Categories	1	2	3	4	5	6	7	8	9	10
General Response to Setting										
1. Enters setting willingly (specify which areas involved—big block area [BBA], reading area [RA], etc.)	① 2									
2. Enters setting reluctantly										
3. Refuses to enter setting										
General Response to Environment										
4. Uses equipment/materials freely										
5. Limited or sporadic use of equipment/ materials										
6. No use of equipment/materials										
General Response to Others					② 7	③ 11	④ 11			
7. Seeks or is in contact with peer(s)										
8. Seeks or is in contact with adult										
9. Avoids or breaks contact with peer(s)										
10. Avoids or breaks contact with adult										
11. Reluctant contact with peer(s); contact lacks motivation or concentration on part of child										
12. Reluctant contact with adult; contact lacks motivation or concentration on part of child										
	1	2	3	4	5	6	7	8	9	10

Children Observed

1. Melissa   3. José

2. Tina   4. Miguel

The example of time sampling just given does not specify details; it merely provides the basis for determining rather broad categories of behaviors—for example, "avoids contact with adults." In practice, all of these behaviors would be *operationally defined*. For example, you could operationally define "avoids contact with adults" as "maintains a physical distance between herself and any adult; initiates no speech with an adult; does not ask for assistance or directions; does not immediately obey an adult's commands or requests." Operational definitions frequently are tested in the field; if there is ambiguity or vagueness, or if there are disagreements between observers as to how to classify given behaviors, the definitions are reworked and refined until they permit accurate decisions by the observer.

Now let us look at Melissa's social behavior within the event sampling format (Table 13-3). Recall that the event sampling is selective and does not record all behaviors. In this example, only Melissa's social contacts or interactions are events of interest. The event sample is presented by itself through narrative description and not in combination with any other technique. Remember, though, that checklists and time sampling could be used in combination with event sampling.

Table 13-3 Event Sampling—Social Behavior

Observer's Name   Carmen Gonzalez (Center Staff)

Child/Children Observed   Melissa

Child's/Children's Age(s)   4 years, 3 months   Child's/Children's Sex   Female

Observation Context (home, child care center, preschool, school)   Mother's Love Child Care Center

Date of Observation   February 12, 1996   Time Begun   9:20 A.M.   Time Ended   9:30 A.M.

Brief Description of Characteristics of Physical and Social Environment

The children are fairly active today—seem to be in a good mood. The teachers and aides also share the children's mood. The activity areas are in a bit of disorder—equipment and materials are strewn about, which might reflect the general emotional mood of the class. The general demeanor is in somewhat sharp contrast with yesterday's emotional climate.

Objective Behavioral Descriptions (OBD) and Interpretations: *Event Sampling*

OBD 1: [Time Begun 9:24 A.M.   Time Ended 9:29 A.M.]

Melissa approaches the reading table where Tina, José, and Miguel are seated. M. sits down, but says nothing to the others. Tina responds immediately to M.'s presence; greets her with "Hi, wanna read a book with me?" M. replies that she (M.) can't read. T. replies that they can look at the pictures. M. agrees with an "OK." Tina smiles and goes for a book. M. does not look at or speak to José and Miguel, nor they to her. T. comes back and tries to sit close to M., who responds by moving away, keeping about 6–8 inches between them. José speaks to the two girls, asking them what they're doing. T. responds, "Never mind, we're busy." M. says nothing but gets up from the table and moves toward the cubby area.

Interpretation 1:

Melissa seems shy, withdrawn, apathetic. She doesn't respond to Tina's greeting, barely even looks at her; seems not even to notice José and Miguel, who also ignore her. M. avoids close contact with Tina; seems to reject physical or psychological proximity. M. is easily distracted, does not focus well socially, as evidenced by her lack of eye contact with Tina and by her looking around the room as T. tries to engage her in a social exchange. M.'s actions don't appear to stem from any dislike of Tina; no evidence of hostility—indeed, M. is emotionally bland. Appears to have no interest in the company of others.

OBD 2: [Time Begun 9:29A.M.   Time Ended 9:30A.M.]
M. breaks contact with Tina and José and walks toward the big block area.

Interpretation 2:
Melissa still seems withdrawn and uninterested; she makes no response to José's friendly overture.

The anecdotal record is one more method that could be used to observe and record the behavior of Melissa (Table 13-4). The anecdotal record might be appropriate if a teacher noticed Melissa's seeming lack of social responsiveness and decided to follow up with some additional observations. This would be a topical use of the record (Irwin and Bushnell 1980) if the teacher wanted to focus just on social behavior. The teacher could also decide to accumulate a series of behavioral incidents with the intention of learning about Melissa from a broader perspective. Our hypothetical teacher might also decide to use a frequency checklist to determine whether Melissa's "nonsocial" behavior occurred very often or whether she was simply having a "bad day."

Table 13-4 Anecdotal Record

Child observed   *Melissa*
Observation Setting   *Preschool Classroom, during free play*
Observer   *Mrs. Thompson*
Date   *February 12, 1996*

Melissa came to school late today. She stood in the doorway to the main classroom and just looked around for about half a minute at the other children involved in various activities. She finally walked across the room toward the reading table, scraping the toe of her right foot for about 6 steps or so. She then picked up her pace up a bit and, on reaching the table, sat down. Tina, José, and Miguel were already seated at the table. Tina had been watching the two boys "read" a book together; she greeted Melissa with a bright "Hi, Melissa, wanna read a book with me?" The boys neither looked up nor said anything. Melissa told Tina that she (Melissa) couldn't read, but Tina replied that they could look at the pictures. Melissa agreed with a softly spoken "ok"; she made no eye contact with Tina—in fact, she looked over toward the block area as she spoke her consent. As Tina went to get a book from the shelf, Melissa began idly flipping through some pages of a book that was lying on the table. Tina returned with a book, saying "I like this one; let's look at this one." She tries to sit close to Melissa, but she moves away slightly, putting 6–8 inches distance between them. José asks, "Hey, you two, wha'cha doin?" Tina responds with "never mind, we're busy." As she says this, she tilts her head upward and sticks out her chin slightly. Melissa makes no response; she gets up from the table and walks slowly toward the big block area.

Mrs. Johnson announces clean-up time, but Melissa again does not make any relevant response; she doesn't participate in clean-up.

Comments

This is the second time in three days Melissa has been late for school. As I recall, on the other occasion, she also seemed different from her "usual self."

Melissa stood in the doorway as though reluctant to leave her position there. I sensed that, momentarily at least, she would have rather been somewhere else.

M.'s response to Tina's suggestion to look at pictures uncharacteristically lacked enthusiasm. She usually likes to look at books.

I can't understand M.'s reaction to Tina's trying to sit close to her. It's almost as though M. is rejecting Tina. The contrast between Melissa's and Tina's behavior seems especially marked.

Note: I'll have to do some follow-up observations of Melissa. Her seemingly apathetic, unsocial behavior needs to be checked—it may just be a bad day for her. Must check with some of my staff; they may have noticed she's become somewhat withdrawn over the past several days. Bring this up at next staff meeting.

CHAPTER FOURTEEN
Interpretation of Observations, Implementation of Findings, and Ongoing Evaluation

Objectives

After studying this chapter, you will be able to

- discuss the relationship among the activities of observation, interpretation, implementation of findings, and ongoing evaluation
- discuss the two roles or types of interpretation
- analyze the concept of bias in interpretation
- discuss the several meanings of implementation of findings
- analyze the components of implementation
- describe the process of ongoing evaluation

This chapter will address the topics of interpretation, implementation, and evaluation. These topics will be discussed to point out the importance of each one in its own right, as well as their relationship to one another.

Interpretation of Observations

Considerable space has already been given to the subject of interpretation, and yet, part of another chapter is devoted to this topic. This is done for two important reasons.

The more fundamental reason is to reemphasize the broad, inevitable role interpretation plays in our lives. Our entire beings are involved in our views of the world, in the way we "see" people, objects, and events. There are no self-evident facts. But, we do become so accustomed to certain "facts" in our world, that they seem self-evident and require no further interpretation or processing. Once we understand what a dog is, we do not attach an interpretation to our every observation of a dog. We simply see a dog.

In this broad sense of interpretation, our knowledge, values, attitudes, and experiences act as "filters" through which what we observe must pass. Naturally, not everything that exists "out there" in the real world gets through our filters. Some things do not even get noticed; we sometimes fail to get a conscious sense impression of an object, person, or event. The incompleteness of our observations is partly the result of our interest at the time, level of concentration, bodily states such as fatigue or illness, what aspects of the situation we think are important, and the amount of time we have to observe. So, we may not see Jerry sharing a toy with Jacob, or Tanya tripping over the corner of the rug, although we may be looking directly at the situation. We are not cameras and cannot merely point our eyes in some direction and register everything that occurs. This is a liberal use of interpretation, and the term personality can summarize the influence of who we are on what we see and on the meaning we derive from what we see.

A stricter use of interpretation involves an additional step. In this use, we interpret something when we consciously try to make it clear and give it a meaning that goes beyond our empirical data. If you can recall, explanation was defined earlier as "making clear or understandable . . . to give or show the meaning or reason for." A major point here is that to explain, to make clear or understandable, often involves moving from something that is directly observable to something that is not directly observable or observed. For example, you repeatedly hear four-year-old Margo asking Mrs. Bergman for approval—something observable—and you conclude that Margo is an emotionally dependent child whose parents probably reinforce that kind of behavior at home—something not observed.

When one interprets, one is really imposing a bias on some fact. The word "bias" is not meant in a negative sense. It refers to the inevitable absence of *total* objectivity and the inevitable presence of the observer's own unique filters. Since no two individuals are exactly alike, no two individuals will see the same phenomenon in entirely the same way or to the exact same extent. Even a mother and father don't see their children in exactly the same way, nor does any child see his parents in the same way as his siblings see them. Indeed, it has been said (but this author can't remember who said it) that "there are as many families as there are family members." Simply translated, even though each family member shares a number of objective similarities with other members, probably none will describe or evaluate in identical ways his or her experiences while growing up. Each of us is a unique individual, and each of us imposes a unique perspective on our experiences. We have referred to "personal biases and perspectives," which again, are made up of our experiences, abilities, attitudes, and knowledge. There is another kind of bias that is more the product of formal learning and purposeful adoption than of forces and influences over which we often have no control. This is the bias (filter) provided and shaped by a theory, hypothesis, conceptual framework, or philosophy.

Theoretical biases may seem more important than personal ones. They are merely different, however, though related and interdependent. Learning a theory and using it to interpret behavior are most assuredly dependent on some of your personal characteristics—intelligence, aptitude, and potential to become a competent observer. Moreover, your values and general views about children can affect which theoretical position you feel most comfortable with emotionally and intellectually. If you believe that children learn on their own if opportunities are provided them, you are not likely to enjoy an educational approach that rigidly structures the classroom and its activities.

Biases formed from theories also have another effect on what you see. They direct your attention only to certain parts of a situation, event, or behavior.

Mussen, Conger, Kagan, and Huston (1984) describe this state of affairs: "Each scholar comes to the infant armed with a set of biases about what qualities are important, puts his or her observation 'lens' closest to those phenomena, and chooses words to describe them." It is not only theoretical biases that create this limited attention; our everyday biases do it, too. Can you imagine a father watching his four-year-old son Billy playing with some children in a schoolyard? Suddenly, while the father is looking right at them, Billy pushes a playmate; a fight breaks out between them and the other child hits Billy on the arm. It is not inconceivable that the father might blame the other child, that he might not "see" Billy as the instigator or the conflict. Indeed, all the father might see is the other boy hitting his son. This is called "selective perception," meaning that people often see only what they want to see, or place importance only on what they think is important, ignoring everything else. The result of this is that just as we assign different degrees of importance to different events in our daily affairs, different theories assign different degrees of importance to various phenomena. Piaget, for example, focused his attention on cognitive or intellectual development, but Freud was interested in personality development. It follows, therefore, that if Piaget and Freud were able to observe a child together, each would concentrate on different facets of the child's behavior, and each would make different interpretations.

In summary, then, even the most simple, straightforward, and informal observations and encounters with the environment involve some form of interpretation. We must put what we see and experience into a relationship with what we already know. We often can do this without much conscious deliberation. More formal interpretations, on the other hand, require us to look at a phenomenon and make sense of it within a particular perspective or conceptual framework—a theory, for example. And this might require conscious thought.

The second reason for discussing interpretation again is that it is the foundation of implementation of findings and ongoing evaluation. Your interpretations will determine the nature of your findings, what you think is significant, or even whether you find anything at all. This is also the case with ongoing evaluation. Evaluation involves making judgments about the value, effectiveness, or appropriateness of something. It stands to reason that such judgments involve some interpretations, and quite possibly both formal and informal interpretations, as previously discussed. In short, implementation and evaluation require you to make sense out of your observations before you can put them to some relevant use. Uses and purposes vary, of course, and can range from merely wanting to understand some facet of a child's development and behavior, to wanting to assess whether an existing program is doing what it claims to be doing, to wanting to initiate a new program.

It bears mentioning, however, that a series of observations, interpretations, and evaluations can still lead to inaccurate or inappropriate conclusions and decisions. The point, though, is that several observations are less likely than just one observation to result in wrong decisions or conclusions. This probably would also be especially true if more than one observer were involved, and if, as a result, interobserver reliability were established. It goes without saying, of course, that much depends upon the skill and experience of the observer(s).

There is one other aspect concerning the issue of interpretation that we will briefly mention but will not discuss at length. This is the effect of our cultural background or heritage on how we see people and events and the meanings they consequently have for us. Although cultural background can have a significant influence on interpretation, we must touch on it only briefly, essentially because it is too difficult and complex a topic to explore in detail in a publication of this kind.

Suffice it to say that culture is a pervasive influence that molds our personalities, values, attitudes, behaviors—in short, everything that is important to, and part of, the human condition. This being so, and given what we have already written about personality as a source of bias and thus an influence on how we "see" things, we would only caution you to try to take your own cultural background and that of others into account when observing and interpreting behavior. Childen's cultural backgrounds should also be considered, especially when their behaviors, values, attitudes, and so forth, differ from our own. Keep in mind, however, that the key word here is "differ" or "different," which should not be translated to mean "better" or "worse."

Implementation of Findings

Implementation is a broad topic. It is probably as broad as the number of reasons for observing and the number of observation methods you can use. This statement is based on the assumption that your reasons for observing should be determined before entering the child's "behavior stream." The phrase "implementation of findings" implies a predesignated purpose and method. In this respect, observation, whether formal or informal, is not very different from a research study or experiment.

An experimental psychologist, for example, has to know certain things before she even enters her laboratory. She must first identify and define a research question or problem. Why does she want to do the experiment? What knowledge does she hope to gain? She must then try to predict under what circumstances or conditions she is likely to find the answers to her question. *Conditions* refer to many factors: the physical and psychological characteristics of the experimental setting (crowded space, stress-provoking experimental tasks); the age, sex, and other characteristics of the subjects participating in the study (IQ, socioeconomic level, level of education, personality traits); how long the experiment will take—simple frequency counts of the occurrences of some response, or perhaps open-ended expressions of personal opinion. She must also decide beforehand how the data will be analyzed; what kinds of statistical tests will be used to determine the reliability and accuracy of the answers to her research problem.

Observation need not be as complicated as all this, of course, but the same fundamental principle applies to observation as to formal research; you have to know why you are observing before you "throw your net into the child's behavior stream." This principle was expressed in an earlier chapter by the statement that observation is not just casually looking *at* something; rather, it is looking *for* something.

To *implement* means to put to some practical use, to perform some action, or to satisfy the conditions of something. Implementing a plan, for example, means to put that plan into action, or to perform the behaviors that are required for the plan to work. This is a very inclusive definition, because there are broad limits to what one can perform, put into effect, or satisfy the conditions of. For that reason, implementation of findings at some point has to be considered in the specific context of your own observation purposes. For instance, you could "satisfy the conditions of" an observation exercise by obtaining a narrative description of a child's behavior during school recess. You might do nothing further with the record, but still have accomplished the goal of gaining experience in describing behavior in a detailed, narrative form. A teacher, however, might use the record to monitor a child's progress in various developmental areas or to establish the basis for modifying the child's behavior.

The word *findings* must be carefully considered. If findings are given too limited a meaning, observation will predominantly serve to support research. This would rule out observing children simply to learn about them, to see if they behave as psychologists describe. In this sense, findings take on a much broader meaning and perhaps can even be defined as objectives or purposes. Implementation of a purpose can be accomplished when you satisfy the condition of learning how Adam responds to the social behaviors of his peers, or when you learn the characteristics of Margaret's speech.

Ongoing Evaluation

Making judgments is an unavoidable activity we all do for various reasons. To evaluate is to make a judgment, and to make a judgment is to make a *comparison* between some event, object, or behavior, and a *standard* or *criterion*. The notion of comparison seems obvious even in the simplest of circumstances. For example, you try a different route to class or work, but you decide that your old route is better than the new one. It is quicker, more scenic, and it passes by a store where you sometimes shop. Your standards here, among possible others, are time, aesthetic pleasure, and the convenience of not having to go out of your way to shop.

Comparisons are essential, for without them, we could not perceive or know anything; we could not even distinguish the familiar from the unfamiliar. We must make comparisons with what we already know to recognize what we do not know. The critical factor in all of this is the *selection* of standard. Selection is the basis of observation itself, of any implementation of findings, as well as of ongoing evaluation. All three of these activities require comparison with a standard. In this general sense, therefore, a standard is any framework or context within which one can make a judgment, decision, or comparison.

Let us return to some familiar territory. Some of our standards are determined by our personalities. We have standards of conduct, for example, by which we judge the acceptability of our own and others' behavior. Such standards could be part of our personality, the result of our upbringing, values, and attitudes. A theory is also a standard by which comparisons, judgments, and decisions are made. Standards based on theory might involve assessing a child's level of cognitive development using knowledge of Piaget's theory: What behaviors are typical of a sensorimotor child—these form the standards or bases of comparison—and how does the child you are observing behave or function in relation to those typical behaviors—or standards? A theory is a formal standard, whereas our personalities might be called informal standards.

If evaluation involves comparison with a standard, then *ongoing* evaluation is a continuous comparison, with the implication that whatever is being evaluated can or will change. It is also possible for the standard to change. Indeed, when evaluating children, the standard has to change. Parents' expectations and demands regarding their child's behavior change as the child's abilities change with maturation and experience. Demands and expectations are therefore standards that are modified to keep step with the child's ability to meet them.

Selection of the standard, as mentioned above, is critical in many cases, because the standard will determine whether the child's performance satisfies the adult's conception of what she can and should be able to do. For example, standards governing toilet training are applied by parents in relation to the child's bowel and bladder control. If the parents are realistic in their assessment of the child's physiological maturity, there may be no problem. The parents will adjust their standard to fit the child. In contrast, the parents could have unrealistic expectations (standards) for their child's toileting behavior, and they could misapply the standard—or apply the wrong standard. They could demand that she sit on the potty, not wet or soil her pants, and tell them when she has to go to the toilet, when the child simply is not capable of such behavior.

Matching the standard to the child's capabilities involves several factors. First, the parents have to know the approximate age a child can be successfully toilet trained. This could be thought to involve an explanation or interpretation, in the sense that success is explained by the concept of *maturational readiness*. Second, implementation of findings is the result of learning about this maturational readiness, evaluating the child's present level of readiness, and then either applying or not applying the standard, depending on the outcome of the evaluation. If the child is not deemed ready for serious toilet training, further evaluation is necessary. The parents might reevaluate her a month or so later, updating their information and making another comparison between the child's apparent readiness and their standards for toileting behavior.

The above example is a simple one. Ongoing evaluation occurs in much more complex ways; but regardless of the level of complexity, the same process occurs as in the toilet training illustration.

Some Practical Examples of Implementation: Although implementation of findings is a broad topic, it does have very specific and very practical effects. Let us look at some hypothetical examples of how observational findings could be used in various contexts.

Illustration # 1

Mrs. Parrish wants to encourage independent behavior among the children in her preschool classroom. She is new to this particular setting, however, and she does not yet know the children and how they play or use the equipment and materials. She believes that independent behavior can be encouraged and fostered by the type and arrangement of the physical objects in the environment. Mrs. Parrish therefore decides to observe the children's play activities and, using an event sampling technique, record instances of dependent behavior displayed by the children. She chooses to observe *dependent* behavior first so as to identify the conditions under which such behavior occurs. She then hopes to modify those conditions in a way that will foster independent behavior.

Mrs. Parrish notices very quickly that every time any child wants to play with a puzzle, the alphabet game, record player, or paints, she has to ask an adult for help. When these materials are involved, the children almost invariably exhibit dependent behavior, simply because the shelves are too high for them to reach. If an adult must hand the materials to the children, Mrs. Parrish concludes, that hardly fosters independence and self-sufficiency.

As a result of this extremely simple observation and interpretation, Mrs. Parrish has the storage shelves lowered to a height accessible to the children. Ongoing evaluation finds that the incidents of children asking for help getting equipment are reduced almost to zero.

Illustration # 2

Most preschools want to encourage cooperation and sharing among the children in their programs. Cooperation and sharing are learned behaviors, however, and one cannot count on them to occur simply as a matter of course. Ms. Crenshaw, the teacher of a class of four-year-olds knew this, but she had to plan ways to allow the children to learn to cooperate. She had to determine how to arrange various classroom situations to bring about cooperative rather than competitive interactions among the children. She decided to observe the children and her staff to see what kinds of situations led to cooperation or competition.

The following scene was observed by Ms. Crenshaw on the morning following her decision to look for instances of cooperative and competitive behavior.

9:30 A.M. It was time for rhythm band activity, and Mrs. Wilson was in charge. She placed the box containing the rhythm instruments on the floor and told the children to get the instruments they wanted to play. (The box contained six triangles, one tambourine, one block and drum stick, and two rattles.) Immediately, there was a scramble toward the box. Martin got there first and grabbed a tambourine. Sally was right behind him and she got her hand on the same tambourine. Martin tugged against Sally's grasp, saying

"It's mine; I got it first." "But I want to play it today," Sally responded. While this battle was going on between Sally and Martin, eight other children were milling around the box trying to get an instrument. Juan picked out the only wooden block and drum stick and ran over to the corner of the room. Carlisle had picked out one of the triangles. Willard also grabbed a triangle, but there were six of those, and so no arguments broke out over that particular instrument. Mrs. Wilson finally had to break up the fight between Sally and Martin. She asked Sally to let Martin play the tambourine today and she could play it tomorrow. Sally reluctantly agreed. Martin walked off, a big smile on his face. Sally picked out the last remaining triangle and walked over and stood beside the children who had got their instruments. After nearly two minutes of rather frantic activity, each child got an instrument, although not without some continued grumbling from the two or three children who did not get the one they desired.

From this observation, Ms. Crenshaw decided there must be a better way to start the rhythm band activity than by putting the box of instruments in the middle of the floor. She came to the conclusion that rather than fostering cooperation and sharing, this approach really created competition. After all, thought Ms. Crenshaw, what other message could the children get when, in effect, they were told "Ok, kids, it's first come, first served, and the fastest and strongest among you will get the instruments you want." She instructed Mrs. Wilson that, in the future, the box was to be passed among the children, permitting each child to choose the instrument he or she wanted that day. The teacher was also to explain that the next time, another child could pick an instrument that he or she was unable to choose the time before. In this way, every child would eventually get to play the instrument he or she desired.

Subsequent observation of this activity confirmed Ms. Crenshaw's interpretation. Except for an occasional complaint from a child who did not want to wait until the next day to play his favorite instrument, the children accepted the new routine. There were even instances when a child would relinquish her turn with an instrument and give it to a friend.

Illustration # 3

Mrs. Gonzales believes that children are active participants in their own development, and therefore should be allowed to direct many of their own activities. Her preschool classroom has a wide variety of equipment and materials selected purposely to accommodate children who vary widely in interests and skills. Mrs. Gonzales also believes that children should be encouraged to "stretch" beyond their present level of ability to promote the development of new skills and interests. Consequently, she uses her observation skills to document each child's behavior and activities in various parts of the classroom. She observes and records data about the equipment and materials the child uses and the skills and knowledge they require of the child. She also observes how long and how often the child plays in any given area. Mrs. Gonzales would like the children to strike a reasonable balance in their use of materials and activities, believing that such a balance will further their overall development.

In the course of her observations, Mrs. Gonzales notices that Victor, a new boy in her class of five-year-olds, plays with the other children using equipment and materials that demand gross motor skills, but he avoids fine motor activities unless he is by himself. From time to time, Victor will watch some of the children as they play with small puzzles, cut out pictures with scissors, or string beads, but he never joins them. If, when he is by himself and in the middle of a fine motor activity, another child approaches, he immediately stops what he is doing and walks away. Mrs. Gonzales notices, however, that Victor's fine motor skills are quite good, and so she tentatively rules out poor coordination as a cause of Victor's behavior. Because she cannot identify anything in the classroom that might contribute to his avoidance of these activities with other children, she decides to consult with Victor's mother or father. She recognizes that a child's experiences at home can affect his behavior at school.

From a conference with Victor's mother, Mrs. Gonzales learns that Victor's older brother (seven years old) is an exceptionally well-coordinated youngster, with motor abilities that are ahead of what one would predict for his age. Unfortunately, however, the brother ridicules Victor's less well-developed fine motor skills, even though Victor holds his own when it comes to running, jumping, climbing, and wrestling. Mrs. Gonzales tentatively concludes (infers) that Victor's self-image is poor in this area because of his brother's frequent disparaging remarks. Apparently, Victor refuses to play with the other children in these activities for fear they will also ridicule him.

Mrs. Gonzales decides to test her interpretation, to implement her findings regarding Victor's home situation. Over the course of several weeks, she manages to draw Victor into a series of activities that increasingly involve fine motor abilities. She always makes it a point to comment favorably on Victor's performance, as well as on the performances of the other children. She has no real concern that anyone will make fun of Victor's fine motor abilities, because she knows that his are as good as most of the other children's in the class. Ongoing observation and evaluation confirm Mrs. Gonzales's interpretation. Within a month, Victor plays with other children in both large and small muscle activities. Now, Mrs. Gonzales notes, Victor is striking more of that balance she thinks is so important.

The first illustration might seem the simplest scenario one could paint. Mrs. Parrish notices that the children cannot reach some of the toys because the shelves are too high. She defines their asking for adults' help in getting the toys as dependency behavior. She then reasons that changing the conditions under which toys can be gotten will change the children's behavior. The shelves are lowered, and the children act independently.

The finding in this first illustration was the relationship Mrs. Parrish saw between shelf height and dependent behavior. She implemented her finding by changing the nature of the relationship from high shelves and high dependency, to lower shelves and independence. What is important to note here, however, is that the "finding" was given a particular meaning; children asking an adult for help in getting toys was interpreted as dependency behavior and evaluated as undesirable. Another teacher might have thought differently, possibly believing that the interests and goals of the preschool are better served by the staff maintaining control over equipment and materials. This second teacher would have looked for dependency in other kinds of behaviors.

The second illustration is only a little more complicated than the first. Much depended on the meaning Ms. Crenshaw put on the children's scrambling for the band instruments. The connection between placing the box on the floor and the children's behavior is not difficult to see. Two key elements, however, are the meaning of the children's responses, and how they should be handled. Ms. Crenshaw saw the milling, shoving, and arguing as unacceptable behaviors that contradicted her goal of fostering cooperation and sharing. She implemented her finding (the connection just mentioned) by structuring the distribution of instruments so that the children had to take turns.

Another teacher might have seen the children's scrambling for the instruments as a natural part of growing up and of learning not only to share, but also to assert themselves. He may have allowed some competition because he believes competition is an inevitable part of life. A second possibility is that the other teacher agrees with Ms. Crenshaw's objective of promoting sharing and cooperation among the children, but disagrees with her method. He might implement his finding by trying to teach the children *general rules* of conduct. Instead of making it impossible to compete by giving each child an instrument, the second teacher might use suggestions or reminders of the rules. As Sally and Martin fought over the tambourine, he might have said something like, "Now Sally, Martin got the tambourine first. What did I tell you children about sharing toys. If someone gets a toy before you do, you have to wait until he is done playing with it, and then it is your turn." The second teacher would be counting on the children to *internalize* the rules and eventually behave cooperatively because it is the appropriate thing to do. In either case, ongoing observation and evaluation would determine the effectiveness of the two teachers' ways of interpreting and implementing their findings.

The final illustration involves more observational data and inferences than the other two illustrations. Mrs. Gonzales sees the children's behavior through her philosophy (and "filter") of balanced activities and providing experiences that help the child progress beyond her current level of ability and development. Within that philosophy, Victor's failure to participate in fine motor activities with the other children violated the balance she thought so important. She progressively, though tentatively, ruled out various possible explanations of Victor's behavior. She finally made the inference that some situation at home might be the cause. When she learned about Victor's brother, she interpreted Victor's behavior as being a result of a poor self-image and fear of being ridiculed by his peers in school. She acted on that interpretation (implemented her finding) by gradually involving Victor in activities that increasingly required small muscle skills. When he learned that the other children did not make fun of him as his brother did, Victor became a regular participant in fine motor activities.

Summary

Interpretation can be thought of in terms of personality and formal theory. In either case, interpretation is the foundation of implementation of findings and ongoing evaluation. A finding is a finding only if it has some meaning, which can then be applied to a specific situation or problem. Ongoing evaluation depends on interpretation, because evaluation involves making a comparison between something observed and a standard. This, in turn, requires making sense out of your observational data and seeing the relationship between the data and the standard you have selected.

Implementation involves a performance, satisfying the conditions of something, or putting something into effect. If you find that Fred fights with Elizabeth whenever they are together in the big block area, you might implement that finding by directing one of them into a different activity. Your response implies that you have certain objectives for the children's behavior, and you interpret or see their behavior in terms of those objectives. Implementation, therefore, is based on a predetermined purpose.

Ongoing evaluation requires comparisons. Comparisons are essential, because without them we could not perceive or know anything. Selection of the standard is critical to observation, implementation, and evaluation; all of these activities require some sort of standard. In this broad sense, therefore, a standard is any framework within which one can make a judgment, decision, or comparison. Our personalities are informal standards, and theories are formal ones. Ongoing evaluation often necessitates modifying the standard one applies to a situation. This is especially true when evaluating children's behavior, which naturally changes as they grow and develop.

Study Questions

1. How do observation, interpretation, implementation of findings, and ongoing evaluation depend on one another? Describe their interrelationship.
2. What is meant by the term "bias" as it is used in this chapter? List some of your biases, and describe how they might affect what you see when you observe children, and your interpretations of your observations.
3. What happens when an observational finding is implemented? Describe the steps involved, the roles of observation, and interpretation.

Observation Exercises

PART 3

Chapter Fifteen
Observing the Newborn: Birth to One Month

Chapter Sixteen
Observing the Infant (One to Twenty-Four Months)

Chapter Seventeen
The Young Child: Ages Two to Six

Introduction and Preparation

Your observation exercises emphasize behavior and development. The major goal of the exercises will always be for you to learn about the child, whether from a broad developmental viewpoint or the immediate and more narrow viewpoint of the child's situation and setting. A related goal will be to enable you to do something with the information you gain from the observations. What you do with that information depends on your reasons for observing and the meaning the information has for you.

Many textbooks on children divide the life span into developmental or functional areas such as physical, motor, social, emotional, and language. This way of studying the child might give the impression that these areas are independent of one another. This is not the case. It is for the convenience of the psychologist, teacher, and others who are involved with children, that the child's development is segmented in this way. This procedure is useful and perhaps even necessary, because it brings the study of the child down to a manageable size. No one can examine simultaneously every facet of development and behavior. Nonetheless, a child is a unified, integrated whole, and his physical self is part of his intellectual self, which are parts of his social self, and so on.

As you observe children of different ages, you will be conducting something similar to a *cross-sectional* study. You will be gathering data that could be used to compare, for example, children's language development from infancy to about six years of age. You could also use this data to determine how closely a particular child's behavior matches the norms for that behavior. For example, does eighteen-month-old Jamie walk by himself, as norms predict he probably will? Or, do the social behaviors of four-year-old Christine agree with normative descriptions of four-year-olds?

There is one other important feature of your exercises. Extensive use is made of questions, which serve at least two purposes. First, they give you information about some of the specific *content* of the developmental areas. They help you focus on specific behaviors as targets of observation and recording. Remember, however, that such a focus may not always be necessary, depending on the methods you use. Consider the narrative description, where any behaviors the child exhibits while you are in her "stream" are suitable for recording.

A second reason is that the questions can be useful aids in interpreting or classifying recorded behaviors. For example, the question "How capable is the child of balancing?" not only gives you information about an observable feature of motor behavior; it also suggests that if you observe a child walk across a balance beam, you could make some interpretive comments about his coordination and control in that activity. Asking questions is an important part of the observation process.

The observation exercises begin with the period of infancy. You will be asked to observe a newborn (birth to one month of age) and a fifteen-to eighteen-month-old infant. There are several observation exercises dealing with certain aspects of development and behavior for each age period.

The second set of observation exercises covers early childhood, or what is often called the preschool years. This portion of the lifespan begins at age two and goes up through age five. The changes that occur after infancy in areas such as physical growth are relatively slower and steadier than during infancy. Generally speaking, you will see greater differences between a six-month-old and an eigthteen-month-old than you will between a two-year-old and a three-year-old. Therefore, in Chapter 17, you will observe children at intervals of years.

Each observation exercise also provides some brief background information concerning the specific developmental or behavioral area covered.

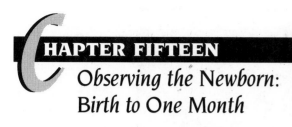

CHAPTER FIFTEEN

Observing the Newborn: Birth to One Month

Exercise 15-1: Physical Characteristics of the Newborn

Background Information

A newborn's physical appearance is easily recognized and typical of most newborns (Table 15-1). The birthweight of the average full-term baby ranges between 5½ and 9½ pounds, the average length between 19 and 22 inches. Characteristically, the skin is wrinkled, blotchy, and covered with fine hairs (*lanugo*) that fall off during the first month. At birth, the skin may be pale to pink in color, or it may have a yellowish appearance due to what is called *normal physiological jaundice*. The eyes of Caucasian babies are generally blue and do not take on their true color until sometime during the first year.

Table 15-1 Physical Characteristics of the Newborn

Body Area	Characteristics
Body weight	Average newborn weighs 5.5 to 9.5 pounds.
Length	Average length is 19 to 22 inches.
Skin	Wrinkled and blotchy; covered with fine hairs (*lanugo*). At birth skin is pale pink in color; or may have yellowish appearance due to normal *physiological jaundice*.
Eyes	Generally blue; take on true color during the first year.
Head	Has misshapen appearance that is gone by the end of the second week. Head comprises one-fourth of total length. Short neck, no chin, flattened nose. Six soft spots (*fontanels*) on top of head (allows skull to grow) that close by about 18 months of age.
External Genitalia	Look enlarged in both sexes.
Legs and Feet	Legs bowed slightly. Feet turn inward at ankles; soles are nearly parallel.

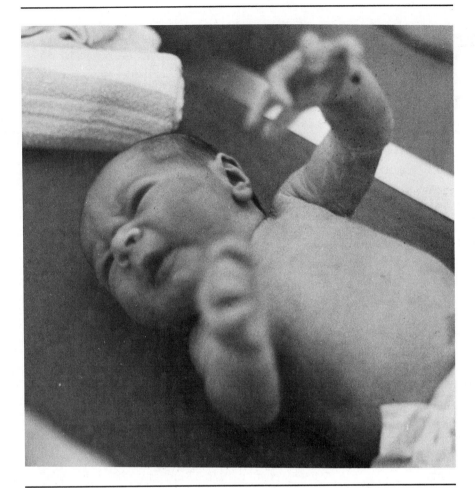

Figure 15-1 Face of a newborn. Note the relatively large head, short neck, and flat nose. (Photo by Warren R. Bentzen)

The head may have a misshapen appearance created by passage through the narrow birth canal, but this disappears by the end of the second week. The head comprises about one-quarter of the newborn's total length, which creates a disproportional appearance. The neonate has a very short neck, no chin, and a flattened nose—what some refer to as a "baby face." There are six soft spots or *fontanels* on top of the newborn's head. These allow the head to change its shape during the birth process, and they allow for brain growth during the first years of life. They close by around 18 months of age.

The external genitalia of both sexes may look enlarged, a temporary condition caused by the mother's female hormones passing to the baby during pregnancy. The newborn's legs are bowed slightly, and the feet turn inward at the ankles until the soles are almost parallel.

Observation Objectives

To observe and describe the physical characteristics of a newborn infant, with the eventual objective of comparing them with an older infant.

Procedure

Describe in as much detail as you can the physical characteristics of a newborn (one month old or less). You will need a measuring tape to measure certain physical features. It is suggested that you write your original notes on ordinary paper, then transfer them to a more formal observation sheet that follows the format provided at the end of the chapter (Observation Exercise 15-1).

Question Guides:

1. What are the newborn's most noticeable physical characteristics? How would you describe her body proportions? facial features? the shape of her legs and their typical positioning?
2. Is there anything about the newborn's physical features that a parent or caregiver might find attractive, or that might motivate a parent or caregiver to feel protective of the newborn?
3. Is there anything about the newborn's appearance that strikes you as unusual? If so, explain.

Exercise 15-2: Infant States and Responsiveness to Stimulation

Background Information

The newborn is frequently described in terms of *states*, which are levels of arousal such as asleep, drowsy, alert, and crying (see Table 15-2). Papalia and Olds (1993) define state as "a periodic variation in an infant's cycle of wakefulness, sleep, and activity" (p. 136). A state has three important characteristics: it is "a behavioral condition that (1) is stable over a period of time, (2) occurs repeatedly in an individual infant, and (3) is encountered in very similar forms in other individuals" (Hutt, Lenard, and Prechtl, 1969, cited in Papalia and Olds, 1979). States are important to the study of the neonate and young infant for several reasons: (1) States describe all infants, which makes them consistent patterns of behaviors; and (2) the infant's state affects the abilities she exhibits and the responses she makes to stimulation at any given time. Besides the characteristics of these states, one can also consider such factors as (1) how frequently a newborn is in a particular state, (2) for how long, (3) what kinds of stimulation put her there, and (4) what amount of stimulation is necessary to arouse her.

There are several forms of stimulation or interaction that are known to quiet a crying baby. Papalia and Olds (1992) note that "the age-old way to soothe crying babies involves steady stimulation—rocking or walking them, wrapping them snugly, or letting them hear rhythmic sounds or suck on pacifiers" (p. 96).

Table 15-2 Infant States

Regular Sleep (quiet sleep)	This state is characterized by closed eyes, regular breathing, and a lack of muscle or eye movements, except for sudden generalized startle responses. Mild stimuli will not arouse the infant who is in this state, which makes regular sleep the low point on the arousal continuum.
Irregular Sleep (active sleep)	The infant's eyes are stil closed, but breathing is irregular and more rapid than during regular sleep. There are slight muscle movements or stirrings from time to time, but no generalized movements. The infant may exhibit facial grimaces, smiles, mouthing movements, and puckering of the lips. There may also be eye movements, which can be discerned through the closed lids.
Periodic Sleep	This state falls between regular and irregular sleep. The infant displays sudden bursts of facial and body movements; there are also changes in the rate of breathing.
Drowsiness	This condition typically occurs when the infant is waking up or falling asleep—what is sometimes called the "twilight zone." The eyelids open and close. If the lids are open, the eyes are unfocused and appear dull or glazed. An infant in the drowsy state will exhibit more activity than when in regular sleep, but less activity than when in irregular or periodic sleep.
Alert Inactivity	Here the infant is awake but not very active. The eyes have a bright and and shiny appearance. A state of *alert activity* can usually be seen after three or four weeks of age. This state is similar to alert inactivity except that the infant displays considerably more motor activity.
Walking Activity or Active Alert (Krantz, 1994, p.134)	In this state one sees frequent bursts of generalized motor activity; the eyes are open; the infant does not cry but may utter other vocalizations such as moans, grunts, or whimpers. Breathing is quite irregular.
Crying	Crying here refers to a sustained or prolonged cry. Facial grimaces, flushing of the face, and closed eyes may accompany the crying. There is frequently generalized motor activity—"vigorous kicking and flailing arm movements w/agitated crying." (Krantz, 1994, p.134)

Based on the work of Wolff (1973). This table adapted from Gander and Gardiner (1981, pp. 109–110) and Krantz (1994, p.134)

Figure 15-2   The Babinski reflex. Note the spread toes. (Photo by Warren R. Bentzen)

In their earlier edition, Papalia and Olds (1979) also cited feeding as a soothing stimulus to a restless infant, as well as "immersing a foot in warm water" and putting the infant "in a warmer place" (Papalia and Olds, 1979, pp. 112–113).

Observation Objectives

To observe states of arousal of the newborn, to describe some of their defining characteristics, and to observe and record how a newborn's state affects his responses to the environment.

Procedure

As a first step, carefully describe characteristics of the physical and social environment that could be sources of stimulation for the newborn—e.g., background noises, talking, objects within sight or reach of the baby, direct stimulation provided by the caretaker (talking to him, caressing him), and so on. This description of the environment is the background against which you will assess the newborn's responsiveness when in various states. As a second step, describe in detail the newborn's behaviors using the narrative description technique. Make note of the small components of responses, such as respira-

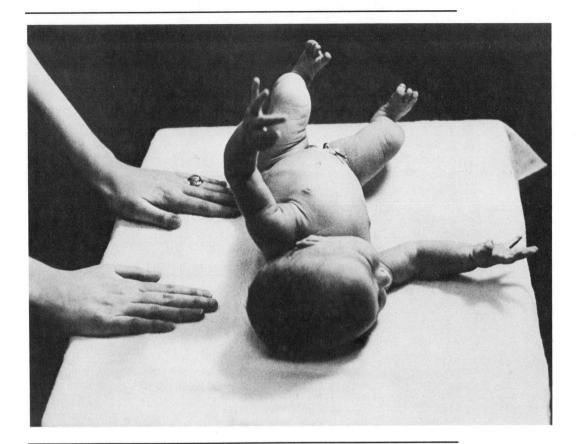

Figure 15-3   The Moro Reflex (Courtesy of Mead Johnson)

tion rate and rhythm, muscle movements, facial expressions, and eye movements (as seen through closed lids if asleep). Classify the behaviors according to the categories defined in Table 15-2.

It is suggested that you observe for about five minutes at a time, striving for at least three five-minute sessions over a total period of an hour to an hour-and-a-half. Since newborns tend to sleep a good part of the day, spacing out your recording sessions will help reduce fatigue and increase your chances of seeing the child in more than one state. (See Observation Exercise 15-2 at the end of this chapter.)

Question Guides:

1. How many different states of arousal does the newborn exhibit during your observation of him?
2. How long does he remain in each state?
3. Is he in one state more than any other? Which one?
4. Is there any one feature of each state observed that best distinguishes it from other states?

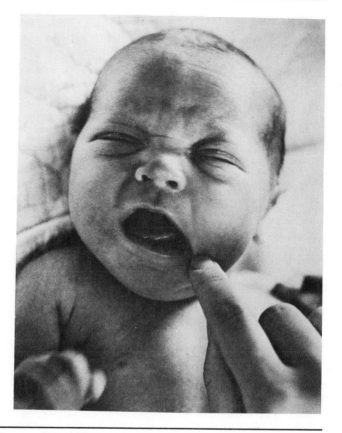

Figure 15-4   Rooting (Courtesy of Mead Johnson)

5. What, if any, stimulation changes the newborn's state? How does his state affect his response to stimulation—is there an apparent general relationship between state and responsiveness to stimulation? What is it?
6. How does the parent or caregiver respond to the newborn while he is in various states? Is the parent or caregiver aware of the newborn's differing sensitivity to stimulation when in various states?

Exercise 15-3: Individual Differences and the Newborn

Background Information

Psychologists speak of individual differences even among newborns. Individual differences exist in such areas as spontaneous behaviors, soothability states, physical characteristics, and temperament.

Figure 15-5   The Plantar Reflex (Courtesy of Mead Johnson)

Spontaneous behaviors are internally generated rather than responses to outside stimuli. They include such observable behaviors as "random startles, fleeting smiles, kicking, erections, and random mouthing and sucking movements" (Gander and Gardiner 1981). As Gander and Gardiner note, infants differ markedly in how often these behaviors occur, their type, and the sequences in which they occur. *Soothability* refers to how easily a crying or upset infant is comforted by such adult responses as holding, rocking, swaddling, warming, or giving a pacifier.

Perhaps the most interesting assessment of individual differences was made by the research team of Thomas, Chess, and Birch (1968, 1970). They describe infants by the terms "easy," "slow-to-warm-up," and "difficult." These descriptions are the result of infants' and children's responses on six personality dimensions: activity level, rhythmicity, approach/withdrawal, adaptability, intensity of reaction, and quality of mood. The infant or child is rated as either high or low on each dimension, depending on the characteristic ways she responds to various situations. These characteristic responses identify the child's *temperament.* Temperament is an important concept, because the infant's response tendencies can interact with the personalities of her parents and with the environment. This interaction can result in either a compatible or an incompatible relationship between the infant and her physical and social environment. For example, imagine a child with a vigorous, physically active temperament born to parents who are inactive physically. Of course, the relationship would not be determined solely by the temperaments of the parents and child. Nonetheless, temperament can have an effect on the child's development and behavior; and since qualities of temperament seem to be stable over the first ten years of life, they deserve attention. Table 15-4 presents the responses of a two-month-old who would be rated high and low on each of the six personality dimensions identified by Thomas *et al.*

Observation Objectives

To observe the differences in the soothability, spontaneous behaviors, and the temperaments of two newborns.

Procedure

This exercise ideally requires you to observe two newborns; however, if that is not possible, you can complete the exercise with just one newborn. Although the behaviors you will be observing are useful for studying individual differences, they will also give you information about a single child. It is suggested that you use the narrative description format for observing and recording. *Observe each of the two newborns for at least three five- to ten-minute sessions within a total period of 60 to 90 minutes in each case.* If you find it difficult to obtain much

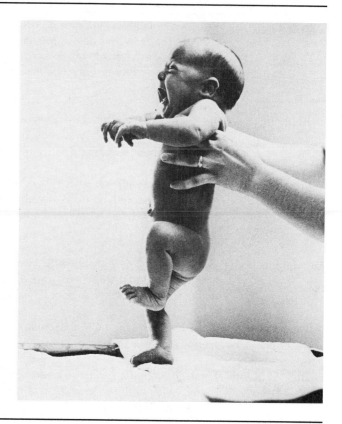

Figure 15-6   The Stepping Reflex (Courtesy of Mead Johnson)

information on the newborns' temperamental qualities just by observing, you may ask the parent or caregiver about the child's typical responses in various situations. For this, refer to Table 15-3, which provides a general description of behaviors related to the Thomas *et al.* nine personality dimensions (also refer to Table 15-4). (See Observation Exercise 15-3 at the end of the chapter.)

Question Guides:

1. What spontaneous behaviors does the newborn exhibit? How frequently do these occur? About how long do they last? Do they seem to follow a recurring sequence or pattern?
2. Does the parent or caregiver respond to any of the spontaneous behaviors exhibited? If so, describe.
3. Is the newborn easily soothed or comforted? What seems to soothe her the most? What different tactics does the parent or caregiver use to comfort the baby?
4. What temperamental qualities characterize the baby? Under what circumstances do you observe indications of the newborn's temperament?

Table 15-3 Temperamental Qualities

Activity Level	Activity can begin in the uterus, where an active fetus can kick frequently. Active babies move around in their cribs or basinettes; they prefer to climb or run rather than engage in more placid activities. Other babies show much less vigorous activity levels.
Rhythmicity	Rhythicity is characterized by regular cycles of activity—eating, sleeping, and bowel movements that occur pretty much on schedule. Other infants are not as predictable.
Approach/ Withdrawl	Approach is an attitude of delight or acceptance when confronted with something new—laughter at first bath, readily eating new food. Withdrawl is a refusal to accept new situations.
Adaptability	Characterized by rapid adjustment to change; no severe negative reactions to disruption of normal routines. Some babies do not easily tolerate change or deviations from the familiar.
Intensity of Reaction	Some children laugh loudly, scream when they cry. Others merely smile, whimper, or cry softly.
Quality of Mood	Some children are generally bright and cheerful; they smile easily. Other children seem generally unhappy and discontent; seem constantly to complain.

Adapted from Papalia and Olds (1996, pp. 266–267) and Dwortesky (1987, p.110)

5. Does the parent or caregiver seem aware of the baby's unique responses to situations? If so, how? Do the parents or caregivers of the two newborns observed differ in their responses to the babies' temperaments? How?

Table 15-4 Infant Temperament at Two Months

Temperament	Rating	Behavioral Characteristics
Activity level: the way the infant moves and how much she moves (Papalia and Olds, 1996, p. 266).	Low	Displays no movement while being dressed or while sleep, for example.
	High	A lot of movement during sleep; wiggles or squirms during some caretaking activities (e.g. diapering).
Rhythmicity: concerns the "predictability of biological cycles such as hunger, sleep, and elimination" (P & O, 1996, p. 266).	Regular	Has been on a regular feeding schedule since birth; bowel movements are regular; sleep patterns are consistent.
	Irregular	Does not awake at the same time each morning. Food eaten varies in amount from meal to meal.
Approach/Withdrawl: how the infant initially reacts to new situations or stimuli such as food, objects, persons (P & O, 1996, p. 266).	Positive	Responds smilingly to caretaking activities such as face washing; has never rejected the bottle; no negative or fearful reactions to strangers.
	Negative	May reject food the first time. Shows distress at the approach of strangers.
Adaptability: how easily or quickly child's initial response to new situation can change "in a desired direction" (P & O, 1996, p. 266).	Adaptive	Passive response to some activity (e.g., bathing) changes to enjoyment after initial response.
	Not adaptive	Retains startle response to sudden noises; continues to resist such caretaking activities as diapering, bathing, etc.
Intensity of Reaction: how vigorously infant responds (P & O, 1996, p. 267).	Mild	Does not cry when experiencing mild discomfort (e.g., wet diapers). Hunger evokes whimpering but not crying.
	Intense	Cries when experiencing mild discomfort such as wet diapers or hunger; vigorously rejects food when not hungry.
Quality of Mood: is the infant's behavior typically pleasant and friendly or is it unhappy and unfriendly (P & O, 1996, p.267)?	Positive	Smiles at familiar others. Shows a positive response to a new food—e.g., "smacks lips" (Dworetsky, 1987, p. 110).
	Negative	Is fussy after eating. Some activities/experiences cause crying—e.g., "rocking the carriage" (Dworetsky, 1987, p. 110).

Adapted from Papalia and Olds (1996, pp. 266–267) and Dworetsky (1987, p.110).

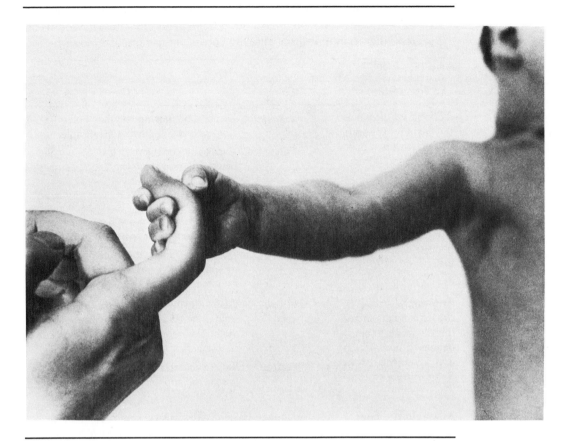

Figure 15-7   Grasping (Courtesy of Mead Johnson)

Exercise 15-4: Motor Responses of the Newborn

Background Information

The newborn's motor abilities are best characterized as reflexive. Discussion of the newborn or infant would be incomplete without mentioning these built-in motor patterns. You may see several of these reflexes during your observations, especially the more common ones such as the startle, orienting, rooting, sucking, swallowing, eye blink, and grasp reflexes (see Table 15-5). Some of these reflexes have survival value; they protect the newborn and young infant from potential harm and enable her to take advantage of the caregiver's efforts to keep her alive. The rooting, sucking, and swallowing reflexes, for example, permit the newborn to eat; the vomiting and eye blink reflexes are protective in nature. Other reflexes appear to serve no special purpose, although pediatricians use them as indications of the child's neurological development. For example, if the Babinski reflex (in which the toes curl upward and fan out when the sole of the foot is stroked) persists beyond six months or so of age, it could indicate damage of the central nervous system.

The newborn's voluntary gross (large) motor activities are limited to lifting up his head while lying on his stomach. Some newborns can lift the head to about a 45 degree angle (*Denver Developmental Screening Test* 1969). Hand functions are limited mainly to the grasp reflex. General, *undifferenti-*

Table 15-5   Infant Reflexes

Reflex	Eliciting Stimulus	Response	Age Ceases
Rooting	Stroking of the cheek with a finger or a nipple.	Infant turns head, opens his mouth, and starts sucking.	9 mos.
Moro	Sudden stimulus such as a loud noise or being dropped.	Infant extends her arms, legs, and fingers; she arches her back and throws her head back.	3 mos.
Grasping	Stroking the palm of the hand.	Fingers close in a strong fist—strong enough for infant to be pulled to an upright position while holding on to something like a stick or one's fingers.	2–3 mos.
Tonic Neck	Infant is put into a supine position (i.e., on his back).	Infant turns his head to one side, extends arms and legs on the preferred side while flexing limbs on the opposite side (so-called "fencer" position).	2–3 mos.
Babinski	Stroke one side of the foot.	Toes fan out and big toe turns upward while foot twists inward.	6–9 mos.
Walking	Hold infant under arms and have his bare feet touch a flat surface.	Makes stepping movements that resemble coordinated walking.	4–8 wks.
Eye Blink	Elicited by a puff of air in the face, a strong odor, a bright light, a loud noise.	Infant blinks eyes.	

Adapted from Papalia and Olds (1996, p. 175).

ated body movements are prominent in the newborn. Even his reactions to focused stimulation, such as a pinprick to the foot, typically involve overall
movements of the arms, legs, and torso, rather than withdrawal of just the stim-
ulated foot and leg.

Keep in mind the general principles that govern motor development.
Muscle control proceeds from the head to the feet (*cephalocaudal principle*),
and from the midline of the body to the outer extremities (*proximodistal principle*). Thus, control of the head and neck (which includes the eyes, mouth, lips,
tongue), comes before control of the trunk, legs, and feet. The infant gains control over the larger arm and shoulder (midline) movements before he can grasp
small objects between thumb and forefinger (extremities).

Observation Objectives

To observe and record a newborn's reflexive and voluntary motor
responses.

Procedure

In this exercise, you will be asked to deviate from a totally naturalistic
approach and try to elicit some common reflexes. It is recommended that the
parent or caregiver stimulate the reflexes so that you will be free to carefully observe and record the responses while they are occurring. Do not overstimulate
the baby, especially when eliciting reflexes that require loud noises or sudden
withdrawal of physical support. You will also observe and record the newborn's
voluntary movements and motor patterns. For this, you will use a narrative descriptive format, since movements of some kind are likely to occur for much of
the time. Observe for five-minutes at a time, and try for at least three five-minute
sessions over a total period of an hour to an hour and a half. (See Observation
Exercise 15-4 at the end of this chapter.)

Question Guides:

1. What reflexes does the newborn exhibit? What specific stimuli elicit the responses? Does he get used to (*habituate*) and stop responding to any stimuli
   that initially cause reflex responses?
2. What non-reflexive movements does the newborn display? What are the
   characteristics of these movements? smooth? jerky or thrashing about? coordinated? Are movements related to one another or are they seemingly independent? Do his movements bring him into any contact with the physical environment? If so, does such contact seem to affect or influence further
   movements?
3. Does the newborn have control over his general movements? over individual parts of his body? Does he have more control over some body parts than
   others? If so, how might this difference in control be explained?
4. Does the parent or caregiver respond to his movements? Does he try to encourage them?

Exercise 15-5: Perceptual Responses of the Newborn

Background Information

Vision   Vision is the sense on which the majority of us depend the most. As Berk (1996) puts it, "Humans depend on vision more than any other sense for active exploration of the environment" (p. 158). But Berk also points out that "vision is the least mature of the newborn baby's senses" (p. 158). This does not mean, however, that newborns are totally incompetent visually. Although their visual acuity is far from what it will be at a later age, newborns can see. What adults can perceive at 660 feet, for example, newborns can perceive at only about 20 feet (Berk, p. 158). Stated in more practical terms, the newborn's optimal range of vision is about 6 to 8 inches. And yet, despite their limited acuity, newborns still actively explore their environment by scanning the visual field for interesting things, and they will try to track moving objects, albeit with slow, inaccurate eye movements (Berk, p. 158).

Bukatko and Daehler (1995) make an interesting and informative observation about newborns' visual capacity and its role in the active exploration of the environment, to wit:

> Because newborns have limited motor skills, we are often tempted to assume that their sensory systems—their eyes, ears, nose, mouth, and skin— must be passive receptors awaiting stimulation. But Eleanor J. Gibson and James J. Gibson convincingly argue that perceiving is an active "process of *obtaining* information about the world" (J. J. Gibson, 1966). We don't simply see, we "look." . . .even neonates mobilize sensory receptors to respond to stimulation flowing from their bustling environment. (p. 218)

Newborns also appear to have some visual preferences and can discriminate between some different visual stimuli. The early work of Fantz (1963), for instance, showed that babies can discern the difference between such patterned visual stimuli as a face, concentric circles, and a newspaper, and such unpatterned stimuli as simple patches of color. Newborns as young as 10 hours to 5 days of age looked at the patterned displays longer than at the unpatterned ones; of the patterned stimuli, they most preferred the face (Schickedanz *et al.*, 1993, p. 135). Willemsen (1979) reports that newborns can "discriminate between solid gray patterns and those composed of five gray stripes."

One final feature of the newborn's vision that we want to mention is that infants younger than about two months of age tend to focus their attention on the outer aspects or contours of a complex stimulus, whereas the older infant tends to look at the internal features of a complex stimulus as well as the outer ones. (See, e.g., Bukatko and Daehler, 1995, for a discussion of this phenomenon.)

Newborns are sensitive to changes in the brightness of the surrounding lighting (Willemsen 1979). Not all psychologists agree on the newborn's visual preferences. Writers such as Craig (1989), report that "infants are selective about what they look at from the beginning. They look at novel and moderately complex patterns and at human faces" (p. 156). Craig (1989) notes that the newborn's preference for the edges of a face changes, with development, to an interest in "the eyes, and even later, at the mouth of a person talking" (p. 156). There does seem to be agreement that newborns prefer to scan the edges and outlines of objects, especially curved outlines. Interestingly, there is evidence that newborns as young as two weeks of age can show a preference for their mothers' faces, even when presented as pictures rather than live (Carpenter 1974, cited in Craig 1983).

Hearing   It was once believed that newborns were deaf, but it is now known that they are sensitive to some aspects of sound. Indeed, Willemsen (1979) notes that they "react to all the major aspects of auditory stimulation—that is, pitch, loudness, timbre, and pattern (rhythm)." Papalia and Olds (1979) report that "the greater the sound intensity, the greater the babies' increase in heart rate and movement," where such increases indicate awareness of the stimulation. Their responses to intense sound helps explain why newborns and babies in general pay attention to high-pitched voices and why adults speak to them in that way. There is also evidence to suggest that newborns can distinguish their mother's voice from that of another female (Fogel 1984). Papalia and Olds (1987) suggest that the infant's "early preference for the mother's voice may be an important mechanism for initiating bonding between a mother and a baby . . . " (p. 161).

Habituation   is another important component of a newborn's response capability. Habituation occurs when, after exposure to a physical stimulus that originally evokes response, the newborn ceases to respond. She gets used to it and it no longer interests her. There are two basic reactions to novel sounds (Papalia and Olds 1979). First, the newborn will exhibit an *orienting response* by turning her head toward the source of the sound. Second, if she is doing anything else at the time, she will stop or *inhibit* that activity. It is as though she can do only one thing at a time, and the novel sound is more important than something that may already be familiar to her. But as Papalia and Olds (1979) point out, it might be difficult to observe an orienting response, because the newborn does not have good control of her eye and muscle movements. Therefore, inhibition of an activity (such as sucking) following a sound, indicates that the newborn is orienting. The inhibitory response reliably accompanies the orienting reflex (Papalia and Olds 1979).

Observation Objectives

To observe and record some of the newborn's behaviors that reflect her perceptual response capabilities.

Procedure

This exercise has two parts. (See Observation Exercise 15-5 at the end of this chapter.) *In Part I, you will be eliciting some responses from the newborn.*

Perform the simple stimulation tasks outlined below, and *record on the checklist provided* whether or not the baby responded. *Immediately follow with a detailed but concise description of the response.* You will need a small flashlight (a penlight is preferable) to test several of the newborn's visual responses.

In Part II, *using a form of event sampling,* observe the newborn for any of the perceptual responses discussed in the section on Background Information. Especially look for behaviors such as the orienting and habituation responses. Notice how the parent or caregiver responds to and stimulates the baby. You may want to perform some causal testing by speaking to the newborn and comparing her reactions to your voice with her reactions to the voice of a familiar person. If there are objects hanging above the crib, observe whether she makes any visual responses to them.

Question Guides:

1. Are there any objects within the newborn's line and range of vision? Does he visually respond to these objects. Does he gaze at it or follow it with his eyes if it is moved slowly in front of his face?
2. Does the newborn respond visually to the general environment? Does the newborn appear to scan the area immediately above him (assuming there are no objects suspended above his crib or bassinet) or to either side of him? If he is held, does he look around the room, as though trying to visually take in his surroundings? What leads you to believe that the newborn has made responses to particular stimuli?
3. Do some body positions seem to evoke more responses to the environment than other positions (e.g., lying on his back, held over an adult's shoulder or on an adult's lap)?
4. Is there any apparent "mismatch" between the newborn's visual competence and the visual stimuli provided for her? For instance, is there a complicated mobile hanging above her crib, when a simple square, circle, or diamond shape might be more appropriate to her ability to process visual information?
5. Does the newborn respond to background sounds? Are there any orienting responses? Has she habituated to these general noises? Why do you think she has made a recognizable response to this aspect of her physical environment?
6. Does the newborn respond to sounds that are not always present in the background? Does she orient? Does she eventually habituate? What leads you to conclude she oriented or habituated to any sounds? To what sounds are these responses made?
7. Does the newborn respond differently to continuous as opposed to intermittent sounds? If so, what are the differences, and what are the specific sounds he responds to.
8. Does the newborn respond to voices? Does she give any indication that she prefers her mother's voice to someone else's voice. If you think so, how does she demonstrate her preference?

Exercise 15-6: Emotional Functioning of the Newborn

Background Information

This last exercise is intended only as a very brief introduction to the area of emotional behavior and functioning, a topic that is continued in Chapters 16 and 17. We draw here on the work of Stanley and Nancy Greenspan (1985), who identified six "emotional milestones." We are primarily concerned in this chapter with the first of these six milestones or stages, but for the sake of providing you with a feeling of continuity and with a larger context, we include the second stage as well.

The first two of these stages or milestones concern the capacities of *self-regulation* and the *use of the senses* to take an interest in the world. The Greenspans refer to these milestones as "two simultaneous challenges" (p. 4). They are challenges because the newborn, after nine months in the darkness and relative quiet of the womb," is suddenly catapulted, as it were, into a world filled with a variety of sensations that are completely new to her. In the first milestone, which takes place between birth and three months of age, the newborn must organize these sensations and at the same time feel comfortable in their presence and actively engage them in ways that are appropriate to her level of developmental maturity—e.g., show interest in the sights and sounds around her and not find them painful (Greenspan and Greenspan, 1985).

This then permits achievement of the second milestone (two to seven months), which is that of "taking a highly specialized interest in the *human* world" (p. 5, italics original). An assumption here is that if the baby does not find these environmental stimuli pleasurable, he may be unlikely to progress to the stage where the world of human beings "is seen as the most enticing, pleasurable, and exciting of all experiences" (p. 4). The pleasure that one wants the baby to feel, say the Greenspans, can be seen in her "enraptured smiles and eager joyfulness" as she "gazes excitedly at your face" while she feels the movements of your body and hears your voice.

Observation Objectives

Your objectives here are quite abbreviated relative to the preceding exercises. We simply want you to attempt to assess how well a newborn is achieving the Greenspans' first emotional milestone. Your objective is to observe and record the newborn's interest in and responsiveness to the sounds, sights, and things that are in his environment. We are aware that responsiveness is already heavily involved in the other exercises in this chapter. Nonetheless, we want to place emphasis on emotions and, in the case of the newborn, on the foundation or precursors of his subsequent emotional growth, development, and behavior.

Procedure

In this exercise, *use the event sampling technique.* Watch a newborn (a child between birth and one month of age and no older) for any behavioral evidence that she is *spontaneously* interested in the sights and sounds around her and that she does not "find them painful" (i.e., she does not appear disturbed or distressed by them). "Spontaneously" means that the newborn is not reacting to *your* efforts to evoke some kind of response from her; she is responding on her own. (See Observation Exercise 15-6 at the end of this chapter.)

Observe for about five minutes at a time over three separate sessions. Pool or combine the information from the three sessions to draw your conclusions or inferences.

Observation Exercise 15-1

The Physical Characteristics of the Newborn

Observer's Name _____

Child/Children Observed _____

Child's/Children's Age(s) _____ Child's/Children's Sex _____

Observation Context (home, child care center, preschool, school) _____

Date of Observation _____ Time Begun _____ Time Ended _____

Brief Description of Physical and Social Characteristics of Observational Setting:

_____

OBJECTIVE BEHAVIORAL DESCRIPTIONS (OBD): *Modified Narrative Description*

Total Length of Newborn _____ Weight of Newborn _____

Length of Head _____ Ratio of Head to Total Body Length _____

Length of Trunk _____ Ratio of Head to Trunk _____

Describe the characteristics of the following:
HEAD AND FACE (shape, eyes, ears, mouth, nose):

TRUNK (e.g., size in relation to head, overall appearance):

ARMS AND LEGS (positioning, shape):

HANDS AND FINGERS (positioning, shape):

SKIN (color, texture, general appearance):

Observation Exercise 15-2

Infant States and Responsiveness to Stimulation

Observer's Name _____

Child/Children Observed _____

Child's/Children's Age(s) _____ Child's/Children's Sex _____

Observation Context (home, child care center, preschool, school) _____

Date of Observation _____ Time Begun _____ Time Ended _____

Brief Description of Physical and Social Characteristics of Observational Setting:

_____

OBJECTIVE BEHAVIORAL DESCRIPTIONS (OBD): *Narrative Description*

OBD Session 1:   [Time begun _____   Time ended _____]
Response to Stimulation

OBD Session 2:   [Time begun _____   Time ended _____]
Response to Stimulation

OBD Session 3:   [Time begun _____   Time ended _____]
Response to Stimulation

Parent's or Caregiver's Responses to Newborn's State Behaviors:

Observation Exercise 15-3

Individual Differences in Newborns (Part I) [Newborn #1 of Two Newborns Observed]

Observer's Name _____

Child/Children Observed _____

Child's/Children's Age(s) _____   Child's/Children's Sex _____

Observation Context (home, child care center, preschool, school) _____

Date of Observation _____   Time Begun _____   Time Ended _____

Brief Description of Physical and Social Characteristics of Observational Setting:

OBJECTIVE BEHAVIORAL DESCRIPTIONS (OBD): *Narrative Description*

OBD Session 1:   [Time begun _____   Time ended _____]

OBD Session 2:   [Time begun _____   Time ended _____]

OBD Session 3:   [Time begun _____   Time ended _____]

PARENT'S REPORT (If needed, identify each area reported on):

Individual Differences in Newborns (Part II) [Newborn #2 of Two Newborns Observed]

Observer's Name _____

Child/Children Observed _____

Child's/Children's Age(s) _____   Child's/Children's Sex _____

Observation Context (home, child care center, preschool, school) _____

Date of Observation _____   Time Begun _____   Time Ended _____

Observation Exercise 15-3

Part II Continued

Brief Description of Physical and Social Characteristics of Observational Setting:

_____

OBJECTIVE BEHAVIORAL DESCRIPTIONS (OBD): *Narrative Description*

OBD Session 1: [Time begun _____ Time ended _____]

OBD Session 2: [Time begun _____ Time ended _____]

OBD Session 3: [Time begun _____ Time ended _____]

PARENT'S REPORT (If needed, identify each area reported on):

COMPARISONS

Newborn # 1: **Summary Description**

Newborn # 2: **Summary Description**

Summary Description of Differences

Soothability:

Spontaneous Behaviors:

Temperaments:

Observation Exercise 15-4

Motor Responses of the Newborn

Observer's Name _____

Child/Children Observed _____

Child's/Children's Age(s) _____   Child's/Children's Sex _____

Observation Context (home, child care center, preschool, school) _____

Date of Observation _____   Time Begun _____   Time Ended _____

Brief Description of Physical and Social Characteristics of Observational Setting:

_____

OBJECTIVE BEHAVIORAL DESCRIPTIONS (OBD): *Narrative Description*

Reflex Elicited _____ **(# 1)**

Stimulation Used _____   **Response** _____

Reflex Elicited _____ **(# 2)**

Stimulation Used _____   **Response** _____

Reflex Elicited _____ **(# 3)**

Stimulation Used _____   **Response** _____

Reflex Elicited _____ **(# 4)**

Stimulation Used _____   **Response** _____

Reflex Elicited _____ **(# 5)**

Stimulation Used _____   **Response** _____

Reflex Elicited _____ **(# 6)**

Stimulation Used _____   **Response** _____

Voluntary Responses (Describe):

Head:

Arms:

Legs:

Trunk:

Overall Description:

Observation Exercise 15-5

Perceptual Responses of the Newborn

Observer's Name _____

Child/Children Observed _____

Child's/Children's Age(s) _____ Child's/Children's Sex _____

Observation Context (home, child care center, preschool, school) _____

Date of Observation _____ Time Begun _____ Time Ended _____

Brief Description of Physical and Social Characteristics of Observational Setting:

_____

Part I: *Modified Checklist Technique*
Stimulation: Loud Hand Clap
Response: Yes _____ **No** _____ **Uncertain** _____
Description:

Stimulation: Soft Hand Clap
Response: Yes _____ **No** _____ **Uncertain** _____
Description:

Stimulation: Loud Voice
Response: Yes _____ **No** _____ **Uncertain** _____
Description:

Stimulation: Soft Voice
Response: Yes _____ **No** _____ **Uncertain** _____
Description:

Stimulation: Object 6" from eyes
Response: Yes _____ **No** _____ **Uncertain** _____
Description:

Stimulation: Object 15" from eyes
Response: Yes _____ **No** _____ **Uncertain** _____
Description:

Stimulation: Tracks moving light
Response: Yes _____ **No** _____ **Uncertain** _____
Description:

Part II: *Event Sampling*

Event Observed _____
Description:

Observation Exercise 15-6

Emotional Functioning of the Newborn

Observer's Name _____

Child/Children Observed _____

Child's/Children's Age(s) _____   Child's/Children's Sex _____

Observation Context (home, child care center, preschool, school) _____

Date of Observation _____   Time Begun _____   Time Ended _____

Brief Description of Physical and Social Characteristics of Observational Setting:

_____

OBJECTIVE BEHAVIORAL DESCRIPTIONS (OBD) AND INTERPRETATIONS: *Event Sampling*

OBD Session 1:   [Time begun _____   Time ended _____]

Interpretation 1:

OBD Session 2:   [Time begun _____   Time ended _____]

Interpretation 2:

Continue with as Many OBDs and Interpretations as Are Needed or Desired.

Summary Comments on Newborn's Emotional Functioning
(Use Greenspan's First Emotional Milestone):

CHAPTER SIXTEEN
Observing the Infant:
One to Twenty-Four Months

Introduction

In the Preface of his *A Primer of Human Development*, T. G. R. Bower (1977), a well known psychologist, researcher, and writer, claims the following:

Few would dissent from the proposition that infancy is the most critical period of human development, the period in which the basic frameworks for later development are established. (Preface)

It will not be of major concern to us whether or not infancy *is*, as Bower claims, "the *most critical* period of human development." We will recognize, however, that researchers and theorists alike deem this initial period of the human lifespan at least to be extremely important.

There are, we suppose, any number of reasons why this is so. We suppose further that some of these reasons are affected or determined by the particular *definition* of infancy that the researcher or theorist is using. Let's look briefly at some definitions or "meanings" of infancy before we discuss further why this period is important.

The first such definitions we offer are based on age or developmental level. We view these definitions as more or less conventional; they are similar to an antique dealer assessing the value of an object on the basis of its age, while essentially disregarding the object's purpose or function per se. In some contrast, we shall offer two additional bases for defining infancy. For these we are indebted to the work of Alan Fogel (1984), a psychologist and writer. First. we shall present briefly Fogel's description of the parental attitudes toward, or perspectives on, children that prevailed in the Western world during the nineteenth century and that prevail today. These attitudes can be thought of as *behavioral definitions*. A behavioral definition is a meaning assigned to something (object, person, event) based on how that thing is *treated* or dealt with by the individual doing the defining. The meaning is determined by how he or she literally behaves toward, or in relation to, the object. For instance, a chair might be defined behaviorally as not only something one sits on, but also as something one stands on to change a light bulb, or as something with which to prop open a door, and so on. In like fashion, an individual's behavioral definition of "child" can be discerned by how he or she actually behaves toward "child," with the meaning of "behaves toward" left undefined at this time.

We shall then turn to a discussion of what Fogel calls nine "areas of competency or types of skill that infants are trying to develop" (p. 5) as a form of *definition based on function*. You should keep in mind, however, that infancy's functions are not separable, at least not easily, from its genetically patterned developmental period from birth to two or three years. Put another way, whereas the adult function or task, let's say, of establishing a family through marriage might *typically* occur during the period of young adulthood, a middle-aged couple can also establish a family, even for a first time. The infant, however, seems destined to accomplish his or her developmental tasks only or predominantly during this relatively short time we call infancy. This reference to a developmental time frame applies to what we call "normal" development. Delays do occur that put some children behind their age peers, just as there are precocious children who move through certain developmental areas at a faster rate than their peers. This manual, however, is interested in the typical rate and path of development, not the atypical ones. This emphasis, however, does rule out the possibility that you may be interested in observing and recording non-normative developmental patterns; we simply do not deal with them here. You will, of course, recognize this "requirement" or time constraint as being a characteristic of a stage.

What is an Infant?

Bower (1977) says that "An infant is literally someone who does not talk" (p. 1). On this view, according to Bower, "The normal duration of infancy, in this strict sense, is about eighteen months" (p. 1). Alan Fogel is not as definitive or as dogmatic as Bower. "The definition of infancy," Fogel writes, "varies, depending upon whom you talk to" (Fogel, 1984, p.1). He clearly disagrees with Bower regarding the age range of the infancy period: "Few experts," Fogel writes, "would answer that infancy covers the period from birth to two years of age" (p. 1). Importantly, however, he also asserts that "Few people in our society would say that a three-year-old is a baby" (p. 1). Fogel decides that *his* book "will cover human development from birth up to the age of three years ..." (p. 1). But Fogel also recognizes that simply knowing the ages that define the period of infancy is not sufficient to understanding this segment of the lifespan. We agree. But we must also settle on some age range within which to confine our remarks. Consequently, we've struck a compromise of sorts between Bower's 18 months and Fogel's 36 months. We shall define infancy chronologically as approximately the first 24 months of life following birth. This will also be in keeping with our treatment of the preschool period (Chapter 17) as comprising the ages two to six years.

We can probably agree that infancy is a significant period of human development. We nonetheless might want to deal a bit further with the question of what an infant is. Any answer certainly has to do with how one "sees" an infant, with one's perspective on such matters. Alan Fogel (1984) devotes an entire introductory chapter to the question of what is an infant, and we have already touched on some of his ideas on this topic in our comments above. Part of Fogel's treatment incorporates an interesting tracing of historical views of children held by the Western world over the past 2400 years. Drawing on the work of Lloyd deMause (1974), Fogel describes six stages that have characterized "parent-child relations" in Western civilization from ancient times to the present day. We shall mention only the last two of these stages, which began in the nineteenth century. Fogel refers to the stages as "modes," which "represent prevailing attitudes of parents toward infants and children ... " (p. 2).

The *socialization mode* (19th to mid-twentieth centuries) emphasized children's conformity to the "goals and standards of adult society," and they were "to be trained and taught in proper ways" (p. 3). Of particular interest is that "Parents believed that children should be loved according to how 'good' or 'bad' they have been" (p. 3). The current mode (mid-twentieth century) is called the *helping mode* and is characterized by the belief that children are "active, creative, and intrinsically valuable" (p. 4). In this context, according to Fogel, "Children should be loved no matter how they behave, and parents should be able to empathize with the child in order to provide whatever is necessary for the child's well-being" (p. 4). In short, the essence of modern parent-child relationships might be said to be involvement and "increasing awareness of children and concern for their welfare ... " (Fogel, p. 4).

It should be clear to you that these modes are ways of "seeing" children, and, as earlier modes have done for the historical periods in which they were prevalent, these last two modes form a foundation for present-day treatment of children. Let's move on to further discussion of a definition of infancy.

We shall hold that a phenomenon (object or event) can be defined according to what it does, what its functions are, or what actions or behaviors are part of its inherent features or attributes. Fogel, again, very nicely provides us with just such a definition according to function. He refers to nine competency areas or "types of skill that infants are trying to develop" that are requisite to the child's becoming "an active, functional member of her society, family, and community" (p. 5). (Please bear in mind that Bower's description of the infant's accomplishments [p. 161] are equally relevant to, though less detailed than, the present discussion.) As it turns out, these areas also afford us a convenient basis for making observations of infants' behavior and for making judgments concerning their abilities and levels of development. Let us treat these nine areas very briefly.

I. *Perceptual/Sensorial Skills*

Involved here are the infant's sensory capacities of hearing, sight, touch, smell, taste, and those distinctly "interior" senses that pertain to balance and to awareness of the location of one's body and its various parts (arms, legs, and so on). Also involved is the way she uses these senses to gain knowledge about the environment. The development (progressive change over time) of the infant's perceptual and sensory skills should be of special interest to you as an observer.

II.   Sensorimotor/Tool-Using

Most simply put, this competence area has to do with the development of motor skills, which include such actions as rolling over, sitting up, standing, walking, running, and so on. Fogel includes Jerome Bruner's (1975) ideas on tool-using skills as "a manifestation of the infant's capacity to understand and manipulate the environment" (p. 6). "Tools" is to be broadly understood as *anything* that can be used as an aid to accomplishing some purpose. Don't restrict your notion of tools to such better known objects as hammers, wrenches, screwdrivers, and the like. In the broad meaning of tool, a stick could be used to pull a toy closer to oneself, thereby making that stick a tool.

III.   Conceptual/Thinking

At about six months of age, infants show the start of an ability to make "conceptual differentiations between classes of objects" (Fogel, p. 6). A beginning awareness of object permanence, which is the understanding that an object's existence does not depend on its being evident to the physical senses, appears at about nine months of age. Fogel notes, however, that (mental) behavior that reflects actual thinking, reasoning, and planning is not evident much before the last part of the second year. Until then, what predominates is trial and error "thinking" in the form of overt acting out rather than mental or internalized selection of courses of action (p. 6). "Internalized selection of courses of action" simply means that the individual can mentally rehearse or anticipate the consequences of various behaviors *without actually performing them*. He can therefore choose an action based on its predicted outcome or effect, although this ability does not rule out the possibility of error.

IV.   Memory

Memory is a critical component of the infant's developing cognitive abilities. Jerome Kagan (1984), a well-known psychologist and author, makes a strong claim for the importance of memory when he writes that "The ability to relate an experience in the present to relevant schemata is one of the central maturing functions of the first year of life. In plainer language, the child becomes able to remember the past" (p. 40). (Schemata is the plural of *schema*, which Kagan defines as "a representation of experience that bears a relation to an original event" [p. 35].) Fogel notes that "nine months of age marks a significant shift in the infant's ability to remember . . . " (p. 6), a shift that leads or contributes to the concept of object permanence and the ability to compare objects in "space, time, and quality" (p. 6).

Kagan discusses three aspects of memory development that constitute the overall ability to remember the past. He refers to these aspects as "recognition of the past, retrieval of the past, and the ability to compare past and present on the stage of active memory" (p. 40). Let's look briefly at these with respect to some normative ages of particular accomplishments.

Kagan says that the three-month-old infant "can recognize a familiar event in her perceptual field because it shares properties with her schemata" (p. 40).

Sharing properties with her schemata means that the familiar event previously encountered by the infant is perceived as being similar in some respects to her memory of that event. During the first six months, however, this recognition will disappear if too much time passes between successive experiences of the event.

The second element of memory development, the ability "to retrieve a schema when there are minimal clues ... in the immediate field" (p. 40), becomes functional, Kagan says, after the fist six months. This ability to retrieve a schema can be measured by hiding an attractive toy and making the infant wait before he is allowed to reach for it. Kagan cites research that found that in a group of infants studied from the ages of eight to twelve months, "no eight-month-old was able to remember the toy's location with a one-second delay ... " (p. 41). By twelve months of age, all of the infants could find the toy when their search for it was delayed for three seconds, and a majority could perform this task even with a seven-second delay.

The third memory achievement involves the ability to retrieve the past over longer and longer lapses of time. Kagan notes that "When older children and adults read a sentence or listen to a conversation, they are able to integrate the incoming information with their knowledge over a period of time that can last as long as thirty seconds" (p. 42). Kagan calls this process of integration *active memory*, which, he says, becomes stronger and more functional around eight months of age (p. 42). Thus it is that "The infant now automatically relates the present to the immediate past, which means she is comparing information from two sources" (p. 42).

V.   Representational/Symbolic

Representation, which is having one thing "stand for" another, possibly quite different, is, says Fogel, the "crowning achievement of cognitive development in the first three years of life" (p. 6). He also includes symbolic thinking, the most significant of which is the use of language. (For a detailed discussion of representational ability, see Chapter 17, Exercise 3.) Of course, one major function of *linguistic symbols* is precisely to represent something else: the word 'chair' stands for the actual object we sit in, 'dog' can stand for a particular furry, four-legged animal we pass everyday on our way to work (or perhaps "Rover" stands for *our* dog). Fogel indicates that it is late into the second year of life before most children can grasp "the relation between the symbol and the actual object ... " (p. 6). This simply means that symbol use is essentially "unthinking" or "uncritical," and it serves predominantly practical purposes, such as in the practical connection between, say, the word 'milk' and the actual glass of white liquid that the parent gives the child following his utterance of the word.

VI.   Communicative/Linguistic

This competency area is close to the representational/symbolic competency just discussed. One important difference is emphasis on the use of language to *communicate*. There is, of course, the complicated business of learning the meaning of words, proper grammar, and so on, but the ultimate use of language is to convey one's ideas, thoughts, and feelings to other people. Communication also involves knowing when to speak and when to listen (the reciprocal character of communication), learning about the environment, understanding what others are trying to make known, and making known one's own messages in socially appropriate ways. In short, language is a social skill as well as an intellectual skill.

VII.   Social/Interactive

Fogel initially emphasizes social/interactive competence in the context of language usage, especially the skill of taking turns in conversation. He mentions the naturally occurring "bursts and pauses in their behavior" as potential forerunners of such conversational skills, but he quickly points out that "any semblance of taking turns seems to be created by the adult partner who learns to skillfully insert her smiles, coos, and words into the natural silences left by the infant" (p. 7). Fogel indicates that the infant's awareness of his or her role as a *partner* in an interaction with an adult does not come about before the age of five or six months. Although there are other facets of social competence, of course (the next basic competency area is one of these other facets), it is important to recognize that infants start to learn social skills far ahead of any learning of words.

VIII.   Expressive/Emotive

Feeling and expressing certain kinds of emotional states is an important element of the infant's social skills (Fogel, p. 7). What emotions an infant can experience apparently depends upon age or developmental level. Fogel says there is general agreement that "infants do not know the feeling of fear before about eight months, and they cannot experience complex feelings like guilt, pride, or shame until they are almost three years old" (p. 7). Control of the kinds of emotions they want to express is not achieved before two or three years of age (Fogel, p. 7). Kagan (1984) offers some informative comments on the relationship between emotional states and age, as well as on the general development of emotion.

> The popular belief that a child's emotions do not change with growth requires the improbable assumption that maturational changes in the brain that produce new cognitive evaluations and special feeling tones have no influence on the older person's emotional experiences. However, because one often uses the same language to name emotions in two- and twenty-two-year-olds, it is easy to believe that the emotional experiences are the same. American mothers also assume, incorrectly I believe, that three-month-olds can experience the emotions of interest, anger, joy, or fear that are attributed to adults. (Kagan, 1984, p. 1972)

IX.   Self-Regulatory/Coping

Whether consciously aware of it or not, parents, teachers, caregivers, and other adults who work with children, are concerned over the practical issues of a child's self-control and her ability to deal constructively with various aspects of the environment; they are also pleased (if not downright relieved) when a child in fact achieves these abilities. As Fogel puts it, "The development of self-regulatory skills is greeted by parents with a sense of relief that goes beyond delight. The ability of an infant to cope with the stresses of everyday life takes from the parent's shoulders a considerable burden" (p. 7). Among the indicators of "successful self-regulation," Fogel lists "sleeping through the night, waiting patiently while a meal is being prepared, handling the fear and distress of separation from the parents, fighting assertively to retrieve a toy from a meddling older sibling" (p. 7).

Although Fogel's indicators of successful self-regulation might suffice to make his point, we want to point out that the infant's ability "... to cope with the stresses of everyday life ..." should not be taken to mean that the infant is therefore stress free. It more accurately means that overall, and on average, the infant is able to handle those "normal" stresses that are characteristic of, and appropriate to, his or her developmental stage. It is also the case with adults that possessing effective strategies for coping with some kinds of stress does not preclude being faced with stress with which one cannot adequately cope.

These skills can be put into the general category of autonomy, which, of course, tends to free adults from some of the tasks associated with being a child's parent or caregiver (see Fogel, p. 8). This freedom gives credence to the relief and delight that adults feel upon the child's achievement of self-regulatory and coping skills.

Some of the preceding descriptions have a Piagetian focus. More recently, however, the theoretical concepts of Lev Vygotsky have come to psychologists' attention. Indeed, his ideas are now competing with Piaget's theory and with an information processing theory (see, e.g. Berk 1993 for a discussion of the weaknesses of Piagetian and information processing theories in explaining cognitive development).

The relevance of Vygotsky's theory lies in its emphasis on the role of the social context in cognitive development. An informative and interesting discussion of Vygotsky's theoretical position is offered by the writing team of Bukatko and Daehler (1995). They write the following:

> A central tenet of Vygotsky's sociohistorical theory is that as children become exposed to and participate in their culture, they begin to internalize and adopt, often with the guidance of a skilled partner such as a caregiver or teacher, more mature and effective ways of thinking and solving problems with respect to their circumstances. Infants, of course, are not born with the tools and ways of thinking that are part of a community's history. These, however, can be transferred to children by those who are skilled or knowledgeable in their use. (pp. 64–65)

These authors go on to say that a critical component of a child's learning consists of social interactions that involve observing how others communicate and solve problems using the resources available to the child's particular culture. Vygotsky also viewed language as a very important cultural tool, because the child internalizes language and uses it to think and to solve problems. Indeed, there is a circular or reciprocal aspect to language use. As the child uses language to think and solve problems, these very activities in turn promote and enhance further development of language skills, that, again in turn, can be used to think in more complex ways and to solve more complex problems.

Why is Infancy Important?

Let us get back briefly to the reasons why infancy is such an important topic of study. Here we shall follow Bower's lead, because he also asks the same question. "Why," he asks, "should 2 percent of lifespan merit such attention?" (p. 1; "such attention" refers, among other things, to his own book on infancy). We like his answers, because they are ones over which probably few would quibble. We offer you an extensive quote from his *Primer*.

> Probably more of the skills that separate human beings from other animals are acquired in infancy than in all the rest of childhood together. By the end of infancy the baby is sociable and cooperative. He has learned what is necessary for language, possibly the most important of all human skills. He can walk on his own two feet. He has refined the manual skills that man shares with no other animal. He can use tools to a limited extent, but an extent greater than any nonhuman. He has acquired some very basic and important concepts of space, causality, number. All this happened in eighteen months, grown from what look like most unpromising beginnings. (pp. 1–2)

David Elkind (1981), a well-known author and Professor of Child Study at Tufts University, also specifies the particular concerns, and therefore the potential accomplishments, of the infancy period. He writes as follows:

> From birth until about two years of age infants are concerned with constructing a world of permanent objects, attaching themselves to significant others, and establishing what now retired Harvard professor Erik Erikson called a sense of "trust." These three attainments constitute the major intellectual, social, and emotional developments of the infancy period. (Elkind, 1981; p. 98)

Have you any doubt that all of these cited accomplishments are indeed important and that they form the very foundation for everything that is to come in subsequent developmental periods?

Of course, the nine competency areas just discussed are, in and of themselves, the occasions for celebrating this first portion of the life span. Although one could argue that the adult also functions within, as well as adds to, these skill areas, he or she does not do so for the first time as an adult (or older child). Let's turn now to a practical application of the ideas presented above.

Exercise 16-1: Physical Characteristics and Motor Abilities of the Infant/Toddler (One to Twenty-Four Months)

Background Information

Physical Characteristics: You will find some striking differences in physical appearance between the newborn and the 15- to 24-month-old infant or toddler. Indeed, you need not wait very long before seeing some dramatic changes. Let's first look briefly at the changes that take place in the child's weight and height. Faw and Belkin (1989), in their excellent college review book on child psychology, report that the first four months of life result in a doubling of birth weight, which brings the infant up to a bodyweight of 14 or 15 pounds. (Craig, 1989, indicates a range from 12 to 15 pounds. We mention this only to point out that such norms will vary at least slightly from source to source; any specific norm probably should not be considered a precise figure.) Weight triples to an average of 20 pounds (Papalia and Olds (1993) report 22 pounds) by the end of the first year. Interestingly enough, subsequent weight gain during the whole second year, according to Faw and Belkin, amounts to only about five pounds. This sharp decrease in gain is attributed to the child's increased physical activity and resulting increased utilization of calories.

Height gains during the first four months come to about 3 to 4 inches (Faw and Belkin, p. 130). By the end of the first year, the child grows yet another 6 inches, achieving a length (on average) of 29 to 31 inches. As with weight increases, growth in height slows down during the second year to a "mere" 4 (to 5) inches. The height of the average two-year-old is 33 to 35 inches (Faw and Belkin, p. 130). Height of the two-year-old, by the way, is approximately one-half of what it will be when he or she is an adult. As you can recall from Chapter 15, the newborn's head is misshapen and disproportionately large relative to her body, which gives the child an appearance that is peculiar if not outright distorted. The growth following this first month or two of life is, say Faw and Belkin, an attempt of the body to "'catch up with' the head" (p. 131). The trunk gains some 50 percent in length during the first two years, while the arms increase their length by 60 to 75 percent (Faw and Belkin, p. 131).

Motor Characteristics and Abilities: At one month, the newborn exhibits a number of involuntary reflex responses, and his voluntary movements are random and poorly controlled. This random aspect of early muscle movement is referred to as mass action and is the opposite of the specific action that refers to the older child's more coordinated muscle movements. Use of the hands is limited to a grasp reflex, and he seems totally unaware that he even has hands. By 18 months, the infant has accumulated the achievements of head control, sitting, rolling over, crawling, creeping, standing, walking, and running. His ability to reach for, grasp, and manipulate objects has also undergone dramatic change. By about 3 months of age, he begins swiping at objects and becomes aware of his hands; by 18 months, he can turn pages of a book one at a time. At one month, his only way to communicate is to cry; by 18 months, he uses words and exhibits other true social behaviors. (See Tables 16-1, 16-2, and 16-3). Of course, all of these accomplishments have depended on the development and maturation of the nervous system, which in turn have depended on many other factors, not the least of which was a supporting and nurturant physical and social environment.

Craig (1989) offers a useful "overview" of an infant's competencies at the ages of four, eight, twelve, eighteen, and twenty-four months. For the area of motor competencies, we shall take advantage of Craig's format and briefly present some of the developmental milestones that are typical at the ages indicated above.

Four Months: The infant can usually hold up his chest when in the prone (on the stomach) position. The four-month-old can also hold his head steady while sitting up supported by an adult. He can roll over from front to back and vice versa. Craig notes that "most four-month-olds can reach and grasp for an object,

---

Table 16-1

Child's Name _____   Age _____

Observer _____   Date _____

DEVELOPMENTAL CHECKLIST

	Yes	No	Sometimes
BY 12 MONTHS: Does the Child			
Walk with assistance?			
Roll a ball in imitation of an adult?			
Pick objects up with thumb and forefinger?			
Transfer objects from one hand to other hand?			
Pick up dropped toys?			
Look directly at adult's face?			
Imitate gestures: peek-a-boo, bye-bye, pat-a-cake?			
Find object hidden under a cup?			
Feed self crackers (munching, not sucking on them)?			
Hold cup with two hands; drink with assistance?			
Smile spontaneously?			
Pay attention to own name?			
Respond to "no"?			
Respond differently to strangers and familiar persons?			
Respond differently to sounds: vacuum, phone, door?			
Look at person who speaks to him or her?			
Respond to simple directions accompanied by gestures?			
Make several consonant-vowel combination sounds?			
Vocalize back to person who has talked to him or her?			
Use intonation patterns that sound like scolding, asking, exclaiming?			
Say "da-da" or "ma-ma"?			

Table 16-2

Child's Name _____   Age _____

Observer _____   Date _____

DEVELOPMENTAL CHECKLIST

	Yes	No	Sometimes
BY 2 YEARS: Does the chld			
Walk alone?			
Bend over and pick up toy without falling over?			
Seat self in child-size chair? Walk up and down stairs with assistance?			
Place several rings on a stick?			
Place 5 pegs in a peg board?			
Turn pages 2 or 3 at a time?			
Scribble?			
Follow one-step direction involving something familiar: "Give me —." "Show me —." "Get a —."			
Match familiar objects?			
Use spoon with some spilling?			
Drink from cup holding it with one hand, unassisted?			
Chew food?			
Take off coat, shoe, sock?			
Zip and unzip large zipper?			
Recognize self in mirror or picture?			
Refer to self by name?			
Imitate adult behaviors in play—for example, feeds "baby"?			
Help put things away?			
Respond to specific words by showing what was named: toy, pet, family member?			
Ask for desired items by name: (cookie)?			
Answer with name of object when asked "What's that"?			
Make some two word statements: "Daddy bye-bye"?			

although they frequently do not make contact" (p. 145). Faw and Belkin (1989) say that the infant of two and one-half months of age is in what they call the "early reaching period," in which she reaches for objects she sees but does so with very poor coordination and control, and frequently her efforts fail. (The development of reaching and grasping behavior will be discussed in greater detail in a separate section below.) These authors report that by the age of four months, "visual reaching and hand reaching become coordinated" (p. 145). This skill is evidenced by infants "visually following their hand and arm as they reach for an object, and their attention alternates between the object to be grasped and the grasping hand itself" (Faw and Belkin, p. 145). Incidentally, Faw and Belkin

Table 16-3 Ages (in Months) of Acquisition of Selected Motor Abilities of Infants and Toddlers. A Summary of Craig's (1989) Data Discussed in this Chapter

Four Months	Eight Months	Twelve Months	Eighteen Months	Twenty-Four Months
Holds chest up from stomach position	Gets into sitting position on his/her own; can maintain sitting posture if put there by another person	Typically takes first unsupported steps	Almost certainly can walk alone. Can carry things in his/her hands while walking	Can walk and run, pedal a tricycle, jump in place with both feet, balance short time on one foot, can throw overhand fairly well
Holds head steady while sitting supported by an adult	One-half of all 8-month olds can stand holding on to a support as well as bring self to a standing position	Can manipulate a number of objects (undo latches, open cabinets, pull toys, twist lamp cords)	Usually can stack from 2 to 4 blocks to build a tower; can scribble with crayon or pencil	Climbs steps and sometimes comes down with help. Crawls into, over, around, and under various objects
Reaches and grasps for an object—contact infrequent	Typically can crawl or creep on hands and knees	Acquires pincer grasp—opposition of thumb and forefinger	Increasing ability to feed self; can partly undress self	Places things into and takes things out of containers; pours water, molds clay, generally manipulates objects to the fullest extent
Visual tracking begins at about 3½ months	Most can pass objects from hand to hand; some can use thumb and forefinger to grasp; most can hand objects back and forth to an adult			Transports items in carts, wagons, carriages, or trucks. Child explores, tests, and probes

view *visual tracking* as a form of visual reaching, even though it is not coordinated with hand and arm movements. Visual tracking is following an object with the eyes, and it appears at about three and one-half months of age.

Eight Months: Craig (1989) reports that most eight-month-olds can get into a sitting position on their own, and almost all infants of this age can maintain a sitting posture once they are put into it by another person. Faw and Belkin (1989) note that most six- to seven-month-olds can sit in a high chair, but that accomplishment comes slightly before the ability to sit without external support. Craig indicates that more than half of all eight-month-olds can stand while holding on to a support, and about half can bring themselves to a standing position (p. 147). Some smaller proportion can move about in a sidewise stepping motion while holding on to the sides of a crib or playpen; some even have the early ability to walk while holding on to a piece of furniture for support, an ability sometimes referred to as "cruising."

The typical eight-month-old can move from place to place by crawling (with the body on the ground) or by creeping on the hands and knees (Craig, p. 147). Faw and Belkin note that at about seven months, infants might thrust "one knee forward as they lie on their stomach." This, say Faw and Belkin, "is the initial step in learning to crawl" (p. 140). These authors claim that by eight months ("34 weeks"), the average child has the capacity to crawl, but they point out that because there is not sufficient arm and leg strength, he cannot yet keep the stomach off the ground by creeping on the hands and knees.

With regard to hand and arm control, Craig indicates that most eight-month-olds can "pass objects from hand to hand, and some are able to use the thumb and finger to grasp" (p. 149). She also reports that infants of this age can usually "bang two objects together ... " (p. 149). Craig also notes that most eight-month-olds can hand an object back and forth to an adult, an activity they very much enjoy doing.

Twelve Months: Faw and Belkin (1989), distinguishing between "supported walking" and "independent walking," (p. 141) report that children typically take their first unsupported (independent), albeit unsteady, steps a short time after their first birthday. Subsequent development of the ability to locomote progresses quickly from that milestone accomplishment, say Faw and Belkin. Craig writes that twelve-month-olds "actively manipulate the environment. They are able to undo latches, open cabinets, pull toys, and twist lamp cords" (p. 149). She also mentions the acquisition of a *pincer grasp,* which should be distinguished from the *ulnar grasp,* which Berk (1989) describes as "a clumsy motion in which the fingers close against the palm" (p. 147). The pincer grasp enables the infant to oppose the thumb and forefinger. This *cortical opposition* ability, in turn, enables the child to pick up quite small objects such as hairs, pins, coins, and so on. With this and other new abilities, however, the child can also get into many more things (and much more trouble) than she could heretofore: she can "turn on the television set and the stove,... explore kitchen cupboards, open windows, and poke things into electrical outlets" (Craig, 1989; p. 149).

Eighteen Months: Children eighteen months of age are almost without exception walking alone. They often like to carry things in their hands or push or pull some kind of object as they walk (Craig, 1989, p. 150). They have a very hard time as yet doing such things as kicking a ball, jumping, or pedaling a tricycle (Craig, p. 150).

Eighteen-month-olds, according to Craig, are generally capable of "stacking from two to four blocks to build a tower, and often they can manage to scribble with crayon or pencil" (p. 150). At this age, children frequently show increased ability to feed themselves and can even partly undress themselves (Craig, p. 150). Dressing oneself, however, is apparently an appreciably more difficult task than taking clothes off, and for that reason, dressing comes later in development.

Twenty-Four Months: The gains in abilities between 18 and 24 months of age seem quite astonishing. As Craig (1989) puts it,

> Two-year-olds can not only walk and run, but they can usually pedal a tricycle, jump in place on both feet, balance briefly on one foot, and accomplish a fairly good overhand throw. They climb up steps and, sometimes, come down again with assistance. They crawl into, under, around, and over objects and furniture; they manipulate, carry, handle, push, or pull anything they see. They put things into and take things out of large containers. They pour water, mold clay, stretch the stretchable, and bend the bendable. They transport items in carts, wagons, carriages, or trucks. They explore, test, and probe. (Craig, 1989; p. 151)

Perhaps her concluding statement is of the greatest importance, to wit: "All this exploration provides a vital learning experience about the nature and possibilities of their physical world" (p. 151). This, of course, is what development is all about.

To bring this section of this first exercise or unit to a close, we would like to present in summary form Faw and Belkin's discussion of the "phases of object manipulation." We do this because the ability to reach for, grasp, and manipulate objects is such a critical ability. Indeed, it could be argued that our hand or manual dexterity is among *the* central attributes that set us apart from the rest of the animal kingdom, with language or symbol use certainly being another key distinguishing characteristic of human behavior and ability.

The authors identify a "prereaching period" and an "early reaching period" (p. 144). The first period comprises about the first two or two and one-half months, during which time the newborn or infant does not reach for objects but merely stares at them if they come into view. (See also Laura Berk, 1989, for reference to, and a discussion of, prereaching.) The second, early reaching period, begins at about two and one-half months of age, when "children begin to reach for objects that they see" (p. 144). Again, however, such behavior is poorly controlled and usually fails to hit the intended target. Let's look now at the two phases discussed by Faw and Belkin.

Phase I, say Faw and Belkin, evidences "various stages of object manipulation," but they write in terms of the characteristics of the skills that represent those stages. Phase I characteristics follow.

Phase I

1. Reaching and grasping are not engaged in as separate acts. That is to say, they lack *differentiation* and demonstrate instead the characteristics of *mass action*. Faw and Belkin also point out that this aspect of hand use demonstrates the principle of *proximo-distal development*. This is simply development that proceeds from the midline (proximo) of the body outwards to the extremities (distal).
2. The infant in Phase I cannot yet use two arms at the same time.
3. Control of hand and arm movements is relatively absent. Once initiated, the infant in Phase I cannot stop a reaching movement, nor can she adjust a reaching movement if it is inaccurate and off target.
4. Grasping in this Phase is not performed in conjunction with how the object feels to the infant. Instead, reaching and grasping are directed by the visual presence of the object as well as by the object's visual relationship to the hand.

Adapted from Faw and Belkin (1989, p. 144).

Faw and Belkin indicate that the "obvious switching of attention back and forth between the grasping hand and the object to be grasped" ends by five months of age, and the infant now "moves his or her hand directly to the object" (p. 145). The authors note that although the movements are well coordinated, they nonetheless still belong in Phase I, because "the reach and grasp are controlled by the visual presence of the object sought and are a unitary action rather than two separate actions" (p. 145). They also note, importantly, that a grasping response will still be made once the reaching is initiated, even if the hand does not actually touch the object. This phenomenon occurs because the infant cannot yet completely control bodily actions. It's as though once begun, a movement or gesture simply must be finished, despite the fact that nothing will be accomplished by it.

Five months of age, say Faw and Belkin, denotes the division or transition between Phase I and Phase II. Phase II has the following characteristics.

Phase II

1. In this phase, infants reach and grasp with two hands, not just one.
2. Infants are able to correct errors in reaching once they are detected.
3. Reaching and grasping now become separable activities and each can be engaged in independently of the other.
4. Visual presence of the object is no longer the primary impetus for grasping; now contact with the object is the controlling factor.

Adapted from Faw and Belkin (1989, p. 146).

Some of the objectives found in this chapter will provide you with a number of options that are absent in the other exercise chapters. The age span from one to twenty-four months comprises a large number of developmental changes that cannot be observed and recorded by any single individual. Moreover, it's also likely that you will have less opportunity to observe infants and toddlers than you will children of preschool age. This fact almost necessitates that we give you enough alternatives so that you can observe the behavior of at least one child in this important first stage of life.

Observation Objectives

(1) To observe and describe the physical characteristics of a child anywhere between one month and twenty-four months of age and compare them with the physical characteristics of the newborn observed in Exercise 15-1; *and/or* (2) to observe and record the motor behavior of an infant between one and twenty-four months of age. This objective should be done in conjunction

Figure 16-1   Face of a toddler. See the difference in proportion as compared to the newborn. (Courtesy of Mead Johnson)

with objective (1) above, which means that you can observe the same infant for both parts of the assignment; *and/or* (3) to compare and contrast the motor skills *of at least two infants who are of appreciably different ages* (e.g., 10 months and 18 months)—the goal here is to chart, in a cross sectional way, the developmental progress an infant makes over the space of several months.

Procedure

For objective (1) of this exercise, measure the child's weight, total height, and the length of the head, trunk, and legs. Compare these measurements with those you obtained on a newborn and summarize the differences. Also compare the toddler's height and weight with the figures given above for the fiftieth percentile. If a comparison with a newborn is not possible, simply determine whether the infant's physical characteristics correspond to what you would normatively expect for his or her age.

For objective (2) of this exercise, *use the event sampling format* and observe and record all of the infant's motor behaviors *for two or three five-minute periods.* Distribute your observations so as to get a varied sample of the infant's abilities rather than an extended display of pretty much the same behaviors. In other words, try to get examples of reaching and grasping, crawling or creeping, walking, cruising, and so on, depending on the infant's age or developmental level. Compare the infant's abilities with norms for his or her age.

For objective (3), you will observe and record *in event sampling format two infants'* large and fine motor skills as specified in the observation exercise sheet. You may have to encourage the infants to exhibit some of the skills listed if they do not display them spontaneously. Encourage here means demonstrating what you want them to do. We shall permit such encouragement in this instance because we want you to compare and contrast the two infants' abilities *on the same tasks.*

You should have on hand such items as a few raisins, 4–6 small blocks, a small container with lid (large enough to hold several of the blocks), beads and a piece of string, a book or magazine, playdough, and a crayon. Some of these items may already be part of the infants' or toddlers' toy collection. Observe and record the following fine motor tasks: (1) stacking several blocks (determine how many they can stack); (2) picking up a raisin (what grasping technique do they use?); (3) placing some of the blocks in the container and removing them again; (4) pulling, squeezing, or pounding playdough; (5) turning the pages of a book; and (6) scribbling with a crayon. The larger motor skills you are to observe are self-explanatory. *Ideally, pick subjects who are old enough to display at least some of the behaviors described above, but who are sufficiently different in age to show developmental differences in performance or competence.*

This exercise falls under Fogel's sensorimotor/tool-using competency area. Can you observe the infants using an object in any way that qualifies as tool use? Naturally, the probability of tool-using behavior increases as the infant's age increases. Therefore, don't look for such behavior in a very young infant.

There is no set amount of time you are to observe, but complete the exercise.

Question Guides:

The following questions use language that seemingly emphasizes the observation of two infants. If you cannot perform that objective, simply refer to the questions in terms of one infant; none of the meaning will be lost.

1. If you observe a toddler, does he or she possess any physical-motor characteristics that might explain the term "toddler"?
2. What is the *overall* character or quality of the two infants' large muscle actions? generally smooth and accurate, or rough and imprecise? How do they differ? What differences would you predict based on their respective ages or developmental levels?
3. Are there large muscle actions that the infants perform easily and others they have difficulty with? Is there any apparent relationship between their abilities and the kinds of activities they choose? That is, do they try things that they do not do very well, or do they seem to stay with those activities they do best?
4. Do the infants show any signs of preferring one foot over the other? one hand over the other? If so, how do they demonstrate their preference (e.g., kicking a ball, the foot they lead with when stepping up a stair, the hand they use to pick up objects)?
5. How many blocks can the infants stack? What best characterizes their efforts to stack blocks? quick and sure? slow and uncertain?
6. When picking up a small object such as a raisin, which fingers do the infants use? What part do their thumbs play? Are they at first unsuccessful in their efforts and then succeed by changing their approach or grasping style?
7. Are there any differences between the way the infants grasp a large object such as a block and a small object such as a raisin?
8. How do their large and fine motor skills compare with the norms for children their age? What skills or responses would you predict they could do fairly well, and which would you predict they could not do at all? Can you rank them in order of increasing difficulty, based on the norms provided, and then rank order them based on how well they actually performed? How do the two rankings compare with each other?
9. What locomotor skills do the infants exhibit? If an infant is just beginning to walk, what proportion of time does she spend walking as opposed to crawling or creeping?
10. Which of Faw and Belkin's phases of reaching and grasping development describe the two infants? On what specific behaviors do you base your conclusion?

Exercise 16-2: Social Behavior of the Infant (One to Twenty-Four Months)

Background Information

When two or more persons take each other into account and influence each other in some way, their behavior is social behavior. The infant most assuredly influences others, and, in an elementary way, he also takes others into account. The infant exerts influence every time an adult responds to his crying, smiling, and vocalizing. When the child changes his behavior to adjust to someone else's characteristics and responses, he is taking that person into account.

There are a few infant behaviors that adults consider especially significant socially. Crying is an important response from the moment of birth; it signals that something is wrong and requires attention. Throughout childhood, crying continues to be a form of communication; it is often disturbing to adults, who take quick action to stop it. Smiling, along with specific eye contact, is particularly gratifying to adults, and the first true social smile—which appears by around six weeks—often makes parents ecstatic. Bower (1977) offers several reasons why infants smile: "(1)... human beings around them. (2)... any high contrast stimuli, which elicits attention from those around them and causes the infant to link the human face with pleasure. (3)... at discovering a relationship between their behavior and events in the external world" (from Travers, 1982, p. 56).

Discussion of the infant's social behavior and competence often include the subject of *attachment*. Attachment is considered present when one person is dependent on another person for emotional satisfaction. One psychologist defines attachment as "... an affectional tie that one person forms to another specific person, binding them together in space and enduring over time ... " (Ainsworth, 1973, p. 1, cited in Travers, 1982, p. 329). Seifert and Hoffnung (1987), also citing Ainsworth, emphasize an additional aspect of attachment by indicating that attachment is "a relationship that is characterized by reciprocal affection and *a shared desire to maintain physical closeness*" (p. 271; italics added).

Attachment develops in stages that have been described by a number of researchers. It is thought to be essential to healthy development, and some psychologists believe that attachment forms the basic foundation for much of the child's future social development and relationships. Table 16-4 depicts some typical characteristics and behaviors associated with attachment, and Table 16-5 presents Mary Ainsworth's (1967, 1973) three stages in the development of attachment (adapted from Travers, 1982, p. 331).

The concept of basic trust versus mistrust is another aspect of social behavior. *Trust versus mistrust* is the first of eight *psychosocial* stages in Erik Erikson's theory of personality development. Psychosocial stages, according to Craig (1989), are "periods in life during which the individual's capacities for experience dictate that he or she must make major adjustments to the social environment and the self" (p. 41). The adjustment to be made, however, is determined by the individual's developmental level and receptiveness to experience.

Basic trust versus mistrust should be resolved during the first 18 months to two years. If things go well, the infant will resolve this first conflict by establishing a stronger sense of trust in his physical-social environment than of mistrust. Whether trust or mistrust becomes the stronger feeling depends on how the infant is treated and on whether or not he sees the world as a predominantly safe, nurturing, and reliable place. Achieving feelings of trust requires interactions between the adult and child that are consistent and effectively match the psychological characteristics of both of them. As Gander and Gardiner (1981) put it,

Table 16-4 The Development of Attachment: Bowlby's Four Phases

Age	Attachment Phase	Behavioral Characteristics
0–6 wks.	Preattachment phase	Infant displays a number of signals that bring the caregiver into close proximity—smiling, crying, grasping, visual contact. The infant's positive responses to the caregiver—feeling comforted, cessation of crying—motivates her to stay with the infant and to continue the caregiving activities. Infant not yet attached, however, since he or she does not mind being left with an unfamiliar person or the mother's absence (shows no stranger or separation anxiety).
6 wks. to 6–8 mos.	Attachment-in-the-making phase	Now infant evidences different responses to a familiar caregiver(s) than to a stranger; she responds to mother in ways that clearly demonstrate recognition of the mother. Infant begins to learn a sort of cause-and-effect relationship between what she does and her mother's responses to her behaviors—she is learning that she has an effect on her environment. Also begin to develop Erikson's sense of trust. A clear-cut attachment still not present, however, since child does not yet show separation anxiety in the mother's absence.
6–8 mos. to 18–24 mos.	Clear-cut attachment phase	Infant shows unequivocal signs of separation anxiety. This reaction indicates that the infant has the concept of object (person) permanence. Child uses mother or other attachment target as a secure physical and psychological base from which to explore the environment and from which to receive emotional support and assurance. Child makes deliberate efforts to keep mother/attachment figure close to him or her.
18 mos. to 24 mos. and beyond	Formation of a reciprocal goal-directed relationship or partnership	Child's increasing cognitive skills enable her to understand some of the factors that play a role in the parents' activities and responses to the child. These cognitive and social skills permit more of a negotiating style of interacting with the parent rather than protesting, crying, or constantly seeking physical proximity to the parent in order to get what the child wants.

Based on the work of Bowlby (1969). Table adapted from Berk (1996, pp. 266–267)

Table 16-5 Stages in the Development of Attachment

Stage	Characteristics
Stage 1	During the first months after birth, there is increasing social responsiveness on the part of the infant. She does not yet distinguish her primary caregiver from others in the environment who may pick her up or care for her.
Stage 2	At abouth six months, the infant engages in *active proximity seeking,* which is evidenced by such responses as consistently seeking attention and contact with the mother or other primary caregiver, and/or by stranger anxiety. This behavior continues through the second year.
Stage 3	Near the age of three years, child exhibits *partnership behavior;* she tries to participate in the mutual give-and-take aspects of social interactions. Also has an identity separate from the parent.

Based on the work of Ainsworth (1967, 1973) and cited in Bigner (1983, pp. 185–86)

"Trust results when mother and infants coordinate their behaviors to one another's temperaments and needs and are consistent and reasonable" (p. 201). The physical environment must also be perceived as reasonably safe and predictable. This perception is affected by the infant's learning that his behaviors have predictable consequences. For example, he shakes his crib and a mobile above him moves. Or, as he learns to control his body, he increases his sense of security and confidence as he functions in a world of space, objects, and natural laws.

Observation Objectives

To observe and record: (1) the infant's general social behaviors and interaction patterns with others; (2) behaviors that indicate attachment; and (3) the effect of observed and reported qualities of the infant's temperament on the interactions between her and others in her familiar surroundings. Also, to use data from different recording methods to draw conclusions about the child's social behavior and temperament, and about the usefulness of different methods in a particular situation.

Procedures

This is a three-part exercise. Each part, however, can stand as an independent exercise. *In Part I, you will use the narrative description method* of recording. You should *observe for about three ten-minute sessions within a 60- to 90-minute period,* depending on your circumstances. Refer to the guide questions that are provided. You will be asked to record your interpretive comments. Make certain your inferences are related to your observed data: Do not make an interpretation that is not supported by your objective behavioral description. *The information from Part I will also be used in Parts II and III.*

In Part II, you will use a time sampling and frequency count format. You will also be using the observation data obtained in Part I. You will note on the checklist whether the infant displays attachment behaviors during the specified time intervals. In this part of the exercise, you are asked to determine the observing and recording intervals to be used. As a general procedure, you may want to divide your recording time into a series of equal intervals, such as ten ten-second periods. Choose another short period of time (e.g., ten seconds) between each recording interval during which you will only observe. Wait for a time (perhaps five minutes) and repeat the process at least twice more. For this part of the exercise, the parent or another familiar caregiver must be with the child or he is not likely to show attachment behaviors. After you have collected your data, answer the questions that follow Part II.

Part III requires you to integrate information on the infant's general social responses and interaction patterns, which you will have obtained in Part I, and information on the child's temperament. Data on temperament will be acquired from your observations and the parent's report. Table 16-6 describes the characteristics of various temperaments. First observe and record the infant's behavior over two or three ten-minute sessions using the narrative description format. When the data are collected, analyze the record for examples of behaviors and descriptions of characteristics that fit any of the information on temperament in Table 16-7. In the second phase of this exercise, ask the parent specific questions about the child's temperament. The information given in Tables 16-6 and 16-7 can help you formulate these questions.

Finally, answer the questions that follow Part III. It is in answering these questions that you will integrate the two sets of information referred to above.

Questions, Part I:

1. Does the infant initiate social contacts with others in the environment? How does he go about it? by verbalizing? by establishing physical contact? by crying? by sharing a toy?
2. How does the other person react to the infant's social behaviors? Does the adult *focus* her attention on the infant and try to sustain the interaction, or does she cut short her response to him as though his overtures were an inconvenience?
3. Does the infant smile? How frequently, and at what? How do others react to his smiling? Does their reaction have any observable effect on the child's subsequent behaviors?
4. How does the infant respond to you, the observer? Does he show fear and uncertainty? withdrawal? Does he approach and try to engage you in play or other interaction? If he approaches you, how long does it take him to do so? Is there a period of "adjustment" on his part? How long is that period?
5. Which physical features of the infant or toddler do you think *might* be attractive to the adult in his setting or to adults in general? Does the adult

Table 16-6 Temperamental Qualities

Activity Level	Activity can begin in the uterus, where an active fetus can kick frequently. Active babies move around in their cribs or basinettes; they prefer to climb or run rather than engage in more placid activities. Other babies show much less vigorous activity levels.
Rhythmicity	Rhythicity is characterized by regular cycles of activity—eating, sleeping, and bowel movements that occur pretty much on schedule. Other infants are not as predictable.
Approach/ Withdrawl	Approach is an attitude of delight or acceptance when confronted with something new—laughter at first bath, readily eating new food. Withdrawl is a refusal to accept new situations.
Adaptability	Characterized by rapid adjustment to change; no severe negative reactions to disruption of normal routines. Some babies do not easily tolerate change or deviations from the familiar.
Intensity of Reaction	Some children laugh loudly, scream when they cry. Others merely smile, whimper, or cry softly.
Quality of Mood	Some children are generally bright and cheerful; they smile easily. Other children seem generally unhappy and discontent; seem to complain constantly.

Adapted from Berger (1980, pp. 91–92)

present during your observations make any comments about baby features she finds appealing? If so, does she respond in any way to those features?

6. What is the adult's response to the child's crying? How tolerant does the adult seem to be of the baby's crying? Is the adult's response immediate, delayed slightly, delayed for a long time? How does the infant respond to the adult's efforts to stop his crying? If the adult is successful, does she stop her interactions with the child, or does she take the opportunity to engage in further social contacts? Does the child seem to cry excessively?

7. Is there specific eye-to-eye contact between the adult and the infant? How does each respond to such contact? How long does the baby maintain this contact? How and for how long does the adult try to establish contact if he is not immediately successful?

8. Where does the child fit in terms of Fogel's social/interactive area of competence? Does the infant have any concept of sharing or taking turns? Is the infant old enough to be aware of his role as "a partner in an interaction with an adult"?

Table 16-7 Temperamental Qualities at One and Two Years

Temperament Quality	Rating	Behavioral Characteristics	
		One Year	**Two Years**
Activity level:	Low	Slow to finish bottle; falls asleep without a fuss; does not resist caretaking activities such as diapering or nail cutting.	Plays quietly with toys; can attend to an activity for long periods of time (e.g., listening to a record, or watching TV)
	High	Moves quickly; enjoys eating; gets into everything—climbing, crawling, and so on.	Still gets into everything; curious about things, explores; might do such things as resist going to bed by repeatedly getting up out of the bed (Dworetsky, 1987, p. 111).
Rhythmicity:	Regular	Regularly naps after a meal and takes a bottle before bedtime. Shows similar regularity and predictability of other bodily functions—bowel movements, waking and sleeping.	Eating patterns regular and predictable; eats heartily every day, snacks before bedtime
	Irregular	Very slow in falling asleep; bowel movements unpredictable. Other bodily functions also unpredictable.	Inconsistent nap times. Unpredictable bowel movements make toilet training difucult (Dkworetsky, 1987, p. 111).
Approach/ Withdrawal:	Positive	Not afraid of strangers; not leary of new foods, objects. Sleep not disturbed by new surroundings.	"Slept well the first time he stayed overnight at grandparents' house" (Dworetsky, 1987, p. 111).
	Negative	Cries at new activities, experiences. Sleep disturbed by strange surroundings. Cries or withdraws at presence of strangers.	Resists new experiences. Does not readily interact with strange children. "Whimpers first time at beach. Will not go into water" (Dworetsky, 1987, p. 111).
Adaptability:	Adaptive	Initial fear or hesitation with strange toys or objects fairly quickly overcome. Initial rejection of new food also replaced by acceptance.	"Obeys quickly" (Dworetsky, 1987, p. 111). Will remain in a place for a long time without feeling anxious—e.g., "stays contentedly with grandparents for a week" (Dworetsky, 1987, p. 111).
	Not Adaptive	New foods, experiences continue to be resisted, rejected. Generally lacks positive response to new things.	Obedience lacking or not readily displayed (Dworetsky, 1987, p. 111). Strongly resists some caretaking activities—e.g., getting haircut (p. 111).

Table 16-7 *(continued)*

Temperament Quality	Rating	Behavioral Characteristics	
		One Year	Two Years
Intensity of Reaction:	Mild	Response to various experiences is not strong or vigorous; does not protest having things done to him or her—e.g., clothing pulled over head (Dworetsky, 1987, p. 111).	Responds mildly to other's behavior directed at him or her, for example, being hit, having a toy snatched away (Dworetsky, 1987, p.111)
	Intense	Emotional and behavioral responses generally strong, vigorous. Rough and tumble play evokes loud laughter, screaming; also resists such things as having temperature taken (Dworetsky, 1987, p. 111).	Loudly displays excitement when playing or pleased with something. Shows strong protest if denied something such as a toy.
Quality of Mood	Positive	Enjoys eating; reaches for bottle and shows positive affect. Strong reaction to interaction games such as peekaboo (Dworetsky, 1987, p. 111).	Plays with sibling and shows positive feelings. Displays satisfaction when successful at accomplishing a task—e.g., putting shoes on (Dworetsky, 1987, p. 111).
	Negative	Does not like being left alone. Cries at mildy painful experiences such as injections (Dworetsky, 1987, p. 111).	Resists such experiences as haircuts; displays separation anxiety when mother leaves.

Adapted from Dworetsky (1987, p. 111)

Questions, Part II: *(These are not guide questions. They are questions you are to answer in writing.)*

1. What percentage of the total time observed did the infant exhibit each of the attachment behaviors sampled? What percentage of the total time observed did the child exhibit non-attachment behaviors? How do these frequencies compare with each other and what is the ratio between them?

2. Analyze your narrative description data (from Part I) for attachment behaviors. If there are any, count how often they occurred. How does this frequency count compare with the count obtained from your time sample? Do you feel more comfortable with one set of figures than with the other? If so, why? Was time sampling an appropriate method to use under the circumstances? Why or why not?

3. On the basis of Ainsworth's three stages of attachment (Table 16-5) and the information given in Table 16-5, can you tell from your time-sampled data which stage of attachment the infant is in? Can you tell from your narrative description? Is one a better basis for judgment than the other? If so, which one, and why?

Questions, Part III: (*These questions are to be answered in writing.*)

1. How do your decisions or judgments regarding the child's temperament compare with the parent's reported descriptions of her temperament? Going back to your narrative description data, whose conclusions about the child's temperament seem more accurate?

2. Does the child's behavior as you observed it correspond with the parent's report? That is, could you have used the parent's perceptions of the child to predict the infant's behaviors with reasonable accuracy?

3. What general conclusions do you reach about the usefulness of the concept of temperament? Why do you draw the conclusions you do?

Exercise 16-3: Cognitive and Language Behavior of the Infant (One to Twenty-Four Months)

Background Information

Many of the behaviors you have observed to this point are related to the infant's cognitive and language development. From Piaget's theoretical perspective, motor and perceptual functions (the essential components of the *sensorimotor period*) are the foundation of cognitive development. Early motor responses first allow the infant to handle objects, to bang, pull, push, drop, and roll them. These are necessary activities, says Piaget, because the child learns about objects by doing something with them. He cannot yet learn about the world by thinking and reasoning. Eventually, the infant becomes mobile, which puts him into more direct contact with the environment. Progressing from having objects brought to him, to going to objects on his own, changes both the quantity and the quality of his experiences.

The infant, like everyone else, gets information about his world through seeing, hearing, touching, tasting, and smelling. But merely receiving information is not enough; he must do something with it. Language and cognition, which includes thinking, knowledge, memory, problem solving, reasoning, and concepts, provide the means of processing and using information.

There are several aspects of cognitive behavior that are relevant to the infant. One aspect is *concept*. Gander and Gardiner (1981) write that "A *concept* may be thought of as a mental representation or memory of something" (p. 143, emphasis original). Ault (1977) notes that concepts "represent the attributes common to several different events" (p. 89). Piaget's *schema* is a mental representation of events in the world. Concepts, however defined, provide ways of classifying and organizing our sensory information; they bring together features and qualities that are shared by concrete things or abstract ideas. For example, dog is a concept. When someone says "dog," we might think of such things as many different species (collie, German shepherd, terrier), four-legged animal, fur bearing, carnivorous, domesticated house pet, and "Rover."

It is generally assumed that infants do not have the same kinds of concepts as adults do, that the infant's concepts are not as sophisticated or as abstract as those of adults. If babies can think, Piaget argued that they do so primarily in sensorimotor ways—that is, through active hands-on involvement with objects in their environment—without the benefit of mental operations or use of the symbolic function (language). We won't debate the issue here, but it is not unreasonable to maintain that infants do have and use at least rudimentary concepts. Certainly they can distinguish among many objects and people in their surroundings: They know their parents from strangers or friends, food that they may eat from things that they may only be able or allowed to mouth, and so on. In Piaget's terms, infants have and use schemes, which are mental representations of things, and we mention these again next.

Habituation is used by some psychologists (see Willemsen 1979, or Sroufe and Cooper 1988, for example) to infer the presence of concepts or memory even in the newborn. "When something new is perceived in the environment," write Sroufe and Cooper (1988), "attention tends to be focused on it. If it is repeated over and over, it loses its ability to draw attention" (p. 149). This is the phenomenon of habituation. If the infant (or anyone else) *reorients* to a *new* stimulus, it is logical to believe that he must have a concept of the first stimulus to know that the second one is different in some way. Sroufe and Cooper (1988) note that habituation "has provided the basis for a very powerful research technique used to study infants" (p. 150). Stranger anxiety also requires the possession of concepts. The child has to recognize that what he perceives about a stranger is somehow different from his concept of a familiar person.

For Piaget, *object permanence* is the crowning achievement of the sensorimotor period and provides the basis for all further cognitive development. When a child has the concept of object permanence, he understands that objects continue to exist even when out of sight or hearing. "Out of sight, out of mind" characterizes the infant who has not yet achieved object permanence. Object permanence develops through a series of stages (see Table 16-8) and is complete by the end of the sensorimotor period at about two years of age.

The sensorimotor period is divided into the six subperiods depicted in Table 16-9. Piaget used the idea of *sensorimotor schemes*, which are organized actions or sequences of actions that permit the individual to interact with the environment. Schemes become modified through learning and provide the foundation for more complex schemes and learning.

There are two other Piagetian concepts that help explain cognitive development and behavior throughout the lifespan: *assimilation* and *accommodation*. Assimilation occurs when the person attempts to make a stimulus or event fit what she already knows or knows how to do. The infant deals with reality by using existing sensorimotor schemes. For example, if she can pick up objects with a palmar grasp, she may try to pick up small, flat ones in the same way. But, if efforts to assimilate do not succeed, then progress depends on the infant's making changes in her sensorimotor scheme. She has to *accommodate* to the novel features of the situation. The infant in the above example will have

Table 16-8 Piaget's Stages of Object Permanence

Stage	Appointment Ages	Chief Characteristics
I.	0–1 month	No object permanence
II.	1–4 months	No object permanence or organization of space
III.	4–8 months	Start of permanence; infant begins to grasp for objects, but does not continue to search for hidden objects
IV.	8–12 months	Continues search for hidden objects but in a random, haphazard fashion
V.	12–18 months	Searches for hidden objects in correct place, but is confused if object's location is changed
VI.	18 months up	Has image of object and searches for it in various places

accommodated if she changes her grasping scheme from a palmar grasp to a thumb and forefinger (pincer) grasp to pick up the small, flat object. Accommodation does not occur automatically; the child must be developmentally ready for it.

The reinforcement theory of learning has also had a significant impact on developmental psychology. This view holds that individuals behave as they do because their behavior has led to consequences they found rewarding: the response is *reinforced*. This form of learning is known as *operant conditioning*. A key point about operant conditioning is that an individual is more likely to repeat a behavior if its consequences are satisfying than if they are unpleasant and punishing.

A second major type of learning is *classical conditioning*. An important aspect of classical conditioning is that it involves involuntary behavior, which is behavior over which we have little to no control. What is especially significant about classical conditioning is that emotional responses can be learned in this way. Classical conditioning begins with an event that naturally causes a response (as when hunger causes a dog to salivate in the presence of food). This event can become associated with a second event that does not cause the response (e.g., the *sound of a bell*, does not cause salivation). Through a pairing of these two events, the second event (the bell) can acquire the ability to produce the response (the salivation) originally produced only by the first event (hunger). Imagine a child who is constantly punished by her uncle. Punishment causes anxiety and fear. Those emotions become associated with the uncle, and, eventually, his mere presence makes the child anxious and fearful.

Language   Language could be the single most significant accomplishment of the human species. Language is a complex set of written or spoken symbols that are combined according to special rules of grammar or syntax to communicate various kinds of information.

Table 16-9 The Six Substages of Piaget's Sensorimotor Period (Including the Stages of Object Permanence)

Substage	Age	Principal Characteristics
I: Reflexive substage	0–1 mos.	Infant mostly uses her reflexes, over which she gradually gains control. She cannot yet demonstrate sensory coordination—i.e., she cannot, for example, recognize the same object by using information coming from two or more of the five physical senses at the same time. No evidence of object permanence.
II: Primary Circular Reactions	1–4 mos.	Infant capitalizes on chance occurences of actions. He engages in repetitive behaviors (thus the term"circular") that primarily involve his own body—e.g., sucking the fingers, watching her hands and feet—rather than the external environment. No evidence of object permanence.
III: Secondary Circular Reactions	4–8 mos.	Interactions with the *external environment* assume importance. Infant repeats behaviors that involve objects in the environment. Infant shows the beginning of *intentional behavior* which she repeats because she enjoys the consequences of her actions. Infant shows the beginning of object permanence by starting to grasp for objects, although he will not continue to search for an object that is hidden.
IV: Coordination of Secondary Schema	8–12 mos.	Infant now combines existing behaviors in order to achieve some goal. He uses specfic behaviors as a means to achieve a goal (ends). Infant will now continue to search for hidden objects, but his search is not organized or methodical; is random and haphazard.
V: Tertiary Circular Reactions	12–18 mos.	Infant repeats actions because they are novel or unfamiliar. She devises and experiments with new means to achieve various ends. Infant can search for and successfully find hidden objects in one location, but is confused if the object is moved to a different place.
VI: Beginning of Thought	18–24 mos.	Infant is ready to enter the preoperational stage of cognitive development. He moves from sensorimotor intelligence to representational intelligence, which means he can deal with symbolic or mental representations of objects. He uses thought to develop and achieve new goals. Infant has a true concept of the object and will search for it even if it is moved from one location to another and she does not witness the transfer.

Adapted from Travers (1982) and Wadsworth (1984)

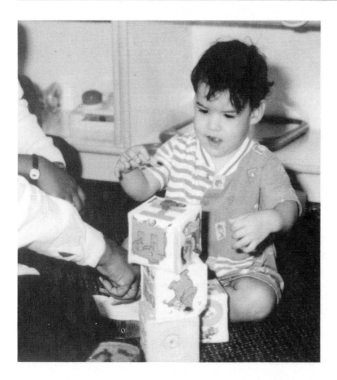

Figure 16-2   Sensorimotor behavior is displayed by the child using this stacking toy.

Language is acquired in a predictable series of stages that can be distinguished according to whether or not the child speaks intelligible words. Vocalizations that occur prior to speech are called *prelinguistic,* and those that include true words are called *linguistic.* Thus, we have two distinct periods of language development that are further subdivided into stages. These periods and stages are depicted in Table 16-10 and Table 16-11.

Observation Objectives

To observe and record various behaviors that indicate the level and characteristics of the infant's cognitive and language functioning, including such abilities as memory and conceptual thinking. To identify situations in which operant and classical conditioning might be occurring.

Procedure

This exercise has three parts. *In Part I, you will test the infant's concept of object permanence.* You will need an attractive toy and two pieces of cloth large enough to completely cover the toy. Your test consists of the following steps: Step (1) Seat the child in a chair and, after holding a toy in front of her so

Table 16-10 Stages in the Development of Language

Prelinguistic Speech	Characteristics
Undifferentiated Crying	A reflexive action; form of communication by which infant signals her needs.
Differentiated Crying	After one month, crying more precise; different patterns, intonations, intensities, and pitches reflect different emotional states.
Cooing	Six weeks, chance utterances of vowel sounds occur; become part of infant's expression of contentment.
Babbling	About 3–4 months, playful repetition of simple consonant and vowel sounds (ma-ma-ma, ba-ba-ba, etc.).
Echolalia	About 9–10 months, infant consciously imitates sounds of others, but without understanding.

Linguistic Speech	Characteristics
Holophrases thought	About 12 months, uses single word to express a ("ball" to mean "play ball with me," or "this is a ball," etc). Average 1-year-old has 4 to 5 word vocabulary; 10-word vocabulary at about 15 months, and 50-word vocabularies by 19 months, by some studies (Nelson 1973).
Telegraphic Speech	At about 24 months, child strings 2 or 3 words together to form a sentence. Only essential nouns and verbs are used.
Grammatically Correct Speech	By around three years, child may have a vocabulary of some 900 words; uses longer sentences with all parts of speech. Has grasp of grammatical principles, although his sentence constructions follow the rules too literally.

she can see it, drop the toy on the floor. Observe and record her response (refer to the Guide Questions). Step (2) Seat the child at a flat surface. Show the child the toy, making certain she sees it; then place the toy under the cloth while the child watches you do it. Observe and record her response. Step (3) As the child watches, move the toy from under the first cloth and hide it under the second cloth (*visible displacement*). Observe and record her response. Step (4) Hide the toy under the cloth as the child watches. Then, while she cannot see what you are doing, hide the toy under the second cloth, but leave the first cloth in its original position (*invisible displacement*). Observe and record her response. (In all of these steps, refer to the Question Guides for Part I.)

Table 16-11 Summary of Development of Eye-Hand Skills

Age in Months	Manipulative Ability
1.5	Manual control consists only of grasp reflex; no coordinated grasping possible at this stage.
3	Uncoordinated swiping at objects is now possible. Infant also observes her own hands.
5.5	Infant can now reach for and grasp an object and bring it to the mouth. Might hold a bottle; bangs toys, manipulates such objects as a rattle.
6.5	Increased manipulation of objects; done with greater skill and coordination.
9.5	Shows the start of the pincer grasp, i.e., infant opposes the thumb and forefinger and can pick up relatively small objects.
10	Gains a number of new skills: can take the lid off a box; pokes or points with the index finger; has the ability to let go of objects intentionally; can begin to show a preference for the right or the left hand.
11.5	Infant can hold a crayon; she can remove small objects from a container such as a cup; intentional release of an object now easily accomplished and can be done for a purpose; can imitate scribbling.
13	Infant can now put small objects into a container as well as take them out; can build a tower 2 to 3 blocks high.
16	Infant can build a tower of 3 to 4 blocks; he can scribble with a crayon or pencil; turns pages of a book, but does so 2 to 3 pages at a time.
18–24	Infant now has a definite preference for one hand over the other; tower building increases to 4 to 6 blocks; can turn one page at a time.
24–30	Infant can now put a few beads on a string; she can mold clay by rolling, pounding, squeezing, and so on.

Adapted from Gander and Gardiner (1981, pp. 125–126)

In Part II, observe the child for two to three ten-minute sessions and record in narrative description form the child's behaviors and relevant characteristics of the context. When you have completed your observations, analyze the narrative description for behaviors that indicate anything about what she has learned and her level of cognitive functioning. Look for behaviors that indicate whether the child is in Piaget's sensorimotor period; look for behaviors that identify which *substage* of the sensorimotor period the child is in. Also look for occasions when operant or classical conditioning might be occurring, such as when the parent responds with "Good boy, Billy!" when the child brings her a favorite toy, or when the parent punishes the child. (Refer to Question Guide Part II.)

In Part III you will be using an event sampling procedure to observe and record the infant's language behavior. *Spend about 20 or 30 minutes in the child's context,* but remain as inconspicuous as possible. Record verbatim the child's speech, to whom he speaks and under what circumstances, and the reactions of others to his communications. Also note behaviors that reflect the child's *speech reception* abilities—how much speech he *understands.* Also take note of the physical gestures the child might use in his efforts to communicate. (Refer to Question Guide Part III.)

Question Guides, Part I:

1. How does the child respond visually when the toy is dropped? Does she look for it? Does she look in the right place; that is, does she seem to know the path the toy will take as it falls?
2. How does the child respond when you hide the toy under the cloth in Step (2)? Does she look for the toy under the cloth or somewhere else? Does she make any emotional or motor responses, for example, facial expressions that indicate delight or amusement, or gross muscle movements that indicate excitement?
3. How does the child respond to Step (3)? Does she continue to look under the first cloth where she first saw you hide the toy, or does she look under the second cloth? Again, what emotional or motor responses does she make as she participates in this game?
4. How does the child respond to the invisible displacement of the toy? Does she persist in looking under the first cloth, or does she go immediately to the second cloth?
5. Given the child's age, what responses would you predict from her in the area of object permanence (what do the norms indicate about her probable level of response)? What stage is the child in with respect to the development of object permanence?

Question Guides, Part II:

1. What evidence is there that the infant is in Piaget's sensorimotor stage of cognitive development? That is, what responses seem typical of the infant, and how do these responses fit into Piaget's theory?
2. What responses does the infant make that are classifiable as sensorimotor schemes? Why do they fit that category rather than the category of random or unpatterned activity?
3. Are there any indications that the infant possesses concepts? What behaviors can be interpreted as showing possession of concepts?
4. What evidence does the infant show that he or she remembers?
5. Are the infant's behaviors being reinforced in any way? What responses are reinforced, and how does the reinforcement occur—by a smile from the adult, by picking the child up and making a fuss over her? What behavior changes result from the reinforcement (changes in the basic nature of the behavior)? in its frequency?
6. Are there any indications that classical conditioning could be taking place? What are the circumstances of the conditioning process? What is the orig-

inally neutral stimulus, and what stimulus is substituted for it? What is the resulting change in behavior? emotional changes? changes in motor activity? avoidance of an object or person?

7. Does the infant give evidence of accommodation; for example, does he change his approach to a problem when the initial approach does not succeed? If the child accommodates, how does her behavior change as a result? What behaviors indicate that assimilation is occurring? Does the infant show signs of Fogel's "internalized selection of courses of action"?

8. Are there any occasions for learning created just by the adult's normal caregiving activities; for example, verbalizing about an event or object while she changes the infant's diapers? What kind of learning might be taking place? What specific adult activities contribute to the infant's learning opportunities?

Question Guides, Part III:

1. What in the physical or social environment stimulates vocalizations? inhibits them? What are some possible explanations for either of these effects?

2. What are the main characteristics of the infant's vocalizations? Are they babbling sounds? one-word phrases? telegraphic speech? What effect do these vocalizations have on others? How do they respond? Do their responses affect the infant's subsequent vocalizations?

3. When does the infant cry? What happens when he cries? Do the effects of his crying on adults change the crying pattern? Does he use crying often as a means of communication, or does he more often use language to communicate?

4. What physical gestures does the infant use to try to get his meaning across to others? Does he point? take the person by the hand and lead her to the "situation"? Do his gestures seem to match or fit his verbalizations; that is, does he seem to coordinate the timing of his gestures with his speech?

5. What responses give evidence of the infant's ability to understand language; that is, what are his receptive skills? What commands and directions is he able to understand and obey? Are his reception and production abilities different from each other? Does the infant understand more than he can speak, or the opposite?

Exercise 16-4: Emotional Development and Behavior in the Infant (Two to Eighteen Months)

Background Information

Emotions are an extremely important part of human behavior, and as Greenspan and Greenspan (1985) make clear, emotional development begins almost from the moment of birth. You can recall from Chapter 15 that the *first milestone* of emotional development (which occurs between birth and three months of age), involves the newborn's capacity of self-regulation. This first milestone also involves the infant's taking an interest in the world. The Greenspans put it this way:

> Your newborn is faced with two fundamental and simultaneous challenges during the first weeks of life. The first is self-regulation—the ability to feel calm and relaxed, not overwhelmed by his new environment. The second is to become interested in the world through his senses—what he hears, sees, smells, tastes, and touches, and what he experiences through his sense of movement. (p. 14)

These tasks are challenges because the newborn, after nine months in the "darkness and relative quiet of the womb," is suddenly catapulted, as it were, into a world filled with a variety of sensations that are completely new to her. The newborn must organize these sensations and at the same time feel comfortable in their presence and actively engage them in ways that are appropriate to her level of developmental maturity—for example, show interest in the sights and sounds around her and not find them painful (Greenspan and Greenspan, 1985). This then permits achievement of the second milestone, which is that of "taking a highly specialized interest in the *human* world" (p. 5, italics original).

The *second milestone* (from about two to seven months) is described by the Greenspans as "falling in love." They write that

> As your newborn moves along into the second, third, and fourth months of life, she will begin to show selective interest in the most special part of her world, namely, you.

It's assumed that if the baby does not find environmental stimuli pleasurable, he may be unlikely to progress to the stage where the world of human beings "is seen as the most enticing, pleasurable, and exciting of all experiences" (p. 4). The pleasure that one wants the baby to feel, say the Greenspans, can be seen in her "enraptured smiles and eager joyfulness" as she "gazes excitedly at your face" while she feels the movements of your body and hears your voice. They indicate further that the "baby is now becoming more responsive to external social interactions, whereas earlier she was more influenced by her inner physical sensations (e.g., hunger, gas bubbles)" (p. 41).

The *third milestone*, which occurs between three and ten months of age, is founded on this special interest in the human world, but now the baby in effect says "love alone is not enough—I now want a dialogue" (p. 4). Dialogue here does not mean sitting down and talking with the adult. It refers instead to such things as the baby smiling in *response* to the parent's smile, or reaching for an object that is held out to him, or making sounds in response to the parent talking to him. The baby is communicating in his own way, and the communication is *intentional*. Indeed, the authors call this milestone "developing intentional communication." The Greenspans also note that the baby is learning that the world is "a cause-and-effect world" (also a cognitive achievement on the baby's part), which means he learns that his behaviors lead to behaviors from others, when he smiles, for example, so does his mother or father. He is also learning some negative emotions, such as anger when you try to take away a toy.

The *fourth milestone*, which occurs between the nine and eighteen months of age, is characterized as the "emergence of an organized sense of self." In this stage the child extends her "emotional dialogue" another step and "learns to connect small units of feeling and social behavior into large, complicated, orchestrated patterns" (p. 5). The increased skill becomes especially evident near the middle of the fourth stage, which is at fourteen or fifteen months of age, when the child can integrate or combine newer and more complex behaviors with behaviors accomplished earlier. If Susan wants to play, for instance, she is no longer confined to pointing to a toy and making sounds that her mother may or may not understand. Instead, Susan can pick up the toy and carry it to her mother, thereby making her intentions rather clear.

The ability to combine relatively complex social and emotional patterns also indicates increasing cognitive abilities. As the Greenspans write, "The emerging ability to piece together many small activities and emotions into a pattern, known as the ability to organize, is crucial to the development of higher-level thinking and planning" (pp. 83–84). In the example of Susan just above, she demonstrated that she knew the "meaning" of objects, the toy, in this case, and of the action of taking the toy to her mother to play. Again, as the Greenspans put it, "This is the beginning of a 'conceptual' attitude toward the world. Objects now have functions" (p. 5). Equally important, however, people, especially parents, also come to have functions for the child; they serve special purposes. Furthermore, they "take on attributes" (p. 5). Parents show feelings and display actions whose functions or meanings the child eventually recognizes.

Observation Objectives

The objective of Part I is to observe and record behaviors that indicate an infant's level of emotional development according to Greenspan and Greenspan's (1985) second, third, and fourth "emotional milestones." The objective of Part II is simply to observe and record *the general emotional responses or behaviors* of two infants between 2 and 18 months of age. Here, the focus is not on Greenspans' emotional milestones, but rather on what most of us would think of as a baby's "normal" feelings as expressed in crying (for various reasons), smiling, cooing, looking about with curiosity, and the like.

Procedure

We suggest you observe an infant between the ages of 2 and 18 months to maximize the possibility of getting data that are relevant to the stages of emotional development specified in the objectives above.

We shall suggest that you *use the event sampling technique.* Specifically look for those behaviors or capacities that define the emotional milestone (stage) that corresponds to the age of the infant you have chosen. We suggest that you observe *for at least three or four ten-minute periods;* this should give you ample opportunity to see the behaviors that are of interest to you. *Try to get a varied sampling of emotional behaviors,* behaviors that demonstrate more than just one aspect of your particular infant's stage of emotional development. In Part II, use the *event sampling technique* to record the general emotional responses of *at least two infants* between the ages of 2 and 18 months. In this exercise, focus on such things as crying, displays of anger or annoyance, fear responses, contentment or delight, and so on. Be sure to record the circumstances or contexts in which these responses occurred. Then compare and contrast the emotional behaviors of the two infants: How did they differ? How were they alike? If you can observe them under the same or similar circumstances, did the two infants behave differently or similarly under relatively the same conditions?

Question Guides:

1. What specific behaviors did the infant exhibit that led you to classify his or her level of emotional development as you did?
2. Did the infant exhibit any behaviors that are found in the next higher stage? If so, were they too infrequent to allow you to put him or her into that next stage? Or, did you classify the infant in the lower stage because of his or her age?
3. Was the infant ahead of his or her age with respect to emotional development? Was he or she behind?

Observation Exercise 16-1

Physical/Motor Characteristics and Skills of the Infant or Toddler (1–24 Months)

Observer's Name _____

Child/Children Observed _____

Child's/Children's Age(s) _____   Child's/Children's Sex _____

Observation Context (home, child care center, preschool, school) _____

Date of Observation _____   Time Begun _____   Time Ended _____

Brief Description of Physical and Social Characteristics of Observation Setting:

_____

Objective (1): Physical Characteristics

Total Length of Newborn _____   Weight of Newborn _____

Length of Head _____   Ratio of Head to Total Body Length _____

Length of Trunk _____   Ratio of Head to Trunk _____

Describe the characteristics of the following:
HEAD AND FACE (shape, eyes, ears, mouth, nose, etc.):

TRUNK (e.g., size in relation to head, overall appearance, etc.):

ARMS AND LEGS (positioning, shape):

HANDS AND FINGERS:

Comparisons with newborns (these may be made using established norms if actual observations of a newborn are not possible or wanted):

Length:

Weight:

Ratio head to total body length:

Ratio head to trunk:

Child's height and weight relative to norms cited:

Observation Exercise 16-1

Continued

Objective (2): Motor Skills of the Infant (1–24 Months)

Observer's Name _____

Child/Children Observed _____

Child's/Children's Age(s) _____ Child's/Children's Sex _____

Observation Context (home, child care center, preschool, school) _____

Date of Observation _____ Time Begun _____ Time Ended _____

Brief Description of Physical and Social Characteristics of Observation Setting:

_____

OBJECTIVE BEHAVIORAL DESCRIPTIONS (OBD) AND INTERPRETATIONS: *Event Sampling*

OBD Session 1: **[Time begun _____ Time ended _____]**

Interpretation 1:

OBD Session 2: **[Time begun _____ Time ended _____]**

Interpretation 2:

Continue with OBDs and Interpretations for as long as feasible or needed.

Comparison of Infant's Functioning with Age Norms:

Observation Exercise 16-1

Continued

Objective (3): Fine Motor Abilities [If children were tested by observer, describe how they were persuaded to perform]

Fine Motor Tasks

Child 1: (Age_____)

Event and description of Response (OBD): *Event Sampling*

Stacking Blocks:

Picking Up Raisin:

Putting Blocks in Container; Removing Them:

Stringing Beads:

Response to Playdough:

Scribbling with Crayon:

Turning Pages:

Hand and Leg Preference:

Indications of Tool Use:

Child 2: (Age_____)

Stacking Blocks:

Picking Up Raisin:

Putting Blocks in Container; Removing Them:

Stringing Beads:

Response to Playdough:

Scribbling with Crayon:

Turning Pages:

Hand and Leg Preference:

Indications of Tool Use:

Comparison (Similarities) of Child 1 and Child 2:

Contrast (Differences) Between Child 1 and Child 2:

Observation Exercise 16-1

Continued

Gross Motor Abilities

Child 1: (Age_____)

Event and description of Response (OBD): *Event Sampling*

Walking:

Running:

Climbing Stairs:

Walking Sideways, Backwards:

Jumping From Low Height (one step):

Other (crawling, creeping, scooting, etc.):

Child 2: (Age_____)

Event and description of Response (OBD): *Event Sampling*

Walking:

Running:

Climbing Stairs:

Walking Sideways, Backwards:

Jumping From Low Height (one step):

Other (crawling, creeping, scooting, etc.):

Comparison of Child 1 and Child 2:

Contrast Between Child 1 and Child 2:

Observation Exercise 16-2

PART I: Social Behavior of the Infant (1–24 Months)

Observer's Name _____

Child/Children Observed _____

Child's/Children's Age(s) _____   Child's/Children's Sex _____

Observation Context (home, child care center, preschool, school) _____

Date of Observation _____   Time Begun _____   Time Ended _____

Brief Description of Physical and Social Characteristics of Observation Setting:

<hr>

SOCIAL BEHAVIORS AND INTERACTION PATTERNS

OBJECTIVE BEHAVIORAL DESCRIPTIONS (OBD) AND INTERPRETATIONS:
Narrative Description

OBD Session 1:   [Time begun _____   Time ended _____]

Interpretation 1:

OBD Session 2:   [Time begun _____   Time ended _____]

Interpretation 2:

OBD Session 3:   [Time begun _____   Time ended _____]

Interpretation 3:

Continue with OBDs and Interpretations for as long as possible or needed.

Observation Exercise 16-2

Continued

PART II: Social Behavior of the Infant (1–24 Months)

Observer's Name _____

Child/Children Observed _____

Child's/Children's Age(s) _____ Child's/Children's Sex _____

Observation Context (home, child care center, preschool, school) _____

Date of Observation _____ Time Begun _____ Time Ended _____

Brief Description of Physical and Social Characteristics of Observation Setting:

_____

Time Sampling of Attachment Behaviors

Recording Intervals — Behavior Categories	1	2	3	4	5	6	7	8	9	10
Looks at Caregiver										
Makes Physical Contact with Caregiver										
Smiles at Caregiver										
Shows Object to Caregiver										
Moves Closer to Caregiver										
Establishes Visual Contact with Caregiver										
Cries When Caregiver Leaves Room										
Negative Reaction to Stranger's Approach										

INTERPRETIVE COMMENTS:

_____

Partly adapted from Willemsen (1979, p. 250).

Observation Exercise 16-2

Continued

PART III: Social Behavior of the Infant (1–24 Months)

Observer's Name _____

Child/Children Observed _____

Child's/Children's Age(s) _____   Child's/Children's Sex _____

Observation Context (home, child care center, preschool, school) _____

Date of Observation _____   Time Begun _____   Time Ended _____

Brief Description of Physical and Social Characteristics of Observation Setting:

_____

OBJECTIVE BEHAVIORAL DESCRIPTIONS (OBD): *Narrative Description*

Session 1: [Time begun _____   Time ended _____]

Qualities of Temperament Noted:

Session 2: [Time begun _____   Time ended _____]

Qualities of Temperament Noted:

Session 3: [Time begun _____   Time ended _____]

Qualities of Temperament Noted:

PARENT INTERVIEW:

Question Asked Parent(s) (#1):

Parent's Response (#1):

Question Asked Parent(s) (#2):

Parent's Response (#2):

Observation Exercise 16-3

PART I: Cognitive and Language Development of the Infant (1–24 Months)

Observer's Name _____

Child/Children Observed _____

Child's/Children's Age(s) _____   Child's/Children's Sex _____

Observation Context (home, child care center, preschool, school) _____

Date of Observation _____   Time Begun _____   Time Ended _____

Brief Description of Physical and Social Characteristics of Observation Setting:

PART I: Object Permanence: *Event Sampling*

Tested Event and Description of Response Observed

Step (1) Dropping the toy:

Step (2) Hiding the toy while the child watches:

Step (3) Visible displacement of the toy:

Step (4) Invisible displacement of the toy:

Comments:

Observation Exercise 16-3

Continued

PART II: Cognitive and Language Development of the Infant (1–24 Months)

Observer's Name _____

Child/Children Observed _____

Child's/Children's Age(s) _____   Child's/Children's Sex _____

Observation Context (home, child care center, preschool, school) _____

Date of Observation _____   Time Begun _____   Time Ended _____

Brief Description of Physical and Social Characteristics of Observation Setting:

_____

OBJECTIVE BEHAVIORAL DESCRIPTIONS (OBD) AND INTERPRETATIONS:
  Narrative Description

OBD Session 1: [Time begun _____   Time ended _____]

Interpretation 1:

OBD Session 2: [Time begun _____   Time ended _____]

Interpretation 2:

OBD Session 3: [Time begun _____   Time ended _____]

Interpretation 3:

Continue with OBDs and Interpretations for as long as needed.

Observation Exercise 16-3

Continued

PART III: Cognitive and Language Development of the Infant (1–24 Months)

Observer's Name _____

Child/Children Observed _____

Child's/Children's Age(s) _____ Child's/Children's Sex _____

Observation Context (home, child care center, preschool, school) _____

Date of Observation _____ Time Begun _____ Time Ended _____

Brief Description of Physical and Social Characteristics of Observation Setting:

_____

PART III: Language: *Event Sampling*

OBD Session 1: [Time begun _____ Time ended _____]

Interpretation 1:

OBD Session 2: [Time begun _____ Time ended _____]

Interpretation 2:

OBD Session 3: [Time begun _____ Time ended _____]

Interpretation 3:

Continue with OBDs and Interpretations for as long as needed.

Observation Exercise 16-4

Emotional Development of the Infant (2–18 Months)

Observer's Name _____

Child/Children Observed _____

Child's/Children's Age(s) _____ Child's/Children's Sex _____

Observation Context (home, child care center, preschool, school) _____

Date of Observation _____ Time Begun _____ Time Ended _____

Brief Description of Physical and Social Characteristics of Observation Setting:

_____

OBJECTIVE BEHAVIORAL DESCRIPTIONS (OBD) AND INTERPRETATIONS: *Event Sampling*

OBD Session 1: **[Time begun** _____ **Time ended** _____**]**

Interpretation 1:

OBD Session 2: **[Time begun** _____ **Time ended** _____**]**

Interpretation 2:

Continue with as many OBDs as are feasible or needed.

Behavioral Summary:

Infant's Probable Emotional Stage:

Supporting Evidence:

This exercise may be difficult for some individuals to do. Greenspans' emotional milestones are rather abstract in some respects and therefore difficult to put into practical, empirical terms. Consequently, we have provided an alternate exercise which is more traditional in its approach

Observation Exercise 16-4

Continued

Part II: Emotional Development of the Infant (2–18 Months): Alternate Exercise

Observer's Name _____

Child/Children Observed _____

Child's/Children's Age(s) _____ Child's/Children's Sex _____

Observation Context (home, child care center, preschool, school) _____

Date of Observation _____ Time Begun _____ Time Ended _____

Brief Description of Physical and Social Characteristics of Observation Setting:

_____

OBJECTIVE BEHAVIORAL DESCRIPTIONS (OBD) AND INTERPRETATIONS: *Event Sampling*

Context of OBD 1:

OBD Session 1 (Infant #1): **[Time begun _____ Time ended _____]**
Interpretation 1:

Context of OBD 2:

OBD Session 1 (Infant #2): **[Time begun _____ Time ended _____]**
Interpretation 2:

Context of OBD 3:

OBD Session 1 (Infant #3): **[Time begun _____ Time ended _____]**
Interpretation 3:

Continue for as Many OBDs as are Needed or Desired.

Comparisons and Contrasts Between Infants' Emotional Behaviors:

Summary Comments:

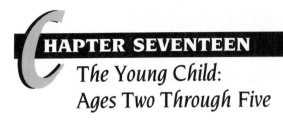

CHAPTER SEVENTEEN

The Young Child:
Ages Two Through Five

Introduction

This chapter focuses your observations and recordings on the period referred to as the preschool years. Although many significant things occur during this span of four years, the rate of growth and developmental change seen during the 18 to 24 months of infancy probably will never again be equaled in any comparable period of time.

The observation exercises in this chapter are approached differently from those in the previous chapters. Unlike the period of infancy, the preschool period will not be divided up into smaller units such as four one-year periods, with separate exercises for each year. The entire preschool period is covered as a single entity, even though it comprises a greater amount of chronological time than infancy.

A second difference in approach concerns the organization of the material. The Question Guides are presented before the Exercise Sheets, and some of the background information is included among the questions, rather than in a separate section. The background information is a starting point for your observations. There are other sources of information you can consult about child development and various theories as additional points of view from which to "see," understand, and interpret children's behavior.

The numbered questions (Question Guides) from Exercises 17-2 on are based in part on the works of Lay and Dopyera (1977) and Lay-Dopyera and Dopyera (1982).

Exercise 17-1: The Preschool Child in the Physical Environment

Background Information

Our physical surroundings exert a powerful influence on all of us. How much space we have, the objects and their arrangement in that space, and the social-psychological "meaning" of the space, combine to determine and direct our behavior. A preschool classroom, a playground, or the child's home are particular spaces with equipment, materials, people, and arrangements that are used even if they are not designed for special purposes. As the child's cognitive and language abilities become more sophisticated, she also comes to understand that spaces have definitions. There definitions dictate what she may do in that space, that is, what others will allow her to do. Also important, however, is the child's learning what she can do in the space because of the physical properties of the objects and materials it contains.

Observation Objectives

To familiarize you with the physical environment in which you are observing and to learn how children respond to and are influenced by their physical surroundings.

Procedure

Your first task is to draw a diagram of the indoor and outdoor environments. On each diagram, name the equipment and materials and show their locations. With your diagram in hand, anyone should be able to walk into the observation setting and find anything that is there (bookshelves, toilets, art area). Similarly, the diagram of the outside environment should locate all of the equipment and materials that are provided for the children's use. Contemporary outdoor environments for young children can be referred to as *playscapes,* "which combine a variety of materials and allow for a range of activities" (Essa, 1996, p. 194). Included in such playscapes might be such things as tricycle tracks, climbers, and sliders. As Essa points out, "Many of today's creative playgrounds contain equipment constructed of such materials as tires, cargo nets, railroad ties, telephone poles, large cable spools, barrels, and drainage pipes" (p. 195). Given such a potential variety of objects, it may not be enough simply to name them. It may be advisable to describe both the items that make up each piece of play equipment, and the uses to which each item or object is put. For example, a drainage pipe should be described in reasonable detail not only with respect to its size and location, but also with respect to how the children actually use it for their play activities: What do they do with such a pipe?

The second part of your assignment concerns how children use the areas available to them, and how different areas have different effects on behavior. Begin by selecting two areas of the classroom or other setting that differ significantly in the activities and behaviors allowed there. For example, one would expect behavior in the big block area to be quite different from that in the dramatic play or story-telling area. The differences can be partly the result of the teacher's enforcement of rules governing behavior. But, spaces themselves also affect behavior. What can be done in a given space is determined by what is there to do something with. If there are no blocks on hand, there obviously will be no playing with blocks. If puzzles are stored on shelves out of the children's reach, playing with puzzles will have to depend on an adult's help.

Observe and record the behavior of two children in the two areas; follow them as they move around the area. Then compare and contrast their behavior in one area with their behavior in the other. Note whether their actions are in keeping with the requirements and expectations of the location.

Summarize the specific ways their behavior changes (if in fact it does) from one location to another. For this exercise, *use the narrative description method,* since you are not looking for any particular event or behavior; you are interested in everything that occurs related to the child in the physical environment.

Question Guides:

1. Do the children's behaviors change from one location to another? If so, how?
2. What behaviors would you expect in each of the two locations you observe the children? Do their behaviors conform to your expectations (or the space's definition)? If so, how? If not, why not? Does the caregiver have to remind the children of the appropriate behavior?
3. What in the environment holds the children's interest? How do they express that interest?
4. How would you assess the overall arrangement of the room or playscape? Is there enough space for the children to move around freely? to engage in the activities for which the space is intended?

Exercise 17-2: Physical Growth and Motor Functioning

Background Information

Physical characteristics and motor abilities are probably the most noticeable and easily measurable aspects of human growth and development. These characteristics and abilities are often of major importance to parents, who point with pride to the gains their child makes in height, weight, and ability to walk, run, and manipulate objects. Since everything we do in some way involves a physical body, it makes sense to say that our physical and motor development and abilities form the foundation for our behavior.

In certain respects, this exercise will be easy to accomplish. Young children of normal ability are usually active physically, and many of their motor behaviors are obvious. On the other hand, there are some subtle aspects to motor behavior that can be overlooked. For example, all "normal" children walk and run, but each does so in her own unique style. For some, walking is smooth and well-coordinated, with no significant peculiarities; for others, toes might point noticeably outward, feet may be somewhat widely spaced, or balance while running might be poor. Moreover, there are behaviors that do not have obvious physical-motor components. Sitting at the snack table eating is not a vigorous activity like free play in the big block areas. And yet, there are things to be considered; for example, the child's posture (does he slouch, sit on one leg, cock his head to one side?), the child's skill in handling eating utensils, pouring juice, or wiping crumbs from the table.

The behaviors of interest in this exercise fall into three general categories: (a) physical characteristics, (b) gross (large) motor movements or abilities, and

(c) fine (small) motor movements of abilities. All of the child's physical-motor functioning will fall into one of these three categories. We would like to make a few brief comments about the questions that are provided throughout this chapter. They are intended to *act as guides*, as a means of directing your observations and your thinking as you approach each of the Observation Exercises. We do not mean for you actually to answer each and every one of these questions. We also fully recognize that some of the questions will not be appropriate to two- and three-year-olds, and maybe not even to some four- or five-year-olds. It could be argued, therefore, that it makes no sense to look for behaviors that are not likely to occur because of a child's particular age or developmental level. Moreover, it could also be argued that it makes no sense to ask questions that are very likely to be answered "yes" precisely because the child *is* of an age or developmental level where particular behaviors or characteristics are commonly observed. In short, why bother to observe for behaviors, skills, or characteristics that are improbable, or for behaviors, skills, or characteristics that are almost certain to occur?

Chapter 17 concerns the ages from two through five years. In that span of time, most if not all of the guide questions presented could, in principle, be answered, or behaviors could be observed that will answer these questions. (Of course, no one individual is likely to see all of the behaviors and skills that are possessed by one or more children.) And there is also the issue of individual differences. One can't assume that three-year-old Melinda will, or will not, in fact exhibit a certain ability simply because developmental norms for three-year-olds predict that she will or that she won't. One of the general goals of observing young children's behavior is to learn what specific children are able to do, as well as to learn about children in general.

Consequently, suppose that you are observing, say, two-year-olds, and you refer to the question "What are the child's abilities to perform rhythmic movements?" If you restrict yourself to the examples of rhythmic movements given in the text, you may not be able to identify any such rhythmic ability. But, the overall objective of the first exercise is to observe and record motor behaviors of any kind. Even the two-year-old can do some rhythmic things—walking, for instance, has a certain rhythm to it. Whatever the case, your goal is to look for all instances of motor behaviors and skills. If you can't specifically respond to a particular question, it's not critical. What is critical is what you do observe and the sense or meaning you derive from your observation.

To reiterate an important point: While observing children's motor skills— *and all other areas of functioning*—it is crucial to take their ages into consideration. It should not surprise you to observe that a two-year-old, who is likely to be two years and some months of age, might prefer large-muscle movements over small ones. This does not mean that a child this age cannot perform small-muscle movements and activities. Indeed, children considerably younger than two years do have some fine motor skills, although they are more rudimentary than those of their older counterparts. If, however, a five-year-old seems to prefer gross over fine-muscle activities, several factors might be at play. The child may not be as skilled or well-developed motorically as his or her age peers; or maybe the child does not find the fine motor activities or opportunities that are available in the setting particularly interesting, which motivates her to play in the large motor areas. (See Tables 17-1 to 17-4 for summaries of motor skills of two- to five-year-olds.)

In light of the above, therefore, the procedure will be to observe at least two children of differing ages (a two- or three-year-old and a five-year-old would be good choices that, generally, would accentuate difference in motor skills.) If you don't have access to children who fall into a two- to five-year range, pick two children who are reasonably active physically and are of normal development.

Observation Objectives

To learn about preschool children's physical characteristics and motor abilities and how they are alike and how they are different from one another in these areas.

Procedure

If possible, select two children of differing ages (a two- or three-year-old and a five-year-old would be good choices). If that is not possible, simply select any two children who are reasonably active physically. *Using an event sampling format,* describe in detail (1) the children's physical appearances and (2) their motor activities as they play during the observation session. *Observe each of the two children for about 10 to 15 minutes.* To make the most pro-

---

Table 17-1 Summary of Motor Skills of the Two-Year-Old Child

- Earlier wide stance while walking replaced by a heel-to-toe movement pattern
- Runs more confidently and with fewer falls
- Climbs stairs without help but cannot yet alternate feet
- Can balance on one foot for a brief time; will still fall when attempting to jump up and down
- Can throw a relatively large ball underhand and does not lose balance
- Can hold cup or glass in one hand
- Can unzip large zippers and unbutton large buttons
- Can turn doorknobs and open doors
- Can hold large crayon with fist; can also scribble
- Can climb up on chair, turn around, and sit down
- Can pour and fill containers with sand, water
- Can stack 4 to 6 objects on top of one another
- Can propel wheeled toys with the feet

Adapted with permission from Allen and Marotz (1994, pp. 78–79)

Table 17-2 Summary of Motor Skills of the Three-Year-Old Child

- Can walk up and down stairs without help; alternates feet; may jump from last step to the floor and land on both feet
- Can briefly balance on one foot
- Can kick a large ball
- Can feed self without help
- Can jump in place
- Can pedal a small tricycle or other wheeled toy
- Can throw a ball overhand
- Can catch a bounced ball with outstretched arms
- Shows improved use/control of crayons and markers while drawing; can make vertical, horizontal, and circular motions
- Can hold a crayon or marker between the first two fingers and thumb, as opposed to the earlier use of the fist to grasp these objects
- Can turn pages of a book one at a time
- Likes to build with blocks
- Can build a tower with 8 or more blocks
- May show preference for either left or right hand
- Can carry a container of liquid without excessive spilling; can also pour from a pitcher into another container
- Can manipulate large buttons and zippers on clothing
- Can wash and dry hands; can brush teeth
- Normally achieves complete bladder control during third year

Adapted with permission from Allen and Marotz, (1994, pp. 89–91)

ductive use of your time, observe the children when they are most likely to display the motor behaviors that you want to see. If your objective concerns large motor activity, observe the children in those areas of the facility that promote or encourage large-muscle movements. Apply the same rationale to small-muscle activities. Then examine your data and compare and contrast (i.e., describe the similarities and differences between) the two children; draw some general conclusions as to their motor skills, degrees of coordination, and preferred activities. The Question Guide provided will give you information about the components of motor development and behavior and will direct your observations and interpretations.

Question Guides (Partly adapted from Lay and Dopyera 1977)

1. Is there anything about the child's body build that sets her apart from the rest of the group?
2. What can you say about how the child holds his body? For example, how does the child stand, sit, walk, and run? Is the child stoop-shouldered? Is the head carried high or does the child look down?

Table 17-3 Summary of Motor Skills of the Four-Year-Old Child

- Can walk in a straight line
- Can hop on one foot
- Can pedal and steer a wheeled toy with skill and confidence; can turn corners and avoid obstacles
- Can climb steps, ladders, trees, and playground equipment
- Can jump over objects 5 or 6 inches high or from a step; lands with both feet together
- Can run, start, stop, and move around obstacles without difficulty
- Can throw a ball overhand
- Can build a tower with 10 or more blocks; uses the dominant hand
- Can form shapes and objects out of clay
- Can reproduce some shapes and letters
- Holds a crayon or marker using first two fingers and the thumb ("tripod grasp")
- "Paints and draws with deliberateness" (p. 99)
- Hits nails and pegs more accurately with a hammer
- Can thread small wooden beads on a string

Adapted with permission from Allen and Marotz (1994, pp. 98–99)

Table 17-4 Summary of Motor Skills of the Five-Year-Old Child

- Can walk backwards heel-to-toe
- Can walk up and down stairs without help; alternates feet
- Is able to learn to do somersaults
- Can touch toes without bending at the knees
- Can walk a balance beam
- Can learn to skip with alternating feet
- Can catch a ball thrown from a distance of three feet
- Displays skilled riding of a tricycle; rides with speed and skillful steering. Some may learn to ride bicycles
- Can jump or hop forward on both feet ten times in succession without falling
- Can balance on either foot with good control for ten seconds
- Can reproduce variety of shapes and letters: square, triangle, A, I, O, U, C, H, L, T, V
- Shows good control of pencil or marker; may start to color within the lines
- Cuts on the line with a scissors, although not perfectly
- "Hand dominance is usually well established"

Adpated with permission from Allen and Marotz (1994, pp. 98–99)

Gross Movements and Abilities   Gross movements and abilities involve the large muscles of the body. Movements controlled by these muscles are large, sweeping movements such as climbing, swinging, walking, running, throwing, and jumping. There is an important consideration for this exercise. When a child is just learning a skill, she tends to practice only that skill, isolating it from others already mastered. This process of learning and practicing a behavior is called *differentiation*. This is the process in which a new skill differentiates or separates out of old, existing skills. During differentiation, the child must devote his entire attention to the unfamiliar task. Once the task is perfected, however, the child can combine the new skill with his existing skills to form an integrated whole. These existing skills are not necessarily physical-motor skills, but may be verbal or cognitive skills. For instance, a child might climb up and down the jungle gym using the hands and feet in a number of different ways, while at the same time shouting to a friend, "Look at what I'm doing." This is an example of *integration*.

When you observe a motor behavior, note if it is combined with other behaviors to form a more complex pattern (integration), or whether the behavior is exhibited by itself and in a repetitive manner (differentiation) (Lay and Dopyera 1977).

Children are capable of a wide variety of motor actions, although individual differences exist. Some children will be able to run, jump, climb, intentionally fall down (with control), and do somersaults and cartwheels. Certain of the child's motor behaviors are basic skills (e.g., walking and running),

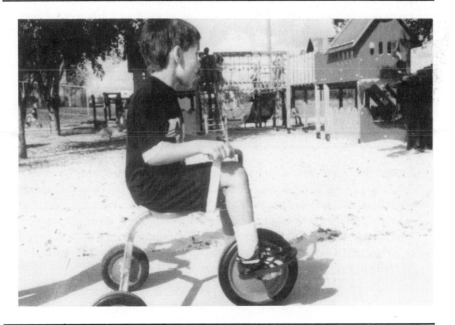

Figure 17-1   Gross motor skills, or use of large muscles is demonstrated by this preschooler on a riding toy.

and some children will be able to perform variations of these basic skills. For example, a child may be able to walk and run backwards or sideways. Be alert to the range or variety of motor actions the child can perform. Remember, developmental level, which is to some degree indicated by age, is a strong determinant of what a child can do.

3. How many different motor behaviors can the child perform?

Children demonstrate their ability to balance in many ways. They walk across balance beams elevated off the floor, they walk on cracks or lines on the ground; they walk stepping from one rock to another. When recording instances of these behaviors, try to indicate how much balancing ability is required. For example, how wide is the beam the child walks across? How quickly does she move on these balancing tasks? Can the child do these things without help, or must her hand be held? How does she compare with the other children? Can the child perform other actions while balancing (integration)?

4. How well does the child perform balancing activities?

You may be able to gauge the child's strength only by seeing how much he can lift, pull, or push compared with his peers. You may not be able to determine his strength in terms of the *most* he can lift, pull, or push. Children demonstrate their strength in a number of ways: they lift and stack blocks, pull each other in wagons, hang from ladders or jungle gyms, and wrestle with each other. What behaviors show the child's strength? How much strength is needed for a particular behavior? For example, how many blocks did the child lift at one time; how many children did she pull in the wagon at the same time, and so on.

5. How strong is the child?

Some children seem to do everything at their top rate of speed, whereas others have a more leisurely pace. How quickly does the child do various things such as walk, run, and climb? Does his rate of movement vary depending on the particular activity or piece of equipment used (keeping in mind that such things as rate of movement also depend upon the child's level of skill)? Are the child's movements coordinated and well timed, or does he do things faster than his coordination will allow?

6. How quickly can the child move or perform various activities?

How long can the child perform a given activity without resting? Can the child go from one activity to another without seeming to get tired? How many times can the child perform a given movement without stopping to rest? Endurance may be partly determined by comparison with the child's peers.

7. How much endurance or stamina does the child appear to have?

Many activities require a sense of rhythm, an ability to move one's body in a properly timed sequence (e.g., in dancing). What evidence is there that the child has this rhythmic capacity? Can she keep time with music and bounce a ball? Can she hop or skip half way across the room without losing the correct pattern of motion? Can the child perform one non-rhythmic activity while simultaneously performing a rhythmic one; for example, can she talk with someone while at the same time make dance movements to music?

8. What are the child's abilities to perform rhythmic movements?

Fine Motor Movements and Abilities   This category involves movements of the small muscles of the body; for example, those used in picking up small objects, zipping a jacket, writing with crayon or pencil, and buttoning a shirt. Fine motor behavior evolves or differentiates out of gross motor movements; it therefore occurs later in the motor development sequence.

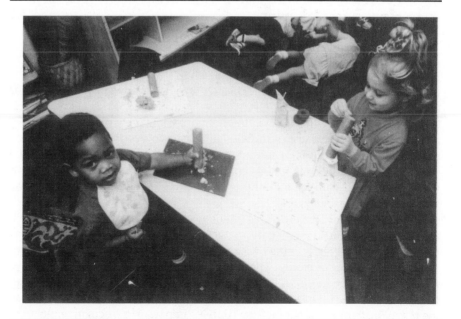

Figure 17-2   Fine motor skills, the use of small muscles, are demonstrated by this child.

Activities such as eating, dressing, and general grooming typically require small muscle skills. To what extent can the child dress himself? This includes buttoning and zipping shirts and jackets, putting on one's socks and shoes, tying laces, and putting on shirts. Eating requires many small muscle actions: holding a fork or spoon and bringing it to the mouth in a controlled manner; pouring liquid; cutting meat with a knife; and serving food from a larger dish onto a plate. General grooming involves combing one's hair, washing one's face and hands, drying oneself with a towel, and brushing one's teeth.

9. What is the range and variety of the child's fine motor skills involved in self-help behavior?

The preschool environment is full of materials that provide opportunities for small-muscle activities. There might be tools such as screwdrivers, hammers, and pliers; jigsaw puzzles with small parts to be fitted together; small blocks to build. Simply turning the pages of a book requires fine-muscle skills. Be alert to the child's functioning in these areas. Try to draw some conclusions regarding his skill in various activities, as well as the extensiveness of his small-muscle abilities.

10. What is the child's ability to handle and use various kinds of toys, objects, and tools? How extensive are his abilities in this area?

Exercise 17-3: Cognitive and Intellectual Development and Behavior

Background Information

This exercise is concerned with the child's mental functioning: how he perceives and thinks about the world, and the factual knowledge the child has and how he uses it. Jean Piaget distinguishes between two kinds of knowledge: (1) knowledge of specific facts and information, which he called knowledge in the "narrow sense"; and (2) knowledge that involves the child's thinking processes and how she reasons about reality, which he called knowledge in the "broad sense." Knowledge in the broad sense also concerns the relationships that the child forms among the various facts he has learned in the narrow sense (see Kamii and DeVries 1977).

One of the characteristics of children's thinking has to do with what Piaget called egocentrism. *Egocentrism,* which is perhaps the best known of the cognitive contents, is concerned with the extent to which children view themselves as the center of reality. Charles Brainerd (1978) offers an interpretative rule of thumb when he writes that "Any behavior that suggests children are preoccupied with themselves and/or unconcerned with things going on around them may be termed egocentric" (p. 103). It's important to recognize that egocentrism results from the young child's *cognitive inability* to take someone else's point of view or to separate himself from various aspects of his environment. Don't confuse this with *egotism,* a label we usually reserve for older children or adults who are intellectually capable of seeing the world from another's perspective, but for whatever reason choose not to do so.

Egocentrism can be expressed by the child who makes a remark about another child, not realizing that the remark could hurt that child's feelings. Or, a child might tell you a story and mention names or describe events only she knows about; yet, she assumes you are as aware of these persons and events as she is.

1. Look for examples of egocentric behavior.

   There are many cognitive abilities that adults take for granted. For the young child, however, these abilities must develop over a long period of time. Piaget argued that some abilities cannot be taught directly; rather, they are the result of maturation, a lot of general experience, learning from others (social transmission), and the processes of assimilation and accommodation.

   One of these cognitive abilities is known as *classification.* This is the process of sorting objects into groups according to perceived similarities. Classification requires that the child notices similarities and differences in the properties of objects. Then he must group those objects on the basis of their similarity on a particular property—for example, color, size, shape, or function. Properties of objects are also called *stimulus dimensions.* There are many dimensions that can form the basis of classification.

   For example, does the child put all the toy sheep in one group in the "barnyard" and all toy cows in another group? Does the child put square things and round things into two different, mutually exclusive groups? Can the child sort objects on the basis of more than one attribute at a time—according to *both* size and shape, for example?

2. Observe how the child sorts objects. How does she perceive things to be alike or different? On what basis does she note similarities and differences?

   Another important cognitive ability concerns the concept of *number.* Number includes the ability to count, but it also involves such things as one-to-one correspondence and conservation of number. *One-to-one correspondence* is the process of matching two groups of objects, lining up one object of one group with one and only one object of the other group. A child who has this ability can, for example, give each child at the snack table one glass of juice, or place a chair at the table for each child there. Note that this ability does not require counting, but only the ability to see that each child is to get one glass, one chair, or what have you.

   Conservation of number is the understanding that the way objects are arranged in space has no effect on their quantity—if no objects are added to or subtracted from the group, their total number remains unchanged. For example, you show a child two equal rows of pennies (say, five in each row). She agrees that the rows are "the same." Then, while she watches, you spread out the pennies in one row so they take up more space than the other row. If the child cannot conserve number, she will tell you the altered ("spread out") row has more pennies than the unaltered row. If she can conserve number, she will not be fooled by the altered row's appearing to have more pennies, and she will tell you the two rows are still the same.

3. Can the child put objects into one-to-one correspondence? Can you give an example? Does he have the concept of number? How does he show that understanding? If he does not understand the number concept, what does he do that indicates the absence of the number concept?

Another cognitive ability that interested Piaget is called seriation. *Seriation* involves the sequential arrangement of objects or ideas according to a particular attribute. Specifically, seriation requires the child to compare and coordinate differences among objects. Thus, arranging sticks of different lengths from shortest to longest is an example of object seriation. Knowing that if Billy is older than Tommy, and Tommy is older than Mary, then Billy is older than Mary, is an example of an abstract seriation.

4. Can the child seriate? According to what criteria does the child arrange objects or events? How many objects can the child arrange in some kind of order?

A child may be able to arrange three sticks according to length, but has difficulty with more than three sticks. He may simply put a larger group of sticks into several groups of three each, although each set of three may be seriated correctly. For example, given nine sticks of different lengths, the child may sort the sticks into three groups of three sticks each, but each smaller group may be seriated correctly.

The concept of conservation applies not only to number but to anything that can be measured; for example, amount of liquid and amount of substance. In these cases, does the child understand that putting equal amounts of liquid into two differently shaped containers does not change their quantities. Or, given two balls made of equal amounts of clay, does the child understand that flattening one of them into a pancake does not change its quantity?

5. Does the child have any understanding of conservation of liquid and substance? How does she show this understanding?

The concepts of causality, space, and time are also important aspects of cognitive functioning. *Causality* is the child's comprehension of cause and effect relationships and how he attempts to explain various phenomena. For example, does the child see the relation between the weather and how one should dress? Or, how does the child try to explain why one object floats and another one sinks?

According to Charles Brainerd (1978), there are three "general features of preoperational children's causality concepts: *finalism, artificialism,* and *animism*" (italics original; p. 106). We would like to deal with these in some detail so that you will be able to recognize their presence in children's thinking.

Brainerd (1978) discusses Piaget's definition of *Animism* as follows:

> By 'animism,' Piaget means more or less the same thing that the dictionary means—i.e., preoperational children attribute life to things that are not actually alive. Or, more precisely, they attribute life to things that adults do not believe are alive (p. 108).

Animism can, we believe, be a bit difficult to discern in children. This is because it's tempting to confuse or equate animism with symbolic play. In the latter, the child simply *pretends* a doll is alive, for example, but does not *literally* believe it is alive. Furthermore, as Brainerd points out, Piaget's definition poses some problems, because adults don't always agree among themselves about what is alive and what is not.

It might be worthwhile to give you a brief description of the four substages through which Piaget believed the development of animism must pass. The first two substages occur during the preoperational stage of cognitive development, whereas the last two occur during the period or stage of concrete operations. We'll give you these as well in case you observe a precocious child who might be exhibiting an advanced development of animism relative to his preoperational peers. For this discussion, we draw on Brainerd's descriptions (pp. 108–109).

Substage I: In substage I, the essential criterion for life is "the effect that an object has on people." If an object can do anything at all that has some consequences for humans, it's said to be alive and to have a will of its own. Lamps, bicycles, cars, and stoves (Brainerd, p. 108) would qualify as having life under this criterion.

Substage II: Here, life has the necessary attribute of mobility: "To be viewed as living, an object must be capable of moving" (p. 109). But as Brainerd points out, movement must be "one of its [the object's] normal functions" (p. 109), even though it need not move spontaneously or by itself. Thus, tables and lamps would not qualify as living things because they do not (ordinarily) move. Interestingly enough, a stone would be considered alive because it can move "by rolling" (p. 109).

Substage III: In this substage movement plays a continuing role, but now it must be spontaneous movement, movement that does not require the intervention of human beings. Stones and bicycles no longer qualify, as they did in substage II, but the sun does since it moves (albeit only apparently) on its own around the earth.

Substage IV: Life in this substage is attributed only to plants and animals, which are the categories of objects that adults normally think of as alive.

The second causality concept is *finalism,* which, says Brainerd, is "the manner in which preoperational children answer the interrogatives 'why,' 'what,' 'where,' and 'how'—but especially the interrogative 'why' " (p. 106). According to Brainerd, Piaget believed that most adults attribute two basic meanings to "why." One of these refers to the goals or purposes of one's behavior. This meaning is captured in the question "Why did you do that?" (p. 106). The second meaning relates to the causes of events. This meaning is captured in the question "Why does the sun shine?" (p. 106). In sum, the first meaning of "why" has to do with effects, or as Brainerd puts it, with "where things are going" (p. 106). The second meaning concerns causes, or as Brainerd again puts it, with "where things come from" (p. 106).

Piaget apparently argued that preoperational children are not able to distinguish between the cause and effect meanings of "why," which can explain the difficulty adults have answering questions to children's satisfaction. Children deal simultaneously with causes and effects, and they talk about these two variables as though they were interchangeable.

Finalism also involves the preoperational child's belief that everything has an identifiable cause. As Brainerd writes, "When Piaget says that preoperational thinking is 'finalistic,' he means that it searches for a simple and direct cause for even the most trivial and accidental occurrences" (p. 107). Simply put, finalism does not account for the basic principle that "*some events happen entirely by chance*" (p. 107).

The third causality concept is *artificialism.* This is the belief that everything that exists has been created by human beings or by a god who builds the way people do, which is according to some blueprint or plan. Natural phenomena such as lakes and mountains are seen as having been purposely constructed by humans for human uses. Brainerd notes that artificialism, like finalism, "implies that no event can occur spontaneously" (p. 107). Everything has a place in some overall plan or design. From this belief, says Brainerd, comes a concept of causality that "fails to differentiate physical causes from psychological ones" (p. 107).

6. Does the child show animism, finalism, or artificialism in his thinking? What behaviors give evidence for this kind of thinking? What evidence is there for the child's general understanding of causality, of cause and effect relationships.

The *space* concept involves awareness of how objects are located in space, of objects' relative positions, and of the amount of space needed to accommodate or contain an object. Some concept of space is needed just to move from place to place without bumping into things, or to find one's way without getting lost.

The concept of *time* involves an understanding of past, present, and future, and of duration, which is how long something lasts. Does the child refer to something he did yesterday or is going to do tomorrow? Does he have a grasp of relational terms such as *before, during,* and *after*? Does he say such things as, "I have to wash my hands before I eat" or "Daddy always drinks coffee after he eats"?

7. Does the child demonstrate an understanding of space and time? How does he show this understanding? How complete does it seem to be?

You should also be alert to the child's factual knowledge. What general kinds of information does she have? Can the child name many objects, persons, or animals? Does she know where she lives (address, city); does she have knowledge of some events that are current in the news? This factual information is knowledge in the "narrow sense" and can be thought of as part of the child's intellectual development and behavior.

8. What factual information does the child have, and how does he use those facts in his dealings with others?

There are other cognitive "contents" that are relevant to the "preschool period" of the lifespan, but we obviously cannot cover all of these. There is one other kind of ability, however, that we feel is especially appropriate to your understanding of preschool children's intelligence, namely the ability to represent mentally the world and its various aspects. Ruth Saunders and Ann Bingham-Newman (1984) offer an excellent account of six characteristics of representation ability. These characteristics can be said to identify the types or levels of representation that are possible for the preoperational child (and for older children and adults, as well). Let's look at these briefly (please see Saunders and Bingham-Newman, pp. 137–138).

(1) The ability to have three-dimensional objects represent or stand for other objects. This ability can be expressed under at least three conditions or circumstances: (a) when both objects are very much alike (p. 137), (b) when both objects are not much alike, and (c) when the child constructs a model of some real object by using a variety of other objects.

(2) The ability to recognize and use two-dimensional objects such as pictures or drawings to represent another real object or setting. The authors cite an example of "using a picture of a doctor's office to create the atmosphere for a dramatic play episode" (p. 137).

(3) The ability to denote objects by exhibiting actions that are usually performed on or with those objects, such as "making a pounding motion to stand for a hammer or a dribbling motion to stand for a basketball" (p. 137).

(4) The ability to represent beings that are alive by mimicking actions or behaviors that are associated with them—for example, moving one's arms to imitate an elephant's trunk (p. 137).

(5) The ability to represent a real event through the use of an abbreviated action or series of actions. This can involve making just a few movements to

stand for a lot of movements that, in an actual situation, take a considerably longer period of time. Saunders and Bingham-Newman give the example of a child bringing "a spoon to the mouth three times to stand for eating breakfast" (p. 137).

(6) The ability to express an idea in a number of different ways.

Observation Objectives

To sensitize you to the way children think and to the kinds of information they might know and are capable of learning. To observe how children differ in their cognitive abilities and styles. To become aware of how preschool, preoperational children mentally represent their world.

Procedure

If you can, select two children of different ages as the subjects of your observations. A five-year-old and a two- or three-year-old would be best. If this is not possible, randomly select two children who are in the observation setting. *Using the narrative description method,* record in as much detail as you can the children's behaviors and the context of those behaviors. *Devote about 10 or 15 minutes to each child.* Then examine the narrative description and describe each child's cognitive characteristics. Write a summary cognitive profile of the two children. How well do the children fit Piaget's sensorimotor stage of development? What representational abilities do the children demonstrate? Describe specifically the behaviors or characteristics that, to you, indicate functioning within a particular category of representational ability. As a final step, compare the two children's level of mental functioning. What can the older child do that the younger one cannot? Which child demonstrates more egocentric behavior? How do they differ in the way they mentally represent the world and its objects or events? As well, how are they alike in all of these areas of cognitive functioning?

Exercise 17-4: Language Development

Background Information

Language is one of the more prominent behaviors in the preschool child. The preschooler is rapidly acquiring speech vocabulary and is refining his grammar and syntax to conform more closely to adult speech patterns. For many people, language is an indication of intellectual and social progress. In this exercise, you will be concerned with describing and analyzing the child's speech, determining such things as the depth and variety of her vocabulary, characteristic sentence structure, and the syntactical forms the child is capable of using. In later exercises, you will be asked to observe and record children's social uses of language beyond the present unit's emphasis on egocentric and sociocentric speech.

Let us look at the child's speech in terms of Piaget's concepts of egocentrism and sociocentrism. *Egocentric speech* is speech that does not take the other person into account; it is speech that, for all practical purposes, is private. There is no real effort to communicate with the other person; therefore, whatever is said is meaningful only to the speaker. Piaget identified three types of egocentric speech: (a) *monologue*, in which the individual talks only to himself and with no other persons present; (b) *repetition*, in which the individual repeats words and phrases over and over again as if to practice them or as if he simply enjoyed making the sounds; and (c) *collective monologue*, in which two or more persons are talking together but none of them is paying attention to what the others are saying. Each "conversation" is independent of the other conversation.

Socialized Speech, on the other hand, is public speech. It is intended to communicate with someone and each person takes into account what the others are saying and responds accordingly.

1. Does the child engage in egocentric or socialized speech? What are the circumstances under which these types of speech are used?

   Vocabulary is the foundation of speech. We communicate by putting individual words together into properly constructed sentences and paragraphs. Presumably, the greater the number of words in our vocabularies, the greater the number and variety of sentences and ideas we can utter and transmit to others. Words have different meanings and serve different purposes. Moreover, words must be placed in the correct position within a sentence; thus, there are rules of grammar and syntax.

2. What do you observe about the child's vocabulary?

   In particular, examine the child's speech for words that express relations and oppositions, for example, words such as *and, or, not, same, different, more, less, instead, if, then,* and *because.* Also, how varied or rich is the child's vocabulary when she talks about the world and the people and things in it? Think in terms of general classes or categories of objects, persons, and events, and then assess how many different words the child uses to discuss those categories. For example, one can talk about animals, people, colors, shapes, vehicles, feelings, weather, food, and buildings, among many others. Each of these words (or concepts) represents a general class of phenomena. Therefore, how many different animals can the child specifically name or talk about: dog, cat, squirrel, tiger, fox, sheep, lamb, and so forth? The child may have only a few specific words representing members of the class, animals. Assess the child's ability in the other categories in the same way.

   Sentence structure is also an important aspect of speech. Structure refers to such things as the *types* of sentences the child uses: questions, imperatives (i.e., commands or directions), sentences that contain a subject and an object. Does the child form compound sentences (two sentences separated by a conjunction); sentences containing a main clause and a subordinate clause (e.g., "I'll go with you if you play with me first."); and sentences containing *relative clauses* (e.g., "The boy who hit me is over there.").

3. Examine the child's speech for the type of sentences he uses. What is the apparent extent of such usage; that is, does the child have a wide or narrow variety of sentence types?

Finally, there is the area of *syntactical forms*. These refer to how various types of words are used within a sentence to convey meaning. Syntactical forms also refer to how various words in a sentence are positioned relative to one another to convey meaning. For example, we speak of forms of *to be*, as illustrated by sentences such as "Johnny *is* big" and "My mommy *was* here." There are also words that take the "ing" ending: "Sam is hitt*ing* Billy" and "The children were walk*ing* across the street." Then there are words that take the *infinitive form*, such as "I want *to watch* TV" and "He wanted *to go* with his mother." There are also the various *tenses*; past, present, and future, to mention only the simple tenses. ("I *went* to the store"; "She *is playing* here with me"; "My mother *will go* to work on Monday.")

4. What kinds of syntactical forms does the child use in her speech? What can you say about how she uses the various parts of speech that include:

singular and plural forms: one bird and two birds; one man and two men.

possessive forms: my book; their house; his car.

verb forms (singular and plural): They don't eat here. He doesn't come very often. The boxers hit each other hard.

pronouns: you, me, they, us, I, him.

adverbs: She walked *slowly* across the room. He ate *quickly* and left.

adjectives: The *red* shoes; the *big* building.

prepositional forms or phrases: He went *to* the blackboard; The cat hid *under* the couch.

Observation Objectives

To learn about the language production abilities of preschool children, and how children of preschool age use language as a means of social interaction.

Procedure

In this exercise, you will most likely be performing a group observation. You are to choose *two to three children* who are playing together or are involved with each other in some way. (A legitimate exception to a group observation is any occasion when a child is talking to him- or herself, such as in the case of self-regulation of behavior, or in language play [see Exercise 17-5 for a description of this kind of play], or in other circumstances in which the child is exhibiting language skills outside of a social context.) If the group breaks up during the observation session, complete your notes and then find a similar group and repeat the process. Your purpose is to observe and record the language behaviors of children who are engaging in social exchanges. You will be using the *event sampling method* to record instances of language use. You will also record the children's specific use of language to communicate with one another. As much as possible, record their speech word for word; also be sure to include data about the social and emotional aspects of the situation.

Exercise 17-5: Play

Background Information

Play is considered by some psychologists to be the most important activity in which the young child engages. Indeed, play activities pervade the lives of children from infancy throughout childhood. Some play seems obviously linked to the child's observation of adults; other play seems to stem from the child's fantasies and from experiences that she finds particularly enjoyable.

There are a number of explanations of the major purpose of play. These range from play as getting rid of excess energy to play as a means of socio-emotional expression. Play can be a group or an individual activity. Play is dis-

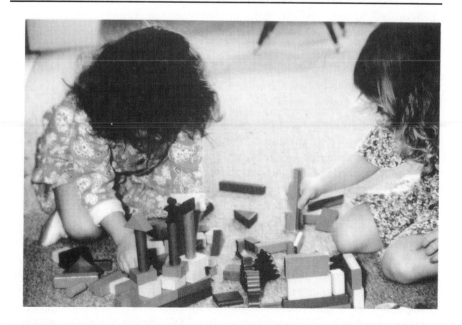

Figure 17-3   Children engaged in parallel play—playing beside but not with each other.

tinguished from non-play behavior by its special characteristics, the most important of which are its voluntary nature and its complete structuring by the participants, with little regard for outside regulation. When play is governed by consistent rules, we say children are playing *games*. These rules give play a social dimension. The participants must put their own personal wishes into the background and abide by the requirements of the game and the wishes of the larger group.

Some might argue that everything that children do is play. "Play is children's work," as the saying goes. We take the position that play is indeed serious business and that it serves a critical role in children's development. But it is not unreasonable to argue that even in young children, play can be distinguished from non-play. For example, if play, as has been theorized, must have the characteristic of *voluntary behavior for its own sake*, then any activity that is "forced" or promoted and monitored by adults is not, technically speaking, play. In this view, then, is a child who is bouncing a ball because he was told by his mother to "go outside and play with the ball," actually playing? We would only propose that it would not be inappropriate to classify some behaviors as falling into the category of play if reasonable justification can be found for the decision. In any event, the categories and forms of play we have provided should make the decision relatively easy to make.

Grace Craig (1989) specifies six categories or *forms* of play that depend on particular characteristics and functions. As Craig notes, these categories of play will overlap with one another; they are not mutually exclusive or exhaustive:

1. *Sensory Pleasure.* "The aim of this kind of play," says Craig, "is sensory experience in and for itself" (p. 255). This kind of play instructs children regarding their "bodies, senses, and the qualities of things in their environment" (p. 255).

2. *Play with Motion.* This is physical movement enjoyed for its own sake. As Craig points out, "play with motion is often begun by an adult and provides infants with some of their earliest social experiences" (p. 255).

3. *Rough-and-Tumble Play.* Craig notes that although this kind of play is often discouraged by teachers and parents, there is evidence that it is beneficial to children. Along with exercise and the release of energy, rough-and-tumble play teaches children how to "handle their feelings, to control their impulses, and to filter out negative behaviors that are inappropriate in a group" (p. 255). It also provides large-muscle exercise.

4. *Play with Language.* This kind of play involves experimentation with language rhythms and cadences, the mixing up of words to make new meanings, the use of language to poke fun at the world and to verify their grasp of reality (Craig, p. 255). There apparently is no concern with using language to communicate; children concentrate on the language itself by manipulating its sounds, patterns, and meanings. Interestingly enough, Craig also notes that children use language play "as a buffer against expressions of anger" (p. 255).

Figure 17-4 Solitary play—the child is focused exclusively on his own activity.

Citing Judith Schwartz (1981), Craig describes three kinds of language play.

1. There is the regular repetition of "letters and words in a steady beat: La la la / Lol li pop / La la la / Lol li pop" (p. 257).
2. There is play consisting of patterns of words "as if they were practicing a grammatical drill or sentences using the same words: Hit it / Sit it / Slit it / Mit it. And: There is the light. / Where is the light? / Here is the light" (p. 257).
3. There is "the less frequent kind of play" in which "children play with the meaning of words or invent words to fit meanings" (p. 257). She gives the examples of "San Diego, Sandiego, Sandi Ego / San Diego, Sandi Ego / Eggs aren't sandy!" (p. 257).

Craig proposes that children engage in language play because it is funny, it gives them the opportunity "to practice and master the grammar and words they are learning," and it allows them "to control their experiences" (p. 257). She notes that older children use language to structure their play, perhaps through the use of rituals that, when followed, allow them to control the experience.

5. *Dramatic Play and Modeling.* The taking on of roles or models is considered a major type of play. This involves such activities or behaviors as playing house, imitating a parent going to work, pretending to be a policeman, nurse, or truck driver (Craig, p. 257). What's entailed here, says Craig, is not just an imitation of whole patterns of behavior, but also such elements as "fan-

tasy and novel ways of interaction" (p. 257). She notes further that children come to understand various social relationships, rules, and other aspects of their culture by way of imitative play.

6. *Games, Rituals, and Competitive Play.* This last type of play is perhaps the most sophisticated. It involves rules and specific goals, decisions about taking turns, setting up guidelines about what is and is not allowed, and so on. These games and the activities they require help to develop cognitive skills— learning rules, understanding the sequence of cause and effect, realizing the results of various actions, learning about winning and losing, and learning to fit and adjust one's behavior to certain permissible patterns and rules (in Craig, p. 257; see also Herron & Sutton-Smith, 1971; Kamii & DeVries, 1980).

John Dworetsky (1987) cites what he calls "five descriptors" of play. He draws from the work of Rubin, Fein, & Vandenberg (1983) and Smith & Vollstedt (1985), who conclude that "the greater the number of descriptors that can be applied to any given situation, the more likely people are to call those circumstances play" (Dworetsky, p. 368). Let's look briefly at these descriptors, which in essence simply isolate different aspects of behavior that are considered to be indicative of play.

1. *Intrinsic motivation.* This simply means that behavior is motivated or prompted from within the individual, and it's "done for its own sake and not to satisfy social demands or bodily functions" (p. 369).
2. *Positive affect.* Play is pleasurable or fun to do.
3. *Nonlaterality.* This means that the behavior "does not follow a serious pattern or sequence"; it has a pretend quality about it (p. 369).
4. *Means/end.* Here the means are emphasized rather than the ends of the activity. Primary interest is in the behavior itself and not in any goals or outcomes that may be achieved.
5. *Flexibility.* This simply means that the behavior isn't rigid but shows pliability in form and context across various situations.

Observation Objectives

To study play behavior from a group or an individual perspective. To analyze children's behavior according to specific descriptive criteria and thereby determine whether that behavior is play or non-play; and to analyze the content of children's interaction patterns and determine into which of Parten's six classifications of play or social interaction those patterns can be put.

Procedure

This exercise consists of two parts. In Part I, you will be using a *narrative description format.* You may observe and record individuals, groups, or both. *Observe at least three individual children, or two groups, for 10 to 15 minutes on each occasion.* Then analyze your descriptive data and draw conclusions as to whether the activity you have recorded is play or non-play activity. Support your decisions by interpreting your data according to Craig's six types of play and Dworetsky's five descriptors discussed above. Indicate, where possible, the kind of play you have observed in each instance and which of the descriptors seem to apply to the behaviors you have recorded. If you believe a behavioral episode is not play, explain also why you reached that decision.

In Part II of this exercise you will be using the *event sampling format*. Your purpose is to look for behavioral events that fit into Parten's six categories of play or social interaction (see Table 7-3c). You will not necessarily observe particular preselected individual children or groups of children, as you did in Part I. Rather than taking in all behavior as it occurs (narrative description), you will have to wait for the occurrence of a particular behavioral event that fits into one of Parten's categories (event sampling). Putting a behavior into a specific category will, for the purposes of this exercise, be the equivalent of making an interpretation. Consequently, there are no spaces specially designated for interpretive comments.

Exercise 17-6: Emotional Behavior

Background Information

Emotions are such a basic part of our psychological beings that we sometimes take them for granted. Some of our emotions are clearly identifiable by us. We know when we are angry, frightened, or joyous. At other times, however, we can have feelings that are not so clear; we may not be able to label what we feel. Whatever the case, emotions are internal experiences that are private and directly accessible only to the individual experiencing them. This being so, we cannot state with certainty what emotion another person is feeling. She must tell us, or we must infer the emotion on the basis of the individual's behavior, facial expressions, and the event that preceded and might have caused the feeling. A child's emotional behaviors become more refined and extensive as she matures. Therefore, a four- or five-year-old will typically be more emotionally expressive than a two-year-old. But, what is the role of emotions; what is their significance? Let us examine for a moment the concept of emotions from a more developmental or perhaps theoretical perspective.

Carroll Izard, in his book *Human Emotions* (1977), asks whether there is a need to study emotions. He notes that "there is a wide range of scientific opinion regarding the nature and importance of emotions" (p. 3). He goes on to give some of these scientific opinions, but very early on, he reaches his own conclusion: "My view is that the emotions constitute the primary *motivational system* for human beings" (italics added, p. 3).

Regardless of your own specific opinion on this question, it's a fact that emotions are here to stay. It's also a fact that on a personal level, emotions—our own and those of children—are extremely important. They are also important on a "professional level." Traditionally, for example, early childhood education programs emphasized children's social and emotional development, and the current stress on cognitive development is of relatively recent origin.

Stanley Greenspan, a practicing psychiatrist involved in research in infant and child development, and his wife Nancy Thorndike Greenspan, a health economist, wrote a book entitled *First Feelings* (1985), in which they deal with the emotional development of children from birth to age four years. Of interest to us are the six "milestones" that characterize or define children's emotional growth and development. In this chapter, we shall briefly discuss only the fifth and sixth emotional milestones, which begin at 18 months of age and go through 48 months of age. This span covers the preschool years, and we intend that you use them as guidelines for determining a child's approximate stage of emotional development or maturity. The earlier stages (1 through 4) are covered in Chapters 15 and 16. The Greenspans' six emotional milestones were arrived at by "closely observing babies' behavior, emotional reactions, and ways of relating to us" (pp. 3–4). You will be asked to do something similar, but in your case, the theoretical groundwork has already been laid. You will only be asked to put your observations into this theoretical framework and to draw some tentative conclusions regarding a child's level of emotional development.

Let us point out again, however, that our major purpose is not to provide you with a means of *intervening* in children's lives as therapists, or even as teachers. Rather, in this exercise, we want to give you a theoretical framework within which to observe and record children's actions in the particular area of emotional development and behavior.

Emotional Milestones During the Preschool Years

The fifth stage or milestone identified by the Greenspans' occurs between eighteen and thirty-six months of age. By the time children reach this stage, they have learned how objects work, and they continue to improve their ability to "organize complicated social and emotional patterns . . . " (p. 5), an ability that becomes evident in stage 4. This stage 4 competence increases to enable the child to "create. . .objects in his own mind's eye" (Greenspan and Greenspan, p. 5). Mental images of his mother, for example, allow him to deal with her—and with objects—even in her absence. As the Greenspans also point out, this ability to form mental images and impressions (to "create [one's own] experiences" or "construct her own ideas," say the Greenspans) also gives the child the ability to dream "in an adult way" (p. 6). This occurs later than fifteen months of age—perhaps by about two or two and one-half years of age. A child in this stage can also engage in pretend play.

The sixth and final milestone, which occurs between thirty and forty-eight months, takes children into what the Greenspans describe as "the emotional realms of pleasure and dependency, curiosity, anger, self-discipline or setting their own limits, even empathy and love" (p. 6). Additionally, children learn "to separate make-believe from reality and are able to work with ideas and to plan and anticipate" (p. 6). In this stage, according to the Greenspans, a three-and-a-half-year-old child can say such things as "I dreamed there were witches under my bed. Tonight I'm going to dream about kittens" (p. 6).

It's important to emphasize here that the child's emotional development and his intellectual development go hand in hand, so to speak. As the Greenspans put it, the child

"... will now begin to organize and manipulate his ideas into a cause-and-effect understanding of his own emotions and the world that *begins to take reality into account* ... "

And,

"... just as your child learned to combine blocks to make an original house, now he can combine emotional ideas. He may create new feelings of shame and, eventually, guilt based on his own feelings about his "bad" wishes and behavior."

Further,

"He now emerges with the 'cause-and-effect' logic at the level of emotional ideas that he developed earlier at the level of behavior" (p. 173; italics added).

The Greenspans' work reveals the developmental course of the emotions, and it gives a hint of some of the changing content or focus of a child's emotional behavior. Therefore, part of your observation task will be to identify the specific content, character, and developmental level of children's emotional responses.

There is a broad range of emotions that children are ultimately capable of displaying. Since we have relied on such a considerable proportion of the Greenspans' work on this critical aspect of development, we shall adopt for use the seven areas of emotional functioning that they identify. These areas of functioning are "dependency, pleasure, love and intimacy, curiosity, assertiveness and exploration, protest and anger, and self-discipline." Also noted are the emotions that are related to these areas: "(feelings of) loss, sadness, anxiety, fear, shame, and guilt" (Greenspan and Greenspan 1985, p. 8).

We will briefly discuss only a few of the above-mentioned emotions or areas of emotional functioning. We want to deal with aggression (which, in the context of the Greenspans' terminology, can be thought of as assertiveness, protest, and anger), dependency, and fear. We hesitate to focus on the negative feelings or behaviors, but they are usually of some concern to parents and adults. Inappropriate aggression might be of particular concern to parents and teachers, especially aggression that threatens the safety of others or that is directed against adults.

Aggression, like some other types of behaviors, is used both to identify particular behaviors that have specific characteristics and to describe a particular personality *trait*. A trait is a tendency to behave in certain ways under certain circumstances. Each of these uses has accompanying problems. Aggressive behavior is frequently defined as behavior that is intended to physically or psychologically hurt another person (or oneself) or to damage or destroy property. An important issue is whether a behavior is *intentionally* aggressive or simply an accidental occurrence. Further, it is argued by some that for a behavior to be termed aggressive, the aggressor must feel anger or hostility toward the "victim" and must derive satisfaction from hurting the victim. This kind of aggression is called *hostile aggression*. In contrast to hostile aggression, there can be cases where the aggressor is interested only in getting some object from the victim or achieving some goal. This is called *instrumental aggression*, and it need not involve anger or hostility.

Be certain that you label as hostile aggression only those behaviors that you believe are purposely intended to hurt another person (include both physical and verbal aggression).

1. Observe the child's behavior for instances of aggression, either toward another child or an adult, or toward objects in the environment.

2. What kinds of situations or frustrations make the child angry? What behaviors by other people anger the child? How does she express her anger?

Dependency consists of such behaviors as clinging or maintaining proximity to adults or other children, seeking approval, recognition, assistance, attention, and reassurance, and striving for affection and support. It is important to recognize that all of us are dependent. The issue is to what degree and under what circumstances we show our dependency. It is also useful to distinguish between two basic types of dependency: (a) *instrumental dependency*, which essentially is the necessary reliance we have on others for certain things that are beyond our capacity to do; and (b) *emotional dependency*, which is a need to be near others and to have their support, affec-

Figure 17-5   A face can say a lot to a teacher

tion, and reassurance. It can also be the unwillingness or the self-perceived inability to do things for oneself that one can or should be able to do.

It is important that, where possible, you distinguish instrumental dependency from emotional dependency behaviors. It is also important to note that as children mature, the characteristics of their dependency behaviors change. Very young children are likely to show clinging and proximity-seeking behaviors, whereas older children, who also have greater cognitive abilities, will likely seek attention and approval.

3. In what situations or activities is the child dependent, and, for example, seeks the presence, direction, or assistance of others? In what situations is the child independent and does not seek direction or assistance from others?

Fear is demonstrated by such behaviors as crying, withdrawing, seeking help, and avoiding the fear-producing situation. Fear can promote both dependency and aggressive behaviors. Nonetheless, fear can be expressed in such a way that it, and not aggression or dependency, is the primary emotion.

4. What kinds of objects or situations appear to scare the child? In what ways does the child express his fears? How does he deal with his fears (e.g., by withdrawing, confronting the fearful situation, seeking help)?

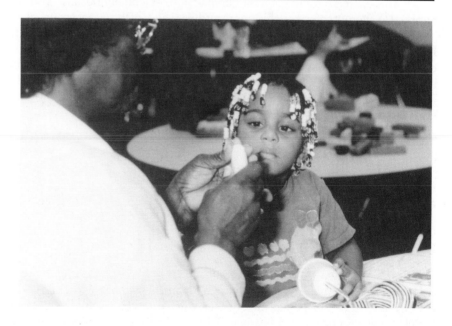

Figure 17-6 Instrumental dependency. This child relies on her teacher to complete a task she cannot handle herself.

In addition to the emotional behaviors just discussed, there are other feelings that children are capable of experiencing and expressing. You should be alert to as many of the child's affective states as possible. For example, there are the feelings of pleasure and displeasure, frustration, boredom, and sadness. Like adults, children will differ as to how accurately they can identify what they feel and, like adults, children differ in how they explain their feelings. However, children may lack the ability to verbally express their feelings.

5. What kinds of things does the child appear to find pleasant? What activities, play materials, stories, games, and so on, seem to be particularly attractive to the child? How does he express that pleasure?

6. What kinds of things are unpleasant or uncomfortable for the child? In what situations does the child appear to be ill at ease? How does she express her displeasure?

As a final topic, and one that pertains to all of the preceding, consider the following question:

7. Are all or most of the child's feelings expressed with equal strength, or does their intensity vary with the particular feeling or situation?

This exercise could get a bit complicated, essentially because you will be asked to attempt some conclusions regarding which of the Greenspans' stages of development your particular child or children can be placed. Additionally, in this exercise you will be trying to gain some general understanding of the child's emotional behaviors, of the range of her emotions and the kinds of situations that prompt these behaviors. Again, you can only infer what the child is feeling from the overt behaviors you have witnessed; you cannot observe emotions directly.

Observation Objectives

To learn about the differences in children's emotional behaviors and the range of emotional responses in preschool children. To determine the level of a child's emotional development according to stages five and six of Greenspan and Greenspan's six milestones or stages of emotional development.

Procedure

There are two parts to this exercise. *In Part I, select three children* and, using the *event sampling technique,* watch for and record behaviors or patterns of behavior that would indicate or reflect at which milestone a child's emotional development can be located. Objectively describe those behaviors, and specify as precisely as you can why you think the behaviors you've recorded do in fact indicate a particular level of emotional development.

In Part II, *staying with the same three children as in Part I,* and using the *narrative description technique,* observe and record each child's behavior for a period of *10 to 15 minutes.* Record in as much detail as possible, and be sure to include descriptions of the physical and social context as they apply to the emotional behaviors observed. Interpret or comment on each child, using the questions and background information provided as guides. Finally, compare the three children. Look at the range of emotional expression, intensity of expression, and what evokes emotional responses. In short, summarize how the children differ from one another in this area of functioning.

Exercise 17-7: Social Development and Peer Interactions

Background Information

Some believe that social development should be the most important concern of the early education curriculum in particular, and the early childhood years in general. It is during this period of life that the child's horizons are expanding dramatically, and his cognitive and emotional abilities are becoming more and more suited to interacting socially with others.

Social behaviors are behaviors that are oriented toward and influenced by other persons. A *social interaction* is a situation where two or more individuals take one another into account. So, for example, Alex and Thomas are in a social interaction when Alex influences Thomas and is also influenced by Thomas.

The concept of *social skills* is familiar to most of us. Social skills include such things as the ability to get along with others, to influence or persuade others without aggression, to resolve conflicts and disagreements in a socially approved way, and generally to be able to imitate and sustain friendships and social interactions. Social skills can involve the ability to be a leader in a group, as well as a follower who can work for the group's best interests.

Social skills are a product of decreasing egocentrism and increasing sociocentrism. Both of these are supported by increasing cognitive and intellectual skills, along with increased contact with others in social situations.

There are many areas of development and behavior that pertain to social behavior. It should also be noted that much of what the child does during the preschool day is done within a social context. Consequently, most if not all of your observation exercises in this chapter have a social component.

1. How does the child show awareness of and sensitivity to others? How does she express concern for others' feelings and needs?

2. How does the child respond in a situation in which he is a follower? Does he follow the directions of the leader or does he refuse to cooperate? Is the child sensitive to the needs of the group and is he willing to play a follower role where it is appropriate? In this regard, does the child follow whatever rules appear to be operating in the situation? Does the child share, take turns, and so on?

3. If the child is a leader, how does she behave in that role? Does she offer suggestions or does she make demands on others? How do the other children respond to her efforts to lead? Does the child instill confidence in others or does she tend to alienate them?

4. How does the child initiate contact with other children? That is, how does he try to join a group, start a new activity or participate in one already going on, or strike up a friendship? How do others respond to the child's efforts?

5. How does the child settle arguments or conflicts—with physical force, verbal threats, efforts to compromise, appeal to an adult, and so on?

Observation Objectives

To identify the social "statuses" of various children in a group. To learn about children's differing styles of social interaction.

Procedure

There are two parts to this exercise. In Part I, try to identify the leaders in particular social/peer interaction situations. Observe and record the behaviors of these leaders and the behaviors of the other children in the group. Do the following:

1. Compare and contrast the leadership styles or behaviors of the several different leaders you have observed. "Style" here simply refers to the way in

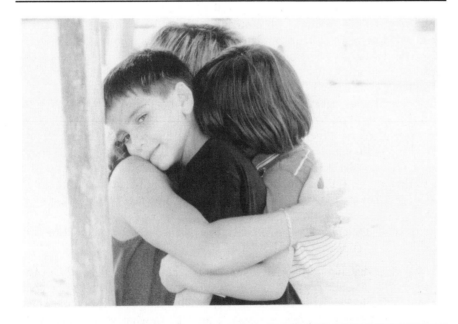

Figure 17-7   Proximity-seeking behavior, a sign of emotional dependency.

which the child asserts his or her leadership: through force, verbal persuasion, "charisma" or sheer positive force of personality, and

2. Compare and contrast the behaviors of the leaders with the behaviors of the followers or others in the group. How are they different? How are they alike? How do the leaders get the others to follow them? Is a child a leader in one group or situation, and a follower in another?

In Part II, construct a chart or diagram (perhaps the best such diagram would be a *sociogram*) that will enable you to determine who are the most and the least popular children in the group—popular in the sense of such indications as the number of social interactions in which they engage, and the number of other children who seek them out or show signs of wanting to be with them. Then observe and record the behaviors of the most popular child and the least popular child in the group. Examine your data record and compare the interaction styles and general behavioral characteristics of these children.

By the way, the sociogram was developed by a psychiatrist named J. L. Moreno. Sociograms, says sociologist Rodney Stark (1985), are "charts showing the social networks within a group" (p. 22). Networks are relationships within a group. Sociograms are often constructed by asking members of a group questions such as: Who are your closest friends? Whom do you admire the most? With whom would you most like to take a trip? Asking such questions may not be possible or desirable with preschoolers; you therefore may have to observe the interactions and social exchanges that occur among the children and calculate a sociogram from that data. A sample sociogram is given immediately below.

Observation Exercise 17-1

Part I: The Preschool Child in the Physical Environnment

Observer's Name _____

Child/Children Observed _____

Child's/Children's Age(s) _____ Child's/Children's Sex _____

Observation Context (home, child care center, preschool, school) _____

Date of Observation _____ Time Begun _____ Time Ended _____

Brief Description of Physical and Social Characteristics of Observation Setting:

_____

DIAGRAMS OF PHYSICAL ENVIRONMENTS

Inside

Outside

Observation Exercise 17-1

Continued

Part II: The Preschool Child in the Physical Environment

Observer's Name _____

Child/Children Observed _____

Child's/Children's Age(s) _____ Child's/Children's Sex _____

Observation Context (home, child care center, preschool, school) _____

Date of Observation _____ Time Begun _____ Time Ended _____

Brief Description of Physical and Social Characteristics of Observation Setting:

_____

OBJECTIVE BEHAVIORAL DESCRIPTIONS (OBD) AND INTERPRETATIONS:
  Narrative Description

OBD 1:   [Time begun _____   Time ended _____]

Interpretation 1: Location 1:

OBD 2:   [Time begun _____   Time ended _____]

Interpretation 2: Location 2:

OBD 3:   [Time begun _____   Time ended _____]

Interpretation 3: Location 3:

Continue with OBDs and Interpretations for as long as needed.
Summary of Behavioral Differences:

Observation Exercise 17-2

Physical Growth and Motor Functioning

Observer's Name _____

Child/Children Observed _____

Child's/Children's Age(s) _____   Child's/Children's Sex _____

Observation Context (home, child care center, preschool, school) _____

Date of Observation _____   Time Begun _____   Time Ended _____

Brief Description of Physical and Social Characteristics of Observation Setting:

_____

OBJECTIVE BEHAVIORAL DESCRIPTIONS (OBD) AND INTERPRETATIONS: *Event Sampling*

OBD 1: Child 1 (age   ):   [Time begun _____   Time ended _____]

Interpretation 1: Child 1

OBD 2: Child 2 (age   ):   [Time begun _____   Time ended _____]

Interpretation 2: Child 2

Continue for as many OBDs as are needed or desired.
Comparison of Children's Motor Behaviors:

Observation Exercise 17-3

Cognitive and Intellectual Behavior

Observer's Name _____

Child/Children Observed _____

Child's/Children's Age(s) _____ Child's/Children's Sex _____

Observation Context (home, child care center, preschool, school) _____

Date of Observation _____ Time Begun _____ Time Ended _____

Brief Description of Physical and Social Characteristics of Observation Setting:

_____

OBJECTIVE BEHAVIORAL DESCRIPTIONS (OBD) AND INTERPRETATIONS:
 Narrative Description

OBD 1: Child 1 (age): **[Time begun** _____ **Time ended** _____]

Interpretation 1: Child 1

OBD 2: Child 2 (age): **[Time begun** _____ **Time ended** _____]

Interpretation 2: Child 2

Continue for as many OBDs as are needed or desired.
Summary Child 1:

Summary Child 2:

Comparison: Child 1 with Child 2:

Contrast Between: Child 1 and Child 2:

Observation Exercise 17-4

Language Development and Behavior

Observer's Name _____

Child/Children Observed _____

Child's/Children's Age(s) _____   Child's/Children's Sex _____

Observation Context (home, child care center, preschool, school) _____

Date of Observation _____   Time Begun _____   Time Ended _____

Brief Description of Physical and Social Characteristics of Observation Setting:

_____

OBJECTIVE BEHAVIORAL DESCRIPTIONS (OBD) AND INTERPRETATIONS: *Event Sampling*

OBD 1:   [Time begun _____   Time ended _____]

Interpretation 1:

OBD 2:   [Time begun _____   Time ended _____]

Interpretation 2:

Continue for as many OBDs as are needed or desired.

Descriptive and Interpretive Summary of Group's Language Behavior:

Observation Exercise 17-5

Play: Part I

Observer's Name _____

Child/Children Observed _____

Child's/Children's Age(s) _____ Child's/Children's Sex _____

Observation Context (home, child care center, preschool, school) _____

Date of Observation _____ Time Begun _____ Time Ended _____

Brief Description of Physical and Social Characteristics of Observation Setting:

_____

OBJECTIVE BEHAVIORAL DESCRIPTIONS (OBD) AND INTERPRETATIONS:
Narrative Description

OBD 1: [Time begun _____ Time ended _____]
Interpretation 1:

OBD 2: [Time begun _____ Time ended _____]
Interpretation 2:

OBD 3: [Time begun _____ Time ended _____]
Interpretation 3:

OBD 4: [Time begun _____ Time ended _____]
Interpretation 4:

Continue for as many OBDs as are needed or desired.
Summary of Interpretive Comments:

Observation Exercise 17-5

Continued

Play: Part II (Parten's Play/Social Interaction Classifications)

Observer's Name _____

Child/Children Observed _____

Child's/Children's Age(s) _____   Child's/Children's Sex _____

Observation Context (home, child care center, preschool, school) _____

Date of Observation _____   Time Begun _____   Time Ended _____

Brief Description of Physical and Social Characteristics of Observation Setting:

_____

Part II: Play Description and Classification (Parten's Six Categories; see Table 7-3c):
   Event Sampling

Unoccupied Behavior:

Solitary Play:

Onlooker Behavior:

Parallel Play:

Associative Play:

Cooperative Play:

Summary of Interpretive Comments:

Observation Exercise 17-6

Part I: Level of Emotional Behavior or Development

Observer's Name _____

Child/Children Observed _____

Child's/Children's Age(s) _____ Child's/Children's Sex _____

Observation Context (home, child care center, preschool, school) _____

Date of Observation _____ Time Begun _____ Time Ended _____

Brief Description of Physical and Social Characteristics of Observation Setting:

_____

Part I: OBJECTIVE BEHAVIORAL DESCRIPTIONS (OBD) AND JUSTIFICATION OF EMOTIONAL LEVEL CHOSEN: *Event Sampling*

OBD 1 Child 1: [Time begun _____ Time ended _____]

Probable or Perceived Emotional Level:

OBD 2 Child 2: [Time begun _____ Time ended _____]

Probable or Perceived Emotional Level:

OBD 3 Child 3: [Time begun _____ Time ended _____]

Probable or Perceived Emotional Level:

Continue for as many OBDs as are needed or desired.

Summary of Differences in Level of Emotional Development (if any):

Observation Exercise 17-6

Continued

Part II: Emotional Behavior

Observer's Name _____

Child/Children Observed _____

Child's/Children's Age(s) _____   Child's/Children's Sex _____

Observation Context (home, child care center, preschool, school) _____

Date of Observation _____   Time Begun _____   Time Ended _____

Brief Description of Physical and Social Characteristics of Observation Setting:

_____

OBJECTIVE BEHAVIORAL DESCRIPTIONS (OBD) AND INTERPRETATIONS:
   Narrative Description

OBD 1 Child 1:   [Time begun _____   Time ended _____]

Interpretation 1:

OBD 2 Child 2:   [Time begun _____   Time ended _____]

Interpretation 2:

OBD 3 Child 3:   [Time begun _____   Time ended _____]

Interpretation 3:

Continue for as many OBDs as are needed or desired.
Summary of Behavioral Differences:

Summary of Behavioral Similarities:

Observation Exercise 17-7

Part I: Social Development and Peer Interaction

Observer's Name _____

Child/Children Observed _____

Child's/Children's Age(s) _____ Child's/Children's Sex _____

Observation Context (home, child care center, preschool, school) _____

Date of Observation _____ Time Begun _____ Time Ended _____

Brief Description of Physical and Social Characteristics of Observation Setting:

_____

OBJECTIVE BEHAVIORAL DESCRIPTIONS (OBD) AND INTERPRETATIONS:
Narrative Description

Leader 1:   [Time begun _____   Time ended _____]

Interpretive Comments 1:

Leader 1:   [Time begun _____   Time ended _____]

Interpretive Comments 2:

Leader 1:   [Time begun _____   Time ended _____]

Interpretive Comments 3:

Followers Situation 1:   [Time begun _____   Time ended _____]

Followers Situation 2:   [Time begun _____   Time ended _____]

Followers Situation 3:   [Time begun _____   Time ended _____]

Observation Exercise 17-7

Continued

Comparisons of Leaders:

Comparisons of Leaders and Followers:

Continue for as many OBDs and Interpretations of Leaders and Followers as are needed or desired.

Part II: Social Development and Peer Interaction

Observer's Name _____

Child/Children Observed _____

Child's/Children's Age(s) _____   Child's/Children's Sex _____

Observation Context (home, child care center, preschool, school) _____

Date of Observation _____   Time Begun _____   Time Ended _____

Brief Description of Physical and Social Characteristics of Observation Setting:

OBJECTIVE BEHAVIORAL DESCRIPTIONS (OBD) AND INTERPRETATIONS:
   Narrative Description

OBD 1 (Least Popular Child):   [Time begun _____   Time ended _____]

Interpretation 1: (Least Popular Child):

OBD 2 (Most Popular Child):   [Time begun _____   Time ended _____]

Interpretation 2: (Most Popular Child):

Continue for as many OBDs and Interpretations as are needed for Least and Most Popular Child.
Comparison of Least and Most Popular Child:

Middle Childhood—
The School-Age Years

PART **4**

Chapter Eighteen
The School-Age Years: *The Six-Year-Old Child*

Chapter Nineteen
The School-Age Years: *The Seven- and Eight-Year-Old Child*

Introduction and Preparation

The National Association for the Education of Young Children (NAEYC) defines early childhood as comprising the years from birth through eight. The latter three years in this age range typically would place children in the first, second, or third grades in the school system. Certainly six-, seven-, and eight-year-olds spend time in places other than the school classroom, but we think most would agree that, except for the summer, the majority of a school-age child's weekday is spent in the formal classroom setting. With regard to observation, therefore, we will assume that at least some of the forthcoming observation exercises will be accomplished in some kind of formal education setting.

Although it depends on the particular school, of course, it is also probable that observations done in a school classroom will be more structured and controlled than those performed in a preschool classroom or a child care center. This means that you will have less latitude or freedom to move around or participate in the children's activities than you would have in a preschool or child care setting. A possible exception to this, of course, is if you are a teacher, a student teacher, or are in some way officially "connected" to the class, although regardless of your official or unofficial status, you will have to abide by the ethical standards that must govern all interactions with children. By all means, however, keep in mind that children of any age can be observed in settings of almost any number and description. Indeed, you have much to gain in your understanding of children of any age if you do observe them in many different kinds of settings and situations.

It is our pleasure, therefore, to offer the reader two new chapters that will cover the first three years of the period called *middle childhood.* We shall address most of the same functional behavioral areas that were addressed in the previous chapters. The years six through eight continue to see developmental changes in physical and motor abilities and behavior. Language and intellectual skills move along a rather inexorable path, barring any physical, emotional, or medical problems that would slow or interfere with their developmental course. Social and emotional behaviors change through the combination of experience and maturation. And yes, children of these ages even continue to play, although their play content and motivations are dramatically different from what they were just a few years earlier.

The general format for the following series of observation exercises—Chapters 18 and 19—will be similar to the format of the exercises in the previous chapters. There is one functional/behavioral area that we addressed previously that will not be dealt with in this section, namely, the child's response to particular characteristics and requirements of the physical environment (see Observation Exercise 17-1).

The observation exercises will cover relevant behavioral and competency areas in a general way, which means that you are at liberty to apply them in whatever situations and in whatever manner suits your *legitimate* purposes. The premise is that, with regard to observation as observation, and leaving aside such aspects as language's social, pragmatic functions, language—to take just one behavioral domain— is language, whether it is displayed, observed, recorded, and interpreted during a classroom learning activity or during a pickup game of soccer in a school play yard. We acknowledge, however, that you may be more interested in how the child talks about academic subject manner than in how he gives instructions to a teammate on how to score a goal. Nonetheless, in principle, not much will significantly change from one situation to the other with respect to the observation and recording skills that are required.

Chapter 18 deals only with the six-year-old child. The final chapter (Chapter 19) will combine the years seven and eight. This "separation" and combination have a precedent in other developmental texts. We can't speak for other authors' rationales, but one motive guiding the present text rests on Piaget's assertion that the period of concrete operations begins at about seven years of age (and ends at about eleven years of age). This means that, more or less technically, the six-year-old has not yet quite made the full transition out of the pre-operational period. This statement must be put into the context of a general assumption that does not apply to all six-year-olds. Piaget's hypothesis simply provides one line of demarcation among many others. Although we don't adopt Piaget as the ultimate authority on children's cognitive development, his ideas still have a prominent place in the developmental literature, a fact that should not be ignored despite the theories that are vying with his for attention and credibility.

HAPTER EIGHTEEN

The School-Age Years:
The Six-Year-Old Child

I. Physical Growth and Motor Functioning

Background Information

This is a time of transitions and significant gains in all of the developmental and behavioral areas. This transitional and "time-of-improvement" character can be discerned when one reads the child development literature. At least some authors describe the skills, abilities, and characteristics of school-age children by comparing and contrasting them with preschool children. Krantz (1994) *for instance,* provides us with a good summary of what physical growth and motor functioning are like during the general period of middle childhood. He notes that *although* "children's growth rate slows during the preschool years, significant changes in body size and proportion dramatically affect their motor skill development" (p. 371). This is a *useful* comparison that points out that even during the earlier preschool period, rapid changes influence the way a child looks and the way she functions or behaves. Growth slows even more after the preschool years, and children during the school-age years show significant ("extraordinary") gains in physical and motor development (Krantz 1994, p. 371). He states further: "Physical changes in size, proportion, strength, and endurance provide the foundation for significant improvements in children's motor skills" (p. 371).

Bukatko and Daehler (1995) also attest to the changes in motor skills and development that occur over a period of about two or three years. These changes are summarized in Table 18-1.

The tabular description is very brief, and it may not immediately suggest the scope of the behavioral differences that are displayed between the ages of four and six. We would suggest, however, that tying shoes and writing some numbers and words represent a rather significant jump in fine (small-muscle) motor ability. Keep in mind, too, that the six-year-old keeps all of the skills she had before she was six, which demonstrates the *cumulative* nature of development.

Bukatko and Daehler (1995) also note that during middle childhood motor skills improve with respect to the speed and complexity of movements. The child demonstrates more coordination and displays physical skills in a greater variety of situations and contexts than was possible at an earlier age (p. 187).

Table 18-1 Summary of Changes in Motor Skills and Development

Age	Functional or Skill Area
4–5 Years	The child • can walk down steps by alternating his feet. • can gallop and skip while leading with one foot and using the rear leg to propel himself forward • when throwing a ball, uses his body by transferring his weight forward to add force to the throw • tries to catch a ball with her hands instead of involving the arms and body • can eat with a fork • can engage in self-help skills such as dressing by herself
5–6 Years	• has the ability to walk across a balance beam • can long jump about three feet, and he can jump vertically into the air for about a foot • can now throw and catch much like an adult
6–7 Years	• can tie her shoes • can write some words and numbers

Adapted from Bukatko and Daehler (1995, p. 186)

Berk (1993) identifies and describes four "basic motor capacities" in which school-age children show significant gains. The first of these is *flexibility,* which Berk also describes through comparison and contrast. She notes that "compared to the movements of preschoolers, those of school-age children are more pliable and elastic, a difference that can be seen as children swing a bat, kick a ball, jump over a hurdle, or execute tumbling routines" (p. 403). *Balance* is the second capacity to see improvement. Although some preschoolers can walk a balance beam, for example, the school-age child walks a narrower beam than the younger child. Better balance is important, because it allows improvement in many other kinds of athletic performance: "...running, hopping, skipping, throwing, kicking, and the rapid change of direction required in many team sports" (Berk, 1993; p. 403). The third area of improvement is that of *agility.* Agility is reflected in quickness and accuracy of movement (p. 403). A number of activities the child engages in shows off his or her agility: jumping rope, hopscotch, and the multidirectional movements required in such activities as tag and soccer (Berk, pp. 403–404). Finally the *force* with which children perform their movements increases dramatically from early childhood. School-aged children throw and kick harder, jump farther, and run with greater speed and force than when they were preschoolers. Table 18-2 is a summary of some of Berk's descriptions.

Table 18-2 A Summary Description of Some Gross Motor Skills of a Child Age Six Years

Motor Area	Characteristics
Running	• Child's running speed is approximately 12 feet per second (Berk, p. 403); has good balance while running; can change direction fairly easily; enjoys vigorous physical activity such as running. skipping, jumping, an so on.
Jumping and Variations	• Can jump vertically about 4 inches; can long jump 3 feet from standing position (Berk, p. 403). By age 7 can jump with some accuracy from one square to another, as in hop scotch (Berk, p. 403).
Throwing	• Speed, accuracy, and distance in throwing increases more in boys than in girls. Differences in speed measured in feet per second (fps) are reflected by 39 fps for a ball thrown by a six-year-old boy versus 29 fps for a six-year-old girl. (Actual speed of throwing will not be possible to determine, but subjectively you should be able to detect differences when compared with a preschooler's throwing style and ability.)
Catching	• Child can now catch smaller balls and over greater distances than when he or she was a preschooler.
Batting	• "Batting motions become more effective with age, increasing in speed and accuracy and involving the entire body" (Berk, p. 403).
Dribbling	• Arm movements in dribbling are more sophisticated—smoother, more controlled and coordinated—than the earlier movements that are awkward and "slapping" in nature.

Adapted from Berk (1993; p. 403)

II. Cognitive and Intellectual Development and Behavior

Background Information: The "Cognitive Revolution"

Middle childhood is an interesting time, from a cognitive and intellectual point of view. Piaget's theory claims that the period of concrete operational thinking, which is the third of his four stages of cognitive development, extends from seven to about eleven years of age. Based on this then, technically, the six-year-old is in the "last phase" of the *preoperational period*. This does not mean that no six-year-old can function in the period of concrete operations, only—at least if Piaget is correct—that it is not typical for the six-year-old to function *primarily* in the later stage. Despite the possibility that the children you will observe will still be in the preoperational period, we will give you some background information that goes beyond the preoperational six years of age and into Piaget's stage of *concrete operational thinking*.

Steinberg and Meyer (1995) refer to what they call the "cognitive revolution" that occurs between 5 and 7 years of age. These authors identify some of the gains children make cognitively and intellectually during this period. These gains include a grasp of *conservation*, improved reasoning about *causation*, increasing *classification* skills, and an increasing ability to *manipulate symbols* (pp. 347–348).

According to Piaget, the preoperational child's reasoning is illogical and unsystematic, whereas the middle-childhood period allows just the opposite style of reasoning, namely, *the beginning of* logical and systematic *thinking and reasoning* (e.g., see Krantz 1994). It's important to note, however, that moving from one kind of reasoning to the other involves a gradual shift or transition, not an abrupt one. Here, the term "cognitive revolution" can be replaced by the term "5-to-7 shift" or "5-to-7 transition." Krantz (1994) points out that for Piaget, "children's reasoning during the 5-to-7 shift [is] *intuitive*..." (p. 397; bold-face type original). As Krantz puts it, "With intuitive reasoning, children often get the right solutions to problems but without understanding the underlying principles" (p. 398). He describes two other characteristics of intuitive thought that are worth mentioning: It is *inconsistent across situations,* and it is *tentative* even when a solution is correct. The first characteristic means that a cognitive skill or decision "breaks down" or is abandoned if the original situation in which the child reasons correctly is changed. The second characteristic means that the child is easily persuaded from his or her decision about a solution to a problem. The child is insecure and uncertain about the correctness of his or her problem solution.

Information Processing and Sociocultural Theory

Piaget's theory is not the only one to try to explain children's cognitive development. Information processing theory and Vygotsky's sociocultural theory of cognitive development also compete for psychologists' attention and perhaps loyalty. Vygotsky's views are discussed in the text *Child Psychology* by Vasta, Haith, and Miller (1995). Note in this passage the brief, but significant, comparison with Piaget.

> For him [Vygotsky], the individual's development is a product of his or her culture. Development, in Vygotsky's theory, referred largely to mental development, such as thought, language, and reasoning processes. These abilities were assumed to develop through social interactions with others (especially parents) and thus represented the shared knowledge of the culture. Mental abilities and processes similarly were viewed in terms of the historical sequence of events that produced them. *Whereas Piaget believed that all children's cognitive development follows a very similar pattern of stages, Vygotsky saw intellectual abilities as being much more specific to the culture in which the child was reared* (p. 23; italics added).

Vygotsky's emphasis on cultural influences on cognitive development is significant. Spodek and Saracho (1994) discuss Vygotsky's distinction between natural development and cultural development. *Natural development,* as the term might suggest to you, is development that is the result of maturation, whereas *cultural development* "relates to language and reasoning ability" (p. 77). Spodek and Saracho discuss the interaction between language and thought as follows:

> ... an individual's thinking patterns are products of the activities practiced in the culture in which the individual grows up. Moreover, advanced modes of thought (conceptual thinking) need to be verbally communicated to children; thus, language is an essential tool in determining a person's ability to learn to think. Children's informal and formal education, using a language medium, determines their conceptual thinking level. If children experience a language climate of direct speech and mass communication media that is dominated by simplistic or "primitive" language, then their thinking will be simplistic or primitive. On the other hand, if the children's language environment includes varied and complex concepts, the children's thinking will be diverse and intricate, provided that their biological equipment (the senses, central nervous system, and so on) is not disabled. (p. 77)

Vygotsky also proposed the concept of the *zone of proximal development,* which seems to be similar to what Hunt (1961) some years ago called the "problem of the match." The zone of proximal development (ZPD) refers to tasks that the child cannot master by himself, but can eventually master with the help and guidance of an adult or an older, more skilled child (Santrock, 1993, p. 287). The ZPD further leads to the concept of *scaffolding,* which is the support or guidance offered by the adult and upon which the child builds—"scaffolds"—his own functional skills and competencies, eventually to be incorporated into his individual repertoire.

One implication or prediction from Vygotsky's theory is that children from different cultures will show different rates of development and different contents to their thinking and reasoning. When observing children from different cultural backgrounds, awareness of these differences may require you to modify what you expect in the way of the child's behavior, attitudes, values, and performance in the various developmental areas.

Information processing theory has become rather popular because, say Bukatko and Daehler (1995), psychologists have become "disenchanted with learning, Piagetian, and other perspectives for explaining behavior" (p. 53). Information processing theory attempts to explain how the mind actually functions; it assumes that humans are really very much like computers. We deal with symbols just as computers do; we have cognitive structures such as short- and long-term memories. We can use various mental processes such as learning and memory strategies, rules, and plans that influence our "attention, decision-making, remembering ..." (Bukatko and Daehler, 1995; p. 53).

One critical aspect to information processing theory's perspective is its assumption that humans have a *limited capacity.* This means that there are only so many mental resources at our disposal. Two important conditions stem from this limited capacity. First, engaging in one activity limits our ability to engage in another one; and second, some mental activities need more mental resources than others. With development, practice, and experience, the child's mental functions become more efficient and effective (Krantz, 1994; pp. 407–408). Krantz identifies "three key aspects of children's cognitive functioning ..." (p. 408) that underlie the increases in this efficiency and effectiveness: (1) the child's increasing use of strategies; (2) his expanding knowledge base; and (3) an increasing awareness and control of his mental abilities.

Strategies

Briefly, Krantz defines *strategies* as "goal-directed operations that individuals use to deliberately facilitate their memory, attention, and problem solving" (p. 408). *Rehearsal,* which essentially is going over something again and again in one's mind, is a type of strategy. *Organization* is also a type of strategy, whereby the individual places objects or events into meaningful conceptual categories—e.g., placing all things that can be eaten into the category "food," and so on. A third strategy is that of *elaboration,* which can be used "when items cannot be easily grouped into familiar categories" (p. 408). Elaboration involves "relating objects to one another with absurd or fanciful images" (p. 408). This involves creating in one's mind a mental image of various objects—that must be remembered or recalled—and that are in some kind of absurd, ridiculous relationship to one another. The example Krantz offers is that of a child having to memorize the words "book, boy, horse, field, rain." Through elaboration, the child could imagine "A boy riding his horse across a field, reading his book in the rain" (p. 408).

One might ask whether six-year-olds use such strategies. Apparently they do not, at least not consistently or spontaneously. Krantz (1994), for example, reports that children can be taught simple strategies to "facilitate attention and memory" by the time they reach kindergarten or first grade. However, they appear to stop using the strategies after the specific training sessions are ended, a phenomenon known as *production deficiency* (Krantz, p. 409).

An Expanding Knowledge Base

An expanding knowledge base, most simply put, means that the middle-age child has more facts, information, and knowledge at his command than he did when he was younger, an accomplishment that stands to reason when considering the fundamental nature of developmental change. This expansion of knowledge can easily be determined simply by talking to a three- or four-year-old and seeing what he or she knows compared to a six-year-old. Relatively extensive factual knowledge and expertise, however, usually must wait for additional maturation, experience, and further improvements in the child's use of learning strategies.

Metacognition

The third key aspect identified by Krantz also deserves some discussion, namely the child's increased awareness and control of his or her mental abilities. This new ability is called *metacognition* (Krantz, 1994). As Krantz describes the term, "It includes what you know, knowing what you do not know, and knowing what to do with what you know to solve problems" (p. 410). Put more simply, it's knowing both what you do and do not know and being able to benefit from that knowledge to solve problems, make decisions, and so on. It's important to note the two main components of metacognition. The first of these components is *self-appraisal*; this refers to an awareness of whether or not one knows or does not know something, the ability to determine what one needs to learn to accomplish a task (for instance), and the ability to reach a conclusion as to whether or not one has done the necessary work to perform adequately a given task or assignment (Krantz, p. 411). *Self-management*, the second component of metacognition, involves the ability to perform the necessary behaviors that will enable one to succeed at a given task. So, for instance, does six-year-old Alyce realize that she does not adequately comprehend a playmate's instructions, that she must ask her friend questions, and does she know what she subsequently must do to successfully perform the desired actions or behaviors? This could also apply to a child's understanding a teacher's class assignment, and so on. Thinking about thinking, which is metacognition, is a significant addition to the child's store of intellectual resources.

A Little More About Piaget

Despite the growing popularity of competing theories, many texts still place heavy emphasis on Piaget's theory, which, the criticisms against some of his ideas and conclusions notwithstanding, still has merit and is worthy of continued consideration. In that light, we present a table that summarizes some of the characteristics of the child's thought during the period of middle-childhood. We are indebted to Harris's (1993) summary of these characteristics, from which we heavily draw for our own presentation of this topic.

Piaget's stage of concrete operations typically is said to begin at about seven years of age, which appears to make Table 18-3 irrelevant to the observation of six-year-olds. Our premise, nonetheless, is that for the beginning student, learning first-hand what children cannot do can in some instances can be as important as learning what they can do. Moreover, the age ranges that mark off the stages in any theory are never definitive or absolute, which leaves open the possibility that there are some six-year-olds who will be able to function at some level within the stage of concrete operations. Finally, the observer is not restricted to Piaget's theory for data on children's cognitive functioning, and so if necessary, Table 18-3 can be disregarded.

Summary of Cognitive Abilities

As one last source of information about the six-year-old child's cognitive-intellectual development and capabilities, we present in Table 18-4 some of the summarizing data found in Brewer's (1995) text *Introduction to Early*

Table 18-3 Summary of Some Characteristics of Concrete Operational Thought

Characteristics of Concrete Operational Thought (The School Years)

- Understands the general rules that underlie or lead to specific outcomes (idea of cause and effect)

- Has the ability to decenter, i.e., simultaneously take into account more than one feature or dimension of an object or situation

- Understands the concept of mental and physical operations and the fact that they are reversible (e.g., the child understands that liquid poured from a short, wide jar into a tall narrow one can be poured back into the short, wide container and no amount of liquid is added or taken away during the "operation." The child is not as vulnerable to the appearance of things)

- Can transfer learning (rules or principles) gained from solving concrete problems to solving problems in "real life"

- Are not fooled by perceptions or by what appears to be true, but can rely on what they know to be true

- Are more logical and can reason inductively—can form hypotheses or educated guesses based on what they have experienced (they can reason from the specific case to a general theory, of sorts)

- Are more sociocentric than egocentric—they can take someone else's viewpoint or perspective and are not restricted to their own point of view

- "Change the facts to fit their hypotheses rather than changing their hypotheses to fit the facts (a *new* egocentrism)" (Harris, p. 529)

Adapted from Harris (1993, p. 529)

Childhood Education: Preschool Through Primary Grades. So that you can make some informative comparisons and contrasts, we also include information concerning the age ranges from four to five and from seven to eight, ages that immediately precede and immediately follow the target age of six years.

III. Language

Background Information: Vygotsky on Language and Thought

We first want to comment very briefly on Vygotsky's views concerning language and its relation to thought, a relationship that has fostered some controversy or differences of opinion among theorists. Piaget believed that thought, and cognitive development in general, preceded language. Language, in this view, is essentially a vehicle for expressing one's thoughts or for "manipulating" one's ideas or intellectual content. Thus, for example, Piaget thought that a child did not use expressions such as "on top of" or "beside" until she under-

Table 18-4 Summary of Cognitive Abilities and Characteristics of the Child from Three to Eight Years of Age

Three to Four Years	Five to Six Years	Five to Six Years
• Understands and follows instructions with as many as two commands	• Attention span is lengthening; can attend to stimuli for longer, uninterrupted periods of time	• "Differences in reading and language abilities widen" (Brewer, 1995, p. 13)
• Judgments are not thought out and mistakes are frequent	• Knows how to seriate objects—she can, for example, arrange objects according to their length	• Begins transition to concrete operational thinking—Piaget's third stage of cognitive development
• Vocabulary increases rapidly	• Knows how to put objects into groups according to some predetermined criteria	• "Talking and discussion are important"—uses language to solve problems and exchange ideas
• Uses numbers but has no understanding of their meaning—lacks number concept	• Thinking is more deliberate, judgments less impulsive; child can predict the outcome of his behavior before actually performing it	• Knows how to plan, one of the characteristics of concrete operational thinking
• Confuses fantasy and reality; may believe, for example, that dreams come into his head from the outside	• Distinguishes between fantasy and reality; knows difference between dreams and actual experiences, for instance	• Interest in activities endures over long periods of time
• Has the beginning of classification, especially according to the function or purpose of an object	• Uses language to categorize things, does so consciously	• Cause and effect begin to be comprehensible
• Has some use of abstract functional words	• Has knowledge of the representational function of words and pictures (knows they stand for real objects)	• Understanding of time and money increases, which abstract thinking
• Incessant use of "why" questions; wants to know how things work, why they behave as they do	• Shows interest in numbers and letters	• Uses slang and profane language
• Thinking is predominantly egocentric—i.e., it centers on the self, difficult for child to take another's point of view	• Can name colors	• Increased understanding and use of abstract terms
	• In memory tasks, rehearsal is not a spontaneous strategy but must be induced or suggested	• Demonstrates more awareness of the larger community, world
	• Can follow three unrelated commands or instructions	
	• Some children may start to demonstrate conservation of number and length	

Adapted from Brewer (1995, p.13)

stood what such words or phrases meant. Vygotsky conceptualized language and thought as developing independently of each other at first, but merging later on (see Santrock, 1993, p. 289).

Vygotsky's views on cognitive development also stressed the importance of language. In discussing Vygotsky's theory and the role of culture in influencing cognitive development, Vasta, Haith, and Miller (1995) write about the "*dialectical process*," a process whereby learning takes place when the child shares problem-solving experiences with another person (p. 38). Interactions with other people is the dominant mechanism for cognitive growth, and although these interactions can take many forms, Vygotsky emphasized "language interchanges" (Vasta *et al.*, p. 38). These authors' additional remarks are worth inclusion here.

> It is primarily through their speech that adults are assumed to transmit to children the rich body of knowledge that exists in the culture. As learning progresses, the child's own language comes to serve as his or her primary tool of intellectual adaptation. Eventually, for example, children can use internal speech to direct their own behavior in much the same way that the parents' speech once directed it. (Vasta *et al.*, p. 38)

Vygotsky called this transfer of control from parent to child *internalization*. "Bodies of knowledge and tools of thought at first exist outside the child, in the surrounding culture. Development consists of gradual internalization—primarily through language—of these forms of cultural adaptation" (Vasta *et al.*, p. 38). The above comments and citations help to explain why Vygotsky's theory is called a sociocultural or sociohistorical theory. Maybe the simplest and most understandable description of Vygotsky's view of the relationship between language and thought comes from Graves, Gargiulo, and Sluder (1996), who write that Vygotsky "... viewed the language acquisition process as follows: Adults provide names for objects, give directions and suggestions, and gradually reduce the level of their language assistance as children gain more competence and confidence with language" (p. 297). It is here that the zone of proximal development comes into play, a concept we discussed earlier.

Metalinguistic Awareness

Berk (1993) summarizes rather nicely the general characteristics of the school-age child's language achievements and his or her relative position on the language continuum; to wit:

> Language continues to develop in middle-childhood, although the changes that take place are less obvious than those that occurred at earlier ages. Vocabulary, grammar, and pragmatics expand and become more refined. In addition, children's attitude toward language undergoes a fundamental shift. School-age children attend to language much more directly. They develop *language awareness*. (Berk 1993, p. 437, italics original)

Santrock (1993), in addressing the same phenomenon, puts it this way:

"During the middle and late childhood, a change occurs in the way children think about words. They become less tied to the actions and perceptual dimensions associated with words, and they become more analytical in their approach to words . . . . The increasing ability elementary children have in analyzing words helps them to understand words have no direct relationship to their own personal experiences. This allows children to add more abstract words to their vocabulary . . . . Also, children's increasing analytic abilities allows them to distinguish between words such as *cousin* and *nephew,* or *city, village,* and *suburb* (p. 422, italics original).

Part of this achievement described by Berk and Santrock can be accounted for by the following explanation:

"They . . . develop an intuitive awareness of how language works, known as *metalinguistic awareness,* that emerges about age 5 and develops throughout middle-childhood . . . . Metalinguistic awareness refers to intuitions about language that enable children to know, for example, whether a sentence is correct or detect that an ambiguous sentence has two meanings." (Zigler and Stevenson 1993, p. 427)

Bukatko and Daehler (1995) also describe this awareness phenomenon. They write that "Older children—for example, those in the first or second grade—show the ability to detect problems in the messages of others and can even suggest revisions" (p. 261). Schickedanz *et al.* (1993) add an important, clarifying piece to the meaning of metalinguistic awareness, noting that such awareness is being able to "pay attention to the form of language—to the structures used to convey meaning—instead of the meaning itself . . ." (p. 484).

There are two components of metalinguistic awareness of interest to us: Humor and metaphor. *Humor* might seem to be self-evident, but children of six have humor that differs significantly from that of older children and adults. Bukatko and Daehler (1995) use the term "language play" in discussing humor and metaphor. By language play they mean "creating funny words, telling jokes or riddles, or using words in a figurative sense" (p. 263). Schickedanz *et al.* (1993) refer to one aspect of language play as *phonologically based ambiguity,* which is ambiguity or uncertainty about how words are pronounced. They offer an interesting, and to a six-year-old, humorous example of a phonologically ambiguous joke:

> "'Knock, knock."
> "Who's there?"
> "Duane."
> "Duane who?"
> "Duane the tub . . . I'm dwowning.'" (p. 485)

Schickedanz *et al.* also identify *lexically based ambiguity,* which is uncertainty about the meaning of words, and *syntactically based ambiguity,* which has to do with the actual structure of the sentence itself. These authors illustrate the lexically based ambiguity by the following joke:

"'Why did the farmer name his hog Ink?'"
"'Because he kept running out of the pen.'" (p. 484)

The syntactically based ambiguity is nicely illustrated by the following:

"'Do you know how long cows should be milked?'"
"'How long?'"
"'As long as short ones, of course.'" (p. 485)

The ambiguity consists in the double meaning of the word "long," which functions as either an adjective or an adverb.

Schickedanz *et al.* (1993) point out that understanding and using the various ambiguities follow a sort of stage-like progression: Children learn phonological ambiguity first at about 6 or 7; lexical ambiguity comes next, and syntactical ambiguity is not comprehended until about 11 or 12 years of age (p. 486).

Vocabulary and Some Syntax

The average six-year-old's vocabulary ranges between 8,000 and 14,000 words (see, e.g., Berk 1993; Harris 1993; Allen and Marotz 1994). Despite this rather impressive number of usable words they have at their command, six-year-olds have not yet mastered all of the facets of language usage. Papalia and Olds (1992), for example, note that "Even though six-year-olds speak on a rather sophisticated level, using complex grammar and several thousand words, they still have a way to go before they master the niceties of syntax—the way in which words are organized in phrases and sentences" (p. 257). They say further that "During the early school years, they [six-year-olds] rarely use the passive voice, verbs that include the form *have*, or conditional ("if . . . then") sentences" (p. 257; italics original).

Drawing on the work of Carol S. Chomsky (1969), not to be confused with Noam Chomsky, Papalia and Olds (1992) cite three kinds of sentence structures, the difficult concepts they contain, and the age at which children typically acquire an understanding of these concepts. The information is presented in Table 18-5.

Table 18-5 Acquisition of Complex Syntactic Structures

Structure	Difficult Concept	Age of Acquisition
The dog is easy to hear.	Who is doing the hearing?	5.6 to 9 years
Allen promised Fran to help.	Who is doing the helping?	5.6 to 9 years
Bill asked Anthony what to say.	Who is saying it?	Some 10-year-olds have not learned this (Papalia and Olds, 1992).
She knew that Amy would get into trouble.	Does the "she" refer to Amy?	5.6 years

Adapted from Papalia and Olds (1992, p. 257)

Metacommunication

We want to discuss one last aspect to language ability and functioning that is *relevant* to the forthcoming observation exercises. Our overall discussion of language has necessarily been very brief and incomplete. Indeed, fuller treatments of all of the behavioral and developmental domains must be left to the human or child development textbooks. This last language topic is called *metacommunication,* which refers to an individual's understanding of the processes of communication. Papalia and Olds (1992) seem to have captured at least some of the essence of this concept and what it means to children and to adults who work with children.

> Young children do not understand all of what they see, hear, or read, but often they do not know that they do not understand. They may be so used to not understanding things in the world around them that this does not seem unusual. Adults therefore need to be aware that children's understanding cannot be taken for granted. For the sake of children's safety, well-being, and academic progress, we have to find some ways to determine whether children do, in fact, know what we want them to do (p. 258).

A sound piece of advice, indeed. It's relevant to note, here, that sometimes children can fool us into believing that they know more than they actually do or are more sophisticated than they actually are because of the language they use. The deception, which is not deliberate on their part, is made possible by our failure to recognize the difference between a child saying particular words and her understanding the concepts those words represent. Can you imagine, for example, a six-year-old saying to you, "I would like some milk, please, because I believe I am suffering from a calcium deficiency"? The point here is, would a six-year-old, really comprehend the meaning of "calcium deficiency?" The example need not be as esoteric as that just given. Put the issue in the context of a teacher giving a first grade child an instruction or direction. Can the teacher be certain that the instruction or direction has been fully understood? The answer to this question is particularly critical if or when the child's safety and well-being are at stake.

IV. Social and Emotional Development

This is the last functional/behavioral area to be covered. We have chosen to combine social and emotional behavior under a working assumption that much of an individual's emotional expression occurs in a social context of one kind or another. Moreover, the norm in developmental textbooks seems to be to make the same combination, treating social and emotional development within a one-chapter format. Furthermore, putting social and emotional development and behavior under one rubric emphasizes the interactive character of human growth and development.

This "interactive character" of the developmental and behavioral domains is nicely pointed out by Steinberg and Belsky (1991), who write that "Middle childhood is a time of developing psychological and social competence in a world that is both expanding and demanding, and middle-childhood is a time when psychosocial and cognitive development *strongly interact"* (p. 377; italics added). Thus it is that the many advances of the school-age child are made possible by the intellectual gains she has made. These authors also add that "cognitive gains provide impetus for social development, and social development, in turn, provides impetus for further cognitive gains" (Steinberg and Belsky, p. 377).

One important element of social and emotional development is *social role-taking ability,* which is defined by Schickedanz *et al.* (1993) as "The ability to put oneself in someone else's place and anticipate what that person is likely to feel or do . . ." (p. 504). These authors describe social role-taking ability as one of the significant milestones or "hallmarks" of the school-age child's social and emotional development. Furthermore, social role-taking ability "Leads children to a greater understanding of others as well as of themselves, since they can now think of themselves from the point of view of others." This ability involves such skills as "understanding emotions, understanding intentions, and understanding thinking" (Schickedanz *et al.,* p. 504). *Social cognition* is the concept used to explain this new social and intellectual skill; it is the ability to understand "a broad range of social and interpersonal events" (Schickedanz *et al.,* p. 504).

Social cognition also includes an ability to define oneself as well as others. In this regard, Bee (1995) writes that ". . . by age 5 or 6, most children define themselves along a whole range of dimensions." Bee also notes that such early self-descriptions are strongly tied to the here-and-now (p. 296). With age and increasing developmental maturity, their descriptions move toward "a more abstract, more comparative, and more generalized self-definition" (Bee 1995, p. 296). Children's descriptions of others also become more abstract, comparative, and generalized. As the term social cognition implies, social, interpersonal skills rely heavily on intellectual skills, thereby creating the occasion or opportunity for interaction between these two sets of abilities.

To keep the observation exercises within reasonable bounds, we shall focus on the six-year-old's relationship with peers, specifically friendships.

Relationships with Peers: Friendships

Middle-childhood is a time when peer groups start to take on a singular importance. This importance is contributed to by the increasing influence of other, non-familial, individuals and groups who assume significant roles in the child's socialization. The school-age child's social interactions are in sharp contrast to those of the preschooler, for example, whose circle of friends is usually limited to siblings, neighborhood children, classmates in his or her preschool or child-care center, and so on. It's important to recognize that although preschool children's relationships are based at least in part on feelings, which makes friends more important than non-friends, it is still the parents who meet most of the child's important emotional needs (Krantz 1994, p. 438). This arrangement changes during middle-childhood, however, in part because of the child's growing independence from her parents. Now the child is likely to choose as a friend someone who possesses personality characteristics that are able to fulfill her emotional needs (Krantz, p. 438).

The school-age child also experiences greater physical mobility and more extensive contacts with other children, all of which result in an enlargement of his circle of potential friends (Krantz 1994). School-age children choose friends largely on the basis of personality characteristics, but the criteria by which friends are selected change with age and maturity. Specific traits or characteristics come to be valued more than others. For instance, Krantz (1994) reports that "Children in the early grades [i.e., first and second] select friends on the basis of self-serving needs: Who is a good, reliable play partner? Who is willing to share resources, such as toys and video games?" (p. 439). Other considerations apply as well, and some of these are gender-based. Although school-age children in general choose friends who are similar to themselves in terms of race, age, social class, sex, and social status (Krantz 1994, p. 439; also see Ramsey and Myers, 1990, among others), "boys tend to emphasize similarity in superficial behaviors, such as interest in comic books or sports . . . ." Girls, on the other hand, emphasize ". . . similarity in personality traits, such as kindness or friendliness" (Krantz, p. 439; also see Erwin 1985).

Selman and Selman (1979), and later Selman (1981), have studied the progression of friendships. Selman and Selman (1979) depicted friendship as occurring in five stages, with some considerable overlap among the age ranges. Selman's later publication identifies four stages, and the ages are more precisely delineated. Their descriptions are interesting and informative, and both versions are presented in Tables 18-6a and 18-6b.

Table 18-6a Three of Selman and Selman's Five Stages of Friendship (1979 Publication)

Stage	Ages	Characteristics
"0 Momentary playmateship (undifferentiated)" [P & O, p. 284].	3–7	Child is egocentric and sees friendship primarily in terms of what he or she can get from it. Child defines or chooses friends in terms of how close they live; child also sees value in what a friend can offer in the way of material resources or possessions such as toys.
"1 One-way assistance (unilateral)" [P & O, p. 284].	4–9	Child defines a good friend as someone who is obedient to his or her wishes, who does what he or she wants the "friend" to do.
"2 Two-way, fairweather cooperation (reciprocal)" [P & O, p. 284].	6–12	Although there is some mutual reciprocity in the friendships at this age and stage, friends are still defined by each individual's self-interests rather than by common interests.

Adapted from Papalia and Olds (1992, p. 284)

Table 18-6b Two of Selman's Four Stages in the Development of Friendship (1981 Publication)

Stage	Ages	Characteristics
1	6 and under	Friendships are based on such things as where the child lives (geographical location) or on the other's physical characteristics or appearance. Child is egocentric (self-centered) and has difficulty seeing things from another person's perspective.
2	7 to 9	Child begins to form friendships based on others' feelings and on the principle of reciprocity—each doing for the other. Friendships also begin to be conducted on the basis of social behaviors and involve mutual evaluation by each other.

Adapted from Craig and Kermis (1995, p. 558)

Craig and Kermis (1995) hasten to point out, however, that some researchers disagree with Selman's model. They write that "... there is evidence that young children implicitly know more of the rules and expectations of being a friend than they are able to tell an interviewer" (p. 558). Also noted is the fact that "... real friendships are quite complicated and are constantly changing" (p. 558)

The cognitive and social skills needed by the school-age child to form and maintain friendships are considerably greater than (and are different from) the skills needed by the younger child to form and maintain his friendships. There are two specific elements involved in making and keeping friends: *social comparison* and *peer reputation* (Krantz, p. 439).

Social Comparison

Social comparison is a cognitive skill that permits the individual to "describe, rate, and rank peers on various traits and attributes" (p. 439). It is reported that school-age children devote substantial amounts of time comparing their peers. In doing so, they consider abstract qualities such as likes and dislikes, thoughts and feelings (Krantz 1994, p. 439; see also Diaz and Berndt 1982).

These social comparisons serve important functions and have some important consequences. Accurate comparisons enable children to assess how well they can meet their peers' needs and motivations; the ranking that takes place also guides children's social interactions. Furthermore, children hold a sort of mirror—or standard—up to other children by which they can judge their own competencies. These self-judgments also affect children's social behavior (see Krantz 1994, pp. 439–440).

Peer Reputation

All of us know the importance of reputation and how effectively our own and others' reputations influence the way others deal with us and the way we deal with them. Krantz (1994) defines peer reputation as ". . . the relatively stable characterization of a child shared by members of the peer group" (p. 441). It is significant that children learn how to influence their own reputation. They can do this by controlling the impression they make on others—through such things as personal grooming and dressing, displaying attributes that are valued by a peer, or by behaving in ways that contradict a negative reputation (Krantz, p. 441).

Keeping Friends and the Emotions

In this area we briefly raise the topic of emotional behavior, an issue to which we have thus far given short shrift. It is one thing to establish a friendship, but it can be quite another to keep it alive and vital.

Establishing a friendship requires certain social skills, which we have already discussed. Once established, however, other skills come into play, because the relationship itself makes certain demands that are more or less continuous and that require careful monitoring and adjustments on the part of the participants. Krantz (1994) identifies as a critical skill the managing of one's emotions ". . . in the context of increasingly intimate and reciprocal relationships" (p. 441). This management of the emotions involves several abilities or accomplishments. First, the child, let's call him Andrew, must be able to control emotional outbursts that might jeopardize the friendship by intimidating and overpowering Rebecca, his would-be friend. Second, Andrew must be sensitive to Rebecca's own changing emotions and adjust his behavior accordingly. Rebecca must reciprocate in this regard, of course, since sensitivity is a two-way street. Sensitivity to and understanding of the other person's feelings and their possible context paves the way for the expression of empathy and emotional support. A third aspect, which seems closely related to the second ability just mentioned, requires what Krantz describes as ". . . learning to attune or to match their emotions and the tempo of their behavior to that of their friends" (Krantz 1994, p. 442; see also Field *et al.*, 1992). Thus, Rebecca may have to temper or tone down her excitement and joy at a good piece of news, because Andrew's mood is less than joyous. As Krantz would put it, "attunement" might require Rebecca to be less buoyant in her emotional expression and Andrew to be a little more upbeat if their interaction is to go relatively smoothly (Krantz, p. 442). Finally, Andrew and Rebecca "must learn to avoid persistent nagging and complaining" that one or both may find annoying (Krantz, p. 442).

One more facet of friendship deserves some attention, namely that of popularity. Researchers have established categories they refer to as social status that reflect children's popularity among their peers. Citing such researchers as Bukowski and Hosa (1989) and Coie, Dodge, and Coppotelli (1982), Krantz (1994) discusses five such social categories and their respective characteristics.

The first of these categories is called *popular children,* who can be described as children "who are liked by most of their peers and disliked by no one" (p. 443). *Rejected children* are those "who are disliked by most of their peers and liked by very few" (p. 443). Then there are *neglected children,* "who are neither actively liked nor disliked by anyone" (p. 443). There are children "who are liked by many of their peers and disliked by many others," and they are called *controversial children* (p. 443). Finally, there are so-called *average status children,* "who are liked by a few peers and disliked by some others" (p. 443).

There is yet one more set of descriptors that is associated with a method of studying relationships within a group, a method called *sociometry.* Steinberg and Meyer (1995) specify four groups that can be placed on a continuum of popularity via the use of this sociometric technique. The first of these groups contains children who are *stars,* who can be described as children who "... are very well liked and have considerable status and influence in the peer group." The authors add to this description by noting that stars, in addition to being "smart and attractive ... have better social skills and are more likely to act as leaders" (p. 421). They are socially active and tend to take charge of planning activities and initiating social events.

Amiables, the second group in order of popularity, are "liked by others, but they have less status and impact than the stars" (p. 421). Next in popularity are the *isolates,* who "... are neither liked nor disliked; these children are often simply ignored" (p. 421). At the bottom of the popularity totem pole, so to speak, are the *rejects,* children who "... are actively disliked by others and have a negative impact on their peer group" (p. 421). You might find it instructive to compare and contrast the two sets of categories for describing popularity. We shall return to them in the observation exercises on the social and emotional behavior of the six-year-old.

This ends our presentation of the background information on the four behavioral and developmental areas covered in this section of the manual. We have discussed physical and motor development, cognitive and intellectual development, language development, and social-emotional development. All that remains are the observation exercises that accompany each of these domains.

Observation Exercise 18-1: Physical Growth and Motor Functioning

Observation Objectives

In this exercise your objective will be to learn about the six-year-old's gross (large) and fine (small) motor abilities as well as his or her general physical characteristics.

Procedure

As mentioned earlier in the presentation of background information, a great deal of discernment and understanding can be gained through the process of noting similarities (comparing) and noting differences (contrasting) between a six-year-old and a younger, preschool child. Therefore, your objective can be accomplished in one of two ways: (1) actually observe at least two three- to four-year-olds and compare and contrast their physical characteristics and their motor abilities with those of at least two six-year-olds; or (2) observe at least two six-year-olds and compare and contrast their physical characteristics and motor abilities against written observation reports on preschoolers that you may have already completed for another assignment. If you can neither observe two preschoolers nor have access to observation reports already completed on some preschoolers, simply select at least two six-year-olds as the targets for your observation and recording.

Part I—Physical Characteristics of the Six-Year-Old: Using an *event sampling format,* do the following things: (1) describe in detail the preschoolers' general physical characteristics and the six-year-olds' general physical characteristics; (2) compare and contrast the older and the younger children's physical characteristics; in addition, however, compare and contrast the two six-year-olds with each other. The intent here is to observe any individual differences that might exist between the two children. Any such differences might be more apparent or pronounced if you observe a boy and a girl rather than two boys or two girls. In the former case, gender differences in motor skills and development will tend to be evident; in the latter case, non-gender related individual differences among children will be manifested, if there are any.

Part II—Gross and Fine Motor Abilities of the Six-Year-Old: Using an *event sampling format,* follow the same pattern as explained immediately above, except now you will be observing and recording instances of large and small muscle abilities or skills, not physical characteristics. You might also want to refer to Chapter 17, Observation Exercise 17-2, for descriptions of various kinds of motor behaviors that you might observe. Be aware, however, that not all the descriptions found in Exercise 17-2 will apply to the six-year-old. Be discriminating when selecting examples of motor behavior that you want to apply to the children you observe in this exercise. By referring to these descriptions, you will again be engaging in a form of comparison and contrast; what does not fit the six-year-old's motor skill repertoire will be a reminder of how the child has changed since his or her preschool days.

Observation Exercise 18-2: Cognitive and Intellectual Development and Behavior

Observation Objectives

This overall exercise could have a number of objectives, primarily because this functional area is so rich in possibilities for observation and study. We have selected two objectives, designated as Parts I and II, leaving you or your instructor (if you are in a formal educational setting) to devise other practical exercises on your own if more are needed or desired. The two objectives are based on two of the three approaches to the study of cognitive development and functioning discussed above: Piaget's theory (Part I) and information processing theory (Part II).

PART I: *Observation Objectives*

To determine whether the children being observed display any of the characteristics of Piaget's concrete operational thought.

Procedure

For this first objective (Part I-A), we will ask you to refer back to Chapter 17, Observation Exercise 17-3, for additional information on Piaget's theory of cognitive development, information that covers his stage of preoperational thinking. *Observe at least two six-year-olds.* You have several options open to you in this first objective. If you believe that merely observing the children, without intervening in any way, will yield you enough information, then use that approach. We believe that either the *narrative description* or the *event sampling* technique is the appropriate one to use, since they are the least selective of the techniques available, and they provide the most raw data that can then be interpreted. You will have to depend on your own judgment and assessment of the observation setting to tell you which method will yield the most information in the most effective and efficient manner.

Bear in mind that the event sampling method relies more heavily than the narrative description on the target behavior occurring fairly frequently. You may simply want to casually watch the children for a short time to see whether they exhibit any of the behaviors or skills that are of interest to you. If they do, then naturalistic observation might suffice as a plausible approach to the exercise. If it appears that the children, or the particular conditions of your situation, will not lend themselves to naturalistic observation, then you may have to take what might be called a "testing approach" (Part I-B). Remember, however, that to test is to interrupt the usual manner in which things are done in the children's environment. In a school setting, you may not interfere in any way with the official routine or activities that are taking place. Of course, if you are the teacher, or if you are a legitimate part of the classroom, you might have considerable latitude concerning what you are allowed to do. Otherwise, you may have to wait for recess or for some other occasion when your testing will not cause a disruption of normal routine.

Look at Table 18-3, which summarizes some of the characteristics of concrete operational thought. Observe the two children you have selected and determine whether they exhibit any of the abilities described in Table 18-3. For example, does either or both of them understand the notion of cause and effect; can either or both sort objects according to more than one criterion at a time, and so on? On the other hand, does either or both of them show more of the characteristics of preoperational thought than of concrete operational thought? What would you conclude regarding which stage of cognitive development predominates?

PART II: *Observation Objectives*

The second objective emphasizes the information processing approach to understanding cognitive behavior. The purposes of this assignment are (1) to determine what if any strategies the child uses to "facilitate memory, attention, and problem solving" (such strategies include *rehearsal, organization,* and *elaboration*); and (2) to explore the child's knowledge base, which is to say, to find out the kinds of information and facts the child has at his or her command.

Procedure

Select at least two children for the *first objective* of this exercise (Part II-A), but choose different children than the ones you observed for the previous exercise. You will use a combination of a *modified checklist* and the *event sampling techniques.* You should recognize that event sampling really also serves as a form of checklist, inasmuch as every time you observe and record the behaviors that make up the desired event, you are also keeping a running tab of the relative frequency with which those behaviors occur. This exercise is simply the first time in this manual that you have specifically been asked to use the checklist. Simply place an "X" or a checkmark in the box to the right of the strategy that you observe the child using. Then describe (as an OBD) how the child used the strategy—what he or she did specifically, under what circumstances or conditions, and so on.

Recall, also, that use of the event sampling method requires you to decide on the spot whether or not the child is using a strategy. If you were using the narrative description, of course, everything would be recorded, and only later would you have to determine whether or not the child employed strategic thinking. We recognize, however, that learning frequently takes place silently and is not a publicly obvious affair. Consequently, you can't know if a child is using a learning strategy if she is sitting at her seat and silently rehearsing information that she must remember at a later time. This being so, you may have to resort again to some sort of testing or interaction approach to accomplish this exercise's objective. The decision must be yours, of course, but remember that you are always to be as unobtrusive as possible, and you must always obey the ethical principles that govern our relationships with children.

For the *second objective* of this exercise (Part II-B), you will use the *event sampling format.* It might be informative and interesting if you were to *pick two children* who, although both being in their sixth year, were separated in age by a number of months. The purpose of this criterion for making your choice would be to see if the age difference between the two children yielded any difference in how each functioned cognitively. The greatest difference, if there is any at all, might be in the amount of knowledge and information the older child has simply by virtue of his or her having had more time to "experience life," as it were. Perhaps the best approach here is simply to listen to what the children have to say to their teachers, to one another, or to you, if the occasion demands that you directly interact with them. Listen for such things as the kinds of information or general knowledge they have at their command; the accuracy of that information, if you can determine it; the kinds of special knowledge they possess, which is knowledge that is not necessarily common to or shared by many other children in the group, and so on. Although we are not necessarily recommending it, a tape recorder can be a useful tool in situations where recording speech word for word is desirable. We do not, however, recommend that an electronic instrument replace the skills needed to observe and record speech behavior using only pencil and paper.

Observation Exercise 18-3: Language

Observation Objectives

There are three objectives to this overall exercise, and they deal with the three main topics discussed above in the background information: (1) metalinguistic awareness, specifically, the child's use of metaphor and humor; (2) vocabulary and the child's practical understanding of syntax; and (3) metacommunication, but in the simplest terms of how well the child understands what is expected of him or her. These three objectives are designated as Parts I, II, and III.

PART I—Metalinguistic Awareness: Objectives

The major objective of Part I is to observe and record instances of the use of humor and metaphor. Humor may be the easier of the two to witness, although listening even to casual conversation will probably reveal some figurative speech if the child uses any. Put another way, metaphoric or figurative speech will generally not require special circumstances, since people frequently speak in metaphors without taking special thought. Metaphor seems to be a rather natural linguistic occurrence. Humor should not be restricted only to specific instances of joke telling or asking the answers to riddles. We take the approach that anything children find funny is worth noting and perhaps analyzing for its content.

Procedure

Select several children, the exact number we leave to you based on how easily you are able to witness examples of humor or metaphor. It might be interesting to compare what different children think is funny and to compare how different children use figurative speech and under what circumstances. You may not be able to observe the use of both humor and metaphor. This is not critical; if you can get examples of only one or the other, that will suffice.

We suggest that you use the *narrative description format*. By so doing, you may also get an idea of the relative proportion of the children's speech that is humorous or metaphorical compared to that which is, let us say, more "ordinary."

PART II—*Vocabulary and Syntax*: *Objectives*

The objectives of Part II are (1) to determine the extent and characteristics of the children's vocabulary, and (2) to determine the syntactical characteristics of the children's speech.

Procedure

For both objectives of Part II, *select at least two children,* and as nearly as you can, record verbatim the children's speech using the *narrative description technique.* Your goal is to obtain as much information as you need or desire and then analyze the speech content for vocabulary, for grammar—the use of such forms as past tense, adverbs, adjectives, verbs, etc.—and for sentence structure or syntax. If you have access to any observational records that you may have completed for preschool children, they will give you the opportunity to compare and contrast the language skills possessed by children within these two age periods.

This exercise will give you the opportunity to test Papalia and Old's (1992) assertion that "During the early school years, they [six-year-olds] rarely use the passive voice, verbs that include the form *have,* or conditional ("if . . . then") sentences" (p. 257).

You may need to refresh your memory regarding examples of grammatical forms—parts of speech such as adverbs, prepositions, and adjectives—and issues concerning sentence structure and syntax.

PART III—*Metacommunication*: *Objectives*

The objective of this last part is to observe and record instances when the child must follow directions or instructions, either as given by a teacher, adult, or another child. We recognize that children much younger than six also have to learn to follow directions. Nonetheless, it is our working premise that if you are observing in a school classroom or other kind of formal academic setting, directions and instructions will be a common aspect of the teacher-child relationship. Furthermore, the consequences of following or not following such instructions will differ from those that might occur in a child care center, preschool, or in the home. Additionally, comparatively speaking, the complexity of instructions given to a six-year-old is greater than those given, say, to a toddler or preschooler. Thus, cognitive, social, and emotional behaviors play a more sophisticated role with a six-year-old than with a younger child.

Procedure

Select two or three children, within a school setting, if possible. Using the *event sampling format,* look for occasions when the children are given specific directions or instructions. Observe and record how they carry out those instructions. How well do they understand what is expected of them? If they do not seem to understand, how do they deal with their misunderstanding? Do they ask questions, or do they move ahead anyway by experimenting, as it were, with a trial-and-error approach? You may also have the opportunity to compare and contrast the children's proficiency in this area of language functioning, since it is likely that the children you observe will not all function at the same level of ability.

Exercise 18-4: Social and Emotional Development

General Observation Objectives

The overall objectives of this final exercise are, naturally enough, to learn how children of this age behave socially with adults and peers, and how they respond emotionally, either in the company of others, or when alone and confronted by various circumstances. We put the primary emphasis on *social* development and behavior, however, and ask you to deal with emotional behavior essentially in the context of social interactions—which is where many emotional expressions will occur anyway.

We have already stressed in the preceding presentation of background information the significance of social functioning for the school-age child. One of the areas that takes on special significance is that of peer relationships and friendships. It is on this facet of middle-childhood behavior and change that we shall base the concluding observation exercises. We shall leave to your creativity and imagination the devising of other exercises and recording formats that deal with the remaining aspects of social and emotional functioning, an approach that heretofore we have not used. It stands to reason, however, that there are likely to be occasions when you will have to create a format for recording the behavior of children of various ages, for various purposes, and in various settings and situations. We give you an opportunity to do so now, if it presently serves your best interests.

PART I—*Children's Popularity (Social Status Categorization)*: *Observation Objectives*:

The objective of Part I of this exercise is to observe and record children's social or interpersonal interactions and assess their relative popularity with their peers. These observations and assessments are based on Krantz's (1994) discussion of five categories of social status that indicate or reflect popularity among one's peers.

Procedure

Select three or four children and using the *event sampling format* or technique, look for behaviors and interaction patterns that help identify into which social status category each child might be placed. You want to look for at least two things: (1) the responses of other children toward the "target" children you have selected for observation, and (2) the behaviors of the target children that might help explain the other children's reactions toward them. Put another way, what might explain why Roxanne is a popular child, yet Jody is a rejected child, and so on?

Read carefully the brief descriptions of these five categories provided in the background information. Identifying each child's respective category depends upon your understanding the behavioral characteristics associated with each category.

In this exercise, also look for examples of emotional expression, especially with respect to how each child responds emotionally to various situations and individuals in the setting. In your interpretations, comment on any differences in the emotional behavior of children you have placed in different social or popularity categories. That is, does the "controversial child" behave differently emotionally than, say, the "neglected child," or the "average status child?"

PART II—Sociometric Analysis of Children's Popularity and Friendships

Objectives

The objective of this final exercise is to observe and record children's interpersonal behaviors and from the data gathered, construct a *sociogram* using Steinberg and Meyer's (1995) four popularity groupings: *stars, amiables, isolates,* and *rejects.* This may seem like a repetition of Part I, but it differs for two reasons: (1) it uses a slightly different set of popularity descriptors, and (2) it involves the method called *sociometry.* Sociograms are defined as "charts showing the social networks within a group" (Stark 1985, p. 22). In a sociogram, each child is represented by a circle or a square—with his or her name written inside it. The circles or squares—children—are connected by lines or arrows that represent a contact with another child. The head or point of the arrow is drawn where the line touches the circle, and the arrowhead indicates the direction in which the contact occurred. Look at the following brief example:

The arrow from Billy to Tonya indicates that Billy initiated social contact with Tonya; the arrow from Tonya to Alicia indicates that Tonya initiated a contact with Alicia; and so on with the remaining children and arrows. The figure with the greatest number of arrows going to it is the most popular child, provided that the "popular" child's social overtures were responded to in a positive way by the other children. There can be more than one very popular child, by the way, but the sociogram will reveal this fact.

Procedure

Using the *narrative description format, observe and record the behavior of as many children as you can* without being overburdened by the task. If the size of the group is rather large, you might want to do this exercise over the course of several days, where on successive days you observe a different subgroup of children. When your observation records are complete, analyze your data and from them construct a sociogram that depicts the children who are stars, amiables, isolates, or rejects. You might want to devise your own coding system by which you can tell not only who initiated contact with whom, but also how the child who was contacted first responded to the other child's efforts. Thus, in the example given above, you know that Billy contacted Tonya, but did Tonya respond positively to Billy's overture? And so it is that a circle might have a lot of arrows going from it to other circles, but it's no evidence that the other children reacted positively to that child's initiations. Perhaps there are no arrows going back to that circle (child).

Observation Exercise 18-1

Part I: Physical Characteristics of the Six-Year-Old

Observer's Name _____

Child/Children Observed _____

Child's/Children's Age(s) _____   Child's/Children's Sex _____

Observation Context (home, child care center, preschool, school) _____

Date of Observation _____   Time Begun _____   Time Ended _____

Brief Description of Physical and Social Characteristics of Observation Setting:

_____

OBJECTIVE BEHAVIORAL DESCRIPTIONS (OBD) AND INTERPRETATIONS: *Event Sampling*

OBD 1 (six-year-old):   **[Time begun _____   Time ended _____]**

Interpretation 1:

OBD 2 (six-year-old):   **[Time begun _____   Time ended _____]**

Interpretation 2:

OBD *A* (preschooler):   **[Time begun _____   Time ended _____]**

Interpretation *A*:

OBD *B* (preschooler):   **[Time begun _____   Time ended _____]**

Interpretation *B*:

Continue with OBDs and Interpretations for as many as possible or needed.

Comparison of six-year-olds and preschoolers:

Contrast between six-year-olds and preschoolers:

Comparison and contrasts of six-year-olds with each other:

Summary comments or descriptions:

Observation Exercise 18-1

Continued

Part II: Motor Abilities of the Six-Year-Old

Observer's Name _____

Child/Children Observed _____

Child's/Children's Age(s) _____   Child's/Children's Sex _____

Observation Context (home, child care center, preschool, school) _____

Date of Observation _____   Time Begun _____   Time Ended _____

Brief Description of Physical and Social Characteristics of Observation Setting:

_____

OBJECTIVE BEHAVIORAL DESCRIPTIONS (OBD) AND INTERPRETATIONS: *Event Sampling*

OBD 1 (six-year-old): [Time begun _____   Time ended _____]

Interpretation 1:

OBD 2 (six-year-old): [Time begun _____   Time ended _____]

Interpretation 2:

OBD A (preschooler): [Time begun _____   Time ended _____]

Interpretation A:

OBD B (preschooler): [Time begun _____   Time ended _____]

Interpretation B:

Continue with OBDs and Interpretations for as many as possible or needed.

Comparison of six-year-olds and preschoolers:

Contrast between six-year-olds and preschoolers:

Comparison and contrasts of six-year-olds with each other:

Summary comments or descriptions:

Observation Exercise 18-2

Part I-A: Cognitive Functioning of the Six-Year-Old: Piaget's Theory (Naturalistic Observation)

Observer's Name _____

Child/Children Observed _____

Child's/Children's Age(s) _____ Child's/Children's Sex _____

Observation Context (home, child care center, preschool, school) _____

Date of Observation _____ Time Begun _____ Time Ended _____

Brief Description of Physical and Social Characteristics of Observation Setting:

_____

OBJECTIVE BEHAVIORAL DESCRIPTIONS (OBD) AND INTERPRETATIONS:
   Narrative Description or Event Sampling

OBD 1:   [Time begun _____   Time ended _____]

Interpretation 1: (In what cognitive stage does the child appear to be functioning?):

OBD 2:   [Time begun _____   Time ended _____]

Interpretation 2:

Continue for as long or for as many OBDs as are required.

Summary of Descriptive Data:

General Conclusions as to Children's Predominant Level of Cognitive Functioning:

Observation Exercise 18-2

Continued

Part I-B: Cognitive Functioning of the Six-Year-Old: Piaget's Theory ("Testing" Approach)

Observer's Name _____

Child/Children Observed _____

Child's/Children's Age(s) _____ Child's/Children's Sex _____

Observation Context (home, child care center, preschool, school) _____

Date of Observation _____ Time Begun _____ Time Ended _____

Brief Description of Physical and Social Characteristics of Observation Setting:

_____

Testing Method or Approach Used (Interaction) and Interpretation of Results (Describe what you did to get child to respond, questions you asked, and so on.)

Interaction 1: [Time begun _____ Time ended _____]

Interpretation 1 (Level of Cognitive Functioning):

Interaction 2: [Time begun _____ Time ended _____]

Interpretation 2:

Continue for as long or for as many testing episodes as are required.

General Conclusions Regarding Children's Level of Cognitive Functioning:

Observation Exercise 18-2

Continued

Part II-A: Cognitive Functioning of the Six-Year-Old (Information Processing Approach): Use of Strategies

Observer's Name _____

Child/Children Observed _____

Child's/Children's Age(s) _____ Child's/Children's Sex _____

Observation Context (home, child care center, preschool, school) _____

Date of Observation _____ Time Begun _____ Time Ended _____

Brief Description of Physical and Social Characteristics of Observation Setting:

_____

OBJECTIVE BEHAVIORAL DESCRIPTIONS (OBD) AND INTERPRETATIONS: *Checklist and Event Sampling, or "Testing" Approach*

    Rehearsal ☐   **Organization** ☐   **Elaboration** ☐

OBD 1: **[Time begun _____ Time ended _____]**

    Rehearsal ☐   **Organization** ☐   **Elaboration** ☐

OBD 2: **[Time begun _____ Time ended _____]**

    Rehearsal ☐   **Organization** ☐   **Elaboration** ☐

OBD 3: **[Time begun _____ Time ended _____]**

Continue for as long or for as many OBDs or events as are needed or desired.

Summary of Observations and Interpretations (Summarize briefly the kinds of strategies that were used and under what circumstances each strategy was used):

Observation Exercise 18-2

Continued

Part II-B: Cognitive Functioning of the Six-Year-Old (Information Processing Approach): Extent of Children's Knowledge Base

Observer's Name _____

Child/Children Observed _____

Child's/Children's Age(s) _____ Child's/Children's Sex _____

Observation Context (home, child care center, preschool, school) _____

Date of Observation _____ Time Begun _____ Time Ended _____

Brief Description of Physical and Social Characteristics of Observation Setting:

_____

OBJECTIVE BEHAVIORAL DESCRIPTIONS (OBD) AND INTERPRETATIONS: *Event Sampling*

OBD 1: Child One's Age in Years and Months _____

  [Time begun _____ Time ended _____]

Interpretation or Comments 1:

OBD 2: Child Two's Age in Years and Months _____

  [Time begun _____ Time ended _____]

Interpretation or Comments 2:

Continue for as long or for as many OBDs as are needed or desired.

Summary Remarks (Comparisons and Contrasts of the Children):

Observation Exercise 18-3

Part I: Metalinguistic Awareness

Observer's Name _____

Child/Children Observed _____

Child's/Children's Age(s) _____ Child's/Children's Sex _____

Observation Context (home, child care center, preschool, school) _____

Date of Observation _____ Time Begun _____ Time Ended _____

Brief Description of Physical and Social Characteristics of Observation Setting:

_____

OBJECTIVE BEHAVIORAL DESCRIPTIONS (OBD) AND INTERPRETATIONS:
   Narrative Description

OBD 1: **[Time begun _____ Time ended _____]**

Interpretation 1: (Did the child use metaphor—figurative speech—or humor? Into which of Schickedanz *et al.*'s categories of humor can you place the child's humorous speech?)

OBD 2: **[Time begun _____ Time ended _____]**

Interpretation 2:

Continue for as many OBDs as needed or desired.

Summary Comments (Include the circumstances under which metaphor or humor was used):

Observation Exercise 18-3

Continued

Part II: Vocabulary and Syntax

Observer's Name _____

Child/Children Observed _____

Child's/Children's Age(s) _____ Child's/Children's Sex _____

Observation Context (home, child care center, preschool, school) _____

Date of Observation _____ Time Begun _____ Time Ended _____

Brief Description of Physical and Social Characteristics of Observation Setting:

_____

OBJECTIVE BEHAVIORAL DESCRIPTIONS (OBD) AND INTERPRETATIONS:
   Narrative Description

OBD 1:   [Time begun _____   Time ended _____]

Interpretation 1: (An assessment of the child's speech with respect to vocabulary, sentence structure, and so on.)

OBD 2:   [Time begun _____   Time ended _____]

Interpretation 2: (Same procedure as Interpretation 1 above)

Continue for as many OBDs as are needed or desired.

Summary Comments:

Observation Exercise 18-3

Continued

Part III: Metacommunication

Observer's Name _____

Child/Children Observed _____

Child's/Children's Age(s) _____   Child's/Children's Sex _____

Observation Context (home, child care center, preschool, school) _____

Date of Observation _____   Time Begun _____   Time Ended _____

Brief Description of Physical and Social Characteristics of Observation Setting:

_____

OBJECTIVE BEHAVIORAL DESCRIPTIONS (OBD) AND INTERPRETATIONS: *Event Sampling*

OBD/Event/Child 1:   [Time begun _____   Time ended _____]

Interpretation 1:

OBD/Event/Child 2:   [Time begun _____   Time ended _____]

Interpretation 2:

OBD/Event/Child 3:   [Time begun _____   Time ended _____]

Interpretation 3:

Continue for as many OBDs as are needed or desired.

Summary Comments (Include any Comparisons and Contrasts between or among the children observed):

Observation Exercise 18-4

Part I: Children's Popularity (Social Status Categorization)

Observer's Name _____

Child/Children Observed _____

Child's/Children's Age(s) _____ Child's/Children's Sex _____

Observation Context (home, child care center, preschool, school) _____

Date of Observation _____ Time Begun _____ Time Ended _____

Brief Description of Physical and Social Characteristics of Observation Setting:

_____

OBJECTIVE BEHAVIORAL DESCRIPTIONS (OBD) AND INTERPRETATIONS: *Event Sampling*

OBD 1: (Record observed child's behaviors and other children's responses to the child. Continue this procedure for each OBD.) [Time begun _____ Time ended _____]

Interpretation 1: (Identify a possible social status category into which the child might be put, and include reasons why you believe the observed child falls into the category you have chosen.)

OBD 2: [Time begun _____ Time ended _____]

Interpretation 2:

OBD 3: [Time begun _____ Time ended _____]

Interpretation 3:

Continue for as many OBDs as are needed or desired.

Summary Comments Comparisons and Contrasts among the observed children):

Observation Exercise 18-4

Continued

Part II: Sociometric Analysis of Children's Popularity and Friendships

Observer's Name _____

Child/Children Observed _____

Child's/Children's Age(s) _____ Child's/Children's Sex _____

Observation Context (home, child care center, preschool, school) _____

Date of Observation _____ Time Begun _____ Time Ended _____

Brief Description of Physical and Social Characteristics of Observation Setting:

_____

OBJECTIVE BEHAVIORAL DESCRIPTIONS (OBD) AND INTERPRETATIONS:
Narrative Description

OBD 1: [Time begun _____ Time ended _____]

Interpretation 1:

OBD 2: [Time begun _____ Time ended _____]

Interpretation 2:

Continue for as many OBDs as are needed or desired.

Summary Comments:

Observation Exercise 18-4

Part II Continued

SOCIOGRAM

CHAPTER NINETEEN

The School-Age Years:
The Seven- and Eight-Year-Old Child

I. Physical Growth and Motor Development

Background Information

In Chapter 18, we sometimes presented data that did not always specifically pertain to the six-year-old. Some of what we discussed dealt with children younger than six and some with children older than six. This attests to the continuous quality of age, which is totally unlike counting the number of apples in a bag and coming up with a nice discrete whole number. It's not always easy or possible—indeed, it may be impossible—to define precisely where the gains of the sixth year of life end and those of the seventh year begin, and so on through the entire life span. (As you well know, changes are frequently reported within age ranges, even though efforts are sometimes made to attach changes to specific ages.) In any event, rather than repeat all of this information when it applies to seven- and eight-year-olds, we will refer you to the material that is relevant to those ages. In this chapter, although we present some of the physical changes that take place in seven- and eight-year-olds, we are not interested in physical changes for their own sake. We want to place such changes primarily in the context of the child's motor development and functioning.

As stated in Chapter 18, physical growth during this period is steady and sustained, much as it is during early childhood, and it is unlike the rapid growth that occurs during infancy. Many of the changes in physical characteristics and motor skills in the one to two years from six to eight appear to be increases in the sophistication of the child's chosen activities and improvements in such things as "agility, balance, control of motor skills, and endurance" (Allen and Marotz 1994). Table 19-1 summarizes some of the physical and motor characteristics of the seven- and eight-year-old child.

We did not discuss play in Chapter 18, even though the period of middle-childhood accentuates the importance and changing character of this activity. In Chapter 17, we discussed play more in terms of its social implications and components than its physical or motor ones. In this chapter, we want to reverse this emphasis and treat play among seven- and eight-year-olds primarily in the context of their motor development. We remind the reader that the seven- and eight-year-old child's changing play is the product not only of his or her

Table 19-1 Summary of Physical and Motor Characteristics of the Seven- and Eight-Year-Old Child

Physical Characteristics	Motor Abilities
• Gains an average of 5 to 7 pounds per year	• Participates eagerly in competitive activities
• Height gains of 2.5 inches per year on average. Average height of girls is 46 to 49 inches; boys 48 to 52 inches	• Enjoys such activities as dancing, skating, swimming, running, wrestling, and sports such as soccer, and baseball
• Arms and legs grow longer, thus giving child a thin, lanky appearance	• Shows significantly more agility, balance, motor ability control, and endurance; is able to balance on one foot, jump rope, and catch a ball.
• Straighter, more erect posture	
• Permanent teeth more prominent now than baby teeth	• The tight grip on a pencil at seven years of age becomes more relaxed by eight
• Suffers minor illnesses less frequently	• Deliberate and confident writing of letters and numbers; character size becomes more consistent and uniform
	• Uses knife and fork when eating
	• Engages in repeated practice of new found skills

Adapted from Allen and Marotz (1994, pp. 127–128)

increased physical and motor skills, but also of his or her equally increasing cognitive abilities and social and emotional maturity. As Berk (1996) puts it, "... greater cognitive and social maturity permits older children to use their new motor skills in more complex ways" (p. 409). We also want to discuss briefly the issue of sex differences in motor development, some of which, having begun in the preschool years, become more pronounced during middle-childhood (see, e.g., Berk 1996). Let us begin with these differences.

Some Gender Differences in Motor Development

Berk (1996) reports that girls stay ahead of boys in fine motor development throughout those years. This includes handwriting and drawing. Interestingly enough, says Berk, girls are ahead of boys in those gross (large) muscle skills that involve "balance and precision of movement," which are required in activities such as "skipping, jumping, and hopping" (p. 413). As for most other motor skills—running, throwing, catching, kicking, batting, dribbling, and so on—boys confirm traditional thinking and perform better than girls (Berk, p. 409). Berk takes pains to point out, however, that it is not genetics alone that account for boys' superior performance in gross motor activities. The environment, she believes, "plays a much larger role" (p. 413), an issue we will not take up here. As we shall note, girls and boys also differ in the characteristics of their rough-and-tumble play.

Games, Rules, and Motor Functioning

It is intuitively reasonable that with greater physical size and strength and constantly improving motor skills, the physical activities of children in the middle-childhood years should also become more sophisticated and more organized, characteristics contributed to in no small way by the child's increasing cognitive and social skills. In this context, we see an interaction between the quality of their play and the character of their physical activities. Although not limited to the period from seven to eight years of age, organized games with rules become more standard fare in children's daily lives, and games demand different things from children than are demanded by the simpler forms of play engaged in by younger, preschool children.

Not all games with rules, of course, are physically demanding; many make their demands in the cognitive and social realms—board games, card games, and the like. On the other hand, games like kick the can, tag, hide-and-seek, leapfrog, and prisoner's base, require physical-motor skills as well as their fair share of interpersonal skills, role and perspective-taking skills, and so on. The critical significance of play can be captured by Steinberg and Meyer's (1995) succinct assertion that "*Play is the work of childhood*: When children play, they produce, whether it's a fantasy or a product" (p. 292; emphasis added). But again, our interest in play at this moment is in the opportunity it affords the child to exhibit his or her growing physical attributes and motor skills. Therefore, disregarding play's testimony to changing peer relations, cognitive abilities, and other dimensions of human behavior, let's look at the body-muscle aspects of play among seven- and eight-year-olds.

Rough-and-Tumble Play

There are many forms of play, of course, but since we are concerned with play that makes demands on the child's motor abilities, the very name "rough-and-tumble" begs for attention. We should point out, however, that rough-and-tumble play is not the only form of what can be called "physical play." Berger (1991), for instance, discusses "three types of play that are especially well-suited to the development of motor skills." These are *sensorimotor play, mastery play,* and *rough-and-tumble play* (p. 254). We are concerned with the latter.

Bukatko and Daehler (1995) call rough-and-tumble play "a special form of play," which, they say, "emerges around age two years and becomes more visible during the elementary school years, especially among boys" (p. 566). Berk (1996) indicates that rough-and-tumble play "is a good-natured, sociable activity that is quite distinct from aggressive fighting" (p. 414). Bukatko and Daehler make the same distinction: "... children do not intend to hurt one another and it often occurs between children who like each other" (p. 566). From this brief description, you can see the strong social components even of such a physically vigorous form of interaction.

Although boys of this age engage in rough-and-tumble play more than girls do, Berk (1996) notes that girls do have their brand of this type of play, which consists mostly of running and chasing, whereas boys prefer playful wrestling and hitting (p. 414).

In the observation exercises that are to come, you will be asked to focus your attention on those activities children engage in that make special demands on their physical attributes and motor skills. We have chosen play as one vehicle for the exercise of these skills, but we will advise you not to restrict yourself unnecessarily to play. There are many avenues for the display of motor behaviors, and you should take advantage of this fact. Put another way, the above discussion is necessarily limited in scope, but don't impose those same limitations on how you complete the exercises.

II. Cognitive and Intellectual Development and Behavior

Background Information

If Piaget is correct, the "typical" seven- and eight-year-old child is in, or has progressed significantly toward, the period of concrete mental operations. In the last chapter, we discussed several perspectives on children's intellectual behavior and development, and at least some of that information can be applied to the seven- and eight-year-old. We will not duplicate all of that material in the present chapter. Table 19-2 outlines some of the characteristics of

---

Table 19-2 Summary of Some Characteristics of Concrete Operational Thought

---

Characteristics of Concrete Operational Thought (The School Years)

- Understands the general rules that underlie or lead to specific outcomes (idea of cause and effect)
- Has the ability to decenter, i.e., simultaneously take into account more than one feature or dimension of an object or situation
- Understands the concept of mental and physical operations and the fact that they are reversible (e.g., the child understands that liquid poured from a short, wide jar into a tall narrow one can be poured back into the short, wide container and no amount of liquid is added or taken away during the "operation." The child is not as vulnerable to the appearance of things)
- Can transfer learning (rules or principles) gained from solving concrete problems to solving problems in "real life"
- Are not fooled by perceptions or by what appears to be true, but can rely on what they know to be true
- Are more logical and can reason inductively—can form hypotheses or educated guesses based on what they have experienced (they can reason from the specific case to a general theory, of sorts)
- Are more sociocentric than egocentric—they can take someone else's viewpoint or perspective and are not restricted to their own point of view
- "Change the facts to fit their hypotheses rather than changing their hypotheses to fit the facts (a *new* egocentrism)" (Harris, p. 529)

Adapted from Harris (1993, p. 529)

Piaget's period of concrete operational thought. Also as a reminder, "concrete" here means that "... children are bound by immediate physical reality and cannot transcend the here and now" (Vander Zanden 1993, p. 302). In other words, much of the concrete operational child's thinking has to occur in the presence of the actual objects of thought, and she cannot deal easily with issues or events that are far from her own experiences, that are hypothetical, or that are too far in the future.

In Chapter 17 we addressed the issue of whether or not children in the period of early childhood could "conserve" such things as number, substance, or volume. That is, do children of this age understand, for example, that if there are two equal rows of pennies, and if one row is spread out so as to take up more space than the other row, there are still the same number of pennies in each row? This is a typical *conservation-of-number* task, and if the child answers that the number of pennies is unchanged, he has conserved number. Until fairly recently, the consensus of opinion was that children under 6 years of age could not conserve such things as number. Now research strongly suggests that very young children can perform some conservation tasks if the problem is presented in ways that are appropriate to their developmental level and prior experience. Bukatko and Daehler (1995), for instance, confirm that infants' and young children's abilities have indeed been underestimated. Reporting on the findings of various researchers, they note that simplifying or restructuring cognitive tasks and observing children under more naturalistic conditions than artificial laboratory settings, "they [children] display cognitive skills at much earlier ages than Piaget believed possible" (p. 296). Some of this research goes back to 1969, when Gelman demonstrated that five-year-olds could conserve number and length when they were tested for this ability through the use of different stimuli. Gelman (1972) later found that children as young as three and four could, with training, learn to conserve number (Bukatko and Daehler 1995, p. 297).

In Table 19-3 we present the approximate ages at which children acquire various conservation abilities. Some of these go beyond the age parameters of early childhood, but we will include them anyway to maintain a sense of continuity, as well as to provide for the possibility that your observations might disclose a child or children whose level of cognitive functioning is higher than their seven- and eight-year-old peers. It is more likely, however, that Table 19-3 can serve as a guide to developmentally appropriate practice and developmentally appropriate expectations. You may recall from Chapter 14 the discussion of the concept of standards. There we wrote that "Selection of the standard ... is critical in many cases, because the standard will determine whether the child's performance satisfies the adult's conception of what she can and should be able to do." Each of the conservation skills is standard, and, therefore, you would not expect a seven-year-old to be able to conserve weight or volume, skills that are ordinarily achieved between 9 and 14 years of age.

Other cognitive and intellectual functions applicable to seven- and eight-year-olds have been discussed in the previous chapter: Information processing theory, Vygotsky's theory, Piaget's theory, and some of the major ideas that

Table 19-3 Order of Acquisition of Conservation Skills

Conservation Skill	Characteristics of Conservation Skill
Number (Ages 5–7)	• The number of objects is independent of how they are arranged in space, provided none is added or taken away.
Substance (Ages 7–8)	• The amount of a substance—such as clay or playdoh—remains unaffected by how that substance is shaped (e.g., the amount of clay in a ball does not increase or decrease if it is flattened out into the shape of a pancake).
Length (Ages 7–8)	• The length, say, of a piece of string is not changed merely by changing how it is arranged (e.g., a string laid out in a straight line keeps its original length when it is formed into a circular shape).
Area (Ages 8–9)	• The amount of total area of a space is not changed by rearranging any of the component parts of that total area (e.g., four one-foot square blocks arranged to form one large square comprising four square feet of area, does not gain or lose any amount of area if the individual squares are rearranged to form a different geometric shape).
Weight (Ages 9–10)	• The weight or heaviness of an object does not change merely by changing the shape of that object (e.g., four one-pound blocks stacked on top of one another, which weigh a total of four pounds, will still weigh a total of four pounds if they are placed side by side).
Volume (Ages 12–14)	• The amount (volume) of liquid in a container, for example, does not depend on the shape of the container (e.g., a quart of water in a short, wide jar is still a quart of water when put into a tall, narrow jar).

Adapted from Vander Zanden (1993, p. 305)

accompany those perspectives. In the present chapter, we emphasize the concept of conservation, it can serve as one example of how the child's cognitive abilities become more and more sophisticated over the course of development.

Consequently, to complete this section of the chapter, we offer a brief tabular summary of some skills, behaviors, or abilities that appear to characterize the overall mental status of the seven- and eight-year-old child (Table 19-4). Keep in mind, however, that when it comes time to perform your observations, anything that is relevant to a child's cognitive functioning can be relevant.

III. Language

Background Information

We have already written quite a lot about language and its developmental characteristics. In fact, language is one of those functional areas of such significance that it's hard to imagine saying too much about it, other than running the risk of prolonging discussion beyond a reasonable and tolerable length.

Table 19-4 Cognitive Development and Achievements of the Seven- and Eight-Year-Old Child

Some Activities and Interests Demonstrated by the Seven- and Eight-Year-Old Child Indicative of Cognitive Functioning

- Child collects things and organizes and displays them in accordance with a more complex system of classification than used when younger; also engages in bargaining with friends to acquire more items.

- Child can identify and name denominations of coins and paper currency.

- Child becomes more sociocentric—other-centered; that is, he or she takes an interest in what other people think and do, which is reflected in an interest in "different cultures, far away places" (Allen and Marotz 1994, p. 129).

- Child can delay gratification as well as plan ahead (e.g., putting off doing something pleasant until later, more appropriate time).

- Child can utilize some logic in efforts to understand how things work or to accomplish a goal (e.g., systematically searches for a lost object).

- Child can tell time and knows the correct day, month, and year.

- Child understands the idea of cause and effect; he knows how one event can affect or influence another event.

- Child is learning addition and subtraction of numbers.

- Child uses words to express ideas more efficiently and accurately.

- Child can recall details from stories and experienced events with considerable accuracy.

- Child now enjoys reading and does so more on his or her own without need for outside help or supervision.

Adapted from Allen and Marotz (1994, p. 129)

Vocabulary: As a general premise, we can say that the seven- and eight-year-olds' language skills continue to improve beyond those held when they were six. In the area of vocabulary alone, marked increases seem to be the norm. Berk (1996), for example, asserts that

> Because the average six-year-old's vocabulary is already quite large (about 10,000 words), parents and teachers usually do not notice rapid gains during the school years. Between the start of elementary school and its completion, recognition vocabulary increases fourfold, eventually reaching about 40,000 words. On the average, about 20 new words are learned each day—a rate of growth that exceeds that of early childhood. (p. 446)

This rapid expansion of vocabulary is the result of gains in other related areas of functioning. For instance, Berk (1996) notes that "... school-age children enlarge their vocabularies through an increasingly powerful ability to analyze the structure of complex words." She gives the example of the child being able to take words such as "happy," "wise," and "decide," and discern or derive "the meanings of 'happiness,' 'wisdom,' and 'decision'" (p. 446).

Another gain comes in the form of increased conceptual knowledge, which in turn forms the foundation for concomitant gains in vocabulary. Berk

(1996) reports that "Five- and 6-year-olds give very concrete descriptions that refer to functions or appearance—for example, knife: 'when you're cutting carrots'; bicycle: 'it's got wheels, a chain, and handlebars'" (p. 446). But, by the end of the elementary school years, "... their definitions emphasize more general, socially shared information. Synonyms and explanations of categorical relationships appear—for example, knife: 'something you could cut with. A saw is like a knife. It could also be a weapon'" (p. 446). Eventually, by fifth and sixth grade, children can acquire new vocabulary words merely by being given a definition (Berk 1996, p. 446). Children also increasingly appreciate the multiple meanings of words. Such multiple meanings include psychological meanings as well as physical ones, which allows a richer, fuller use of the ambiguous character of language. This grasp of the double meanings of many words, of course, further allows the use of more sophisticated metaphors than was possible at an earlier age or level of language development. In turn, according to Berk (1996), children's humor changes rather dramatically, whereby "... riddles and puns requiring children to go back and forth between different meanings of the same key word are common" (p. 446).

Grammar: Another aspect of language development and functioning is that of grammar. We refer the reader to the lengthier discussion of language in Chapter 18, if and when more information is required than what is provided here.

Grammar, along with syntax, are what make language—spoken or written—intelligible. Grammar is the rules governing the correct usage of words and their relationships to one another in sentences. *The American Heritage Talking Dictionary* (1994) defines grammar as "The system of rules implicit in a language, viewed as a mechanism for generating all sentences possible in that language ... A normative or prescriptive set of rules setting forth the current standard of usage for pedagogical or reference purposes ... The study of how words and their component parts combine to form sentences."

One grammatical construction of some note is the use of the passive voice—"The ball *was hit by* Alonzo."—as opposed to the active voice—"Alonzo *hit* the ball." Berk writes that "... full passives are rarely used by 3- to 6-year-olds," but that "they increase steadily over middle-childhood" (p. 447). Also noted by Berk is the fact that "Older children also apply their understanding of the passive voice to a wider range of nouns and verbs" (p. 447).

Middle childhood also sees an understanding of infinitive phrases, which allows the child to distinguish the difference between the sentences "John is easy to please" and "John is eager to please" (Berk, p. 447). All of the above accomplishments are partly the result of increased cognitive skills and partly of an "improved ability to analyze and reflect on language" (Berk, p. 447). The confusion arises over who exactly is doing what, or who exactly has what characteristics. In the sentence "John is eager to please," who is doing the pleasing, or who wants to please? It is difficult for children younger than 5 or 6, which are the estimated beginning ages of acquisition of this syntactical structure (see, e.g., Papalia and Olds 1993, p. 417), to distinguish between this sentence and the sentence "John is easy to please." Here, John is the *potential recipient* of actions that will *please him*, whereas before, John is the *potential doer* of actions that will *please others.*

A final aspect of language of concern to us is that of *pragmatics,* which has to do with what Berk (1996) calls "the communicative side of language" (p. 447). Here, the individual has to deal with the practical tasks associated with making herself understood by others. One such task is to take into account the particular needs or situation of the listener. For example, pragmatics would require the child to know what his conversational partner knows about the topic under discussion, or about the context of the conversation. Failure to take such matters into account might be partly explainable by invoking Piaget's concept of egocentrism. The younger, more egocentric child might fail to provide enough information for the other person to understand what is being communicated, or needed, in the situation. Giving instructions, for instance, will not result in meaningful action if those instructions are incomplete, vague, or ambiguous. The older child can realize or discern the gaps in her directions and adjust them accordingly, something the preschooler is unable to do.

This ability to give adequate instructions develops through a gradual progression. The older child just referred to probably is a child of about ten or eleven years of age. Berger (1991), for instance, discusses this issue in the context of a study by Sonnenschein (1986) that involved first- and fourth-grade children giving instructions to a playmate on how to find a toy. As Berger reports the findings "... Only the fourth-graders' instructions were consistently well-suited to finding the toy; those of the first graders included both helpful and irrelevant additional information" (p. 380).

The relevance of these findings to your observations is that you can expect seven- and eight-year-olds to demonstrate at least some ability to provide a listener with meaningful information in particular situations.

Another important facet of pragmatics is the child's improved ability to understand "the distinctions between the form and meaning of utterances" (Berk, p. 447). This is an interesting phenomenon, since it is an aspect of our daily interactions involving language that probably goes unnoticed by most of us. Think of it in terms of the following example of an 8-year-old. Josie's mother wants her to clean her room. Several times her mother has asked her to perform this household chore. She usually phrases her request as "Josie, clean your room." Josie has responded with "OK, Mom," but has left the job undone. Finally, in desperation and frustration, her mother says "Josephine Markowitz, clean your room." Now Josie hops to it, knowing that her mother's rephrasing of her request signals some anger and urgency. And this realization on Josie's part was derived from her mother's simple use of Josie's full name, along with a probable rise in the volume and tone of her voice.

Berk, again, provides an informative illustration of this communication skill, to wit:

Even 3-year-olds know that a playmate who says "I need a pencil," is not just making a statement. She is asking for a pencil. But 8-year-olds understand more unconventional expressions of meaning. For example, the day after she forgot to take the garbage out, Lizzie knew that her mother's statement "The garbage is beginning to smell," really meant "Take that garbage out." Making subtle inferences about the relationship between an utterance and its context is beyond the ability of preschoolers. (p. 447)

Your observation exercises will, we hope, provide you the opportunity to witness and record some of these linguistic skills and to compare the seven- and eight-year-old's skills in this area with those of the younger child.

IV. Social and Emotional Behavior

Background Information

The school-age years (6 to 12) are when the child acquires and even masters certain basic competencies, many of which are functionally related to formal education. It is feasible to place these competencies and their accomplishments under the general rubric of "personality changes." We take our lead in this assumption from Berk's (1996) statement that "According to Erikson (1950), the *personality changes* [emphasis added] of the school years build on Freud's *latency stage* [emphasis original] . . ." (p. 466). The psychosocial crisis or task in Erikson's theoretical perspective of middle-childhood is that of developing either a sense of *industry* or a sense of *inferiority.* It is the sense of industry that enables the child to accomplish the educational tasks associated with formal schooling, among other demands made in other contexts and situations. As Berk puts it, "In school, children engage in productive work beside and with other children" (p. 466). For our purposes, it is this engagement in meaningful, productive activity that captures the essence of industry.

A sense of inferiority can be captured by the ideas of pessimism or inadequacy, which interfere with the development of competence and mastery, critical components of industry (e.g., Berk 1996). The concepts of both industry and inferiority lend themselves quite nicely to the concepts of, and issues associated with, self-esteem, self-concept, moral behavior and reasoning, and cooperation with others in such endeavors as accomplishing tasks. As you can readily see, this latter set of issues goes to the heart of personality and social relationships.

Self-Concept and Self-Esteem

Self-concept should be distinguished from self-esteem. For our purposes, *self-concept* refers to the manner in which an individual describes herself; that is, what qualities or attributes does the child assign to herself? We may think of self-concept as a more or less objective assessment of who we are, our strengths and weaknesses, our personality characteristics, and so on. Berk (1996) writes that "During the school years, children organize their observations of behaviors and internal states into general dispositions that they can verbalize to others, with a major change taking place between ages 8 and 11" (p. 467). Berk offers an informative comparison between two children's descriptions of themselves, a 7-year-old boy and an 11 1/2-year-old girl. Note the rather significant differences between these two self-descriptions.

> *A boy age 7*: I am 7 and I have brown hair and my hobby is stamp collecting. I am good at football and I am quite good at sums and my favorite game is football and I love school and I like reading books and my favorite car is an Austin. (Berk 1996, p. 467; cited from Livesley & Bromley 1973, p. 237)

> *A girl age 11 1/2*: My name is A. I am a human being. I'm a girl. I'm a truthful person. I'm not pretty. I do so-so in my studies. I'm a very good cellist. I'm a very good pianist. I'm a little tall for my age. I like several boys. I like several girls. I'm old-fashioned. I play tennis. I am a very good swimmer. I try to be helpful. I'm always ready to be friends with anybody. Mostly I'm good, but I lose my temper. I'm not well-liked by some girls and boys. I don't know if I'm liked by boys or not. (Berk 1996, p. 467; cited from Montemayor and Eisen 1977, pp. 317–18)

Bukatko and Daehler (1995) discuss self-concept—or what they call "self-definition"—in terms of the *categorical self.* They note that "... during the preschool years, knowledge of self extends beyond physical features to include activities the child likes and is good at, his possessions, and his relationship to others" (p. 441). In developing a categorical self, children "... classify themselves in terms of membership in certain groups based on their sex, age, skills, what they own, where they live, and who their friends are" (p. 441).

In rather sharp contrast to the preschooler and the seven-year-old, the 11-year-old moves beyond a listing of specific behaviors and describes general competencies and categories of characteristics. As Berk also points out, the younger child—as with younger children in general—does not identify any psychological traits, while the older child describes her personality (p. 467).

Self-esteem refers to one's sense of personal worth or value. So, for example, although the girl described above considers her academic abilities or performance only "so-so," she might still have a positive sense of personal worth that is essentially unaffected by her less than exemplary scholastic competence or accomplishments.

Berk reports that "By age 7 to 8, children have formed at least three separate self-esteems—academic, physical, and social—that become more refined with age" (p. 468). This refinement consists in part of academic self-worth dividing into performance relative to different school subjects and social self-worth dividing into peer and parental relationships. Physical self-esteem builds on physical ability and physical appearance (Berk 1996, pp. 468–469).

Conventional wisdom dictates that high or positive self-esteem contributes more to higher levels of confidence and performance than does low or negative self-esteem. But research also suggests that children's self-esteem becomes more realistic as they grow older and engage in more social comparisons with other individuals. "Self-esteem drops during the first few years of elementary school" (Berk 1996, p. 469). The decline results from such things as the evidence provided by the child's actual performance and from the adjustments the child makes in his self-judgments so as to make them more congruent with other people's opinions of him (Berk 1996, p. 469).

For the school-age child, there is an aspect of children's behavior that is particularly germane to academic performance; and it is an aspect that is, we think, fairly easily accessible to more or less direct observation. We are referring here to the reasons we—people in general—offer as explanations for our behavior. In the present context, they are reasons that are labeled by Berk as "achievement-related attributions" (p. 470). These attributions are among the influences that contribute to the child's self-esteem (Berk 1996). Berk identifies two basic attributions that children make with respect to their "academic self-esteem": (1) *Mastery-oriented attributions*, and (2) *learned helplessness*, which results in attributions that are made by the child himself and are critical and derogatory of his own abilities.

Children with high academic self-esteem, writes Berk, ". . . believe their successes are due to ability—a characteristic they can count on in the future when faced with new challenges. And when failure occurs, they attribute it to factors about themselves or the environment that can be changed and controlled, such as insufficient effort or a very difficult task" (p. 471). In sharp contrast, the learned helpless child attributes her failures to the lack of ability, but, interestingly enough, she attributes her successes to luck rather than to ability. In either circumstance, learned helpless children eventually believe that ability is a "fixed characteristic of the self that cannot be changed" (Berk 1996, p. 471). Consequently, in their minds, effort doesn't count for much and will not have an appreciable effect on competence. As a further consequence, future difficult tasks merely increase their sense of incompetence and their feelings of loss of control, a condition that leads to Erikson's sense of inferiority (Berk 1996, p. 471).

This concludes the background segment of this chapter. We have attempted to select developmental and behavioral occurrences in the lives of seven- and eight-year-olds that are either reasonably open or accessible to naturalistic observation or, where they are not, to some form of intervention or testing that might reveal the behaviors of interest. Again, constraints of time and space have forced us to make choices that might not have been made by others. You should always feel free to make your own decisions as to what and how to observe. We can only offer a few guidelines to direct you down a few pathways among the many that exist in the context of young children's growth, development, and behavior.

Before getting into the observation exercises, we want to remind you that unless you are already officially associated with the school or other facility in which you will do your observations, prior permission is required to enter that facility and observe the children. Getting such permission must be one of the first tasks on your agenda. The actual process involved will undoubtedly already have been established by the appropriate authorities at the observation site. Consult with them before embarking on any of your assignments.

Observation Exercise 19-1

Part I: *Physical Growth and Motor Development*: Observation Objectives

The purposes of this exercise are at least two-fold: (1) to observe seven- and eight-year-olds' motor behavior in the context of their play activities, and (2) to compare and contrast the characteristics of girls' and boys' play and motor functioning. Two factors are assumed to operate here. First, there is the assumption that children seven and eight years of age of both genders tend to play with more sophistication and complexity than they did when they were younger, *characteristics that will influence the kind and quality of the motor behaviors a child of either sex will exhibit during the course of play*. Second, there is the assumption that girls play differently than boys, which means that the characteristics of each gender's physical/motor actions will be different from each other. It is these two general classes of differences that we want you to observe and record.

Procedure

PART I: In Part I of this exercise, you will use the *event sampling format* or technique. Find several children—*at least two or three, if possible*—who are playing together and whose play involves significant motor activity. Observe and record their behavior for as long as it lasts, unless its duration is too long and it becomes unfeasible for you to continue.

When you have gathered all of your data, interpret it with respect to the overall characteristics of the children's motor functioning. Try to draw comparisons and contrasts between the kind and quality of these seven- and eight-year-olds' motor skills and preferences and what you know—or can find out—to be the kind and quality of a six-year-old's motor skills and preferences. You might be able to make such comparisons by using the information you acquired via your earlier observations of the six-year-old.

PART II: *Gender-Related Differences in Motor Functioning*: Observation Objectives

Part II of this exercise is concerned with discovering any differences that might exist between boys' and girls' motor behavior—that is, what kinds of games they play (or other activities they might participate in) and the differences in motor skills that these games or activities might require.

Procedure

You will again use the *event sampling technique*. This time, select a small group of girls and a similar group of boys who are engaged in some kind of activity that involves the use of their bodies and their motor skills and abilities.

Your focus here will be less on the individual child and more on how all of the individuals function as a group, but with respect to the physical/

motor demands that the activity makes on the children. The assumption is that because the group as a whole has apparently gotten together to play in whatever game they happen to be playing, each individual child will have at least most of the prerequisite skills needed for that activity. If girls games require different skills than boys games, these differences should become apparent and accessible to your observation and recording.

Observation Exercise II: Cognitive and Intellectual Development and Behavior

PART I: *Concrete Operational Thinking*: *Observation Objectives*

We have stressed Piaget's concrete operational stage of cognitive development both in the Chapter 18 and again in the present one. You might recall that earlier in the text, we mentioned that although theory testing is not one of your usual tasks, in the course of your observations you might very well do just that—test a theory. Part of your assignment in Exercise 18-2 was to determine whether the six-year-old children you observed functioned significantly in the stage of concrete operations. At issue was the claim that the period of concrete operations does not "officially" begin until about age seven. One of the objectives of this present exercise is to compare and contrast the concrete operational thinking of some seven- and eight-year-olds with the concrete operational thinking of some six-year-olds. You are to decide which group of children, as identified by their ages, indeed better represents the cognitive functioning that is characteristic of this third stage in Piaget's theory.

Procedure

Therefore, for Part I of this exercise, select *two or three children* for observation. Use the *event sampling format* or technique and look for examples of cognitive behavior that can be described as concrete operational thinking. Refer to Table 19-2 for more detailed information regarding the important characteristics of this stage. With the information you need at hand, compare your data on seven- and eight-year-olds' level of cognitive functioning with any data you have on the six-year-old's level of cognitive functioning. Are there any sharp differences or similarities between these two age groups? If you do not have prior observation data on six-year-olds, or if you are not able to observe children of this age before completing the present exercise, you may simply compare the information you do have against information available in a textbook or in this manual. Although that information will not have come from your own personal observations, it will be the result of someone's observations, and that fact serves to attest to the importance of observation as a necessary and legitimate activity.

PART II: *General Characteristics of Children's Cognitive Behavior: Observation Objectives*

In Part II of this exercise, you will focus on the overall characteristics of the children's cognitive functioning, with the goal of simply describing in more or less general terms how seven- and eight-year-olds think and process information, the kinds of knowledge they might possess and how they deal with or use this knowledge, and so on.

Procedure

Select at least *three children* and using the *narrative description format,* observe and record their behavior for what we shall simply call a "reasonable length of time." We would add, however, that you should select a situation and setting that lend themselves to witnessing the kinds of behaviors you want to observe. Refer to Table 19-4 for some guidelines regarding the types of cognitive behaviors that are relevant to this exercise.

Observation Exercise 19-3: Language

Observation Objectives

Although our background discussion of language presents rather specific information, the objectives for this exercise are purposely left somewhat open-ended. Your goal will simply be to capture as much information about several children's language behavior as you possibly can and offer a general interpretive description of the basic characteristics of their language. The characteristics of major importance for this exercise are vocabulary, grammar, and pragmatics, as these are discussed above under background information.

Procedure

Select *at least two children* as your "targets." We recommend that both sexes or genders be represented, and if you observe, say, three children, two boys and a girl or two girls and a boy, rather than three boys or three girls, this would be the more desired gender composition of the group. Using the *narrative description format,* record verbatim as much of the children's speech as you can. Then interpret or discuss your data with respect to the children's vocabulary, the grammatical construction of their sentences, and whatever aspect of pragmatics you are able to discern.

Finally, compare and contrast the characteristics of the general language behavior exhibited by a child of each sex. For example, do girls talk about different things than boys? Can you detect significant differences in their respective vocabularies, grammatical constructions, and so on? Is it boys, girls, or neither sex, who have the "better" verbal skills? Do boys and girls differ in their language usage when in the same setting and situation? That is, do boys use more assertive, aggressive, or authoritative language than girls when they are acting as leaders, for example?

Observation Exercise 19-4: Social and Emotional Development and Behavior

Observation Objectives

A primary objective of this exercise is to observe and record evidence of children's self-esteem as they express it in the course of their daily activities and interactions. Such expressions can be made with regard to one or more of the three kinds of self-esteem reported by Berk (1996) and discussed above in the background information: *academic, physical,* and *social* self-esteem. Coinciding with self-esteem is self-concept, which is how a child describes him- or herself. You must understand and maintain the distinction between self-esteem and self-concept in order to complete this exercise successfully.

Procedure

This exercise may be difficult to complete through strictly naturalistic observation, because it requires you to hear and record specifically what children say about themselves—descriptions in terms both of their self-concepts and their self-esteem. In view of this somewhat limiting condition, you may have to resort to some kind of intervention strategy, perhaps directly asking a child to talk about himself or herself, to describe herself to you, to tell you something about himself. You may want to ask the child what he or she is or is not good at in school, for instance, or when playing with peers, and so on. You will have to try to get the child to evaluate himself with respect to his strengths and weaknesses; this evaluation will give you some notion of the worth or value the child places on himself with respect to his academic performance, social skills and status, and physical appearance, if you can tap into all of those areas.

Whether you use naturalistic observation or a "testing" approach is a judgment you will have to make. In any event, use the following procedure if observation alone is feasible and it will give you the information you need to complete the assignment.

Select at least *two children* for this exercise. It might be desirable to observe a boy and a girl rather than two boys or two girls. Use the *narrative description format,* since this technique yields the greatest amount of information per unit of time spent observing. The idea here is to try to witness the children's verbal and behavioral expressions concerning how they feel about themselves, how they rate themselves against various performance, social, and physical criteria, either in relation to themselves or in comparison to their peers.

If you are observing in a formal school setting, the children's academic self-esteem may be put in the context of *mastery-oriented attributions* or the attributions associated with *learned helplessness.* Whatever the specific context, try to obtain information about as many aspects of the children's self-esteem as you can, as well as descriptions of their self-concepts, or how they describe themselves and what qualities or characteristics they assign to themselves. We have been using the phrase "testing strategy" to indicate a means of obtaining information about children other than by naturalistic observation. Even though we have tried to recommend this approach very sparingly, "testing" may still not be quite the appropriate word, since it could suggest a procedure that does not serve the child's best interests, or is too intrusive, or is not really observation in its purer form. In the present context, therefore, we offer the phrase "conversational strategy" or "conversational approach" to replace "testing strategy." Apart from direct, non-intervening observation, and except for one possible alternative approach, it will be through conversation with children that you will have to get the information you need to complete this exercise.

Moreover, if you believe that a conversational approach is the better approach, even if only for part of the exercise, then we leave it up to you to devise an appropriate way of getting the data you need. But we must remind you that the sanctity of the child's feelings, the confidentiality of the information you obtain, and any other ethical issue or concern associated with the observation process, has to be given top priority. This issue is of special relevance in this exercise, because you are delving into children's perceptions of who they are and the value or worth they put on themselves as persons, as students, as physical beings, and as social partners with their teachers, friends, and peers.

Therefore, keep in mind that although the children may make judgments about themselves, you are not to make judgments about the children.

As a final task, it might be interesting to compare the self-concept statements your children make with the self-descriptive statements made by the seven-year-old boy and the eleven-year-old girl reported by Berk. How close do the general characteristics of your children's self-concepts come to those of the children cited in the example?

There are those who would oppose the conversational approach for obtaining information about children's self-esteem and self-concept. If you or those in authority in the observational setting are opposed to such an approach, then out of respect for that point of view, let us suggest yet another possible way to get the data you need. If you are in a formal school setting, talk to a teacher or other *appropriate* staff member about a child's self-esteem and self-concept. What are that individual's perceptions or impressions of the child in that regard? Then, observe the child and look for behavioral indications of the teacher's/staff member's impressions. For example, does the child persevere in the face of difficult tasks? Does the child blame himself or others for his success? his failures? Does the child describe herself in ways that correspond with the teacher's description of the child's self-concept? Instead of a teacher, a parent may be the person to give you this kind of information.

Epilogue

There is only one more thing we have to say at this time: "Congratulations!" How far and how long you have traveled depends on how many of the observation exercises you have completed and how much you have involved yourself in the overall content of this manual. We sincerely hope that your journey has been informative and interesting, even if at times it may have been difficult and time consuming. We believe, nonetheless, that if not now, in the immediate present, then sometime in the future, you will find that your hard work has paid off. If today you are a better, more astute observer of young children's behavior than you were just yesterday, and certainly before you first began, then we have accomplished our primary objective.

Observation Exercise 19-1

Part I: General Physical and Motor Skills of the Seven- and Eight-Year-Old (In the Context of Play or Game)

Observer's Name _____

Child/Children Observed _____

Child's/Children's Age(s) _____ Child's/Children's Sex _____

Observation Context (home, child care center, preschool, school) _____

Date of Observation _____ Time Begun _____ Time Ended _____

Brief Description of Physical and Social Characteristics of Observation Setting:

_____

OBJECTIVE BEHAVIORAL DESCRIPTIONS (OBD) AND INTERPRETATIONS: *Event Sampling*

OBD 1:   [Time begun _____   Time ended _____]

Interpretation 1:

OBD 2:   [Time begun _____   Time ended _____]

Interpretation 2:

Continue for as many OBDs as are needed or desired.

Comparisons of Motor Skills of Seven- and Eight-Year-Olds with Those of Six-Year-Old:

Contrasts Between Motor Skills of Seven- and Eight-Year-Olds and Those of Six-Year-Old:

Observation Exercise 19-1

Continued

Part II: Gender-Related Differences in Motor Functioning

Observer's Name _____

Child/Children Observed _____

Child's/Children's Age(s) _____   Child's/Children's Sex _____

Observation Context (home, child care center, preschool, school) _____

Date of Observation _____   Time Begun _____   Time Ended _____

Brief Description of Physical and Social Characteristics of Observation Setting:

_____

OBJECTIVE BEHAVIORAL DESCRIPTIONS (OBD) AND INTERPRETATIONS: *Event Sampling*
Clearly Indicate the gender composition of the respective groups for each OBD

OBD 1:   [Time begun _____   Time ended _____]

Interpretation 1:

OBD 2:   [Time begun _____   Time ended _____]

Interpretation 2:

Continue for as many OBDs as are needed or desired.

Summary Comments Concerning General Characteristics of Boys' and Girls' Motor Functioning and Play:

Summary Comments Concerning Similarities and Differences Between Boys' and Girls' Motor Functioning and Play:

Observation Exercise 19-2

Part I: Cognitive Functioning in Piaget's Stage of Concrete Operational Thinking: A Comparison Between Six-Year-Olds, and Seven- and Eight-Year-Olds

Observer's Name _____

Child/Children Observed _____

Child's/Children's Age(s) _____ Child's/Children's Sex _____

Observation Context (home, child care center, preschool, school) _____

Date of Observation _____ Time Begun _____ Time Ended _____

Brief Description of Physical and Social Characteristics of Observation Setting:

_____

OBJECTIVE BEHAVIORAL DESCRIPTIONS (OBD) AND INTERPRETATIONS: *Event Sampling*

OBD 1: [Time begun _____ Time ended _____]

Interpretation 1:

OBD 2: [Time begun _____ Time ended _____]

Interpretation 2:

OBD 3: [Time begun _____ Time ended _____]

Interpretation 3:

Continue for as many OBDs as are needed or desired.

Comparisons of the Two Groups of Children (With Respect to Stage of Cognitive Functioning):

Contrasts Between the Two Groups of Children (With Respect to Stage of Cognitive Functioning):

Observation Exercise 19-2

Continued

Part II: General Characteristics of Children's Cognitive Behavior

Observer's Name _____

Child/Children Observed _____

Child's/Children's Age(s) _____ Child's/Children's Sex _____

Observation Context (home, child care center, preschool, school) _____

Date of Observation _____ Time Begun _____ Time Ended _____

Brief Description of Physical and Social Characteristics of Observation Setting:

_____

OBJECTIVE BEHAVIORAL DESCRIPTIONS (OBD) AND INTERPRETATIONS:
 Narrative Description

OBD 1: [Time begun _____ Time ended _____]

Interpretation 1:

OBD 2: [Time begun _____ Time ended _____]

Interpretation 2:

OBD 3: [Time begun _____ Time ended _____]

Interpretation 3:

Continue for as many OBDs as are needed or desired.

Summary Remarks on Children's General Cognitive Characteristics:

Observation Exercise 19-3

Language

Observer's Name _____

Child/Children Observed _____

Child's/Children's Age(s) _____ Child's/Children's Sex _____

Observation Context (home, child care center, preschool, school) _____

Date of Observation _____ Time Begun _____ Time Ended _____

Brief Description of Physical and Social Characteristics of Observation Setting:

_____

OBJECTIVE BEHAVIORAL DESCRIPTIONS (OBD) AND INTERPRETATIONS:
  Narrative Description

OBD 1: Child's Sex ☐ **Male** ☐ **Female** **[Time begun** _____ **Time ended** _____ **]**

Interpretation 1:

OBD 2: Child's Sex ☐ **Male** ☐ **Female** **[Time begun** _____ **Time ended** _____ **]**

Interpretation 2:

OBD 3: Child's Sex ☐ **Male** ☐ **Female** **[Time begun** _____ **Time ended** _____ **]**

Interpretation 3:

Continue for as many OBDs as are needed or desired.

Summary Comments on Children's General Language Behavior, Skills, and so on.

Comparisons and Contrasts Between Boys' and Girls' Language Behavior, Skills, and so on.

Observation Exercise 19-3

Continued

Optional Exercise: Comparisons of Seven- and Eight-Year-Old's Language Skills With those of a:

Six-Year-Old:

Five-Year-Old:

Three-Year-Old:

Please note that there is nothing wrong with comparing and contrasting seven- and eight-year-old children's language skills with, say, the language skills of nine-year-olds. Our assumption is that you may already have, from previous observation assignments, information on three-, five-, and six-year-olds' language abilities. Moreover, these younger ages fall within the definition of early childhood, and the nine-year-old does not.

Observation Exercise 19-4

Social and Emotional Development and Behavior (Self-Esteem and Self-Concept)

Observer's Name _____

Child/Children Observed _____

Child's/Children's Age(s) _____   Child's/Children's Sex _____

Observation Context (home, child care center, preschool, school) _____

Date of Observation _____   Time Begun _____   Time Ended _____

Brief Description of Physical and Social Characteristics of Observation Setting:

_____

OBJECTIVE BEHAVIORAL DESCRIPTIONS (OBD) AND INTERPRETATIONS:
Narrative Description (with Naturalistic Observation)

OBD 1:   [Time begun _____   Time ended _____]

Interpretation 1:

OBD 2:   [Time begun _____   Time ended _____]

Interpretation 2:

OBD 3:   [Time begun _____   Time ended _____]

Interpretation 3:

Continue for as many OBDs as are needed or desired

Summary Comments:

OPTIONAL EXERCISE #1: Compare the self-concept statements you observed with the statements made by the children in Berk's example cited in this manual:

Observation Exercise 19-4

Continued

Alternate Version: Social and Emotional Development and Behavior—Testing Format (Self-Esteem and Self-Concept)

Observer's Name _____

Child/Children Observed _____

Child's/Children's Age(s) _____   Child's/Children's Sex _____

Observation Context (home, child care center, preschool, school) _____

Date of Observation _____   Time Begun _____   Time Ended _____

Brief Description of Physical and Social Characteristics of Observation Setting:

_____

OBJECTIVE BEHAVIORAL DESCRIPTIONS (OBD) AND INTERPRETATIONS:
Conversational Approach

If direct questioning was used, indicate specifically the question(s) you asked the child. Do this for each OBD or whenever the form of the question changes.

Question Asked:

Response of Child 1:

Interpretive Comment 1:

Question Asked:

Response of Child 2:

Interpretive Comment 2:

Continue for as long as needed or desired

Summary Remarks Regarding Children's Self-Esteem and Self-Concepts:

Observation Exercise 19-4

Continued

OPTIONAL EXERCISE #2: Compare a teacher's or parent's description of perception of a child's self-concept and self-esteem with the child's behaviors that presumably reflect or confirm those descriptions or perceptions. In other words, does the child behave in ways that match the adult's perceptions of the child's self-concept and self-esteem?

APPENDIX I
Developmental Checklists

Child's Name _____   Age _____

Observer _____   Date _____

DEVELOPMENTAL CHECKLIST

	Yes	No	Sometimes
BY THREE YEARS: Does the Child			
Run well in a forward direction?			
Jump in one place, two feet together?			
Walk on tiptoe?			
Throw ball (but without direction or aim)? Kick ball forward?			
String 4 large beads?			
Turn pages in book singly?			
Hold crayon: imitate circular, vertical, horizontal strokes?			
Match shapes?			
Demonstrate number concepts of one and two? (Can select one or two; can tell if one or two objects.)			
Use spoon without spilling?			
Drink from a straw?			
Put on and take off coat?			
Wash and dry hands with some assistance?			
Watch other children; play near them; sometimes join in their play?			
Defend own possessions?			
Use symbols in play—for example, tin pan on head becomes a space ship?			
Respond to "Put — in the box," "Take the — out of the box"?			
Select correct item on request: big vs. little; one vs. two?			
Identify objects by their use: show own shoe when asked, "What do you wear on your feet"?			
Ask questions?			
Tell about something with functional phrases that carry meaning: "Daddy go airplane." "Me hungry now"?			

Child's Name _____ Age _____

Observer _____ Date _____

DEVELOPMENTAL CHECKLIST

	Yes	No	Sometimes
BY FOUR YEARS: Does the Child			
Walk on line?			
Balance on one foot briefly? Hop on one foot?			
Jump over an object 6 inches high and land on both feet together?			
Throw ball with direction?			
Copy circles and crosses?			
Match 6 colors?			
Count to 5?			
Pour well from pitcher? Spread butter, jam with knife?			
Button, unbutton large buttons?			
Know own sex, age, last name?			
Use toilet independently and reliably?			
Wash and dry hands unassisted?			
Listen to stories for at least 5 minutes?			
Draw head of person and at least one other body part?			
Play with other children?			
Share, take turns (with some assistance)?			
Engage in dramatic and pretend play?			
Respond appropriately to "Put it beside," "Put it under"?			
Respond to two step directions: "Give me the sweater and put the shoe on the floor"?			
Respond by selecting the correct object—for example, hard vs. soft object?			
Answer "if," "what," and "when" questions?			
Answer questions about function: "What are books for"?			

Child's Name _____ Age _____

Observer _____ Date _____

DEVELOPMENTAL CHECKLIST

	Yes	No	Sometimes
BY FIVE YEARS: Does the Child			
Walk backward, heel to toe?			
Walk up and down stairs, alternating feet?			
Cut on line?			
Print some letters?			
Point to and name 3 shapes?			
Group common related objects: shoe, sock and foot; apple, orange and plum?			
Demonstrate number concepts to 4 or 5?			
Cut food with knife: celery, sandwich?			
Lace shoes?			
Read from story picture book—in other words, tell story by looking at pictures?			
Draw a person with 3 to 6 body parts?			
Play and interact with other children; engage in dramatic play that is close to reality?			
Build complex structures with blocks or other building materials?			
Respond to simple three step directions: "Give me the pencil, put the book on the table, and hold the comb in your hand"?			
Respond correctly when asked to show penny, nickel, and dime?			
Ask "How" questions?			
Respond verbally to "Hi" and "How are you"?			
Tell about event using past and future tense?			
Use conjunctions to string words and phrases together—for example, "I saw a bear and a zebra and a giraffe at the zoo"?			

Child's Name _____ Age _____

Observer _____ Date _____

DEVELOPMENTAL CHECKLIST

	Yes	No	Sometimes
BY SIX YEARS: Does the Child			
Walk across a balance beam?			
Skip with alternating feet?			
Hop for several seconds on one foot?			
Cut out simple shapes?			
Copy own first name?			
Show well-established handedness; demonstrate consistent right or left handedness?			
Sort objects on one or more dimensions: color, shape or function?			
Name most letters and numerals?			
Count by rote to 10; know what number comes next?			
Dress self completely; tie bows?			
Brush teeth unassisted?			
Have some concept of clock time in relation to daily schedule?			
Cross street safely?			
Draw a person with head, trunk, legs, arms and features; often add clothing details?			
Play simple board games?			
Engage in cooperative play with other children, involving group decisions, role assignments, rule observance?			
Use construction toys, such as Legos, blocks, to make recognizable structures?			
Do 15-piece puzzles?			
Use all grammatical structures: pronouns, plurals, verb tenses, conjunctions?			
Use complex sentences, carry on conversations?			

Child's Name _____   Age _____

Observer _____   Date _____

DEVELOPMENTAL CHECKLIST

	Yes	No	Sometimes
BY SEVEN OR EIGHT YEARS: Does the Child			
Participate in competitive activities?			
Show significant improvement from earlier age in agility, balance, control of motor abilities, and so on?			
Produce letters and numbers deliberately and confidently?			
Cut food with knife and fork?			
Name denominations of coins and currency?			
Plan ahead?			
Tell time and know the correct day, month, and year?			
Comprehend cause and effect in developmentally appropriate situations?			
Show some knowledge of addition and subtraction of numbers?			
Recall stories in considerable detail?			
Use adult-like sentences?			
Use gestures to make a point in a conversation?			
Play with two or three close friends of the same age?			
Like to talk with friends on the telephone?			
Want to belong to groups; like to talk in secret code; strongly desire peer acceptance?			

Adapted from Allen and Marotz (1994, pp. 128–131)

1. Initiation of Activity:

   ___ Almost always involves self in constructive activity of own choice; often rejects suggestions.

   ___ Occasionally needs help in initiating activity; accepts it readily.

   ___ Frequently spends long period before initiating activity; sometimes may reject suggestions.

   ___ Rarely initiates activities, or usually rejects suggestions.

2. Attention Span:

   ___ Can stay with a chosen activity for very long periods, even returning the next day.

   ___ Can remain with an age-appropriate task until it is finished.

   ___ Needs encouragement to stay with task until complete.

   ___ Rarely finishes task. Moves rapidly from one to another.

3. Curiosity:

   ___ Interested in new ideas—words and relationships as well as things.

   ___ Actively explores any new things in the room.

   ___ Can be intrigued by really exciting things, but usually uninterested.

   ___ Shows little or no interest in anything new.

4. Frustration Tolerance:

   ___ Is inventive in solving practical problems. If he is completely blocked, shows mature behavior.

   ___ Usually tries hard and accepts failure well, but if severely frustrated may behave immaturely.

   ___ Sometimes reacts to mild frustrations by giving up, crying, or behaving aggressively.

___ Unable to tolerate any level of frustration; gives up, cries, or behaves aggressively.

5. Relationship with Teacher:

___ Self sufficient; may volunteer help or support to teacher.

___ Warm relationship, but asks for help or attention only when appropriate.

___ Sometimes requires unusual amount of help or physical contact; or seeks attention through silly or wild actions; or is occasionally aggressive toward teacher.

___ Continually seeks: help, contact, or attention; or frequently behaves aggressively; or ignores teacher entirely (but clings to avoid some situations).

6. Acceptance of Routines and Limits:

___ Understands and obeys intelligently even when teacher is not present.

___ Usually conforms to limits and routines but can deviate easily when appropriate.

___ Frequently tests limits; or fails to follow routines; or somewhat anxious about changes in routine.

___ Testing of limits and resisting of routines continuous problem; or compulsive about routine, becomes anxious at any deviation from schedule.

7. Reactions to Adults Other Than Teacher:

___ Interested in new adults; will take lead in conversation but not try to monopolize.

___ Does not initiate contact but will accept it and leave room with adult if teacher tells him to do so.

___ Will not respond to initiation; or refuses to leave room until he knows person well; or overly eager for attention from strangers.

___ Cries or hides when stranger approaches; or makes immediate demands for exclusive attention from new adults.

8. Interaction with Other Children:

___ Initiates cooperative play regularly.

___ Occasionally initiates play and usually accepts initiation from others.

___ Often rejects advances of others; or plays more alone than with others.

___ Avoids other children most of the time.

Reprinted, by permission, from Helen Chauvin, Director, Head Start Program, Plattsburgh State University College.

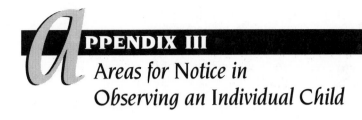

Areas for Notice in
Observing an Individual Child

Physical Appearance

What are the child's general physical features?

Does he seem in good physical health?

Body Movements and Use of Body

Does he move quickly or slowly?

Does he seem at ease with his body, or is he stiff or unsure?

Are his small and large muscle skills and movements about equally developed or is one area more developed than the other?

Does he express his feeling through his body—slouching shoulders, drooping head, slow movements; or quick, jaunty pace, chest puffed out, marked arm swing?

Facial Expressions

Does she use her face to express feelings?

Does her face register her minute-by-minute reactions to what she is experiencing and what is occurring around her?

Does her face show only intense feelings?

Does she typically show a "deadpan" expression?

Speech

How much of his feelings does he express through his tone of voice?

Does he generally keep his voice under control, or does it express changing moods?

When upset, does he talk more or less than usual?

Is speech an important means of communication to the child, or does he seldom speak, preferring to communicate in other ways?

Does he play with speech by making up chants, songs, puns, stories?

Is his speech fluent, average, inarticulate?

Emotional Reactions

How and when does she exhibit happiness, anger, sadness, doubt, enthusiasm, fear?

Does she seem to have too much control over her feelings, too little control, or a good balance?

Play Activities

What activities does he get involved in?

How does he become involved; how do the activities progress; what does he go to next?

Does he play for a long time at one thing or does he move from one activity to another?

Does he play only briefly in some activities but show prolonged attention in others?

Does she avoid any activities?

What does she seem to derive from an activity—the pleasure of being with other children, sensory stimulation or pleasure, a feeling of mastery or problem solving, a sense of creative expression of ideas and feelings?

Do any aspects of an activity seem to especially frustrate or especially please her?

Does the tempo or pace of his play remain even, speed up, slow down? Under what circumstances?

Does he prefer to play alone—never, always, sometimes? Under what circumstances?

Does she express fantasy in her play verbally, through gestures, through play materials?

If she engages in dramatic play, what kind of roles does she like to take—mother, baby, father, dog?

Does he try new things?

Does he show curiosity about his environment, equipment, people?

Does she prefer to confine her play to a relatively small space, or does she expand over a large area?

Does he seem more comfortable playing indoors or outdoors?

Does she have special skills (music, painting, puzzles, dramatic play)?

Basic Needs

Do you notice anything in particular about his habits and feelings about food? elimination? sexuality? sleep? rest?

Emotional Dependency Behavior: Time Sample Procedure

Observer's Name _____

Observation Setting (home, day-care center, etc.) _____

Date _____ Time _____ Activity _____

Brief Description of Setting/Situation:

_____

Recording Intervals	1	2	3	4	5	6	Child

Behavior Signs

Proximity-Seeking

FT	Follows Teacher
FC	Follows Child
CT	Cries when Teacher leaves area
RS	Resists Strangers
CT	Clings to Teacher

Positive Attention-Seeking

AT	Seeks approval from teacher for specific acts done, work accomplished
AC	Seeks approval from child, for acts done, work accomplished
GT	Seeks general acknowledgement from teacher—no specific focus of efforts
GC	Seeks general acknowledgement from child—no specific focus of efforts

Negative Attention-Seeking

WA	Whines for attention
CA	Cries for attention

Recording Intervals		1	2	3	4	5	6	Child

TT   Temper tantrum for attention, or if
     does not get attention
DG   Disrupts group activities to get
     attention

Definitions of Behavior Signs and Procedure

Proximity-seeking consists of behaviors that (1) serve to keep the child physically close to the teacher or another child, or (2) indicate anxiety or displeasure at being apart from the teacher or other child. "Clings to teacher" (or child) involves actual physical contact, whereas "follows" indicates being close without actually touching. "Resists strangers" implies stranger anxiety and an accompanying desire on the part of the child to be near a *familiar* adult or child. Proximity is sought for its own sake and for the emotional security it provides the child.

Positive and *negative attention-seeking* are more specific in their focus, even though they usually require the child to be at least momentarily close to the adult or another child. "General acknowledgement" refers to attention-seeking that has no specific focus or intent; the child simply wants an adult or another child to know he is there or that he has done something. He does not demand actual approval for his accomplishment; and so a mere "I see" from the teacher may be sufficient. Approval-seeking demands a more specific kind of acknowledgement from the teacher or another child—"Yes, John, that's *very good!*" may be the response John wants to hear.

Negative attention-seeking behaviors are behaviors that adults (and sometime children) usually define as unpleasant or unacceptable. Whining, crying, temper tantrums, and generally disruptive behaviors are usually considered negative. The child who displays such behaviors often does so for their attention-getting value; he will even risk punishment, if that is a form of attention he is willing to accept, or if it seems to him to be the only way he can get attention when he wants or feels he needs it. These behaviors can be viewed as attention-seeking if the child stops the behavior when he receives the attention.

Procedure   Observe for 10 seconds and note whether the child is displaying any of the behaviors listed on the observation sheet. Record the behavior using the coding abbreviations; give yourself 20 seconds to make the recording. Then move on to the next child; stay in column "1" until all the children have been observed once. Repeat this process until you have a total of six (6) separate recordings for each child. If you observe 10 children, it will take you five minutes to complete the first round of observations.

Always record the most complex behavior displayed by the child. For example, if the child follows the teacher to get her approval of a drawing she has just completed, mark the incident as AT, since the proximity-seeking only served the primary purpose of getting approval of the drawing.

APPENDIX V

Observational Record (Social Skills)

Date _____

Frequency of Participation

Activities	9:00	9:15	9:30	9:45	10:00	10:15	10:30	10:45	11:00	11:15	Total
Easel-Markers turtle, printing, playdough											
Housekeeping											
Blocks Large Small											
Manipulative toys dominoes counting bears											
Calendar Weather											
Finger plays "8 pigs" "This little cow"											
Pig puppets art (group)											
Name bingo (group)											
Trikes Sand (group)											
Books Music											
Making snack											
Game: Guess who's tapping											

Reprinted, with permission, from Susan Benzon

Comments

Observational Record 1

Totals: _____
_____
_____
_____

Date:	Name	**Social Situations**											
		1	2	3	4	5	6	7	8	9	10	11	12
ART													
MUSIC													
SAND & WATER													
HOUSE KEEPING													
DRAMA PLAY													
BLOCKS													
BOOKS													
PUZZLES													

Reprinted, with permission, from Susan Benzon

Observational Record 2

Date _____

Group Activities

Name	Large Groups		%		Large Groups		%	

Reprinted, with permission, from Susan Benzon

Comments:

Note

Appendices labeled V and VI are used with permission of Susan Benzon, former Director, Humpty Dumpty Preschool, Plattsburgh Air Force Base, Plattsburgh, New York.

APPENDIX VII
Summary of Piaget's First Two Stages of Cognitive Development

Stage 1   Sensorimotor   Child learns to control his body in space. Behaves intelligently, but without use of language; uses his physical senses and his motor capacities to interact with and learn about the environment. Object permanence the capstone achievement of this stage.

Stage 2   Preoperational   Judgments of quantity based on perceptions. Various cognitive operations begin—seriation, classification, concepts of space, time, causality. Egocentric in some thinking and behavior. Language used to express thoughts. Still needs practical, concrete experiences; cannot reason hypothetically. Reasons from particular to particular; cannot reason from the general to the particular.

APPENDIX VIII
Havighurst's Developmental Tasks—
Infancy Through Middle Childhood

Havighurst defined "developmental task" as "a task which arises at or about a certain period in the life of an individual, successful achievement of which leads to his happiness and to success with later tasks, while failure leads to unhappiness in the individual, disapproval by society, and difficulty with later tasks" (Havighurst, R. J. *Human Development and Education*. New York: Longmans, Green. 1953: 2).

Infancy and Early Childhood (first five years)

1. Learning to walk
2. Learning to take solid food
3. Learning to talk
4. Learning to control elimination of body wastes
5. Learning sex differences and sexual modesty
6. Achieving physiological stability
7. Forming simple concepts of social and physical reality
8. Learning to relate oneself emotionally to parents, siblings, and other people
9. Learning to distinguish right and wrong, and developing a conscience

Middle Childhood (from six to twelve years)

1. Learning physical skills necessary for ordinary games
2. Building wholesome attitudes toward oneself as a growing organism
3. Learning to get along with agemates
4. Learning an appropriate masculine or feminine social role
5. Developing fundamental skills in reading, writing, and calculating
6. Developing concepts necessary for everyday living
7. Developing a conscience, morality, and a scale of values
8. Achieving personal independence
9. Developing attitudes toward social groups and institutions

Glossary

Accommodation

a mental process in which the person changes his cognitive structure or sensorimotor scheme to deal successfully with a new situation; for example, a child accommodates when he comes to understand that not every four-legged animal is a "doggie."

Action fragment

a sample of behavior that is not representative and therefore supplies no information about the larger behavior stream; the behavior sample is thus only a fragment of the total action that occurred.

Actions

behaviors; actions form a class or set of items that are recorded by checklists, what Brandt (1972) called action checklists.

Activity versus passivity in development

two opposing points of view regarding the extent to which the child participates in his own development. The passive view holds that the child is primarily a *reactor* to the environment and "soaks up" stimulation like a sponge; the active view sees the child as an *actor* who seeks stimulation rather than passively waiting for it to occur.

Alert Activity (also called active alert, waking activity)

one of the six states or relative levels of infant arousal first identified by Wolff (1966). Alert activity is characterized by such things as irregular breathing and vigorous body movements.

Anecdotal record

an informal observation method often used by teachers as an aid to understanding the child's personality or behavior. It provides a running account of behavior that is either typical or unusual for the child being observed.

Animism

a belief that non-living objects are actually alive and behave like humans.

Artificialism

the belief that everything that exists has been created by human beings or by a god who builds things the way people do according to a plan or blueprint.

Assimilation

a mental process in which the person attempts to make a stimulus or piece of information fit into what she already knows.

Attachment

a condition process in which one person is dependent on another for emotional satisfaction and support; attachment forms with specific other persons and is enduring over time.

Average Status Children

children whom some peers like and some dislike. Average status children appear to differ from the controversials in terms of the number of peers who have feelings one way or another toward them.

Behavior

anything an individual does that can be directly observed by one or more of the five physical senses.

Behavior sampling

this is the general objective and characteristic of all observation; sampling involves taking some portion (sample) of the behaviors out of an individual's behavior stream. Different methods of observing and recording take different sized samples with different amounts and kinds of information.

Behavior stream

a metaphor used by Herbert Wright to capture the continuous quality of behavior; behavior is a lifelong continuum, a stream that can never be seen in its entirety.

Bias

a particular perspective or point of view; biases can be personal or based on a theory or philosophy.

Category system

a type of coding system in which the categories of behavior chosen for observation are both mutually exclusive and exhaustive; that is, each category excludes all other categories, and the categories include the total range of behaviors that a child can exhibit.

Cephalocaudal principle

the principle that describes motor development as progressing in a head-to-foot direction; the child first gains control over the head and neck and proceeds down the body to finally gain control over the legs and feet.

Checklist

an information observation method that denotes the presence or absence of something. In studying children, checklists record whether specific behaviors have occurred.

Classical conditioning

a form of learning in which a neutral stimulus—one that evokes no response—becomes paired with a stimulus that does. Eventually, the neutral stimulus evokes the response; for example, a puff of air on the eye causes the individual to blink, a soft tone does not; if the tone and the puff of air are both administered very close together in time, eventually the tone by itself will cause the individual to blink.

Classification

a process of sorting objects into groups according to perceived similarities; for example, putting all green things into one group, and all red things into another group. Objects (and ideas) can be classified according to a number of dimensions at the same time; for example, according to shape, size, and color.

Closed method

a characteristic of any method that does not preserve descriptions of behavior and events as they originally occurred.

Coding scheme

a means of reducing complex, detailed descriptions of behavior to a simple mark of tally on an observation sheet; coding schemes often record categories of behavior, such as aggression, dependency, or quarrels.

Cognitive structure

Piaget's concept referring to one's mental organization of ideas and facts; an individual's cognitive structure determines his intellectual behavior and abilities at any given stage of development.

Collective monologue

a form of egocentric speech in which two or more persons are talking together but none of them is paying attention to what the others are saying; each conversation is independent of the other conversations.

Concept

a mental representation or memory of something; concepts bring together attributes that are common to several different events; e.g., the concept "dog" represents the attributes of fur-bearing, four-legged, mammal, and domesticated carnivore that characterize collies, terriers, German shepherds, and all other breeds of dog.

Concrete operational thinking

The kind of intellectual ability possible to the child in Piaget's stage of concrete operations. Concrete operational thinking allows the child to adapt to various aspects of his environment through the use of systematic logic. Such thinking is characterized by the ability to (1) reverse mental actions, (2) move away from the appearance of things to their "reality," (3) attend to several aspects of a situation at a time rather than just one, and (4) see others' points of view, i.e., there is a decline in egocentrism.

Confidentiality

a condition of research and observation in which the observer or researcher does not reveal information about any individual to anyone.

Conservation

a general principle that the physical appearance of a substance does not necessarily affect its quantity. The principle applies to such things as substance, volume, number, area, and length; for example, the principle of conservation of number dictates that the physical arrangement of a group of coins has no effect on their number.

Conservation of number

one of several conservation tasks or abilities, conservation of number refers to the fact that two numerically equal quantities of something remain equal even when one of them is changed in some way, provided that nothing has been added or taken away. Changes that do not affect the quantity of something are called irrelevant transformations.

Context

a term that combines setting and situation to include all aspects of an environment—time, space, circumstances, other people, and physical and psychological conditions.

Control

related to structure, control also refers to observing young children's behavior in a patterned, systematic way. The observer controls the observation by knowing her purpose and being able, for the most part, to accomplish her objectives.

Controversial children

children who seem to strike a balance between being liked and disliked. Many of their peers like them, and many also dislike them.

Cumulative change

a characteristic of development in which behaviors build on one another and contribute to the overall character and direction of the developmental process.

Degree of observer inference required

a characteristic of observation and recording methods involving the amount of inference that is required in using a particular method; inference was also discussed in terms of when in the observation process inference is needed. Specimen records require no inferences at the time of initial recording; time sampling using a coding scheme requires inferences at the time of recording.

Degree of selectivity

a characteristic of observation and recording methods that determines how many behaviors are targeted for observing and recording. Methods vary from completely unselective (specimen record) to highly selective (such as the event sample).

Describe

to tell or write about; to give a word picture of some object, event, or idea.

Development

change over time in the structure, thoughts, and behaviors of an individual due to biological and environmental influences.

Diary description

an informal observation method in which records are made daily of selected aspects of a child's growth and development. The topical diary restricts itself to new behaviors exhibited by the child in a particular developmental area, such as language, social and emotional behavior, and so on; the comprehensive diary records in order as much of everything new as it can.

Differentiation

a process in which behaviors that are initially expressed in a diffuse, non-specific way, eventually separate out and become more skilled, specific, and independent of one another. Also refers to learning a new skill and, during that process, having to practice only that skill, isolating it from other skills already mastered.

Duration record

a variation of the frequency count in which the observer times how long a particular behavior lasts.

Egocentric speech

speech that does not take the other person into account and that, for all practical purposes, is private.

Egocentrism

the cognitive inability to take other people's points of view and to recognize their needs and interests; a preoccupation with one's own view of the world.

Elaboration

in information processing theory, elaboration is a memory device that forms absurd associations or connections among items to be remembered. It's the absurdity of the associations that makes remembering the items easier.

Emotional dependency

a need to be near others and to have their support, affection, and reassurance; it can also involve the unwillingness or self-perceived inability to do things for oneself that one can or should be able to do.

Empirical

having to do with things that can be seen, heard, touched, smelled, and tasted; data obtained by direct observation and not through abstract thought processes or theory; tied to the "real" world.

Environmentalism

a point of view that stresses the role of the environment in determining behavior and development, in contrast with the role of heredity.

Errors of commission

errors in which you include more information than is actually present in the situation; reporting behaviors and interactions that did not occur or persons as present who were not.

Errors of omission

errors in which you leave out information that is helpful or necessary to understanding the child's behavior.

Errors of transmission

errors in which you record observed behaviors in the wrong order.

Evaluation

the application of your own values and attitudes to the child's behavior, characteristics, and personality; generally, placing a value on, or judging the worth of something.

Event

behaviors that can be placed into particular categories; for example, hitting to get a toy away from another child is a behavior that can be put into the category "instrumental aggression."

Event sampling

a formal method that observes and records specific kinds of behaviors (events) whenever they occur. It is a sampling technique because it takes out of the behavior stream only preselected behaviors or categories of behaviors.

Explain

to give the meaning or interpretation of; to make clear or plain; to show the relationship among facts or ideas.

Filter

a term used metaphorically to illustrate the idea that things and events "pass through" our personalities, through our individual experiences, values, attitudes, and knowledge; these act as filters that allow certain information to get through to us, while excluding or screening out certain other information.

Five-to-seven shift

the period of gradual transition from the illogical and unsystematic thinking of the preschooler to the more logical thinking of the school-age child.

Formal observation method

a method of observing and recording behavior that is highly structured and controlled; it typically involves a great deal of prior preparation, including the construction of elaborate data forms and training of observers. Formal methods are often used in research studies.

Frequency count

an informal observation method in which the observer simply makes a mark or tally on an observation sheet every time a particular behavior occurs.

Group

a collection of individuals who are organized around a common purpose. Some groups are organized by an outside agency or authority—a school system or church, for example—and these are called institutional groups. Other groups form spontaneously on the basis of mutual interests and common characteristics; these are called peer groups.

Group observation

observations in which (1) the individual is observed in the context of a group and changes in her behavior as she participates in different groups are documented, or (2) the group itself is considered a single entity or unit and its behavior is observed and recorded.

Growth

increase in size, function, or complexity to some point of optimal maturity; associated with quantitative change.

Habituation

a situation where, after being exposed to a physical stimulus that originally evokes a response, the individual ceases paying attention to it; getting used to stimulus and losing interest in it.

Hierarchic integration

a process in which skills and behaviors that are initially separate and independent of one another are combined and can work together as a harmonious unit (e.g., the skill of grasping an object and the skill of moving the hand toward an object, are combined to form the integrated skill of reaching and grasping).

Hostile aggression

aggression in which the aggressor feels anger or hostility toward the victim and derives satisfaction from hurting the victim.

Inconspicuous observation

observation that imposes or introduces nothing into the observation setting and situation (context) beyond what is required to achieve legitimate objectives.

Informal observation method

a method of observing and recording behavior that lacks the strict research format of formal methods; it is less structures than a formal method and is suitable for immediate use by teachers and others who can use the method for day-to-day program operation and interactions with children.

Information processing theory

a model of cognitive functioning that assumes that (1) the mind is similar to a computer in that it stores and processes information; (2) processed information is also transformed by the individual, e.g., from a visual to a verbal or conceptual form; and (3) the individual's ability to process information is limited. (See, e.g., Zigler and Stevenson, 1993.)

Instrumental aggression

aggression in which the aggressor is interested only in getting an object from the victim or in achieving some goal, and he uses aggression to do so; it need not involve anger or hostility.

Instrumental dependency

the necessary reliance we all have on others for certain things that are beyond our own capacities to do.

Interobserver reliability

the degree to which two or more observers agree with one another as to what occurred during an observation session. High interobserver reliability indicates minimal disagreement and relatively few differences in observers' judgments and inferences.

Interpretation

going beyond your objective descriptions and trying to explain or give them meaning; relating something that is directly observable to something that is not directly observable, but which is perhaps based on a theory or hypothesis.

Intuitive

a substage of Piaget's preoperational stage of cognitive development. Intuitive thinking is the type of reasoning that takes place during the 5-to-7 shift. (see glossary for 5-to-7 shift).

Invisible displacement

taking an object from one place of concealment (such as under a piece of cloth) and moving it to another, but not allowing the child to watch you make the change; this is a technique used to test a child's concept of object permanence.

Learning history

an individual's life experiences, which form a unique set of learned associations or stimulus-response bonds; these constitute that person's distinctive history and make her different from everyone else.

Lexically based ambiguity

ambiguity based on the different meanings of words—e.g., "pen" can refer to a writing tool or to an enclosure in which animals are kept.

Linguistic

vocalizations that include actual words.

Maturation

developmental changes over time that are the result of heredity; changes built into the individual that unfold naturally and sequentially with time.

Metacognition

metacognition is thinking about thinking. It's being aware of one's cognitive abilities and exercising some control over them.

Metacommunication

similar to metacognition, metacommunication is communicating about communication. It's the ability, for instance, to talk about what makes a particular communication style effective or ineffective, or to consider how best to communicate a message to someone so that its meaning will not be lost or distorted.

Metalinguistic awareness

the ability to attend to and understand the form that language takes, the structure by which meaning is conveyed. The meaning itself is of secondary importance.

Method

a set of instructions that specifies what one must do to accomplish some task; it may also describe how to do what needs to be done.

Middle childhood

that period of the lifespan that comprises the period from 6 through 12 years of age. It is also frequently called the school-age years.

Monologue

a form of egocentric speech in which the individual talks only to herself, with no one else present.

Narrative Description

a formal method of observation and recording in which you continuously record in as much detail as possible what the child does and says, by herself and in interaction with other persons or objects. *See also* specimen record.

Natural unit

a sequence of behaviors that forms a logical whole or segment within the overall behavior stream; the unit has a distinct beginning, behaviors in the middle that constitute a specific event, and a distinct ending. Event sampling structures the observation environment into natural units. (Wright 1960)

Neglected children

children who are essentially neutral on the scale of liked versus disliked. Their peers neither actively like or dislike them. It might be said that such children's peers are indifferent to them.

Objective description

description of behavior and events that does not contain interpretations, subjective impressions, or speculations, but describes only what you see and hear in such a way that another observer would agree with your report.

Objective permanence

the understanding that objects continue to exist even when out of sight or hearing; this is the most important achievement of the sensorimotor period.

Observation

noting and recording facts and events; looking for something in a controlled, structured way.

Observation plan

a plan that guides all phases of the observation process. The plan determines what behaviors will be observed, how much of the behavior stream will be sampled, and which observation method will be used to achieve the other steps in the plan.

One-to-one correspondence

a matching of two groups of objects in which one object of one group is paired with one and only one object of the other group; for example, a child who has this ability can give each child at the snack table one cookie and one napkin.

Open method

a characteristic of any method that preserves descriptions of behavior and events as they originally occurred.

Operant conditioning

a form of learning in which the consequences of a response determine whether that response is likely to be repeated under the same or similar circumstances; for example, if a child's whining gets her the attention from the teacher that she desires, the child is likely to whine in future situations when she wants attention.

Organization
a strategy from remembering things by placing them into larger categories—e.g., putting all things that can be eaten into the category "food," or all things that one wears into the category "clothing." Remembering the broad category supposedly helps one to remember the specific items in that category.

Orienting response
a response in which the individual turns toward the source of a sound or other stimulus.

Participant observation
when an observer becomes part of the group she is observing and participates in as many of its activities as is appropriate, with the objective of reducing the effects of observation on the group's behavior.

Peer
a companion who is approximately the same age and developmental level.

Peer reputation
the relatively stable and consistent way a child's peers perceive and describe or characterize him or her.

Phonologically based ambiguity
ambiguity in language based on how words sound or are pronounced.

Playscapes
a relatively recent term to describe contemporary playground structures that are "innovative" by combining "a variety of material" (Essa, 1996).

Popular children
children whom most peers like and no one dislikes.

Pragmatics
pragmatics has to do with the practical, communicative side of language. Here, the individual has to deal with the practical tasks associated with making herself understood by others. One such task is to take into account the particular needs or situation of the listener.

Prelinguistic
vocalizations that occur prior to actual speech (cooing and babbling, for example).

Preoperational period
the second stage in Piaget's theory of cognitive development. It is defined primarily by the child's ability to use language and otherwise engage in symbol manipulation (what Piaget called the "symbolic function.") Unlike the later stages, however, the preoperational child is not able to engage in true operational thinking.

Process (noun)
a series of related activities that require time to accomplish.

Process (verb)
to think about, give a verbal label, to, or to put a fact into some meaningful relationship with other facts.

Production deficiency
a term used to describe the case where a child knows how to use a particular strategy but does not spontaneously do so in situations where it would help him solve a problem.

Professional ethics
standards of conduct that serve to protect the privacy, confidentiality, rights, and safety of anyone who is the subject of observation or research.

Proximodistal principle
the principle that describes motor development as progressing from the midline of the body outward to the extremities; thus, chest, shoulders, and upper arms come under control before the hands and feet.

Psychosocial crisis
a concept in Erikson's theory of personality development; a crisis is a conflict, a turning point or time of special sensitivity to particular social influences.

Qualitative change
change in psychological functions such as speech, emotions, and intelligence; involves change in the fundamental organization of behaviors and behavior patterns; change in the child's cognitive structure.

Quantitative change
growth; changes in the amount, number or quantity of something (e.g., increases in height and weight).

Raw data
descriptions of behavior and events as they originally occurred.

Reflex
a built-in, preprogrammed pattern of involuntary motor behavior that is elicited by a specific form of stimulation; e.g., the startle reflex is elicited by a sudden loud noise.

Rehearsal
a strategy that involves going over information again and again in order to remember it at a later time. In information processing theory, rehearsal aids the storage and retrieval processes.

Reinforcement
a condition in which an individual's response to a stimulus has rewarding or satisfying consequences; those consequences provide reinforcement of the re-

sponse, thus increasing the probability that, in the future, the individual will respond in similar fashion to a similar stimulus.

Rejected children
children whom most peers dislike and very few like.

Repetition
a form of egocentric speech in which the individual repeats words and phrases over and over again as if to practice them or as if he simply enjoyed making the sounds.

Representativeness
a desirable feature of behavior samples; representative samples are those that exemplify or reflect the typical characteristics of the larger population or class of behaviors of which the sample is a part.

Role
recurring behaviors and behavior patterns that are associated with specific statuses; teacher's role behaviors include teaching, grading, and counseling students, for example; parents' role behaviors include nurturing, protecting, and socializing the child.

Rough-and-tumble play
rough-and-tumble play is play that involves a lot of strenuous physical activity such as wrestling, running, pushing, and so on. It is, however, good-natured, prosocial activity that is very different from aggressive fighting. In this kind of play, there is no intent to hurt one another, and it's frequently engaged in by children who like each other.

Scaffolding
related to the zone of proximal development, scaffolding is the process whereby an adult gives the child the necessary assistance to allow the child to function on her own. (See, e.g., Krantz, 1994.)

Schema
Piaget's term for a concept or mental representation of events in the world.

Self-concept
the more or less objective assessment of who we are, our strengths and weaknesses, our personality characteristics. Self-concept refers to the manner in which an individual describes himself, e.g., the qualities or attributes that the child assigns to himself.

Self-esteem
self-esteem refers to one's sense of personal worth or value. It is distinguished from self-concept, although it is related to it.

Sensorimotor period
the first stage in Piaget's theory of cognitive development, in this stage, the infant learns about his environment by active manipulation of the objects in it; learning and intellectual development are accomplished by use of the physical senses and motor abilities.

Sensorimotor schemes
organized actions or sequences of actions that permit the individual to interact with the environment.

Sequential change
change that occurs in a lawful, orderly fashion and according to a predetermined series of steps or stages; stage theories hold that change is sequential.

Seriation
a process of arranging objects in some order according to a particular dimension; seriation requires the ability to compare and coordinate differences between objects—for example, arranging a collection of rocks in order of increasing weight, from the lightest to the heaviest.

Setting
the physical environment in which an observation takes place; it includes such factors as physical space, objects in that space, and opportunities and resources that permit people to behave in certain ways.

Sign system
a type of coding system in which the categories of behavior chosen for observation are mutually exclusive; that is, no given behavior can be put into more than one category because each category excludes all others.

Situation
the social and psychological characteristics and conditions that exist in a particular setting—the nature of the children's play, events that occur that may change the character of the ongoing activities, and so on.

Social
an interaction or situation in which each participant takes the others into account, or in which each participant influences and is influenced by the others.

Social autonomy
the ability to rely on oneself for the satisfaction of various needs and desires; self-sufficiency.

Social behavior
behavior between two or more persons who take one another into account and influence one another in some way.

Social cognition
an ability to think about and understand social and interpersonal events of which one is a part. Social cognition includes such things as social role-taking ability (which see), empathy, identification, and vicarious experiencing, among others.

Social comparison

describing, rating, and ranking peers on various characteristics and traits. Most simply put, social comparison involves comparing one's peers (or others) on various aspects of social and personal functioning and attributes.

Social role-taking ability

the ability to understand another person's position or situation and what he or she might be feeling or thinking. It involved such things as understanding emotions, intentions, and thinking. (See, e.g., Schickedanz *et al.*, 1993.)

Sociocentric speech

public speech; speech that is intended to communicate with someone, and each person takes into account what the others say and each responds accordingly.

Sociocentrism

the opposite of egocentrism; the ability to take other's points of view and to recognize their needs and interests.

Sociocultural theory (also sociohistoric theory)

the name given to Vygotsky's theory of mental development in which the emphasis is shifted away from the child in explaining development and to the influence of the individual's social or cultural environment.

Sociogram

a sociogram is a graphic representation of how children in a group feel about one another. Children are often represented by circles, and their interactions with peers are represented by arrows that connect one circle (child) to another.

Sociometry

a technique for studying children's popularity or social status among their peers. The technique can involve asking children to name their best friend or friends, or to identify the child or children who are most liked by the class or group.

Soothability

the ability of a crying or upset infant to be quieted by such adult responses as rocking, holding, swaddling, or giving a pacifier.

Spatial definition

the concept that physical spaces or environments have particular meanings associated with them, and these meanings or definitions determine what one may do when in that space or environment.

Specimen record

a formal method of observation and recording in which you continuously record in as much detail as possible what the child does and says, by herself and in interaction with other persons or objects. *See also* Narrative Description.

Spontaneous behaviors

behaviors that are internally generated and not responses to outside stimuli; they include behaviors such as random startles, fleeting smiles, and erections.

Stage theory

a theory that holds that development occurs in a step-like fashion, with each step or level qualitatively distinct from, and more complex than, previous levels.

Stars

a classification that can be determined from a sociogram (which see) and that identifies or describes a child or children who are well liked and popular among their peers. Such children also have considerable status and influence in the peer group.

States

levels of arousal such as asleep, alert, drowsy, and crying; as they are behavioral conditions that (1) are stable over a period of time, (2) occur repeatedly in an individual infant, and (3) are encountered in similar form in other individuals.

Static descriptor

a descriptive item that pertains to a highly stable characteristic of research subjects or settings (Brandt 1972); age, sex, race, and socioeconomic are examples of static descriptors. These descriptors are often recorded by a checklist.

Status

a position within a social group or organization; teacher, student, child, adult, president, and parent, are examples of statuses.

Stimulus-response bond

a connection or association between an environmental stimulus and an individual's response to that stimulus; the connection is established because the consequences of the response are rewarding or reinforcing to the individual.

Strategies

mental operations that are used to enhance memory, attention, and problem solving.

Structure

in the context of observation, structure refers to observing and recording behavior in a systematic, patterned way such that the observer knows why he or she is in the observation setting and by what method the behaviors of interest will be recorded.

Syntactically based ambiguity
ambiguity based on different interpretations of a sentence. This ambiguity depends on the structure of sentence itself and how that structure allows different meanings to be put on the sentence.

Temperament
a child's characteristic ways of responding to various situations; temperament is described by the child's responses on six personality dimensions: activity level, rhythmicity, approach/withdrawal, adaptability, intensity of reaction, and quality of mood.

Theory
a formal set of general statements or propositions that are supported by data and that attempt to explain a particular phenomenon.

Time sampling
a formal method of observation and recording in which you record selected behaviors during preset uniform time periods and at regularly recurring or randomly selected intervals.

Trait
a tendency or predisposition to behave in certain ways under certain circumstances.

Trust versus mistrust
the first crisis in Erikson's theory; the infant's experiences with his environment and the people in it will determine whether he resolves the crisis or conflict by establishing a stronger sense of trust than of mistrust. A sense of trust will enable the infant to see his world as a predominantly safe, nurturing and trustworthy place.

Validity
pertaining to the accuracy and soundness of an observation or interpretation; the degree to which something measures what it claims to.

Zone of proximal development (ZPD)
a concept in Vygotsky's theory, the ZPD refers to a situation (zone or gap) in which the child finds a task too difficult to accomplish alone but which can be accomplished with the help of an adult or older child. *See also* Scaffolding.

Bibliography

Ainsworth, M.O. The Development of Mother-Infant Attachment. edited by B. Caldweel and H. Ricciuti, *In Review of Child Development Research*, Vol. 3. Chicago: University of Chicago Press. 1973.

Ainsworth, Mary. *Infancy in Uganda: Infant Care and the Growth of Love.* Baltimore: Johns Hopkins University Press. 1967.

Allen, K.E. and Marotz, L. *Developmental Profiles: Prebirth Through Eight,* 2nd ed. Albany: Delmar Publishers. 1994.

Almy, Millie and Celia Genishi. *Ways of Studying Children,* Rev. ed. New York: Teachers College Press. 1979.

Ault, Ruth. *Children's Cognitive Development.* New York: Oxford University Press. 1977.

Barker, R.G. and Wright, H.F. *One Boy's Day.* New York: Harper and Row. 1951.

Beatty, Janice J. *Observing Development of the Young Child.* Columbus: Merrill Publishing Co. 1986.

Bee, H. *The Growing Child.* New York: Harper Collins Publisher. 1995.

Berger, K.S. *The Developing Person.* New York: Worth Publishers. 1980.

Berger, Kathleen S. *The Developing Person: Through Childhood and Adolescence,* 3rd ed. New York: Worth Publishers, Inc. 1991.

Berk, L.E. *Infants, Children, and Adolescents.* Boston: Allyn and Bacon. 1993.

Berk, Laura E. *Child Development.* Needham Heights: Allyn and Bacon. 1989.

Berns, R.M. *Topical Child Development.* Albany: Delmar Publishers, Inc. 1994.

Bigner, Jerry J. *Human Development: A Life-Span Approach.* New York: Macmillan Publishing Company, Inc. 1983.

Bjorklind, D.F. How Age Changes in Knowledge Base Contribute to the Development of Children's Memory: An Interpretive Review. *Developmental Review*, 1987. 7: 93–130.

Bower, T.G.R. *A Primer of Infant Development.* San Francisco: W.H. Freeman and Company. 1977.

Brainerd, Charles J. *Piaget's Theory of Intelligence.* Englewood Cliffs: Prentice-Hall, Inc. 1978.

Brandt, Richard M. *Studying Behavior in Natural Settings.* New York: Holt, Rinehart and Winston, Inc. 1972.

Brewer, J.A. *Early Childhood Education: Preschool Through Primary Grades,* 2nd ed. Boston: Allyn and Bacon. 1995.

Bruner, J. From Communication to Language. *Cognition,* 1975. 3: 255–87.

Bukatko, D. and Daehler, M.W. *Child Development: A Thematic Approach.* Boston: Houghton Mifflin Company. 1995.

Bukowski, W.M. and Hosa, B. Popularity and Friendship: Issues in Theory, Measurement, and Outcome. edited by T.J. Berndt and G.W. Ladd, *Peer Relationships in Child Development.* New York: Wiley. 1989.

Carpenter, G. Mother's Face and the Newborn. *New Scientist.* 1974. 61: 742–44.

Chomsky, C.S. *The Acquisition of Syntax in Children from Five to Ten.* Cambridge: Massachusetts Institute of Technology (MIT) Press. 1969.

Coie, J.D., Dodge, K.A., and Coppotelli, H. Dimensions and Types of Social Status: A Cross-age Perspective. *Developmental Psychology,* 1982. 18: 557–70.

Coombs, C.H. *A Theory of Data.* New York: Wiley. 1964.

Craig, Grace J. *Human Development,* 5th ed. Englewood Cliffs: Prentice-Hall, Inc. 1989.

Craig, G.J. and Kermis, M.D. *Children Today.* Englewood Cliffs: Prentice-Hall. 1995.

Cross, D. and Paris, S.G. Developmental and Instructional Analysis of Children's Metacognition and Reading Comprehension. *Journal of Educational Psychology,* 1988. 80: 131–142.

De Mause, L. The Evolution of Children. edited by L. De Mause, *The History of Childhood.* New York: Pyschohistory Press. 1974.

Diaz, R.M. and Berndt, T.J. Children's Knowledge of a Friend: Fact of Fancy? *Developmental Psychology,* 1982. 18: 787–94.

Dworetzky, John P. *Introduction to Child Development,* 3rd ed. New York: West Publishing Co. 1987.

Elkind, David. *The Hurried Child: Growing Up Too Fast Too Soon.* Reading: Addison Wesley Publishing Co. 1981.

Erwin, P.G. Similarity of Attitudes and Constructs in Children's Friendships. *Journal of Experimental Child Psychology,* 1985. 40: 470–85.

Essa, E. *Introduction to Early Childhood Education,* 2nd ed. Albany: Delmar Publishers. 1996.

Fantz, R.L. Pattern Vision in Newborn Infants. *Science,* 1963. 140: 296–97.

Faw, Terry and Belkin, Gary S. *Child Psychology.* New York: McGraw-Hill Publishing Co. 1989.

Federico, Ronald C. *Sociology,* 2nd ed. Reading: Addison-Wesley Publishing Co. 1979.

Field, T.M., Greenwald, P., Morrow, C., Healy, B., Foster, T., Guthertz, M., and Frost, P. Behavior State Matching During Interactions of Preadolescent Friends Versus Acquaintances. *Developmental Psychology,* 1992. 28: 242–50.

Fogel, Alan. *Infancy: Infant, Family, and Society.* New York: West Publishing Co. 1984.

Gander, Mary J. and Gardner, Harry W. *Child and Adolescent Development.* Boston: Little, Brown and Company. 1981.

Gardner, D. Bruce. *Development in Early Childhood,* 2nd ed. New York: Harper and Row. 1973.

Gaver, Donna, and Herbert C. Richards. Dimensions of Naturalistic Observation for the Prediction of Academic Success. *Journal of Educational Research,* Jan./Feb. 1979.

Gelman, R. Conservation Acquisition: A Problem of Learning to Attend to Relevant Attributes. *Journal of Experimental Child Psychology,* 1969. 7: 167–87.

Gelman, R. Logical Capacity of Very Young Children: Number Invariance Rules. *Child Development,* 1972. 43: 75–90.

Gibson, J.J. *The Senses Considered as Perceptual Systems.* Boston: Houghton Mifflin. 1966.

Goodwin, William R. and Driscoll, Laura A. *Handbook for Measurement and Evaluation in Early Childhood Education.* San Francisco: Jossey-Bass Publishers. 1980.

Graves, S.B., Gardiulo, R.M. and Sluder, L.C. *Young Children: An Introduction to Early Childhood Education.* New York: West Publishing Company. 1996.

Greenspan, Stanley and Greenspan, Nancy T. *First Feelings: Milestones in the Emotional Development of Your Baby and Child.* New York: Viking Penguin. 1985.

Hansen, Norwood Russell. *Patterns of Discovery.* Cambridge: Cambridge at the University Press. 1958.

Harris, A.C. *Child Development,* 2nd ed. New York: West Publishing Company. 1993.

Herron, R.E. and Sutton-Smith, B. *Child's Play.* New York: Wiley. 1971.

Hunt, J.McV. *Intelligence and Experience.* New York: The Ronald Press. 1961.

Hutt, S.J., Lenard, H.G., and Prechtl, H.E.R. Psychophysiology of the Newborn. *Advances in Child Development and Behavior.* New York: Academic Press. 1969.

Ihde, Don. *Experimental Phenomenology: An Introduction.* New York: Paragon Books. 1977.

Irwin, D. Michelle and Bushnell, M. Margaret. *Observational Strategies for Child Study.* New York: Holt, Rinehart and Winston. 1980.

Izard, Carrol E. *Human Emotions.* New York: Plenum Press. 1977.

Kagan, Jerome. *Personality Development.* New York: Harcourt Brace Jovanovich, Inc. 1971.

Kagan, Jerome. *The Nature of the Child.* New York: Basic Books, Inc. 1984.

Kamii, C. and DeVries, R. *Group Games in Early Education.* Washington, D.C.: National Association for the Education of Young Children. 1980.

Kamii, Constance and Rheta DeVries. Piaget for Early Education. *The Preschool in Action: Exploring Early Childhood Programs,* 2nd ed. Boston: Allyn and Bacon, Inc. 1977: 365–420.

Krantz, M. *Child Development: Risk and Opportunity.* Belmont: Wadsworth Publishing Company. 1994.

Krogh, S.L. *Educating Young Children: Infancy to Grade Three.* New York: McGraw-Hill Publishing Co. 1994.

Langer, Jonas, *Theories of Development.* New York: Holt, Rinehart and Winston, Inc. 1969.

Lay, Margaret Z. and John E. Dopyera. *Becoming a Teacher of Young Children.* Lexington: D.C. Heath and Company. 1977.

Lay-Dopyera, Margaret and John E. Dopyera. *Becoming a Teacher of Young Children,* 2nd ed. Lexington: D.C. Heath and Company. 1982.

Lefrancois, Guy R. *Of Children: An Introduction to Child Development.* Belmont: Wadsworth Publishing Co. 1996.

Lerner, Richard. *Concepts and Theories of Human Development.* Reading: Addison-Wesley. 1976.

Martin, Patricia Y. and O'Connor, Gerald G. *The Social Environment: Open Systems Application.* New York: Longman. 1989.

McGhee, P.E. *Humor: Its Origin and Development.* San Francisco: W. H. Freeman. 1979.

Miller, P.H. *Theories of Developmental Psychology,* 3rd ed. New York: W. H. Freeman. 1993.

Montemayor, R. and Eisen, M. The Development of Self-Conceptions from Childhood to Adolescence. *Developmental Psychology*, 1977. 13: 314–19.

Morrison, G.S. *Early Childhood Education Today*, 6th ed. Englewood Cliffs: Merrill Publishing Co. 1995.

Mussen, Paul H., Conger, John J. and Kagan, Jerome. *Child Development and Personality*, 5th ed. New York: Harper and Row. 1979.

Mussen, Paul H., Conger, John J., Kagan, Jerome, and Huston, Aletha. *Child Development*, 6th ed. Philadelphia: Harper and Row. 1984.

Nelson, K. Structure and Strategy in Learning to Talk. *Monographs of Society for Research in Child Development*, 1973. 38:182.

Neuman, W.L. *Social Research Methods: Qualitative and Quantitative Approaches*, 2nd ed. Needham Heights: Allyn and Bacon. 1994.

Papalia, Diane E. and Olds, Sally W. *Human Development*. New York: McGraw-Hill Book Company. 1978.

Papalia, Diane E. and Olds, Sally W. *A Child's World: Infancy Through Adolescence*, 4th ed. New York: McGraw-Hill. 1987.

Papalia, Diane E. and Olds, Sally W. *A Child's World: Infancy Through Adolescence*, 6th ed. New York: McGraw-Hill Book Co. 1993.

Papalia, Diane E. and Sally W. Olds. *Human Development*, 5th ed. New York; McGraw-Hill Book Company. 1992.

Paris, S.G. and Winograd, P. How Metacognition Can Promote Children's Academic Learning. edited by B. Jones and L. Idol, *Dimensions of Thinking*. Hillsdale: Erlbaum. 1990.

Parten, Mildred B. Social Participation Among Pre-school Children. *Journal of Abnormal and Social Psychology*, 1932. 27: 243–269.

Pillari, Vimala. *Human Behavior in the Social Environment*. Belmont: Wadsworth Publishing Co. 1988.

Ramsey, P.G. and Myers, L.C. Salience of Race in Young Children's Cognitive, Affective, and Behavioral Responses to Social Environments. *Journal of Applied Developmental Psychology*, 1990. 11: 49–67.

Richarz, Ann Sherrill. *Understanding Children Through Observation*. New York: West Publishing Company. 1980.

Salkind, Neil. *Theories of Human Development*. New York: D. Van Nostrand Co. 1981.

Santrock, J.W. *Children*, 3rd ed. Madison: Brown and Benchmark. 1993.

Saunders, Ruth and Bingham-Newman, Ann M. *Piagetian Perspective for Preschools: A Thinking Book for Teachers*. Englewood Cliffs: Prentice-Hall, Inc. 1984.

Schiamberg, Lawrence B. *Human Development*, 2nd ed. New York: Macmillan Publishing Co. 1985.

Schickedanz, J.A., Schickedanz, D.I., Hansen, K., and Forsyth, P.D. *Understanding Children*, 2nd ed. Mountain View: Mayfield Publishing Company. 1993.

Schwartz, J.I. Children's Experiments with Language. *Young Children*, 1981. 36: 16–26.

Seifert, Kelvin L. and Hoffnung, Robert J. *Child and Adolescent Development*. Boston: Houghton Mifflin Co. 1987.

Selman, R.L. The Child as a Friendship Philosopher. edited by S.R. Asher and J.M. Gorman, *The Development of Children's Friendships.* Cambridge, UK: Cambridge University Press. 1981.

Selman, R.L. and Selman, A.P. Children's Ideas About Friendship: A New Theory. *Psychology Today,* 1979. 13(4): 71–80, 114.

Sonnenschein, S. Development of Referential Communication Skills: How Familiarity with a Listener Affects a Speaker's Production of Redundant Messages. *Developmental Psychology,* 1986. 22: 549–52.

Spodeck, B. and Saracho, O.N. *Right From the Start: Teaching Children Ages Three to Eight.* Boston: Allyn and Bacon. 1994.

Sroufe, L. Alan and Cooper, Robert G. *Child Development: Its Nature and Course.* New York: Alfred A. Knopf. 1988.

Stark, Rodney. *Sociology.* Belmont: Wadsworth Publishing Co. 1985.

Steinberg, L. and Meyer, R. *Childhood.* New York: McGraw-Hill, Inc. 1995.

Steinberg, L. and Belsky, J. *Infancy, Childhood, & Adolescence: Development in Context.* New York: McGraw-Hill, Inc. 1991.

Stern, V. and Cohen, D. *Observing and Recording the Behavior of Young Children.* New York: Teachers College.1958. (Revised in 1978.)

Stone, L. Joseph and Church, Joseph. *Childhood and Adolescence: A Psychology of the Growing Person,* 4th ed. New York: Random House. 1979.

Stone, L.J. and Church, J. *Childhood and Adolescence: A Psychology of the Growing Person,* 5th ed. New York: Random House. 1984.

Thomas, A., S. Chess, and H. Birch. *Temperament and Behavior Disorders in Children.* New York: New York University Press. 1968.

Thomas, A., S. Chess, and H. Birch. The Origin of Personality. *Scientific American,* 1970. 232(2): 102–09.

Thorndike, R.L. and E.P. Hagan. *Measurement and Evaluation in Psychology and Education,* 4th ed. New York: Wiley. 1977.

Travers, John F. *The Growing Child,* 2nd ed. Dallas: Scott, Foresman and Company. 1982.

Vander Zander, James W. *Human Development,* 4th ed. New York: Alfred A. Kropf. 1989.

Vasta, R., Haith, M.M., and Miller, S.A. *Child Psychology: The Modern Science,* 2nd ed. New York: John Wiley & Sons, Inc. 1995.

Wadsworth, Barry J. *Piaget's Theory of Cognitive and Affective Development,* 3rd ed. New York: Longman Inc. 1984.

Webster's New World Dictionary of the American Language, College Edition. Cleveland: The World Publishing Company. 1960.

Willemsen, Eleanor. *Understanding Infancy.* San Francisco: W.H. Freeman and Company. 1979.

Wolff, Peter H. The Classification of States. *The Competent Infant.* New York: Basic Books. 1973.

Wright, Herbert F. Observational Child Study. *Handbook of Research Methods in Child Development.* New York: John Wiley and Sons, Inc. 1960.

Zigler, E.F. and Stevenson, M.F. *Children in a Changing World: Development and Social Issues,* 2nd ed. Pacific Grove: Brooks/Cole Publishing Company. 1993.

Annotated Bibliography

Children with Developmental Problems or at High-Risk for Developmental Problems (Identification and Intervention)

Adler, S. and King, D., eds. *A Multidisciplinary treatment program for the pre-school exceptional child.* Springfield, IL: Charles C Thomas, 1986.

This text is a comprehensive, interdisciplinary manual on the care, education and treatment of young children with developmental problems; directed to professionals, day care providers and parents.

Allen, K.E. *The Exceptional Child: Inclusion in early childhood education.* Albany, NY: Delmar Publishers, Inc. 1996.

This text provides a comprehensive overview of early intervention and early childhood education for children with developmental problems, as well as their inclusion in the integrated (mainstreamed) classroom.

Blackman, J.A. *Medical aspects of developmental disabilities in children birth to three.* Rockville, MD: Aspen Systems Corp., 1984.

This is an outstanding book for early childhood personnel as it provides well-illustrated and readily understood information about medical issues that affect the developmental progress of young children; highly recommended.

Fallen, N.F. & Umansky, W. *Young children with special needs.* Columbus, OH: Charles E. Merrill, 1985.

This text is especially useful for its focus on the developmentally different child as being in need of a "holistic" approach to early care and education just as is the normally developing child.

Hanson, M,J. and Harris, S.R. *Teaching the young child with motor delays.* Austin, TX: Pro-Ed, 1986.

This easy-to-read handbook bridges the gap between parents and professionals who work with motor-impaired children, birth to three, and includes teaching strategies and therapy activities to be used in the home and in the infant center.

Haslam, R.H.A. and Valletutti, P.J. *Medical problems in the classroom.* Austin, TX: Pro-Ed, 1985.

This book provides teachers and professionals from other disciplines with clues to early identification and points out ways that teachers can assist in the management of these problems.

Krajicek, M.J. and Tomlinson, A.I.T. *Detection of developmental problems in children.* Baltimore, MD: University Park Press, 1983.

Practical and readable, this is a highly acclaimed pediatric nursing text that focuses on early identification, screening and beginning intervention strategies with children with potential or identified developmental problems.

McCormick, L. and Schiefelbusch, R.L. *Early language intervention.* Columbus, OH: Charles E. Merrill, 1984.

A good introduction to both normal and atypical language development and overall communication development with practical examples of programs, procedures and materials for fostering communication skills in young children.

Peterson, N.L. *Early intervention for handicapped and at-risk children.* Denver, CO: Love Publishing Company, 1987.

This is an excellent text for students and professionals in early childhood special education and related disciplines who are working with young children with developmental problems; gives an invaluable perspective on what early intervention actually entails.

Infants, Toddlers and Parents

Apgar, V. and Beck, J. *Is my baby all right? A guide to birth defects.* New York: Trident, 1972.

This continues to be one of the best sources for information about genetic and environmental causes of developmental problems and what the progress and treatment of a problem is from birth on; sensitive and readable.

Brazelton, T.B. *Infants and mothers: Differences in development.* New York: Dell, 1969.

Though this book was published a number of years ago it remains one of the best descriptions of the first year of life. It is written by a sensitive and observant pediatrician who has remained at the forefront of developmental pediatrics.

Brazelton, T.B. *Toddlers and Parents.* New York: Dell, 1974.

Like Brazelton's infant book this is an exceptionally good book, for parents and caregivers of young children; just as sensitively written as the earlier book, this one too, is a treasury of good advice and sensible suggestion about toddlers.

Bricker, D.D. *Early education of at-risk and handicapped infants, toddlers, and preschool children.* Glenview, IL: Scott, Foresman, and Company, 1986.

Written by one of the leading infant specialists, this text offers both students and practitioners a contemporary view of the field with examples of application for those working with atypical infants and children.

Bromwich, R.M. *Working with parents and infants.* Austin, TX: Pro-Ed, 1981.

This remains one of the best books in the field for helping parents learn to work with their handicapped or high-risk children; particularly noteworthy is the inclusion of case histories covering successful, partly successful, and unsuccessful interventions; invaluable for those working with parents.

Caplan, F. and Caplan, T. *The first twelve months of life* and *The second twelve months of life.* New York: Putnam Publishing Co., 1982.

Very readable books that provide excellent descriptions of normal growth and development although their emphasis on month to month changes rather than on developmental sequence may contribute to some undue anxiety in new parents. Includes many practical suggestions for dealing with daily behaviors and routines.

Hanson, M.J. *Atypical infant development.* Austin, TX: Pro-Ed, 1984.

This interdisciplinary text presents students and professionals with a current review of research and literature on both normal and atypical infant developmental problems.

Leach, P. *Your baby and child from birth to age five.* New York: Alfred A. Knopf, 1986.

This book offers parents and caregivers excellent developmental explanations as well as practical suggestions for daily caregiving routines, appropriate play equipment and behavior management.

Marotz, L.; Rush, J. and Cross M. *Health, safety and nutrition for the young child.* Albany, NY: Delmar Publishers, Inc., 1993.

This book provides a comprehensive overview of the factors that contribute to maximizing the growth and development of each child. It includes some of the most current research information and knowledge concerning each of these areas and is especially useful for teachers, caregivers and parents.

Wilson, L.C., Watson, L. and Watson, M. *Infants and toddlers.* Albany, NY: Delmar Publishers, Inc., 1995.

Parents and caregivers will find this book particularly useful in understanding developmental sequences, creating enriching environments and providing appropriate learning experiences for infants and toddlers based on their developmental needs.

Index

Note: Pages numbers with an "f" indicate figures; those with a "t" indicate tables.